# Study Guide to accompany

# Psychology in the New Millennium

Sixth Edition

Spencer A. Rathus

Prepared by Spencer A. Rathus and Joyce Bishop

**Harcourt Brace College Publishers**

Fort Worth  Philadelphia  San Diego  New York  Orlando  Austin  San Antonio

Toronto  Montreal  London  Sydney  Tokyo

*Address Editorial Correspondence To:*  Harcourt Brace College Publishers
301 Commerce Street, Suite 3700
Fort Worth, TX 76102

*Address Orders To:*  Harcourt Brace & Company
6277 Sea Harbor Drive
Orlando, FL 32887-6777
1-800-782-4479 or 1-800-433-0001 (in Florida)

Printed in the United States of America

ISBN: 0-15-503218-6

5678901234 066 987654321

# Contents

# How to Use This Study Guide Effectively

## Your Time Is Valuable.

Invest your study time so you get the greatest benefit!

The following techniques have been shown to increase students' mastery of new information:

- Use as many of your senses and abilities as possible–writing, reading, hearing, speaking, drawing, etc.

- Organize information so it is meaningful to you.

- Study with other people whenever possible.

- Have FUN. We remember what we enjoy!

This study guide has been designed to provide you with ideas and resources in all of these area. This preface explains how to effectively use the sections in each chapter.

### How to Handle Multiple Choice Questions

Checking your progress is an important step in your studying. The *Pretest* measures your starting point and the *Posttest* measures how far you have progressed toward your goal of mastering the material.

Follow directions!

You are usually looking for the answer that best answers the questions. Perhaps no answer is perfect.

Try to answer the question before you look at the choices.

Place a mark next to questions that seem difficult and return to them later. Don't let a tough question consume half the time allotted for the test.

When you see two answers that are opposite in meaning, there's a good chance that one of them is the correct answer.

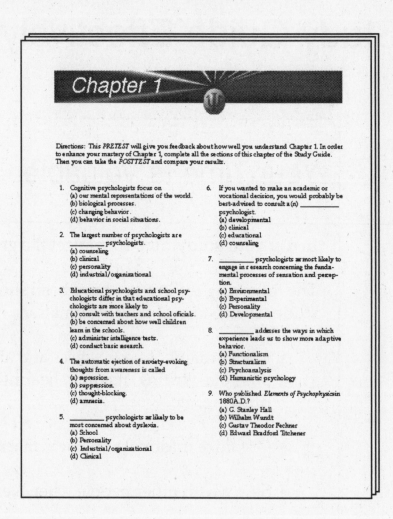

Eliminate any answers you are sure are wrong. Look out for qualifying terms such as *all, completely, never, always,* and *only.* Because these qualifiers severely limit the applicability of the question, they frequently indicate incorrect answers. On the other hand, more moderate qualifiers such as *usually, sometimes, frequently, probably,* and *often* tend to indicate correct choices.

*Getting the Overall Picture of the Chapter*

The overview outlines the material presented in the chapter. The overview summarizes the topics in the chapter and shows how they are interrelated.

Chapter 1 begins with a definition of the science of psychology as the study of behavior and mental processes. Behaviorists focus on behavior, whereas cognitive psychologists focus on our mental representations of the world. There is a discussion of the goals of psychology—the description, explanation, prediction, and control of behavior. When possible, the subject matter of psychology is explained through psychological theories.

Then there is a description of what different kinds of psychologists do—including clinical and counseling psychologists; school and educational psychologists; developmental psychologists; personality, social, and environmental psychologists; experimental psychologists; and psychologists in industry. Emerging fields, such as forensic psychology and health psychology, are also touched upon.

The history of psychology could be said to begin with Aristotle's book *Peri Psyches*, and Socrates' assertion "Know Thyself." The first psychological laboratory was established in Leipzig by Wundt, and he originated the school of structuralism. William James developed functionalism in the United States. John B. Watson looked to the Russian Ivan Pavlov's conditioning experiments as a model, and he developed behaviorism in the United States. Gestalt psychology was brought from Germany to the United States in the 1930s. Sigmund Freud developed his school of psychoanalysis around the turn of the century in Vienna.

Today six major psychological perspectives or viewpoints hold sway in the United States:

• the biological perspective, which searches out relationships between biological structures and the behavior of the organism;

• the cognitive perspective, which focuses on the roles of mental representation and thought in determining behavior;

• the humanistic–existential perspective, which stresses the importance of human experience and the freedom to make choices;

• the psychodynamic perspective, which focuses on the role of inner conflict and ways in which people attempt to evade anxiety;

• learning perspectives, such as behaviorism and social-cognitive theory. Behaviorism sees behavior as largely determined by situational factors. Social-cognitive theory recognizes the importance of situational factors, but finds important roles for cognitive factors, such as observational learning and values; and

• the sociocultural perspective, which fosters the consideration of matters of ethnicity, gender, culture, and socioeconomic status in psychology.

Awareness of the richness of human diversity makes psychology a stronger science and serves the public interest. Learning about the experiences of various ethnic groups in the United States highlights the influences of social forces on the individual. The probing of human diversity enables students to appreciate the cultural heritages and historical problems of various ethnic groups. The study of ethnicity also contributes to our understanding of basic psychological processes. The diversity of human behavior and mental processes—and the commonalities—enhance our understanding of human nature.

Critical thinking helps make us into active, astute judges of other people and their points of view. Critical thinking fosters skepticism, which is central to the scientific perspective. Critical thinking refers to a process of analyzing and probing the questions, statements, and arguments of other people.

The overview defines some of the key terms, but can only provide a broad sketch of what is contained within the chapter. It is not intended to serve as a substitute for reading the chapter, but it can help you learn the material in the chapter better by providing an "advanced organizer".

You may find it worthwhile to read the chapter overview in the Study Guide before reading the chapter itself.

*What You Should Learn from the Chapter*

This section will give you a good idea of what you should know when you have finished studying the chapter. Along with the overview, you may want to read these objectives before you read the chapter in the text.

The learning objectives increase your readiness for the material by fostering recognition of the key points as you proceed in your reading.

When you have finished reading the chapter in the text, it is useful to reread the learning objectives in the Study Guide to determine whether or not you have met the learning objectives. If you have not, you may wish to return to the chapter and seek out this information before you proceed with other aspects of your studying.

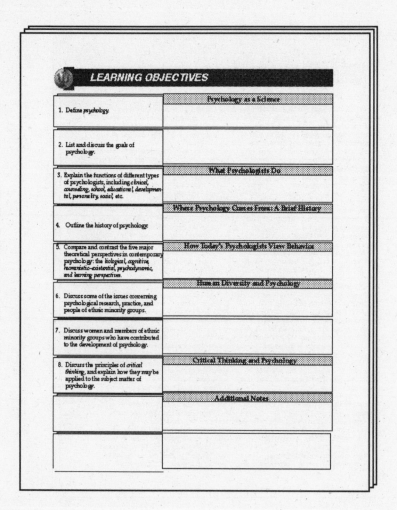

The learning objectives are varied, but most fall into a limited number of categories. Many, for example, ask you to define, compare, and contrast key terms. Some ask you to describe, discuss, or to summarize the results of research studies. Others ask you to list a number of items that are to be memorized. It is helpful to write out the answers to the learning objectives in the boxes to the right of the objectives. This approach will be particularly helpful if your instructor uses essay questions on tests.

## Organizing Your Class and Text Notes

The Lecture and Textbook Outline section is designed so you can take notes on these pages during lecture and also from your reading of the text.

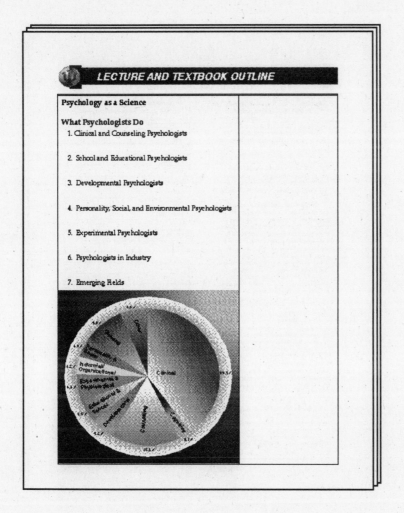

Most students find it useful to read the material and make notes before the instructor covers the material in class.

Before you begin filling out this section decide how you will tell the difference between:
- your ideas
- concepts from the text
- notes from the instructor
- topics the instructor says will be on the exam

*Learn to Study Smart*

The first twelve chapters have study tips. Studying in groups of four to six people has been shown to be the most effective way to study.

Once you form a study group you could divide up the 12 *Effective Studying Ideas* in the study guide and then teach each other. You could learn all 12 study tips by the second week of class with only a small amount of effort.

Think of the study tips as tools. Some of the ideas will work great for you and others will not. Try as many as you can and only keep the ones that fit your needs and personality. Do not try to make too many changes all at once. That can be very overwhelming.

## Important Words or Phrases

Each chapter has a list of "key" or important terms. Most of these terms are found in the running glossary (the words and terms that are defined in the margins of the pages on which they appear) of the text and in the glossary at the end of the text.

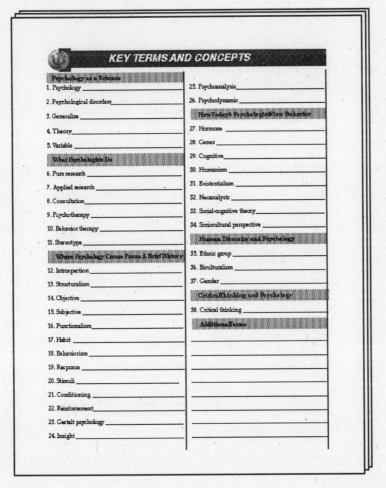

All are found in the reading material of the chapter. Some of these terms are so important they are found in a number of chapters. Repetition shows that these terms–such as "classical conditioning" and "psychoanalysis"–have applications in several subfields of psychology.

Space is provided for you to write in the meaning of each term. You may then check your definition in the running or end-of-book glossary in your textbook. For terms that are not defined in the glossaries, why not use a dictionary or see whether your definition is consistent with the way in which the word or phrase is used in the textbook?

## A Step-By-Step Approach

In the chapter-review sections, you fill in the blanks or circle the correct term as you read an extensive summary of the chapter. These step-by-step summaries are more detailed than the summaries in the textbook.

This section requires your active participation and active learning is more effective than passive learning.

The chapter-review sections make use of many key terms and build concepts in logical sequence. Not every objective is covered in this one section, but rather, can be found in combination with other sections. Most items include "prompts"–that is, a letter or segment of the correct term.

Sometimes the correct answer is used in the following sentence of the review, allowing you to immediately check the accuracy of your answer. The correct answers are provided at the end. Students sometimes complain that the meanings of sentences are unclear when they attempt to fill in the blanks in test items, or that several answers might have been correct. The prompts will help avoid some of this type of confusion. If you do not know the meaning of an answer in the chapter review, check the appropriate chapter of your textbook or the glossary at the end of the textbook.

## Not Just for Those Whose Second Language Is English

Not all students who are taking this course grew up speaking English in their homes or have a strong foundation in English. The bridging-the-gap is designed for any student who could use language support.

This section covers three specific areas:

1. *Idioms* – which are usages of a language that may not be directly translatable into other languages.

2. *Cultural references*– these are people, places, things, and activities that may not be familiar to all people.

3. *Phrases and expressions* (different usage) –lists and explains words which have meanings that differ from their usual meanings or are used as metaphors.

Students whose first language is English are encouraged to read the bridging-the-gap sections for several reasons. These sections, for example, will
- enhance their ability to use idiomatic English,
- remind them of the material in the textbook from which the words were taken,
- increase their sensitivity to the language problems of people whose first language is not English.

# CUT-OUT FLASH CARDS

## Studying Where You Are

Most students have trouble finding enough time to study. Try cutting these flash cards out and carrying them with you. If ever you have to wait remember to pull out a couple of flash cards and you won't waste any time.

During times of stress, flash cards can serve a very useful function. Stress is much worse when we feel over-whelmed; in fact, we tend to shut down and do nothing. At those times divide up what you have to do. For example, rather than panicking because you have an exam over 100 pages, divide up these cards and carry a different set with you each day. That is a lot less overwhelming than sitting down to study 100 pages.

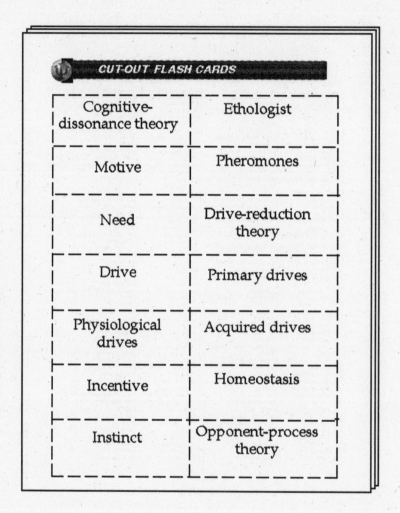

**CUT-OUT FLASH CARDS**

| | |
|---|---|
| Cognitive-dissonance theory | Ethologist |
| Motive | Pheromones |
| Need | Drive-reduction theory |
| Drive | Primary drives |
| Physiological drives | Acquired drives |
| Incentive | Homeostasis |
| Instinct | Opponent-process theory |

Flash cards can be a fun way to study because it can involve friends. If you like competition, you could set up teams in your study group and then compete to see which team can get the most definitions correct from the flash cards. Some students copy the flash cards onto bright colored paper with each chapter being a different color.

# "Secrets" of Learning

There are two "secrets" of learning: 1) Understand the material first because it is much easier to learn what you understand; and 2) repetition, repetition, repetition, repetition, repetition, repetition, and repetition. Most students need to review material at least five to six times to have a good understanding of the information.

We learn through seeing, hearing, and doing. People tend to be strong in one or two of these areas but weak in the other. When do you learn the easiest, is it visual, auditory, or when actually doing something physically? Try to convert what you want to learn into the format that is easiest for you.

Now it's up to you. Psychology is the most exciting part of our lives, and we sincerely hope that you will find it stimulating and rewarding. We are happy to be sharing your journey in Psychology.

Spencer A. Rathus
and Joyce Bishop

Directions: This *PRETEST* will give you feedback about how well you understand Chapter 1. In order to enhance your mastery of Chapter 1, complete all the sections of this chapter of the Study Guide. Then you can take the *POSTTEST* and compare your results.

1. Cognitive psychologists focus on
   (a) our mental representations of the world.
   (b) biological processes.
   (c) changing behavior.
   (d) behavior in social situations.

2. The largest number of psychologists are _____ psychologists.
   (a) counseling
   (b) clinical
   (c) personality
   (d) industrial/organizational

3. Educational psychologists and school psychologists differ in that educational psychologists are more likely to
   (a) consult with teachers and school officials.
   (b) be concerned about how well children learn in the schools.
   (c) administer intelligence tests.
   (d) conduct basic research.

4. The automatic ejection of anxiety-evoking thoughts from awareness is called
   (a) repression.
   (b) suppression.
   (c) thought-blocking.
   (d) amnesia.

5. _____ psychologists are likely to be most concerned about dyslexia.
   (a) School
   (b) Personality
   (c) Industrial/organizational
   (d) Clinical

6. If you wanted to make an academic or vocational decision, you would probably be best-advised to consult a(n) _____ psychologist.
   (a) developmental
   (b) clinical
   (c) educational
   (d) counseling

7. _____ psychologists are most likely to engage in research concerning the fundamental processes of sensation and perception.
   (a) Environmental
   (b) Experimental
   (c) Personality
   (d) Developmental

8. _____ addresses the ways in which experience leads us to show more adaptive behavior.
   (a) Functionalism
   (b) Structuralism
   (c) Psychoanalysis
   (d) Humanistic psychology

9. Who published *Elements of Psychophysics* in 1880 A.D.?
   (a) G. Stanley Hall
   (b) Wilhelm Wundt
   (c) Gustav Theodor Fechner
   (d) Edward Bradford Titchener

10. Who received his doctoral degree from the University of Chicago in 1903?
    (a) B. F. Skinner
    (b) G. Stanley Hall
    (c) Albert Bandura
    (d) John B. Watson

11. Structuralism attempted to define experience in terms of
    (a) habits.
    (b) person and situational variables.
    (c) sensations, feelings, and mental images.
    (d) unconscious ideas and instincts.

12. _____ psychologists have emphasized the roles of insight and understanding in problem solving.
    (a) Psychoanalytic
    (b) Structuralistic
    (c) Behavioral
    (d) Gestalt

13. _____ oriented psychologists use techniques such as CAT scans, PET scans, and electrical stimulation of sites in the brain to show that these sites are involved in thoughts, emotions, and behavior.
    (a) Socioculturally
    (b) Cognitively
    (c) Biologically
    (d) Behaviorally

14. The hormone _____ stimulates maternal behavior in rats.
    (a) oxytocin
    (b) prolactin
    (c) cortisol
    (d) vasopressin

15. Who is a social–cognitive theorist?
    (a) John B. Watson
    (b) Carl Rogers
    (c) Erich Fromm
    (d) Albert Bandura

16. _____ theorists are vitally concerned with the experience of various ethnic groups in the United States.
    (a) Sociocultural
    (b) Social–cognitive
    (c) Humanistic–existential
    (d) Gestalt

17. According to the *Chronicle of Higher Education* (1992), the percentage of _____ Americans in the college population showed the greatest increase between 1980 and 1990.
    (a) African
    (b) Asian
    (c) Hispanic
    (d) Native

18. Who was the first female president of the American Psychological Association?
    (a) Calkins
    (b) Washburn
    (c) Ladd–Franklin
    (d) Strickland

19. In the years 1980 and 1992, the field of _____ psychology had the highest percentage of women.
    (a) clinical
    (b) school
    (c) educational
    (d) developmental

20. A person challenges another person's opinion by insulting the individual who first expressed the opinion. This sort of argument is known as *argumentum ad*
    (a) *baculum.*
    (b) *populum.*
    (c) *hominem.*
    (d) *verecundiam.*

**Answer Key to *Pretest***

| | | | |
|---|---|---|---|
| 1. A | 6. D | 11. C | 16. A |
| 2. B | 7. B | 12. D | 17. B |
| 3. D | 8. A | 13. C | 18. A |
| 4. A | 9. C | 14. B | 19. D |
| 5. A | 10. D | 15. D | 20. C |

Chapter 1 begins with a definition of the science of psychology as the study of behavior and mental processes. Behaviorists focus on behavior, whereas cognitive psychologists focus on our mental representations of the world. There is a discussion of the goals of psychology—the description, explanation, prediction, and control of behavior. When possible, the subject matter of psychology is explained through psychological theories.

Then there is a description of what different kinds of psychologists do—including clinical and counseling psychologists; school and educational psychologists; developmental psychologists; personality, social, and environmental psychologists; experimental psychologists; and psychologists in industry. Emerging fields, such as forensic psychology and health psychology, are also touched upon.

The history of psychology could be said to begin with Aristotle's book *Peri Psyches*, and Socrates' assertion "Know Thyself." The first psychological laboratory was established in Leipzig by Wundt, and he originated the school of structuralism. William James developed functionalism in the United States. John B. Watson looked to the Russian Ivan Pavlov's conditioning experiments as a model, and he developed behaviorism in the United States. Gestalt psychology was brought from Germany to the United States in the 1930s. Sigmund Freud developed his school of psychoanalysis around the turn of the century in Vienna.

Today six major psychological perspectives or viewpoints hold sway in the United States:

- the biological perspective, which searches out relationships between biological structures and the behavior of the organism;
- the cognitive perspective, which focuses on the roles of mental representation and thought in determining behavior;
- the humanistic–existential perspective, which stresses the importance of human experience and the freedom to make choices;
- the psychodynamic perspective, which focuses on the role of inner conflict and ways in which people attempt to evade anxiety;
- learning perspectives, such as behaviorism and social–cognitive theory. Behaviorism sees behavior as largely determined by situational factors. Social–cognitive theory recognizes the importance of situational factors, but finds important roles for cognitive factors, such as observational learning and values; and
- the sociocultural perspective, which fosters the consideration of matters of ethnicity, gender, culture, and socioeconomic status in psychology.

Awareness of the richness of human diversity makes psychology a stronger science and serves the public interest. Learning about the experiences of various ethnic groups in the United States highlights the influences of social forces on the individual. The probing of human diversity enables students to appreciate the cultural heritages and historical problems of various ethnic groups. The study of ethnicity also contributes to our understanding of basic psychological processes. The diversity of human behavior and mental processes—and the commonalities—enhance our understanding of human nature.

Critical thinking helps make us into active, astute judges of other people and their points of view. Critical thinking fosters skepticism, which is central to the scientific perspective. Critical thinking refers to a process of analyzing and probing the questions, statements, and arguments of other people.

| | |
|---|---|
| | **Psychology as a Science** |
| 1. Define *psychology*. | |
| 2. List and discuss the goals of psychology. | |
| 3. Explain the functions of different types of psychologists, including *clinical, counseling, school, educational, developmental, personality, social,* etc. | **What Psychologists Do** |
| 4. Outline the history of psychology. | **Where Psychology Comes From: A Brief History** |
| 5. Compare and contrast the five major theoretical perspectives in contemporary psychology: the *biological, cognitive, humanistic–existential, psychodynamic, and learning perspectives.* | **How Today's Psychologists View Behavior** |
| 6. Discuss some of the issues concerning psychological research, practice, and people of ethnic minority groups. | **Human Diversity and Psychology** |
| 7. Discuss women and members of ethnic minority groups who have contributed to the development of psychology. | |
| 8. Discuss the principles of *critical thinking*, and explain how they may be applied to the subject matter of psychology. | **Critical Thinking and Psychology** |
| | **Additional Notes** |
| | |

# LECTURE AND TEXTBOOK OUTLINE

## Psychology as a Science

## What Psychologists Do

1. Clinical and Counseling Psychologists

2. School and Educational Psychologists

3. Developmental Psychologists

4. Personality, Social, and Environmental Psychologists

5. Experimental Psychologists

6. Psychologists in Industry

7. Emerging Fields

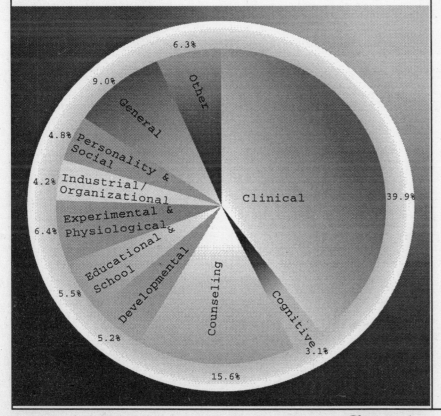

## Where Psychology Comes From: A Brief History

1. Structuralism

2. Functionalism

3. Behaviorism

4. Gestalt Psychology

5. Psychoanalysis

## How Today's Psychologists View Behavior

1. The Biological Perspective

2. The Cognitive Perspective

3. The Humanistic-Existential Perspective

4. The Psychodynamic Perspective

5. Learning Perspectives

6. The Sociocultural Perspective

## Human Diversity and Psychology

1. Ethnic Diversity: A Social Mosaic

2. Gender

3. Other Kinds of Diversity

4. Diversity in American Higher Education

5. Diversity of Contributors to the Development of Psychology

## Critical Thinking and Psychology

1. Principles of Critical Thinking

   - Be skeptical.

   - Examine definitions of terms.

   - Examine the assumptions or premises of arguments.

   - Be cautious in drawing conclusions from evidence.

   - Consider alternative interpretations of research.

   - Do not oversimplify.

   - Do not overgeneralize.

   - Apply critical thinking to all areas of life.

2. Recognizing Common Fallacies in Arguments

# EFFECTIVE STUDYING IDEAS

## Finding Time for What's Important to You

*"Doust thou love life, then do not squander time,
for that's the stuff life is made of."*
Benjamin Franklin

The best way to stay in control of our life is to use a weekly time plan. On the next page is a chart for you to write in advance a time plan for the week and then keep track of how you actually spent your time. At the end of the week, total the number of hours you spent in each category. Use the summary chart on this page to compare what you planned to do with what you actually did.

Once you know what your strengths and weaknesses are, develop a plan for yourself to capitalize on your best time for studying. This is also a good time to make a list of your time wasters, prioritize the list, and then develop a plan to work on them one by one. Most of us make the mistake of trying to change too many things all at once. (Like our impressive exercise program that lasted only three weeks.) Plan changes that you could live with for the rest of your academic career. So you need to be realistic, and be considerate of yourself.

How you choose to spend your time tells a lot about what is important to you. This week think about your goals. Do you invest your time in a way that is supportive of your goals? If not, you need to either change your goals or change your behavior. The study tips in Chapter 10 of this Study Guide give tips in how to change a habit.

Two good books on how to use your time effectively are: *How to Get Control of Your Time and Your Life* by Alan Lakein, and a newer time management book specifically for college students is *Studying Smart* by Diana Scharf.

My goal for this year is _____

_____

_____

Five years from now, I hope to be . . .

_____

_____

## Summary Chart of Time Use

Add up total hours spent per week.
(grand total should be 168 hours)

| Category | Planned | Actual |
|---|---|---|
| Sleep | | |
| Meals | | |
| Grooming | | |
| Chores | | |
| Class | | |
| Work | | |
| Study | | |
| Commuting | | |
| Exercise | | |
| Entertainment | | |
| Television | | |
| | | |
| | | |
| | | |
| | | |
| | | |

Based on the Summary Chart above, write four changes you believe would help you be a more successful student. Place a star by the one you are going to try this week.

| | |
|---|---|
| 1 | |
| 2 | |
| 3 | |
| 4 | |

| Monday __/__/__ | | |
|---|---|---|
| | Planned | Actual |
| | | |
| 7:00 a.m. | | |
| 7:15 | | |
| 7:30 | | |
| 7:45 | | |
| 8:00 | | |
| 8:15 | | |
| 8:30 | | |
| 8:45 | | |
| 9:00 | | |
| 9:15 | | |
| 9:30 | | |
| 9:45 | | |
| 10:00 | | |
| 10:15 | | |
| 10:30 | | |
| 10:45 | | |
| 11:00 | | |
| 11:15 | | |
| 11:30 | | |
| 11:45 | | |
| 12:00 p.m | | |
| 12:15 | | |
| 12:30 | | |
| 12:45 | | |
| 1:00 | | |
| 1:15 | | |
| 1:30 | | |
| 1:45 | | |
| 2:00 | | |
| 2:15 | | |
| 2:30 | | |
| 2:45 | | |
| 3:00 | | |
| 3:15 | | |
| 3:30 | | |
| 3:45 | | |
| 4:00 | | |
| 4:15 | | |
| 4:30 | | |
| 4:45 | | |
| 5:00 | | |
| 5:15 | | |
| 5:30 | | |
| 5:45 | | |
| 6:00 | | |
| 6:15 | | |
| 6:30 | | |
| 6:45 | | |
| 7:00 | | |
| 7:15 | | |
| 7:30 | | |
| 7:45 | | |
| 8:00 | | |
| 8:15 | | |
| 8:30 | | |
| 8:45 | | |
| 9:00 | | |
| 9:15 | | |
| 9:30 | | |
| 9:45 | | |
| | | |

| Tuesday __/__/__ | | |
|---|---|---|
| | Planned | Actual |
| | | |
| 7:00 a.m. | | |
| 7:15 | | |
| 7:30 | | |
| 7:45 | | |
| 8:00 | | |
| 8:15 | | |
| 8:30 | | |
| 8:45 | | |
| 9:00 | | |
| 9:15 | | |
| 9:30 | | |
| 9:45 | | |
| 10:00 | | |
| 10:15 | | |
| 10:30 | | |
| 10:45 | | |
| 11:00 | | |
| 11:15 | | |
| 11:30 | | |
| 11:45 | | |
| 12:00 p.m | | |
| 12:15 | | |
| 12:30 | | |
| 12:45 | | |
| 1:00 | | |
| 1:15 | | |
| 1:30 | | |
| 1:45 | | |
| 2:00 | | |
| 2:15 | | |
| 2:30 | | |
| 2:45 | | |
| 3:00 | | |
| 3:15 | | |
| 3:30 | | |
| 3:45 | | |
| 4:00 | | |
| 4:15 | | |
| 4:30 | | |
| 4:45 | | |
| 5:00 | | |
| 5:15 | | |
| 5:30 | | |
| 5:45 | | |
| 6:00 | | |
| 6:15 | | |
| 6:30 | | |
| 6:45 | | |
| 7:00 | | |
| 7:15 | | |
| 7:30 | | |
| 7:45 | | |
| 8:00 | | |
| 8:15 | | |
| 8:30 | | |
| 8:45 | | |
| 9:00 | | |
| 9:15 | | |
| 9:30 | | |
| 9:45 | | |

| Wednesday__/__/ | | |
|---|---|---|
| | Planned | Actual |
| | | |
| 7:00 a.m. | | |
| 7:15 | | |
| 7:30 | | |
| 7:45 | | |
| 8:00 | | |
| 8:15 | | |
| 8:30 | | |
| 8:45 | | |
| 9:00 | | |
| 9:15 | | |
| 9:30 | | |
| 9:45 | | |
| 10:00 | | |
| 10:15 | | |
| 10:30 | | |
| 10:45 | | |
| 11:00 | | |
| 11:15 | | |
| 11:30 | | |
| 11:45 | | |
| 12:00 p.m | | |
| 12:15 | | |
| 12:30 | | |
| 12:45 | | |
| 1:00 | | |
| 1:15 | | |
| 1:30 | | |
| 1:45 | | |
| 2:00 | | |
| 2:15 | | |
| 2:30 | | |
| 2:45 | | |
| 3:00 | | |
| 3:15 | | |
| 3:30 | | |
| 3:45 | | |
| 4:00 | | |
| 4:15 | | |
| 4:30 | | |
| 4:45 | | |
| 5:00 | | |
| 5:15 | | |
| 5:30 | | |
| 5:45 | | |
| 6:00 | | |
| 6:15 | | |
| 6:30 | | |
| 6:45 | | |
| 7:00 | | |
| 7:15 | | |
| 7:30 | | |
| 7:45 | | |
| 8:00 | | |
| 8:15 | | |
| 8:30 | | |
| 8:45 | | |
| 9:00 | | |
| 9:15 | | |
| 9:30 | | |
| 9:45 | | |

| Thursday __/__/__ | | |
|---|---|---|
| | Planned | Actual |
| | | |
| 7:00 a.m. | | |
| 7:15 | | |
| 7:30 | | |
| 7:45 | | |
| 8:00 | | |
| 8:15 | | |
| 8:30 | | |
| 8:45 | | |
| 9:00 | | |
| 9:15 | | |
| 9:30 | | |
| 9:45 | | |
| 10:00 | | |
| 10:15 | | |
| 10:30 | | |
| 10:45 | | |
| 11:00 | | |
| 11:15 | | |
| 11:30 | | |
| 11:45 | | |
| 12:00 p.m | | |
| 12:15 | | |
| 12:30 | | |
| 12:45 | | |
| 1:00 | | |
| 1:15 | | |
| 1:30 | | |
| 1:45 | | |
| 2:00 | | |
| 2:15 | | |
| 2:30 | | |
| 2:45 | | |
| 3:00 | | |
| 3:15 | | |
| 3:30 | | |
| 3:45 | | |
| 4:00 | | |
| 4:15 | | |
| 4:30 | | |
| 4:45 | | |
| 5:00 | | |
| 5:15 | | |
| 5:30 | | |
| 5:45 | | |
| 6:00 | | |
| 6:15 | | |
| 6:30 | | |
| 6:45 | | |
| 7:00 | | |
| 7:15 | | |
| 7:30 | | |
| 7:45 | | |
| 8:00 | | |
| 8:15 | | |
| 8:30 | | |
| 8:45 | | |
| 9:00 | | |
| 9:15 | | |
| 9:30 | | |
| 9:45 | | |

| Friday __/__/__ | | |
|---|---|---|
| | Planned | Actual |
| | | |
| 7:00 a.m. | | |
| 7:15 | | |
| 7:30 | | |
| 7:45 | | |
| 8:00 | | |
| 8:15 | | |
| 8:30 | | |
| 8:45 | | |
| 9:00 | | |
| 9:15 | | |
| 9:30 | | |
| 9:45 | | |
| 10:00 | | |
| 10:15 | | |
| 10:30 | | |
| 10:45 | | |
| 11:00 | | |
| 11:15 | | |
| 11:30 | | |
| 11:45 | | |
| 12:00 p.m | | |
| 12:15 | | |
| 12:30 | | |
| 12:45 | | |
| 1:00 | | |
| 1:15 | | |
| 1:30 | | |
| 1:45 | | |
| 2:00 | | |
| 2:15 | | |
| 2:30 | | |
| 2:45 | | |
| 3:00 | | |
| 3:15 | | |
| 3:30 | | |
| 3:45 | | |
| 4:00 | | |
| 4:15 | | |
| 4:30 | | |
| 4:45 | | |
| 5:00 | | |
| 5:15 | | |
| 5:30 | | |
| 5:45 | | |
| 6:00 | | |
| 6:15 | | |
| 6:30 | | |
| 6:45 | | |
| 7:00 | | |
| 7:15 | | |
| 7:30 | | |
| 7:45 | | |
| 8:00 | | |
| 8:15 | | |
| 8:30 | | |
| 8:45 | | |
| 9:00 | | |
| 9:15 | | |
| 9:30 | | |
| 9:45 | | |

| Saturday __/__/__ | | |
|---|---|---|
| | Planned | Actual |
| | | |

| Sunday __/__/__ | | |
|---|---|---|
| | Planned | Actual |

# KEY TERMS AND CONCEPTS

## Psychology as a Science

1. Psychology _____

2. Psychological disorders_____

3. Generalize _____

4. Theory _____

5. Variable _____

## What Psychologists Do

6. Pure research _____

7. Applied research _____

8. Consultation_____

9. Psychotherapy _____

10. Behavior therapy _____

11. Stereotype _____

## Where Psychology Comes From: A Brief History

12. Introspection _____

13. Structuralism _____

14. Objective _____

15. Subjective _____

16. Functionalism_____

17. Habit _____

18. Behaviorism _____

19. Response _____

20. Stimuli _____

21. Conditioning _____

22. Reinforcement_____

23. Gestalt psychology _____

24. Insight _____

25. Psychoanalysis_____

26. Psychodynamic _____

## How Today's Psychologists View Behavior

27. Hormone _____

28. Genes _____

29. Cognitive_____

30. Humanism _____

31. Existentialism _____

32. Neoanalysts _____

33. Social-cognitive theory_____

34. Sociocultural perspective _____

## Human Diversity and Psychology

35. Ethnic group _____

36. Biculturalism _____

37. Gender _____

## Critical Thinking and Psychology

38. Critical thinking _____

## Additional Terms

_____

_____

_____

_____

_____

_____

_____

_____

_____

# Matching—Names to Know

Instructions: The names in the first column are of people who have made significant contributions to psychology. The second column lists schools of psychology and other identifying information. Place the letter of the item that is best associated with the person in the blank space to the left of the person's name. Answers are given below.

____ 1. Aristotle
____ 2. Plato
____ 3. Wolfgang Köhler
____ 4. Gustav Theodor Fechner
____ 5. Erik Erikson
____ 6. Edward B. Titchener
____ 7. Abraham Maslow
____ 8. B. F. Skinner
____ 9. Mary Whiton Calkins
____ 10. Carl Rogers
____ 11. Socrates
____ 12. John B. Watson
____ 13. Wilhelm Wundt
____ 14. Jean Piaget
____ 15. Ivan Pavlov
____ 16. Max Wertheimer
____ 17. G. Stanley Hall
____ 18. Kurt Koffka
____ 19. Sigmund Freud
____ 20. Karen Horney
____ 21. Kenneth B. Clark
____ 22. William James
____ 23. Christine Ladd–Franklin

A. Humanistic Perspective
B. Behaviorism
C. Gestalt Psychology
D. Studied ethnicity and influenced a Supreme Court decision on desegregation
E. Psychodynamic Perspective
F. Author, *Elements of Psychophysics*
G. Structuralism
H. Founder of American Psychological Association
I. Introspection
J. Formulated a theory of color vision
K. Functionalism
L. Cognitive Perspective
M. Author, *Peri Psyches*
N. Said "Know thyself"
O. Introduced the method of paired associates and discovered the primacy and recency effects

# Prominent Figures in the History of Psychology

This exercise is based on Table 1.1 in the chapter and provides you with the opportunity to recall people whom psychological historians and department chairpersons rank as having made notable contributions to psychology. Write the missing name in the blank space, and check your answers against the key that follows the exercise.

| Historians | | | Chairpersons | | |
|---|---|---|---|---|---|
| Rank | Figure | Area of Contribution | Rank | Figure | Area of Contribution |
| 1. | Wilhelm (1) W_____ | Structuralism | 1. | B. F. (2) S_____ | Operant Conditioning |
| 2. | William (3) J_____ | Functionalism | 2. | Sigmund (4) F_____ | Psychoanalysis |
| 3. | (5) S_____ Freud | Psychoanalysis | 3. | (6) W_____ James | Functionalism |
| 4. | John B. (7) W_____ | Behaviorism | 4. | Jean (8) P_____ | Cognitive Development |
| 5. | Ivan (9) P_____ | Conditioning | 5. | G. Stanley (10) H_____ | Development |
| 6. | Hermann (11) E_____ | Memory | 6. | (12) W_____ Wundt | Structuralism |
| 7. | (13) J_____ Piaget | Cognitive Development | 7. | Carl (14) R_____ | Self Theory, Person-Centered Therapy |
| 8. | B. F. (15) S_____ | Operant Conditioning | 8. | (16) J_____ B. Watson | Behaviorism |
| 9. | Alfred (17) B_____ | Assessment of Intelligence | 9. | (18) I_____ Pavlov | Conditioning |
| 10. | Gustav Theodor (19) F_____ | Psychophysics | 10. | Edward (20) T_____ | Learning–Law of Effect |

## SECTION 1: Psychology as a Science

**Obj. 1:** Psychology is defined as the study of
(1) <u>b          </u> and mental processes.

(2) <u>          ists</u> limit their investigations to observable behaviors, such as muscular responses or measurement of heart rate. Cognitive psychologists include (3) <u>m          </u> processes, such as images, concepts, thoughts, and dreams. Behaviorists argue that the difficulty in studying mental processes is that they are private events, usually assumed to be present on the basis of the (4) <u>self-          </u> of the person experiencing them.

**Obj. 2:** Psychology seeks to describe, explain,
(5) <u>p          </u>, and (6) <u>c          </u> behavior. But psychologists do not attempt to (7) <u>c          </u> the behavior of other people against their wills. Instead, they help clients (8) <u>m          </u> their own behavior for their own benefit.

Behavior is explained through psychological
(9) <u>t          </u>, which are sets of statements that involve assumptions about behavior. Explanations and
(10) <u>p          </u> are derived from theories. Theories are revised, as needed, to accommodate new
(11) <u>ob          </u>. If necessary, theories are discarded.

## SECTION 2: What Psychologists Do

**Obj. 3:** Some psychologists engage in basic or
(12) <u>p          </u> research, which has no immediate applications. Other psychologists engage in
(13) <u>a          </u> research, which seeks solutions to specific problems. In addition to research, many psychologists are found in (14) <u>          ching</u>.

(15) <u>          al</u> psychologists comprise the largest subgroup of psychologists. Clinical psychologists help people who are behaving (16) <u>          ally</u> adjust to the demands of life. Clinical psychologists help clients resolve problems through (17) <u>          rapy</u> and (18) <u>b          </u> therapy. (19) <u>C          </u> psychologists work with individuals who have adjustment problems but do not show seriously abnormal behavior.

School psychologists assist students with problems that interfere with (20) <u>          ing</u>. School psychologists help make decisions about placement of students in (21) <u>sp          </u> education and
(22) <u>rem          </u> programs. (23) <u>Ed          </u> psychologists are more concerned with theoretical issues concerning human learning.

(24) <u>D          </u> psychologists study the changes that occur throughout the life span. They attempt to sort out the relative influences of heredity and the
(25) <u>en          </u> on growth. Personality psychologists attempt to define human (26) <u>          its</u>. They study influences on our thought processes, feelings, and
(27) <u>b          </u>. (28) <u>S          </u> psychologists study the nature and causes of our thoughts, feelings, and behavior in social situations. Environmental psychologists study the ways in which behavior influences and is influenced by the (29) <u>p          </u> environment.

(30) <u>E          </u> psychologists conduct research into basic psychological processes, such as sensation and perception, learning and memory, and motivation and emotion. Experimental psychologists who seek to understand the relationships between biological changes and psychological events are called
(31) <u>b          </u> psychologists.

Industrial psychologists focus on the relationships between people and (32) <u>w          </u>. (33) <u>          nal</u> psychologists study the behavior of people in organizations. Consumer psychologists attempt to predict and influence the behavior of (34) <u>c          </u>.

Health psychologists are concerned with the ways in which (35) <u>s          </u> and other psychological factors can contribute to diseases. Forensic psychologists apply psychological expertise within the
(36) <u>c          </u> <u>          </u> system.

## SECTION 3: Where Psychology Comes From: A Brief History

**Obj. 4:** The Greek philosopher (37) A_____ was among the first to argue that human behavior is subject to rules and laws. Socrates proclaimed "Know thyself" and suggested the use of (38) _____tion to gain self-knowledge.

Wilhelm (39) W_____ established the first psychological laboratory in 1879. Wundt also founded the school of (40) _____alism and used introspection to study the objective and subjective elements of experience.

William James founded the school of (41) _____alism. Functionalism dealt with observable behavior as well as conscious experience, and focused on the importance of (42) h_____, to which James referred as "the enormous flywheel of society."

John B. Watson founded the school of (43) b_____. Behaviorists argue that psychology must limit itself to (44) ob_____ behavior and forgo excursions into subjective consciousness. Watson pointed to Pavlov's experiments in (45) _____ning as a model for psychological research. Behaviorism focused on learning by conditioning, and B. F. Skinner introduced the concept of (46) _____ment as an explanation of how learning occurs.

Gestalt psychology focused on (47) p_____. Gestalt psychologists saw our perceptions as (48) wh_____ that give meaning to parts. They argued that learning can be active and (49) _____ful, not merely responsive and (50) _____ical, as in Pavlov's experiments.

Sigmund Freud founded the school of (51) p_____. According to psychodynamic theory, people are driven by hidden impulses and distort reality in order to protect themselves from (52) a_____.

## SECTION 4: How Today's Psychologists View Behavior

**Obj. 5:** The six major perspectives in contemporary psychology include the biological, (53) co_____, (54) hu_____–existential, psychodynamic, learning, and sociocultural perspectives. Biologically-oriented psychologists study the links between behavior and biological events, such as the firing of cells in the (55) b_____ and the release of hormones.

Cognitive psychologists study the ways in which we perceive and mentally (56) r_____ the world. Piaget's study of the (57) c_____ development of children has inspired many developmental and educational psychologists. Cognitive psychologists also study (58) in_____ processing—the processes by which information is perceived, stored, and (59) re_____.

Humanistic–existential psychologists stress the importance of human (60) ex_____. They also assert that people have the freedom to make responsible (61) ch_____.

Contemporary psychoanalysts are likely to consider themselves (62) _____lysts. They generally follow Freud's views, but focus less on the roles of (63) un_____ sexual and aggressive impulses and see people as more capable of making conscious choices.

Watson and his followers are referred to as (64) _____ists. Social–cognitive theorists are in the behaviorist tradition because of their strong focus on the role of (65) _____ing in human behavior. Social–cognitive theorists also find roles for (66) ob_____ learning, expectations, and values in explaining human behavior, however.

The sociocultural perspective fosters the consideration of matters of (67) eth_____, gender, culture, and (68) _____economic status in psychology.

## SECTION 5: Human Diversity and Psychology

**Obj. 6:** The profession of psychology is committed to the dignity of the (69) _____dual, but we cannot understand individuals without an awareness of the richness of human (70) _____sity. People's (71) _____nic groups are defined by features such as their common cultural heritage, race, language, and history. People also differ according to their (72) _____er—that is, the state of being male or being female. Today (73: *Circle one*: men or women) account for 54.5% of U.S. postsecondary students.

**Obj. 7:** Psychology's "golden oldies," as listed in Table 1.1, are all white (74: *Circle one:* females or males). Christine (75) Ladd–F_____ formulated a theory of color vision. Mary Whiton (76) C_____ introduced the method of paired associates and discovered the primacy and recency effects. Margaret Floy (77) W_____ wrote *The Animal Mind*. African–American psychologist J. Henry (78) A_____ engaged in research in the perception of heat and cold. Kenneth B. (79) C_____ influenced a key Supreme Court decision on desegregation. Jorge (80) S_____ was among the first to show how intelligence tests are culturally biased.

## SECTION 6: Critical Thinking and Psychology

**Obj. 8:** Critical thinking is intended to foster an attitude of (81) skep_____. Critical thinking refers to thoughtfully (82) _____zing and probing the questions, statements, and arguments of others. It means examining the (83) def_____s of terms, examining the (84) pre_____s or assumptions behind arguments, and scrutinizing the logic with which arguments are developed. Critical thinking within the science of psychology also refers to the ability to inquire about causes and (85) _____cts, and to knowledge of (86) re_____ methods. Critical thinkers are also cautious in drawing conclusions from (87) _____ence. Critical thinkers do not (88) over_____ or (89) over_____.

Critical thinkers also learn to recognize the logical (90) fal_____s in other people's claims and arguments. Critical thinkers, for example, recognize the fallacies in arguments directed to the person [*argumentum ad* (91) _____*inem*], arguments employing force [*argumentum ad baculum*], appeals to authority [*argumentum* ad (92) _____*diam*], and appeals to popularity [*argumentum ad* (93) _____*lum*].

| | |
|---|---|
| 1. behavior | 47. perception |
| 2. Behaviorists | 48. wholes |
| 3. mental | 49. purposeful |
| 4. self–report | 50. mechanical |
| 5. predict | 51. psychoanalysis |
| 6. control | 52. anxiety |
| 7. control | 53. cognitive |
| 8. modify | 54. humanistic |
| 9. theories | 55. brain |
| 10. predictions | 56. represent |
| 11. observations | 57. cognitive |
| 12. pure | 58. information |
| 13. applied | 59. retrieved |
| 14. teaching | 60. experience |
| 15. Clinical | 61. choices |
| 16. abnormally | 62. neoanalysts |
| 17. psychotherapy | 63. unconscious |
| 18. behavior therapy | 64. behaviorists |
| 19. Counseling | 65. learning |
| 20. learning | 66. observational |
| 21. special | 67. ethnicity |
| 22. remediation | 68. socioeconomic |
| 23. Educational | 69. individual |
| 24. Developmental | 70. diversity |
| 25. environment | 71. ethnic |
| 26. traits | 72. gender |
| 27. behaviors | 73. women |
| 28. Social | 74. males |
| 29. physical | 75. Franklin |
| 30. Experimental | 76. Calkins |
| 31. biological | 77. Washburn |
| 32. work | 78. Alston |
| 33. Organizational | 79. Clark |
| 34. consumers | 80. Sanchez |
| 35. stress | 81. skepticism |
| 36. criminal justice | 82. analyzing |
| 37. Aristotle | 83. definitions |
| 38. introspection | 84. premises |
| 39. Wundt | 85. effects |
| 40. structuralism | 86. research |
| 41. functionalism | 87. evidence |
| 42. habit | 88. oversimplify |
| 43. behaviorism | 89. overgeneralize |
| 44. observable | 90. fallacies |
| 45. conditioning | 91. *hominem* |
| 46. reinforcement | 92. *verecundiam* |
| | 93. *populum* |

| Idioms | | |
|---|---|---|
| 4 | to a tee | exactly like you |
| 4 | sacrifice ourselves | give up our life for someone |
| 10 | user friendly | easy to use |
| 11 | best suited | well matched |
| 13 | firmly planted | a definite part of |
| 16 | took up the behaviorist call | started working as a behavioral scientist |
| 16 | slip of the tongue | said something by mistake |
| 16 | seething cauldron | like a boiling pot |
| 17 | taken many turns | changed focus many times |

| Cultural Reference | | Explanation |
|---|---|---|
| 4 | William Shakespeare | English dramatist, died 1616 |
| 4 | cathedrals | large, beautiful churches |
| 10 | automobile dashboards | a panel under the windshield of a car |
| 10 | criminal-justice system | system to enforce our laws |
| 11 | Cornell University | University in Eastern U.S. |

| Phrases and Expressions (Different Usage) | | |
|---|---|---|
| 4 | downright puzzling | confusing |
| 5 | sign language | talk through hand motions |
| 5 | need not justify | do not have to support |
| 5 | concepts interwoven into theories | ideas are put together to make a theory |
| 5 | formulations | make up of |
| 5 | apparent relationships | what seems to be relationships |
| 5 | presumed | believed to be |
| 6 | deprived | not given |
| 6 | predicted | told about before |
| 6 | incapable | not able to do |
| 6 | erroneously | incorrectly |
| 6 | diverse interests | different and broad interests |
| 6 | impacts | effects |
| 7 | spurred onward | pushed forward |
| 7 | enhances | increases |
| 7 | do not engage in | do not do |
| 7 | disseminate | spread |
| 7 | specialize | focus on |
| 7 | maladaptive | not useful |
| 8 | clarify | make understandable |
| 8 | surmounting | overcoming |
| 8 | obstacles | problems |
| 8 | optimizing | making the best possible |
| 8 | facilitate | help |
| 8 | acculturation | take on parts of a new culture |
| 8 | maternal | mother |
| 9 | fundamental | basic |
| 9 | devise strategies | think up new ideas |
| 9 | persuasiveness | ability to be convincing |

| Phrases and Expressions (Different Usage) | | |
|---|---|---|
| 10 | emerging | newly developing |
| 10 | expertise | skills |
| 10 | examine | look at |
| 10 | investigate | study |
| 11 | delved | study deeply |
| 11 | external forces | outside pressure |
| 11 | mottos | guiding principle |
| 11 | differentiate | see as different |
| 11 | rational | logical, reasonable |
| 11 | introspection | to examine our thoughts |
| 11 | profoundly | very much |
| 11 | founded | started, began |
| 11 | miniature | very small |
| 12 | adopted | took on |
| 12 | dealt with | past tense of to deal with |
| 12 | overt behavior | actions that can be seen |
| 12 | organisms | anything that is living |
| 12 | transmit | give |
| 12 | repetition | repeating |
| 12 | meanders | not walking in a straight line |
| 12 | pathway | a long area to walk on |
| 13 | stream of consciousness | flow of thoughts |
| 13 | bridled | got upset at |
| 13 | emission | sending off |
| 13 | salivation | mouth watering |
| 13 | absurd | ridiculous, silly |
| 13 | academic life | working at a university |
| 13 | behave | act |
| 13 | intricate | complex |
| 14 | summation of instances | adding together of time |
| 14 | enumerating | telling item by item |
| 14 | hopeless task | impossible to do |
| 14 | prominent | important |
| 14 | mechanical | like a machine |
| 14 | insight | sudden increase in knowledge |
| 15 | marooned | stuck on an island |
| 15 | mental elements | ideas in the mind |
| 15 | pondering | thinking about |
| 15 | In a flash? | quickly |
| 15 | killing spree | kills many people |
| 16 | hidden impulses | drives they are unaware of |
| 16 | astounded | very surprised |
| 16 | abominable | terrible |
| 16 | absurd | ridiculous |
| 16 | decent | good |
| 16 | delude | fool |
| 16 | gratifying | satisfying |
| 17 | contemporary | modern, current |
| 17 | investigation | study |
| 17 | pivotal | most important |

Chapter 1    What Is Psychology?    35

| | Phrases and Expressions (Different Usage) | | | | Phrases and Expressions (Different Usage) | |
|---|---|---|---|---|---|---|
| 18 | implications | issues | | 29 | postsecondary institutions | colleges and universities |
| 18 | realm | area | | 29 | | |
| 18 | psychology's roots | background | | 29 | cherished | deeply cared about |
| 18 | descendants | people that came after him | | 29 | passive recipients | receive without thinking |
| 18 | retrieved | found | | 29 | dispute | go against |
| 19 | unifies | brings together | | 29 | celebrities | famous people |
| 19 | summation | adding together | | 29 | probing | deeply questioning |
| 19 | have been stamped collectively | labelled as | | 29 | scrutinizing | carefully looking at |
| 19 | poorly suited | not well matched | | 30 | strive | work at |
| 19 | vital | important | | 30 | demonstrate | show |
| 19 | dominated | most important to | | 30 | sparks considerable controversy | start a lot of arguments |
| 20 | watered-down form | weaken | | 31 | bombarded by TV | see many commercials |
| 20 | vernacular | common language | | 31 | tabloids | newspapers that are very sensational but do not always print the truth |
| 20 | ascribe | see as the source | | | | |
| 20 | distinction | difference | | | | |
| 20 | broad guideline | wide guide | | 31 | fallacies | false statements |
| 20 | exemplified | shown as example | | 32 | ingenious | smart, creative |
| 20 | compel | force | | 32 | compassionate | caring |
| 20 | modify | change | | 32 | ushered in | begun |
| 20 | brazen | loud and bold | | 32 | refreshing breezes | new beginnings |
| 21 | pays off | is worth it | | | | |
| 21 | prevalence | occurrence | | | Additional Terms | |
| 21 | biases | prejudice | | | | |
| 21 | diminishes | make smaller | | | | |
| 21 | obstacles | problems | | | | |
| 23 | crucible | container used to melt items | | | | |
| 23 | liquefied and blended into one | melted together as one | | | | |
| 23 | competently | skillfully | | | | |
| 23 | reproductive patterns | patterns in who is having babies | | | | |
| 24 | decade | 10 year period | | | | |
| 24 | denigrated | put down | | | | |
| 24 | erroneously | falsely | | | | |
| 25 | anatomic sex | physical male or femaleness | | | | |
| 25 | complex web of cultural expectation | many interrelated expectations | | | | |
| 25 | overt behavior | behavior that can be seen | | | | |
| 25 | channeled into | led to | | | | |
| 26 | inroads into | improve status in | | | | |
| 26 | are in place | are happening now | | | | |
| 26 | gay males | men attracted to other men sexually | | | | |
| 26 | lesbians | women attracted to other women sexually | | | | |
| 26 | mainstream culture | majority culture | | | | |
| 26 | loath | reluctant, to hesitate | | | | |
| 26 | heightens | increases | | | | |
| 27 | homogeneous | all similar people | | | | |
| 27 | to persuade | to convince | | | | |
| 27 | discourse | discussion | | | | |
| 27 | ultimately | after some time | | | | |
| 27 | pioneered | started, began | | | | |
| 27 | presages | pointed toward | | | | |
| 28 | made their mark | made contributions | | | | |
| 28 | detriment | harmful | | | | |

1. If you wanted to run a study in which you learned about another person's _____, you would rely on that person's self-report.
   (a) heart rate
   (b) mental images
   (c) emission of a brain wave
   (d) muscular responses

2. Applied research is best described as research undertaken
   (a) with human beings.
   (b) with lower animals.
   (c) to find solutions to specific problems.
   (d) for its own sake.

3. If you knew someone who was having an adjustment problem, you would refer that person to a(n) _____ psychologist.
   (a) educational
   (b) developmental
   (c) personality
   (d) counseling

4. If you were to read an article comparing the values of breast-feeding and bottle-feeding, it would probably report research that had been carried out by _____ psychologists.
   (a) clinical
   (b) personality
   (c) developmental
   (d) school

5. _____ psychologists are most directly concerned with the investigation of issues related to gender roles, processes such as repression, and the development of traits.
   (a) Personality
   (b) Clinical
   (c) Organizational
   (d) School

6. Industrial/organizational psychologists are most likely to be consulted to
   (a) assist in the processes of hiring and promotion.
   (b) help workers make educational decisions.
   (c) treat workers showing abnormal behavior.
   (d) investigate the political and social attitudes of workers.

7. The earliest author of a book about psychology is
   (a) Democritus.
   (b) Darwin.
   (c) Sophocles.
   (d) Aristotle.

8. Which of the following schools of psychology was originated in Germany?
   (a) functionalism
   (b) structuralism
   (c) behaviorism
   (d) psychoanalysis

9. Who argued that the mind, like light or sound, was a natural event?
   (a) Carl Rogers
   (b) Sigmund Freud
   (c) B. F. Skinner
   (d) Wilhelm Wundt

10. The school of psychology that focused most directly on perceptual processes is
    (a) psychoanalysis.
    (b) behaviorism.
    (c) humanistic psychology.
    (d) Gestalt psychology.

11. Who founded the American Psychological Association?
    (a) William James
    (b) Edward Bradford Titchener
    (c) G. Stanley Hall
    (d) Mary Whiton Calkins

12. _____ is a neoanalyst.
    (a) Christine Ladd-Franklin
    (b) Erik Erikson
    (c) Albert Bandura
    (d) Carl Rogers

13. Social-cognitive theorists but not behaviorists focus, on the role of _____ in behavior.
    (a) unconscious processes
    (b) cognition
    (c) reinforcement
    (d) learning

14. Who wrote *The Animal Mind*?
    (a) Margaret Floy Washburn
    (b) Elizabeth Loftus
    (c) Christine Ladd–Franklin
    (d) Mary Whiton Calkins

15. Who introduced the methods of paired associates?
    (a) Margaret Floy Washburn
    (b) Elizabeth Loftus
    (c) Christine Ladd–Franklin
    (d) Mary Whiton Calkins

16. Who engaged in research on the perception of heat and cold?
    (a) B. F. Skinner
    (b) J. Henry Alston
    (c) Jorge Sanchez
    (d) Kenneth B. Clark

17. Who influenced a key Supreme Court decision on desegregation?
    (a) B. F. Skinner
    (b) J. Henry Alston
    (c) Jorge Sanchez
    (d) Kenneth B. Clark

18. Who was among the first to show how intelligence tests are culturally biased?
    (a) B. F. Skinner
    (b) J. Henry Alston
    (c) Jorge Sanchez
    (d) Kenneth B. Clark

19. A key value of critical thinking is that it
    (a) provides a data base of knowledge.
    (b) makes individuals argumentative.
    (c) provides people with skills to educate themselves for a lifetime.
    (d) teaches people how to criticize works of art, literature, and music.

20. A student says, "I know this is true because my psychology professor says that it is true." This argument is an example of the *argumentum ad*
    (a) *hominem.*
    (b) *baculum.*
    (c) *verecundiam.*
    (d) *populum.*

**Answer Key to *Posttest***

1. B
2. C
3. D
4. C
5. A
6. A
7. D
8. B
9. D
10. D
11. C
12. B
13. B
14. A
15. D
16. B
17. D
18. C
19. C
20. C

| | |
|---|---|
| Psychology | Psychotherapy |
| Psychological disorders | Behavior therapy |
| Generalize | Stereotype |
| Theory | Introspection |
| Variable | Structuralism |
| Pure research | Objective |
| Applied research | Subjective |

| | |
|---|---|
| The systematic application of psychological knowledge to the treatment of problem behavior. | The science that studies behavior and mental processes. |
| Application of principles of learning to the direct modification of problem behavior. | Patterns of behavior or mental processes that are connected with emotional distress or significant impairment in functioning. |
| A fixed, conventional idea about a group. | To go from the particular to the general; to extend. |
| An objective approach to describing one's mental content. | A formulation of relationships underlying observed events. |
| The school of psychology that argues that the mind consists of three basic elements–sensations, feelings, and images–that combine to form experience. | A condition that is measured or controlled in a scientific study. A variable can vary in a measurable manner. |
| Of known or perceived objects rather than existing only in the mind; real. | Research conducted without concern for immediate applications. |
| Of the mind; personal; determined by thoughts and feelings rather than by external objects. | Research conducted in an effort to find solutions to particular problems. |

| Functionalism | Gestalt psychology |
| --- | --- |
| Habit | Insight |
| Behaviorism | Psychoanalysis |
| Response | Psychodynamic |
| Stimuli | Hormone |
| Conditioning | Genes |
| Reinforcement | Cognitive |

| | |
|---|---|
| The school of psychology that emphasizes the tendency to organize perceptions into wholes and to integrate separate stimuli into meaningful patterns. | The school of psychology that emphasizes the uses or functions of the mind rather than the elements of experience. |
| In Gestalt psychology, the sudden reorganization of perceptions, allowing the sudden solution of a problem. | A response to a stimulus that becomes automatic with repetition. |
| The school of psychology that emphasizes the importance of unconscious motives and conflicts as determinants of human behavior. | The school of psychology that defines psychology as the study of observable behavior and studies relationships between stimuli and responses. |
| Referring to Freud's theory, which proposes that the motion of underlying forces of personality determines our thoughts, feelings, and behavior. | A movement or other observable reaction to a stimulus. |
| A chemical substance that promotes development of body structures and regulates various body functions. | A feature in the environment that is detected by an organism or leads to a change in behavior. A form of physical energy such as light or sound that impinges on the sensory receptors. |
| The basic building blocks of heredity. | A simple form of learning in which stimuli come to signal other stimuli by means of association. |
| Having to do with mental processes such as sensation and perception, memory, intelligence, language, thought, and problem solving. | A stimulus that follows a response and increases the frequency of the response. |

| | |
|---|---|
| Humanism | Gender |
| Existentialism | Critical thinking |
| Neoanalysts | Biological perspective |
| Social-cognitive theory | Cognitive perspective |
| Sociocultural perspective | Learning perspective |
| Ethnic group | Fallacies in arguments |
| Biculturalism | Organizational psychology |

| | |
|---|---|
| The state of being female or being male. | The philosophy and school of psychology that asserts that people are conscious, self-aware, and capable of free choice, self-fulfillment, and ethical behavior. |
| An approach to thinking character-ized by skepticism and thoughtful analysis of statements and argu-ments. | The view that people are completely free and responsible for their own behavior. |
| Assumes behavior and mental processes can be explained in terms of biological processes, such as, nervous system, endocrine system, or genetic factors. | Contemporary followers of Freud who focus less on the roles of unconscious impulses and more on conscious choice and self-direction. |
| Assumes people mentally represent the world and consciously attempt to understand it through mental imagery, information processing, thinking, and language. | A school of psychology in the behav-iorist tradition that includes cognitive factors in the explanation and prediction of behavior. Formerly called social-learning theory. |
| Assumes people are very similar at birth but unique histories of experience and reinforcement guide unique patterns of development of behavior and skills. | The view that focuses on the roles of ethnicity, gender, culture, and socioeconomic status in behavior and mental processes. |
| • Arguments directed to the person;<br>• Appeals to force, authority, popularity | A group characterized by common features, such as cultural heritage, history, race, and language. |
| Organizational psychologists study the behavior of people in organiza-tions, such as business firms. | Competence within two cultures without losing one's cultural identity or choosing one culture over another. |

# Chapter 2

# Research Methods in Psychology

Directions: This *PRETEST* will give you feedback about how well you understand Chapter 2. In order to enhance your mastery of Chapter 2, complete all the sections of this chapter of the Study Guide. Then you can take the *POSTTEST* and compare your results.

1. The Milgram studies employed the _____ method.
   (a) naturalistic–observation
   (b) laboratory observation
   (c) testing
   (d) experimental

2. The current edition of the *Publication Manual of the American Psychological Association* prefers usage of the term *participants* to *subjects* because
   (a) *participants* is more impersonal.
   (b) *participants* acknowledges that individuals in research studies take an active role in the studies.
   (c) *subjects* can be used only in reference to animals such as rats and pigeons.
   (d) the word *subject* is also used in the phrase *subject matter*.

3. Who received electric shock in the Milgram studies?
   (a) learners
   (b) teachers
   (c) researchers
   (d) confederates of the researchers

4. A(n) _____ is a specific statement about behavior or mental processes that is tested through research.
   (a) hypothesis
   (b) scientific method
   (c) theory
   (d) observation

5. An operational definition of a variable is
   (a) easy to measure.
   (b) limited to observable behavior only.
   (c) one that has a causal effect on behavior or mental processes.
   (d) a definition of a variable in terms of the methods used to create or measure that variable.

6. People who exercise regularly are healthier than people who do not. This statement shows that
   (a) exercise causes people to be in good health.
   (b) good health causes people to exercise.
   (c) there is a correlational relationship between exercise and health.
   (d) there is an experimental relationship between exercise and health.

7. Who is a former APA president?
   (a) Lang
   (b) Strickland
   (c) Milgram
   (d) Goodall

8. Research suggests that from _____ of U.S. women will be physically assaulted—slapped, beaten, choked, or attacked with a weapon—by a partner with whom they share an intimate relationship.
   (a) 3% to 9%
   (b) 10% to 20%
   (c) 21% to 34%
   (d) 35% to 50%

9. The Kinsey studies on sexual behavior did not adequately represent
(a) African Americans.
(b) women.
(c) middle class individuals.
(d) people who live in the Midwest.

10. One of the reasons that people who complete and return magazine surveys do not represent the general population is
(a) they were not selected at random from telephone directories.
(b) stratification was not used.
(c) volunteer bias.
(d) magazine distribution is limited in parts of the United States.

11. The majority of participants in a recent survey of college students identified themselves as politically
(a) conservative.
(b) middle of the road.
(c) liberal.
(d) radical.

12. The majority of participants in a recent survey of college students agreed that
(a) government is not doing enough to control pollution.
(b) taxes should be raised to reduce the federal deficit.
(c) marijuana should be legalized.
(d) the death penalty should be abolished.

13. The validity of a test is
(a) its consistency.
(b) the degree to which it measures what it is supposed to measure.
(c) the degree to which test–takers obtain similar scores on separate testing occasions.
(d) the extent of agreement by psychologists that it is valid.

14. A negative correlation between variables means that
(a) there is no relationship between the variables.
(b) there is an antagonistic or belligerent relationship among the variables.
(c) one variable increases as the other decreases.
(d) research on the relationship between the variables will not lead to useful results.

15. According to the text, the Milgram studies are criticized mainly because the
(a) results provide some ugly information about people.
(b) study participants were not selected at random.
(c) identities of the teachers and the learners were sometimes confused.
(d) methods raise ethical questions.

16. Jane Goodall studied chimpanzees by means of the _____ method.
(a) case–study
(b) naturalistic–observation
(c) survey
(d) experimental

17. Cause and effect are best discovered by means of the _____ method.
(a) case–study
(b) naturalistic–observation
(c) correlational
(d) laboratory–observation

18. In experiments, the presence of dependent variables presumably depends on the _____ variables.
(a) control
(b) independent
(c) experimental
(d) hypothetical

19. The results of the *Literary Digest* survey demonstrate the importance of _____ in research.
(a) random sampling
(b) using a control group
(c) carefully stated hypotheses
(d) using blinds

20. The Lang study on alcohol and aggression could not have been carried out without the _____ of study participants.
(a) informed consent
(b) confidentiality
(c) deception
(d) debriefing

**Answer Key to *Pretest***

| | | | | |
|---|---|---|---|---|
| 1. D | 5. D | 9. A | 13. B | 17. D |
| 2. B | 6. C | 10. C | 14. C | 18. B |
| 3. B | 7. B | 11. B | 15. D | 19. A |
| 4. A | 8. C | 12. A | 16. B | 20. C |

Psychology is an empirical science that relies on the scientific method to confirm (or disconfirm) theoretical hypotheses. Psychologists use various methods to observe behavior in research: the case–study, survey, testing, naturalistic–observation, and laboratory–observation methods. The case–study method involves in–depth research into the life of an individual or a small group. The survey method uses interviews, questionnaires, and public records to study the reported behavior of large numbers of people. Psychological tests can be used to study psychological traits. Naturalistic observation occurs in the field—where behavior naturally happens. Laboratory observation allows researchers to observe behavior under controlled conditions. The correlational method shows positive or negative relationships among variables, but cannot be used to learn of cause and effect. The experimental method applies experimental treatments in an effort to determine cause and effect.

The purpose of ethics is to prevent harm from coming to participants in research and to clients in therapy. Animals are sometimes harmed when psychologists believe that the resultant findings will be of broad benefit. Some experiments require the deception of human participants, who are debriefed when the procedures are completed.

## LEARNING OBJECTIVES

| | Scientific Method |
|---|---|
| 1. Describe the features of the *scientific method*. | |
| | **Samples and Populations** |
| 2. Explain how psychologists use samples in an effort to represent populations. | |
| 3. Discuss the use of sampling in psychology to represent human diversity. | |
| | **Methods of Observation** |
| 4. Discuss the *case–study method*. | |
| 5. Discuss the *survey method*. | |

6. Discuss the *testing method*.

7. Discuss the *naturalistic–observation method*.

8. Discuss the *laboratory–observation method*.

## The Correlational Method

9. Define the *correlational method*.

10. Discuss the limitations of the correlational method.

## The Experimental Method

11. Define the *experimental method*.

12. Discuss the use of independent and dependent variables in the experimental method.

13. Discuss the use of experimental and control groups in the experimental method.

14. Discuss the use of blinds and double blinds in the experimental method.

## Ethical Issues in Psychological Research & Practice

15. Discuss ethical issues in conducting research and practice with people and animals.

## Psychology and Modern Life

16. Discuss the various pseudoscientific approaches to understanding and influencing behavior.

**The Milgram Studies**

**The Scientific Method: Putting Ideas to the Test**

**Samples and Populations:**
**Representing Human Diversity**

1. Problems in Generalizing

2. Psychology in a World of Diversity

   • The Wyatt Survey

**Methods of Observation:**
**The Better to See You With**

1. The Case-Study Method

2. The Survey Method

3. The Testing Method

4. The Naturalistic-Observation Method

5. The Laboratory-Observation Method

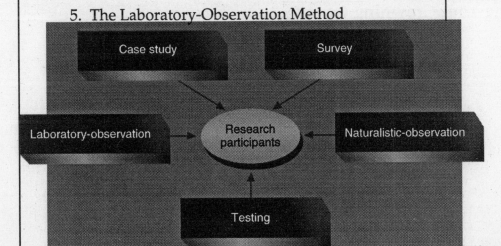

# The Correlational Method: Seeing What Goes Up &What Comes Down

1. Correlation Coefficient   -1.00 to +1.00

2. Positive Correlation

3. Negative Correlation

# The Experimental Method: Trying Things Out

1. Independent and Dependent Variables

2. Experimental and Control Groups

3. Blinds and Double Blinds

# Methods of Studying Your Crowning Glory– The Brain

1. Accidents

2. Electrical Stimulation of the Brain

Psychological theory
Daily experiences
Commonly held beliefs

Research questions

Hypotheses

Examining the research questions

Hypothesis testing

Evidence (observations)

Drawing conclusions

Theory construction or modification

New research questions or hypotheses

3. Lesions

4. Electroencephalograph (EEG)

5. Computerized Axial Tomography (CAT Scan)

6. Positron Emissions Tomography (PET scan)

7. Magnetic Resonance Imaging (MRI)

## Ethical Issues in Psychological Research and Practice

1. Research with People

2. Research with Animals

## Mastering Exams

### Before and During the Test

1. Predict the test questions. Ask your instructor to describe the test format; how long it will be, and what kind of questions to expect (essay, multiple choice, problems, etc.). Also ask what the procedure is for asking questions during the exam. Know the rules for taking the test so you do not create the impression of cheating.

2. Have a section in your notebook labeled "Test Questions" and add several questions to it after each lecture or reading the text. Record topics instructors repeat several times.

3. Arrive early to the exam so you can relax.

4. Scan the whole test immediately. Budget your time based on how many points each section is worth.

5. Read the directions *slowly*. Then **REREAD** them.

6. Answer easiest, shortest questions first. This gives you the experience of success and stimulates associations. This prepares your mind for more difficult questions.

7. Use memory techniques when you're stuck.
   - If your recall on something is blocked, remember something else that's related.
   - Start from the general and go to specific

8. Look for answers in other test questions. A term, name, date, or other fact that you can't remember might appear in the test itself.

9. Don't change an answer unless you are sure, because your first instinct is usually best.

### Machine-Graded Tests

1. Check the test against the answer sheet often.

2. Watch for stray marks that look like answers.

### Multiple-Choice Questions

1. Check the directions to see if the questions call for more than one answer.

2. Answer each question in your head before you look at the possible answers; otherwise, you may be confused by the choices.

3. Mark questions you can't answer immediately, and come back to them if you have time.

4. If incorrect answers are not deducted from your score, use the following guidelines to guess:
   - If two answers are similar, except for a couple of words, choose one of these answers.
   - If two answers have similar sounding or looking words, choose one of these answers.
   - If the answer calls for a sentence completion, eliminate the answers that would not form grammatically correct sentences.
   - If answers cover a numerical range, choose one in the middle.
   - If all else fails, close your eyes and pick one.

### True-False Questions

1. Generally, answer these questions quickly.
2. If any part of the statement is false, the whole statement is false.
3. Absolute qualifiers, such as "always" or "never", generally indicate a false statement.

### Open-Book and Notes Tests

1. Write down key points on a separate sheet.
2. Tape flags onto important pages of the book.
3. Number your notes, write a table of contents.
4. Prepare thoroughly because they are usually the most difficult tests.

### Essay Questions

1. Find out precisely what the question is asking. Don't *explain* when asked to *compare*.
2. Make an outline before writing, or draw a mind-map (explained in the Study Tip for Chapter 5.)
3. Be brief, write clearly, use a pen (erasable pen if acceptable to the instructor), get to the point, and use examples.

# KEY TERMS AND CONCEPTS

### The Milgram Studies: Shocking Stuff at Yale

1. Empirical _____

### The Scientific Method: Putting Ideas to the Test

2. Scientific method _____

3. Theory _____

4. Hypothesis _____

5. Operational definition _____

6. Selection factor _____

7. Replicate _____

### Samples and Populations: Representing Human Diversity

8. Generalize _____

9. Sample _____

10. Population _____

11. Infer _____

12. Random sampling _____

13. Stratified sample _____

14. Volunteer bias _____

### Methods of Observation: The Better to See You With

15. Case study _____

16. Survey _____

17. Reliability _____

18. Test–retest reliability _____

19. Aptitude _____

20. Validity _____

21. Validity scales _____

22. Naturalistic observation _____

23. Unobtrusive _____

24. Laboratory _____

### The Correlational Method: Seeing What Goes Up and What Comes Down

25. Correlational method _____

26. Correlation coefficient _____

27. Positive correlation _____

28. Negative correlation _____

### The Experimental Method: Trying Things Out

29. Experiment _____

30. Treatment _____

31. Independent variable _____

32. Dependent variable _____

33. Placebo _____

34. Blind _____

35. Double–blind study _____

### Methods of Studying Your Crowning Glory— The Brain

36. Homunculus _____

37. Lesion _____

38. Electroencephalograph _____

39. Computerized axial tomography (CAT scan) _____

40. Positron emission tomography (PET scan) _____

41. Magnetic resonance imaging (MRI) _____

### Ethical Issues in Psychological Research and Practice

42. Ethical _____

43. Ethics review committee _____

44. Informed consent _____

45. Confidential _____

46. Debrief _____

47. Breathalyzer _____

### Additional Terms _____

Circle the T or F in each of the following items, to indicate whether the item is true or false. Check your answers in the key given below. It is more important at this time for you to understand why each item is true or false than to get them all right.

T F 1. In the scientific method, study participants are randomly selected and assigned to experimental groups or control groups.

T F 2. A hypothesis is a formulation of the relationships that underlie observed events that allows us to explain and predict behavior.

T F 3. A hypothesis is a specific statement about behavior or mental processes that is tested through research.

T F 4. Historically speaking, most large–scale studies in the field of health have been conducted with men as the study participants.

T F 5. In the Lang study on the effects of alcohol on aggression, aggression was operationally defined as selection of a level of shock to deliver to another person.

T F 6. Samples must be very large.

T F 7. If a sample is not randomly selected, the results of the study are inaccurate.

T F 8. A random sample is selected by picking out telephone numbers in a directory by chance.

T F 9. People who volunteer to participate in research studies differ from people who do not.

T F 10. There is a positive correlation between intelligence and academic achievement.

T F 11. There is a negative correlation between two variables. We can conclude that increasing one variable causes the other to decrease.

T F 12. Researchers attempt to use unobtrusive measures in the naturalistic–observation method so that they do not influence the behavior they are observing.

T F 13. Experimental blinds aim at controlling for the effects of expectations.

T F 14. Case studies differ from surveys in the numbers of individuals studied.

T F 15. It is unethical for a psychologist to breach confidentiality with a client, even when the client states that she or he is going to kill a third party.

## Answer Key to *True–False Exercise*

1. F. This statement describes an experiment. The scientific method is a way of obtaining scientific evidence in which research questions or hypotheses are formulated and tested.
2. F. The statement defines a theory, not a hypothesis.
3. T. 4. T. 5. T. The operational definition of a variable is defined in terms of the methods used to create or measure that variable. 6. F. The most important factor about a sample is that it represent the targeted population.
7. F. The results of the study may be accurate enough for the sample in the study. The results may not be able to be generalized to a target population, however. 8. F. A random sample is defined as a sample that is drawn so that each member of a population has an equal chance of being selected to participate. Telephone numbers may be used in random sampling, but are not essential to the definition of random sampling. 9. T. Sure they do. They may be more willing to help other people, more interested in research, or simply have more time. In the case of sex surveys, they may also be more willing to disclose intimate information. Factors such as these may introduce volunteer bias into the results of a study. 10. T. That is, people who are more intelligent, for example, also tend to obtain better grades in school. Such a correlation does not delve into matters of cause and effect, however. 11. F. We can assume that as one variable increases, the other is *likely* to decrease. Correlation does not demonstrate cause and effect, however.
12. T. 13. T. Double–blind studies, which are the standard for demonstrating the effectiveness of new drugs, attempt to control for the expectations of both the study participants and the researchers. 14. T. Case studies usually address an individual or a small group, whereas surveys may address thousands of people. Ways of acquiring information may be similar, however, including interviews and questionnaires.
15. F. Such situations create ethical dilemmas, but many psychologists—and many states—require that a psychologist warn the threatened party of the danger.

# CHAPTER REVIEW

## SECTION 1: The Scientific Method

**Obj. 1:** The (1) _____fic method is an organized way of going about expanding and refining knowledge. Psychologists usually begin by formulating a (2) r_____ question. A research question may be studied in its question format, or it may be reworded into a (3) _____sis, which is a specific statement about behavior or mental processes that is tested through research.   Psychologists next examine the research question or (4) t_____ the hypothesis through carefully controlled methods such as naturalistic or laboratory observation and the experiment. Psychologists draw (5) _____sions about their research questions or the accuracy of their hypotheses on the basis of their research (6) ob_____s or findings. Research findings often suggest refinements to psychological (7) _____ries and, consequently, new avenues of research.

As psychologists draw conclusions from research evidence, they are guided by principles of (8) cr_____ thinking. For example, they try not to confuse connections (correlations) between the findings with (9) c_____ and effect. As critical thinkers, psychologists similarly attempt to avoid (10) over_____ing or overgeneralizing their results.

Some psychologists include (11) _____cation of research reports in professional journals as a crucial part of the scientific method. Psychologists and other scientists are obligated to provide enough details of their work that other scientists will be able to repeat or (12) _____cate it. Publication also permits the scientific community at large to (13) ev_____, and perhaps criticize, the methods and conclusions of other scientists.

## SECTION 2: Samples and Populations

**Obj. 2:** Samples must accurately (14) rep_____ the population they are intended to reflect. Otherwise, we cannot (15) _____lize from research samples to populations.

The individuals who are studied are referred to as a (16) s_____. A sample is a segment of a (17) _____ation.

**Obj. 3:** Women's groups and health professionals argue that there is a historic bias in favor of conducting research with (18: *Circle one:* men or women). Most large–sample research conducted into life style and health has been conducted with (19: *Circle one:* men or women). Research samples have also tended to (20: *Circle one:* overrepresent or underrepresent) minority ethnic groups in the population. The Kinsey studies on sexual behavior did not adequately represent (21) Af_____Americans, poor people, the elderly, and diverse other groups.

In a (22) r_____ sample, each member of a population has an equal chance of being selected to participate. Researchers can also use a (23) _____fied sample, which is drawn so that identified subgroups in the population are represented proportionately in the sample. A large, randomly selected sample (24: *Circle one:* will or will not) show reasonably accurate stratification.

The concept behind (25)_____teer bias is that people who offer to participate in research studies differ systematically from people who do not.

Gail Wyatt conducted a survey to compare the sexual behavior of White women and (26) _____ American women. When social class differences were mathematically considered, Wyatt found that the ages of initial intercourse for the African American and White women in her sample were (27: *Circle one:* similar or dissimilar). The White women in Wyatt's sample (28: *Circle one*: did or did not) match the population of White women in Los Angeles County.

## SECTION 3: Methods of Observation:
### The Better To See You With

Chapter 2   Research Methods in Psychology   55

**Obj. 4:** Sigmund (29) _____d developed psychodynamic theory largely on the basis of case studies. Problems with the case study include gaps in (30) m_____ and purposeful distortions of the past. Interviewers may also have certain expectations and subtly guide people to fill in gaps in ways that are (31: *Circle one:* consistent or inconsistent) with their theoretical perspectives.

**Obj. 5:** Psychologists conduct surveys to learn about behavior and mental processes that cannot be observed in the natural setting or studied (32) ex_____ally. Psychologists making surveys may employ questionnaires and interviews or examine public (33) re_____s. In responding to surveys, people may inaccurately recall their behavior or purposefully (34) mis_____ it. Some people try to ingratiate themselves with their interviewers by answering in what they perceive to be the (35)_____ly desirable direction. Other people may falsify attitudes and exaggerate problems to draw (36) at_____ to themselves or try to foul up the results.

**Obj. 6:** Psychologists also use psychological tests to measure various (37) t_____s and characteristics among a population. Psychological test results, like the results of surveys, can be distorted by people who answer in a socially (38) _____able direction or attempt to exaggerate problems. For these reasons, some psychological tests have (39) v_____ scales built into them.

**Obj. 7:** The (40) _____istic–observation method observes individuals in their natural habitats. Psychologists and other scientists try to avoid interfering with the behaviors they are observing by using (41) _____sive measures. Jane (42) _____ has extensively observed the behavior of chimpanzees in their natural environment.

**Obj. 8:** Psychologists place lower animals and people into controlled laboratory environments where they can be observed and where the effects of specific (43) con_____s can be discerned.

## SECTION 4: The Correlational Method: Seeing What Goes Up & What Comes Down

**Obj. 9:** Psychologists use the correlational method to investigate whether one observed behavior or measured trait is related to, or (44) _____lated with, another. A number called the correlation (45) co_____ indicates the direction and the magnitude of a correlation between variables. A correlation coefficient can vary between +1.00 and (46) _____.

When variables are (47) _____ly correlated one increases as the other increases. When variables are (48) _____ly correlated one increases as the other decreases. Numerous studies report (49) _____tive correlations between intelligence and achievement.

**Obj. 10:** Correlational research may suggest but does not show, cause and (50) _____. Nevertheless, correlational research can point the way to profitable experimental research.

## SECTION 5: The Experimental Method: Trying Things Out

**Obj. 11:** An (51) _____ment is considered the best research method for answering questions concerning cause and effect. In an experiment, a group of participants receives a (52)_____ment, such as a dose of alcohol. The study participants, or subjects, are then observed carefully to determine whether the treatment makes a difference in their behavior. Experiments allow psychologists to (53) con_____ the experiences of study participants to determine the effects of a treatment.

**Obj. 12:** The presence of an (54) _____dent variable is manipulated by the experimenters so that its effects may be determined. The measured results or outcomes in an experiment are called (55) _____dent variables. The presence of (56) _____dent variables presumably depends on the (57) _____dent variables.

**Obj. 13:** Ideal experiments place participants in experimental and (58) con_____ groups. Participants in (59) _____tal groups obtain the treatment, whereas participants in (60) _____ol groups do not. Every effort is made to ensure that all other (61) _____tions are held constant for participants in both experimental and control groups. In this way, researchers can have confidence that the experimental outcomes reflect the (62) _____ments and not chance factors or chance fluctuations in behavior.

**Obj. 14:** A (63) p_____, or "sugar pill," often results in the behavior that people expect. When participants in experiments are given placebos but think that they have obtained the real (64) tr_____, we can conclude that changes in behavior and mental processes stem from their (65) _____fs about the treatment, and not from the treatment itself.

Well–designed experiments control for the effects of expectations by creating conditions under which participants are unaware of, or (66) _____ to, the treatment they have obtained. Yet researchers may also have expectations. Studies in which both participants and experimenters are unaware of who has obtained the treatment are called (67) _____–_____ studies.

## SECTION 6: Ethics in Psychological Research and Practice

**Obj. 15:** Psychologists adhere to (68) _____cal standards that are intended to promote the dignity of the individual, foster human welfare, and maintain scientific integrity. They also assure that psychologists (69: *Circle one*: do or do not) undertake research methods or treatments that are harmful to study participants or clients.

In order to help avoid harming study participants, human participants must provide (70) _____ consent before they participate in research programs. Psychologists treat the records of study participants and clients as (71) _____tial because they respect people's privacy and because people are more likely to express their true thoughts and feelings when researchers or therapists keep their disclosures confidential.

Many experiments like the Lang study on the effects of alcohol cannot be run without

(72) de_____ing study participants. Psychological ethics require that research participants who are deceived be (73) _____fed afterward to help eliminate misconceptions and anxieties about the research and to leave them with their dignity intact.

**Obj. 16:** Psychologists and other scientists frequently turn to (74) _____mals to conduct harmful or potentially harmful research that cannot be carried out with humans. Although the studies are carried out with animals, psychologists still face the (75) eth_____ dilemma of subjecting study participants to harm. As with people, psychologists follow the principle that animals should be subjected to (76) h_____ .

## Additional Notes

# Answer Key to *Chapter Review*

1. scientific
2. research
3. hypothesis
4. test
5. conclusions
6. observations
7. theories
8. critical
9. cause
10. oversimplifying
11. publication
12. replicate
13. evaluate
14. represent
15. generalize
16. sample
17. population
18. men
19. men
20. underrepresent
21. African
22. random
23. stratified
24. will
25. volunteer
26. African
27. similar
28. did not
29. Freud
30. memory
31. consistent
32. experimentally
33. records
34. misrepresent
35. socially
36. attention
37. traits
38. desirable
39. validity
40. naturalistic
41. unobtrusive
42. Goodall
43. conditions
44. correlated
45. coefficient
46. −1.00
47. positively
48. negatively
49. positive
50. effect
51. experiment
52. treatment
53. control
54. independent
55. dependent
56. dependent
57. independent
58. control
59. experimental
60. control
61. conditions
62. treatments
63. placebo
64. treatment
65. beliefs
66. blind
67. double–blind
68. ethical
69. do not
70. informed
71. confidential
72. deceiving
73. debriefed
74. animals
75. ethical
76. harm

| | Idioms | Explanation |
|---|---|---|
| 42 | tightly knit theories | several theories that work together |
| 42 | vent their rage | show their extreme anger |
| 44 | fits of laughter | very strong laughter |
| 46 | tapping into | reaching |
| 46 | new avenues | new areas |
| 47 | landslide | win by a lot of votes |
| 51 | pool of participants | group of participants |

| | Cultural Reference | Explanation |
|---|---|---|
| 42 | Yale University | highly respected University in Eastern U.S. |
| 49 | sophomores | second year college students |
| 47 | Roosevelt | a president of the U.S. |
| 42 | mental processes | workings of the mind |
| 42 | obsessed | think about all the time |
| 42 | alternate ways | other ways |
| 42 | collaborate | work together |
| 42 | empirical | can be observed |
| 42 | authority figures | people of importance |
| 42 | skeptical | doubt |
| 42 | recount | review |
| 42 | boundless | endless |
| 42 | hideous atrocities | horrible acts |
| 42 | maimed | hurt, injured |
| 42 | their comrades | other soldier they work with |
| 42 | without provoca-tion | without cause or encourage-ment |
| 43 | slaughter | kill |
| 43 | distinguished | very professional |
| 43 | dangling | hanging |
| 43 | pity | feel sorry for |
| 44 | misgivings | negative feelings |
| 44 | reassuring | encouraging |
| 44 | essential | important |
| 44 | barged | go into suddenly |
| 45 | replication | repeat experiments |
| 45 | passionate devotion | strong commitment |
| 46 | folklore | traditions and legends |
| 46 | modify | change |
| 47 | erroneous | wrong |
| 47 | corroborate | work together |
| 47 | routed | defeated |
| 48 | discrepancy | mistake |
| 48 | heralded for | seen as good examples of |
| 48 | agonizing | very painful |
| 49 | drawn from | taken from |
| 50 | accorded | given |

| | Phrases and Expressions (Different Usage) | |
|---|---|---|
| 50 | haphazardly | poorly |
| 50 | systematically | in an organized way |
| 51 | recruited | asked to be a part of |
| 51 | mathematically considered | corrected for with math |
| 51 | disproportionate | not equal |
| 51 | minutia | small idea |
| 51 | factual inaccuracies | not correct |
| 52 | distort | change |
| 52 | consistent | similar |
| 52 | prodding | pushing |
| 52 | mousy | quiet and shy |
| 52 | promiscuous | overly sexual |
| 52 | universality | same around the world |
| 52 | wee hours | very early |
| 52 | suspense | wonder |
| 52 | tallied | counted |
| 53 | smug | self-righteous |
| 53 | borne out | found to be true |
| 53 | pollsters | people who take surveys |
| 53 | may employ | may use |
| 53 | alluded | hinted at |
| 53 | impair | hurt |
| 53 | compiling | gathering |
| 53 | not foolproof | not perfect |
| 53 | ingratiate | to gain favor |
| 53 | foul up | interfere with |
| 53 | recounts | tells about |
| 53 | fascinating | interesting |
| 54 | entitle | give him the right |
| 54 | stance | belief |
| 55 | prowess | skill |
| 56 | became acquainted with | got to know |
| 56 | sound health | good health |
| 56 | while away the hours | send many hours with |
| 58 | assessed | measured |
| 58 | prestige | importance |
| 58 | agemates | people the same age |
| 60 | balked | did want to do it |
| 60 | essential | important to |
| 62 | blistering hot | extremely hot |
| 62 | provocations | upsetting events |
| 62 | "rooting for" | wishing for, cheering for |
| 63 | highball of vodka | tall glass of the alcohol called vodka |
| 63 | discriminated | tell the difference between |
| 63 | dose | amount |
| 63 | folklore | story passed down in families |
| 64 | confer | talk with |
| 64 | farfetched | unbelievable |

Chapter 2 Research Methods in Psychology **59**

| Phrases and Expressions (Different Usage) | | Additional Terms from the Text | | |
|---|---|---|---|---|
| 64 | linking | connecting | | |
| 64 | betterment | improvement | | |
| 65 | elusive | hard to find | | |
| 65 | hang its hat | locate | | |
| 65 | attributed | stated the cause | | |
| 65 | dwelled | lived | | |
| 66 | horrendous | horrible, terrible | | |
| 66 | provocation | irritation | | |
| 66 | gruesome | horrible | | |
| 66 | duly | properly | | |
| 66 | minute amounts | small amounts | | |
| 67 | static images | images that do not move | | |
| 68 | underlying | also happening at the same time | | |
| 68 | anguish | extreme upset | | |
| 68 | adhere to | follow | | |
| 68 | foster | encourage | | |
| 68 | construed | thought of as | | |
| 68 | groaned | to make a loud noise, usually indicating pain | | |
| 69 | skeptical | doubtful | | |
| 69 | console | electronic control box | | |
| 69 | confederates | someone who acts like a subject in the experiment but who is helping the researchers | | |
| 69 | rigged | set up before | | |
| 69 | recruits | people who agreed to be part of the experiment | | |
| 69 | propriety | how proper | | |
| 69 | potential benefits | possible future benefits | | |
| 70 | deceived | fooled | | |
| 70 | debriefing | explain detail later | | |
| 70 | dilemmas | situations | | |
| 70 | contemplate | time about | | |
| 70 | persistent | continuing | | |
| 72 | extraterrestrials | people from other planets | | |
| 72 | phony | not real | | |
| 72 | cited | listed | | |
| 74 | path | way | | |
| 74 | road to riches | way of getting rich | | |
| 74 | long-standing tradition | old tradition | | |
| 75 | are not borne out | do not come true | | |
| 75 | mixed reception | both liked and disliked | | |
| 75 | amass | gain | | |
| 75 | tap | connect to | | |
| 75 | sensationalistic | get a lot of attention for being very unusual | | |
| **Additional Terms** | | | | |
| | | | | |

1. Unobtrusively observing customers at a fast–food restaurant in order to determine how frequently they take bites is an example of the _____ method.
   (a) experimental
   (b) case–study
   (c) survey
   (d) naturalistic–observation

2. If you were to run an experiment on the effects of temperature on aggressive behavior, aggressive behavior would be the
   (a) hypothesis.
   (b) dependent variable.
   (c) treatment.
   (d) correlation coefficient.

3. In the Lang experiment on alcohol and ag-gression, the condition that led to the most aggressive behavior was
   (a) drinking tonic water only.
   (b) drinking vodka and tonic water.
   (c) belief that one had drunk tonic water only.
   (d) belief that one had drunk vodka and tonic water.

4. The Lang study on alcohol and aggression could **NOT** have been carried out without the _____ of study participants.
   (a) informed consent
   (b) confidentiality
   (c) deception
   (d) debriefing

5. Kinsey used _____ in his research on sexual behavior.
   (a) laboratory observations of sexual behavior
   (b) reports of former lovers of the individuals under study
   (c) interview data
   (d) psychological test data

6. A _____ sample is one in which every member of a population has an equal chance of being selected.
   (a) biased
   (b) chance
   (c) random
   (d) stratified

7. The development of psychodynamic theory relied largely on the _____ method.
   (a) case–study
   (b) naturalistic–observation
   (c) survey
   (d) psychological testing

8. Wyatt's research compared the behavior of white women to that of
   (a) white men.
   (b) African American women.
   (c) Hispanic American women.
   (d) Native American women.

9. Psychologists generally agree that the best research method for determining cause and effect is the _____ method.
   (a) naturalistic–observation
   (b) case–study
   (c) correlational
   (d) experimental

10. According to the text,
    (a) there is a positive correlation between intelligence and academic achievement.
    (b) there is a negative correlation between intelligence and academic achievement.
    (c) intelligence provides the basis for academic achievement.
    (d) there is no relationship between intelligence and academic achievement.

11. Which of the following is/are the source(s) of research questions?
    (a) psychological theory
    (b) daily experiences
    (c) folklore
    (d) all of the above

12. A specific statement about behavior or mental processes that is tested through research is termed a
    (a) research question.
    (b) hypothesis.
    (c) theory.
    (d) scientific principle.

13. Psychologists have observed that more–aggressive children spend more time watching TV violence than less–aggressive children. What can we conclude from this observation?
    (a) TV violence causes aggression.
    (b) Aggressive behavior causes the watching of violent TV shows.
    (c) There is a correlation between aggression and watching TV violence.
    (d) None of the above conclusions are possible.

14. According to the text, most of the large–sample research conducted into life style and health has been conducted with
    (a) women.
    (b) men.
    (c) a balance of men and women.
    (d) individuals drawn from ethnic minority groups.

15. The concept behind _____ is that people who offer to participate in research studies differ systematically from people who do not.
    (a) the selection factor
    (b) blinds and double blinds
    (c) the use of placebos
    (d) volunteer bias

16. The case of _____ provides a valuable case study in the processes of language development.
    (a) Genie
    (b) Eve
    (c) Lang
    (d) Jane

17. Validity scales are most likely to be employed in the _____ method.
    (a) naturalistic–observation
    (b) correlational
    (c) testing
    (d) experimental

18. Which of the following is apparently an effect of providing informed consent in psychological research?
    (a) a sense of control
    (b) volunteer bias
    (c) selection factor
    (d) violation of ethical principles

19. Diana Baumrind argues that deception–based research
    (a) is necessary only with people.
    (b) makes experiments less stressful.
    (c) can harm the reputation of the profession of psychology.
    (d) is ethical only when the benefits of the research outweigh the potential harm.

20. The most important factor about a sample is that it
    (a) be large.
    (b) be drawn at random.
    (c) represent the targeted population.
    (d) consist of people who are volunteers.

**Answer Key to *Posttest***

| | |
|---|---|
| 1. D | 11. D |
| 2. B | 12. B |
| 3. D | 13. C |
| 4. C | 14. B |
| 5. C | 15. D |
| 6. C | 16. A |
| 7. A | 17. C |
| 8. B | 18. A |
| 9. D | 19. C |
| 10. A | 20. C |

| | |
|---|---|
| Empirical | Generalize |
| Scientific method | Sample |
| Theory | Population |
| Hypothesis | Infer |
| Operational definition | Random sample |
| Selection factor | Stratified sample |
| Replicate | Volunteer bias |

| To extend from the particular to the general; to apply observations based on a sample to a population. | Emphasizing or based on observation and experiment. |
|---|---|
| Part of a population. | A method for obtaining scientific evidence in which research questions or hypotheses are formulated and tested. |
| A complete group of organisms or events. | A formulation of the relationships and principles that underlie observed events. Theories allow us to explain and predict behavior. |
| Draw a conclusion. | In psychology, a specific statement about behavior or mental processes that is tested through research. |
| A sample that is drawn so that each member of a population has an equal chance of being selected to participate. | A definition of a variable in terms of the methods used to create or measure that variable. |
| A sample that is drawn so that identified subgroups in the population are represented proportionately in the sample. | A source of bias that may occur in research findings when participants are allowed to determine for themselves whether they will be part of a research study. |
| A source of bias or error in research that reflects the prospect that people who offer to participate in research studies differ systematically from people who do not. | Repeat, reproduce, copy. |

| Case study | Naturalistic observation |
|---|---|
| Survey | Unobtrusive |
| Reliability | Laboratory |
| Test-retest reliability | Correlational method |
| Aptitude | Correlation coefficient |
| Validity | Positive correlation |
| Validity scales | Negative correlation |

| | |
|---|---|
| A scientific method in which organisms are observed in their natural environments. | A carefully drawn biography that may be obtained through interviews, questionnaires, and psychological tests. |
| Not interfering. | A method of scientific investigation in which a large sample of people answer questions about their attitudes or behavior. |
| A place in which theories, techniques, and methods are tested and demonstrated. | Consistency. |
| A scientific method that studies the relationships between variables. | A method for determining the reliability of a test by comparing test takers' scores from separate occasions. |
| A number between +1.00 to - 1.00 that expresses the strength and direction (positive or negative) of the relationship between two variables. | An ability or talent to succeed in an area in which one has not yet been trained. |
| A relationship between variables in which one variable increases as the other also increases. | The degree to which a test measures what it is supposed to measure. |
| A relationship between two variables in which one variable increases as the other decreases. | Groups of test items that suggest whether the test results are valid (measure what they are supposed to measure). |

| | |
|---|---|
| Experiment | Homunculus |
| Treatment | Lesion |
| Independent variable | Electro-encephalograph |
| Dependent variable | Computerized axial tomography (CAT) |
| Placebo | Positron emission tomography (PET) |
| Blind | Magnetic resonance imaging (MRI) |
| Double-blind study | Ethical |

| | |
|---|---|
| Latin for the "little man." A homunculus within the brain was once thought to govern human behavior. | A scientific method that seeks to confirm cause-and-effect relationships by introducing independent variables and observing their effects on dependent variables. |
| An injury that results in impaired behavior or loss of a function. | In experiments, a condition received by participants so that its effects may be observed. |
| An instrument that measures electrical activity of the brain. Abbreviated EEG. | A condition in a scientific study that is manipulated so that its effects may be observed. |
| Formation of a computer-generated image of the anatomical details of the brain using X-ray through the head and measuring from different angles the amount of radiation that passes through. CAT scan. | A measure of an assumed effect of an independent variable. |
| Formation of a computer-generated image of the neural activity of parts of the brain by tracing the amount of glucose used by the various parts. Abbreviated PET scan. | A bogus treatment that has the appearance of being genuine. |
| Formation of a computer-generated image of the anatomy of the brain by measuring the signals emitted when the head is placed in a strong magnetic field. Abbreviated MRI. | In experimental terminology, unaware of whether or not one has partaken of a treatment. |
| Moral; referring to one's system of deriving standards for determining what is moral. | A study in which neither the participants nor the persons measuring results know who has received the treatment. |

Directions: This *PRETEST* will give you feedback about how well you understand Chapter 3. In order to enhance your mastery of Chapter 3, complete all the sections of this chapter of the Study Guide. Then you can take the *POSTTEST* and compare your results.

1.  The _____ of the neuron uses oxygen to create energy to carry out the work of the cell.
    (a) axon        (b) dendrite
    (c) soma        (d) myelin

2.  Each cell in the body contains _____ genes.
    (a) 100
    (b) 1000
    (c) 100,000
    (d) 100,000,000

3.  A polarized neuron has a resting potential of about _____ millivolts in relation to the body fluid outside the cell membrane.
    (a) -70        (b) -40
    (c) +40        (d) +70

4.  One of the neurons in your brain receives stimulation from a few neighboring neurons, and, as a result, it fires. The same receiving neuron then receives messages from larger and larger numbers of neighboring neurons. As a consequence, the receiving neuron
    (a) fires more strongly.
    (b) fires more frequently.
    (c) shows no change in its pattern of firing.
    (d) releases more inhibitory than excitatory neurotransmitters.

5.  Receptor sites for neurotransmitters are found on the _____ of receiving neurons.
    (a) dendrites
    (b) synaptic vesicles
    (c) clefts
    (d) axon terminals

6.  _____ is excitatory at synapses between nerves and muscles that involve voluntary movements, but inhibitory at the heart and some other locations.
    (a) ADH
    (b) ACTH
    (c) ANS
    (d) ACh

7.  _____ increase(s) the release of dopamine and norepinephrine, and also impede(s) their reabsorption after neurons have fired.
    (a) Phenothiazines
    (b) LSD
    (c) Amphetamines
    (d) Endorphins

8.  You sit and cross your legs, and a physician taps your leg just below the knee. As a result, you kick reflexively. Which of the following is involved in your reflexive response?
    (a) white matter in the spinal cord
    (b) sensory cortex
    (c) afferent neurons
    (d) motor cortex

9.  People who produce excess amounts of thyroxin may develop a disorder characterized by excitability, insomnia, and weight loss known as
    (a) cretinism.
    (b) giantism.
    (c) hypothyroidism.
    (d) hyperthyroidism.

10. You know someone who is going to have an operation to help control epilepsy. It is likely that a part of his _____ will be removed in this operation.
    (a) cerebellum
    (b) limbic system
    (c) hypothalamus
    (d) myelin sheath

11. Messages from the brain and spinal cord to the _____ nervous system control purposeful body movements, such as raising a hand or running.
    (a) autonomic
    (b) somatic
    (c) sympathetic
    (d) parasympathetic

12. The parasympathetic division of the autonomic nervous system stimulates
    (a) digestive processes.
    (b) the fight–or–flight response.
    (c) the heart rate.
    (d) ejaculation.

13. If a person's abilities to comprehend other people's speech and to think of the proper words to express his own thoughts were impaired, we should suspect damage to _____ area of the brain.
    (a) Levy's
    (b) Delgado's
    (c) Wernicke's
    (d) Gazzaniga's

14. Concerning the left brain/right brain controversy, it is most accurate to conclude that
    (a) the sounds of speech evoke a response in the dominant hemisphere only.
    (b) the sounds of speech evoke a response in the nondominant hemisphere only.
    (c) creativity and intuition are confined to the nondominant hemisphere.
    (d) the hemispheres are similar enough so that each can function quite well independently, but not as well as they function in normal combined usage.

15. Luteinizing hormone is secreted by the
    (a) posterior lobe of the pituitary gland.
    (b) anterior lobe of the pituitary gland.
    (c) adrenal medulla.
    (d) adrenal cortex.

16. In women, prolactin
    (a) regulates maternal behavior.
    (b) causes uterine contractions.
    (c) stimulates production of milk.
    (d) maintains pregnancy.

17. A friend of yours appeared to be suffering from anxiety. However, a thorough medical examination revealed that he actually had the medical condition known as
    (a) hyperthyroidism.
    (b) hyperglycemia.
    (c) hypothyroidism.
    (d) hypoglycemia.

18. Strands of DNA contain all of the following **EXCEPT**
    (a) phenylalanine.
    (b) guanine.
    (c) phosphate.
    (d) sugar.

19. Psychologists usually attempt to carry out adoptee studies in order to
    (a) find siblings whose genetic codes overlap by 50 percent or more.
    (b) study the conditions that lead to adoption.
    (c) better sort out the effects of nature and nurture.
    (d) learn whether traits such as eye color and height can be genetically transmitted.

20. If a single zygote divides into two groups of cells, _____ will be the result.
    (a) fraternal twins
    (b) maternal twins
    (c) identical twins
    (d) spontaneous abortion

**Answer Key to *Pretest***

| | | | |
|------|------|-------|-------|
| 1. C | 6. D | 11. B | 16. C |
| 2. C | 7. C | 12. A | 17. D |
| 3. A | 8. C | 13. C | 18. A |
| 4. B | 9. D | 14. D | 19. C |
| 5. A | 10. B | 15. B | 20. C |

Chapter 3 explores the relationships between biological structures and processes, on the one hand, and behavior and mental processes on the other. Biological psychologists assume that biological structures and processes allow people to develop thoughts and ideas, images, and plans; and to engage in adaptive behavioral responses to environmental stimulation.

## Neurons

Nerve cells or neurons are the building blocks of the nervous system. Neurons have cell bodies, dendrites, and axons. "Messages" enter neurons by the dendrites, travel along the lengths of axons as electrochemical neural impulses, and are transmitted from one neuron to another as chemical substances called neurotransmitters. Some neurotransmitters of interest to psychologists are acetylcholine (ACh), dopamine, norepinephrine, serotonin, and neuropeptides.

## The Nervous System

The nervous system consists of the central nervous system (brain and spinal cord) and peripheral nervous system. The peripheral nervous system is further divided into the somatic and autonomic nervous systems (ANS). The sympathetic and parasympathetic divisions of the ANS are of interest to psychologists because of their role in emotional responses. The hindbrain contains the medulla, pons, and cerebellum. The reticular activating system ascends through the hindbrain and midbrain into the forebrain. The forebrain contains important structures such as the thalamus, hypothalamus, limbic system, and cerebrum.

## The Cerebral Cortex

Each hemisphere of the cerebral cortex contains frontal, parietal, temporal, and occipital lobes. The visual cortex is located in the occipital lobe, and the auditory cortex in the temporal lobe. The sensory cortex lies in the parietal lobe, and the motor cortex in the frontal lobe. Structures that permit comprehension and production of language are located in the dominant (usually left) hemisphere of the cerebral cortex, and damage to these areas produces aphasias.

## The Endocrine System

The endocrine system consists of ductless glands that secrete hormones. Hormones of particular interest to psychologists include growth hormone, prolactin, ADH, and oxytocin (secreted by the pituitary gland); insulin (the pancreas); thyroxin (the thyroid gland); corticosteroids (the adrenal cortex); adrenaline and norepinephrine (the adrenal medulla); testosterone (the testes); and estrogen and progesterone (the ovaries).

## Heredity

Genes, the basic units of heredity, are segments of chromosomes, and chromosomes consist of strands of DNA. Monozygotic twins are of great interest in the study of the genetic transmission of traits. Psychological traits such as extraversion and neuroticism seem to be at least partly inherited. Selective breeding clearly allows breeders to develop certain physical traits over the generations, but the role of heredity in development of psychological traits is less clear. The normal human complement of chromosomes is 46. Deviation from this number gives rise to disorders such as Down syndrome.

| | **Neurons: Into the Fabulous Forest** |
|---|---|
| 1. Describe the parts and functions of the *neuron*. | |
| 2. Explain the difference between *afferent* and *efferent* neurons. | |
| 3. Explain the electrochemical process by which neural impulses travel. | |
| 4. Explain the *"all-or-none principle"* of neural transmission. | |
| 5. Explain the functions of different kinds of *synapses* and *neurotransmitters*. | |
| | **The Nervous System** |
| 6. Explain what is meant by a *nerve*. | |
| 7. Explain the location and functions of the various divisions of the nervous system. | |
| 8. Explain how spinal reflexes work. | |
| 9. Explain ways in which psychologists study the functions of the brain. | |
| 10. List and locate the major structures of the *hindbrain*, *midbrain*, and *forebrain*. | |

11. Explain the functions of the parts of the brain.

12. Summarize the activities of the _____ and *parasympathetic* branches of the autonomic nervous system.

13. Locate the four lobes of the hemispheres of the cerebral cortex, and explain the functions of various parts of these lobes.

**The Cerebral Cortex**

14. Summarize the findings of divided–brain research.

15. Summarize research findings on electrical stimulation of the brain.

16. Explain the functions of hormones secreted by the pituitary gland, the pancreas, the thyroid, the adrenal glands, the testes, and the ovaries.

**The Endocrine System**

17. Explain the glandular disorders: *acromegaly, hyperglycemia,* and *hyperthyroidism*.

**Heredity: The Nature of Nature**

18. Define *genes* and *chromosomes*, and describe the human chromosomal structure.

19. Explain the purposes and methods of various kinds of kinship studies.

20. Differentiate between *dominant* and *recessive* traits.

21. Summarize the results of experiments in *selective breeding*.

22. Discuss the promise of genetic engineering.

23. Discuss the effects of Alzheimer's disease.

24. Discuss the problems of premenstrual syndrome.

**Additional Notes**

## Neurons: Into the Fabulous Forest

### 1. The Makeup of Neurons

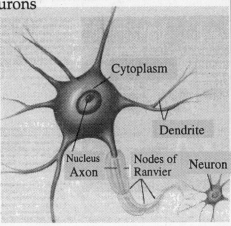

### 2. The Neural Impulse: Let Us "Sing the Body Electric"

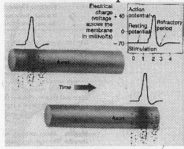

### 3. The Synapse

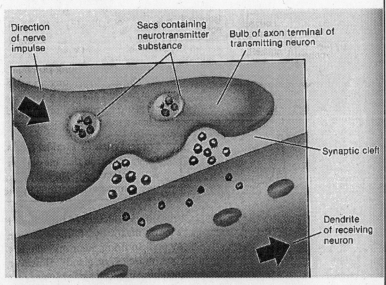

### 4. Neurotransmitters

# The Nervous System

### 1. The Central Nervous System

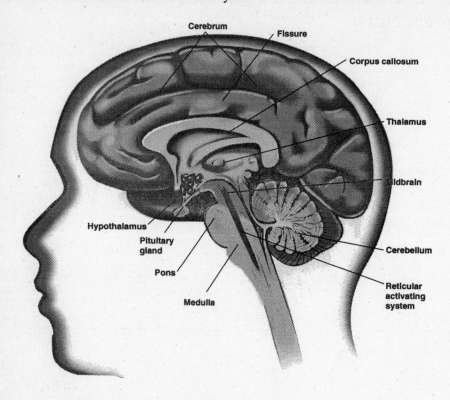

### 2. The Peripheral Nervous System

# The Cerebral Cortex

### 1. The Geography of the Cerebral Cortex

### 2. Thought, Language, and the Cortex

### 3. Left Brain, Right Brain?

### 4. Handedness: Is It Gauche to Be Left-Handed?

### 5. Split-Brain Experiments: When Hemispheres Stop Communicating

### 6. Electrical Stimulation of the Brain

# The Endocrine System

- A Guided Tour of the Endocrine System

  a. Hypothalamus

  b. Thyroid Gland

  c. Adrenal Glands

  d. Testes and Ovaries

# Heredity: The Nature of Nature

1. Genes and Chromosomes

2. The Human Genome Project

3. Kinship Studies

4. Dominant and Recessive Traits

5. Experiments in Selective Breeding

# Psychology and Modern Life

1. Alzheimer's Disease

2. Premenstrual Syndrome

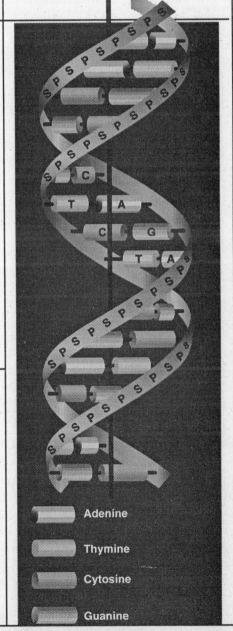

Adenine

Thymine

Cytosine

Guanine

## How to Study

1. Plan two hours study time for every hour you spend in class.

2. Study difficult or boring subjects first.

3. Avoid long study sessions.

4. Be aware of your best time of the day to study.

5. Use waiting time by studying flash cards or listen to taped material.

6. Use a regular study area.

7. Don't get too comfortable.

8. Use the library.

9. Take frequent breaks. Most people need a five minute break every 20-40 minutes with a 30 minute break after a couple of hours. You will need a different number of breaks depending on how interested you are in the topic and how tired you are.

10. Avoid noise and distractions from people.

11. If you are your own worst distraction, read the study tip in Chapter 9. It explains how to stay focused.

12. Make an agreement with your living mates about study time. This includes roommates, parents, spouses, and kids. Make a written contract which states the rules clearly. Come up with a signal so others know you need to study and do not want to be disturbed.

## Studying in Groups

Research has shown that one of the most effective ways to learn is to study with other students. Your grades on exams will be better and you will have a lot more fun doing it!

## How to Form a Group

1. Look for dedicated students who share some of your academic goals and challenges.

2. You could write a note on the blackboard asking interested students to contact you, or pass around a sign-up sheet before class.

3. Limit groups to five or six people.

4. Test the group by planning a one-time-only session. If that session works, plan another.

## Possible Activities for a Study Group

1. Discuss the material right after lecture.

2. Compare notes and fill in any gaps.

3. Have discussions and debates about the material.

4. Test each other with questions brought to the group meeting by each member.

5. Divide up the material among group members, and then next session practice teaching each other. This could also include creating wall size summary charts or mind-maps.

6. Brainstorm possible test questions.

7. Share ideas for overcoming personal problems in the area of money, transportation, child care, time scheduling, or other barriers to learning.

8. Develop a plan at the beginning of each meeting from the list above or any ideas you have.

9. Work in groups of three at a computer. Choose one person to type, another to dictate summaries of lectures and assigned readings, and tlhe third person can check the work and consult other books.

10. Network on campus with other students. Join a club or professional society. Find a mentor and learn about student services available to you on campus.

## Neurons: Into the Fabulous Forest

1. Neuron _____

2. Neurotransmitters _____

3. Glial cells _____

4. Soma _____

5. Dendrites _____

6. Axon _____

7. Terminals _____

8. Knobs _____

9. Myelin sheath _____

10. Node of Ranvier _____

11. Afferent neuron _____

12. Efferent neuron _____

13. Mnemonic device _____

14. Neural impulse _____

15. Polarization _____

16. Resting potential _____

17. Depolarization _____

18. Action potential _____

19. All–or–none principle _____

20. Absolute refractory period _____

21. Relative refractory period _____

22. Synapse _____

23. Receptor site _____

24. Excitatory synapse _____

25. Inhibitory synapse _____

26. Acetylcholine (ACh) _____

27. Hippocampus _____

28. Dopamine _____

29. Noradrenaline _____

30. Serotonin _____

31. Endorphins _____

## The Nervous System

32. Nerve _____

33. Nuclei _____

34. Ganglia _____

35. Central nervous system _____

36. Peripheral nervous system _____

37. Spinal cord _____

38. Spinal reflex _____

39. Interneuron _____

40. Gray matter _____

41. White matter _____

42. Medulla _____

43. Pons _____

44. Cerebellum _____

45. Reticular activating system _____

46. Comatose _____

47. Thalamus _____

48. Hypothalamus _____

49. Limbic system _____

50. Amygdala _____

51. Septum _____

52. Basal ganglia _____

53. Cerebrum _____

54. Cerebral cortex _____

55. Fissures _____

56. Corpus callosum _____

57. Somatic nervous system _____

58. Autonomic nervous system (ANS) _____

59. Sympathetic _____

60. Parasympathetic _____

## The Cerebral Cortex

61. Frontal lobe _____

62. Parietal lobe _____

63. Temporal lobe _____

64. Occipital lobe _____

65. Somatosensory cortex _____

66. Motor cortex _____

67. Association areas _____

68. Aphasia _____

69. Wernicke's aphasia _____

70. Broca's aphasia _____

71. Epilepsy _____

72. Split–brain operation _____

73. Tactile _____

## The Endocrine System

74. Pituitary gland _____

75. Adrenal cortex _____

76. Adrenal medulla _____

77. Duct _____

78. Endocrine system _____

79. Hormone _____

80. Negative feedback _____

81. Growth hormone _____

82. Prolactin _____

83. Antidiuretic hormone _____

84. Oxytocin _____

85. Pancreas _____

86. Insulin _____

87. Hyperglycemia _____

88. Hypoglycemia _____

89. Syndrome _____

90. Thyroxin _____

91. Metabolism _____

92. Hypothyroidism _____

93. Cretinism _____

94. Hyperthyroidism _____

95. Corticosteroids _____

96 Cortisol _____

97. Adrenaline _____

98. Testosterone _____

99. Primary sex characteristics _____

100. Secondary sex characteristics _____

101. Estrogen _____

102. Progesterone _____

## Heredity

103. Heredity _____

104. Genetics _____

105. Behavior genetics _____

106. Extroversion _____

107. Neuroticism _____

108. Genes _____

109. Polygenic _____

110. Chromosomes _____

111. Sex chromosomes _____

112. Nature _____

113. Nurture _____

114. Genome _____

115. Zygote _____

116. Monozygotic (MZ) twins _____

117. Dizygotic (DZ) twins _____

118. Autism _____

119. Concordance _____

120. Dominant trait _____

121. Recessive trait _____

122. Selective breeding _____

## Psychology and Modern Life

123. Alzheimer's Disease _____

_____

## SECTION 1: Neurons: Into the Fabulous Forest

**OBJ. 1:** The (1) n_____ system contains billions of neurons and glial cells. Neurons transmit messages to other neurons by means of chemical substances called (2) _____mitters. (3) G_____ cells nourish neurons and direct their pattern of growth. Neurons have a cell body, or (4) s_____; (5) d_____, which receive transmissions; and (6) a_____, which extend trunklike from the cell body. Chemicals called neurotransmitters travel across (7) s_____ to transmit messages to other neurons.

Many neurons have a fatty myelin (8) s_____. These sheaths are missing at the nodes of (9) R_____. Neural impulses travel more rapidly along myelinated (10) a_____, where they can jump from (11) n_____ to node.

**OBJ. 2:** Sensory or (12) _____ent neurons transmit sensory messages to the central nervous system. Motor or (13) _____ent neurons conduct messages from the central nervous system that stimulate glands or cause muscles to contract.

**OBJ. 3:** Neural transmission is an (14) e_____ process. An electric charge is conducted along an axon through a process that allows (15) s_____ ions into the cell and then pumps them out. The neuron has a (16) r_____ potential of -70 millivolts in relation to the body fluid outside the cell membrane, and an (17) a_____ potential of +110 millivolts. The conduction of the neural impulse along the length of the neuron is what is meant by (18) _____ing.

**OBJ. 4:** Neurons (19) f_____ according to an all–or–none principle. Neurons may fire (20) _____s of times per second. Firing is first followed by an (21) _____ refractory period, during which neurons do not fire in response to further stimulation. Then they undergo a (22) _____ refractory period, during which they will fire, but only in response to stronger-than-usual messages.

**OBJ. 5:** A synapse consists of an axon (23) _____al from the transmitting neuron; a (24) d_____ of a receiving neuron; and a small fluid-filled gap between them that is called the synaptic (25) c_____.

(26) _____tory synapses stimulate neurons to fire. (27) _____tory neurons influence neurons in the direction of not firing.

Neurotransmitters are contained within synaptic (28) _____s. These vesicles are found in the knobs at the tips of the axon (29) _____als. Each neurotransmitter can fit into a specific (30) _____tor site on the dendrite of the receiving neuron.

(31) Ace_____ (abbreviated ACh) is the neurotransmitter that controls muscle contractions. The poison (32) c_____ acts by preventing ACh from lodging within receptor sites. ACh is normally prevalent in a brain structure essential to the formation of memories: the (33) _____pus. (34) _____mer's disease is connected with deterioration of cells that produce ACh. The neurotransmitter (35) _____ine is involved in voluntary movements, learning and memory, and emotional arousal. Deficiencies of dopamine are linked to (36) _____son's disease. It is also theorized that schizophrenic individuals may (37) over_____ dopamine because of a greater–than–normal number of receptor (38) _____s. Deficiencies of (39) _____phrine have been linked to depression. Amphetamines act by increasing the release of the neurotransmitters (40)_____ and (41) _____. Deficiencies of (42) _____nin are linked to anxiety, depression, and insomnia. The drug (43) _____ decreases the action of serotonin, frequently leading to hallucinations.

"Runner's high" may be caused by the release of chains of amino acids called (44) _____ns. Endorphins act like (45: *Circle one:* inhibitory or excitatory) neurotransmitters.

## SECTION 2: The Nervous System

**OBJ. 6:**  A nerve is composed of a bundle of (46) _____ns of neurons. The cell bodies of these neurons are gathered into clumps called (47) n_____ in the brain and spinal cord, and (48) g_____ elsewhere.

**OBJ. 7:** The first major division of the nervous system is into the central and (49) _____al nervous systems. The brain and (50) s_____ _____ compose the central nervous system. The peripheral nervous system is divided into the (51) _____ic and (52) _____ic nervous systems. The somatic nervous system transmits sensory information about muscles, skin, and joints to the (53) c_____ nervous system. The somatic nervous system also controls (54) _____ar activity from the central nervous system. The autonomic nervous system is subdivided into sympathetic and (55) _____tic branches.

**OBJ. 8:**  A spinal (56) r_____ is an unlearned response to a stimulus that does not involve the brain. A spinal reflex may involve as few as two neurons: a sensory or (57) _____ent neuron, and a motor or (58) _____ent neuron. A third kind of neuron, an (59) _____ron, may transmit the neural impulse from the sensory neuron through the spinal cord to the motor neuron.

In the spinal cord, (60: *Circle one:* gray or white) matter consists of small, nonmyelinated neurons that are involved in reflexes. (61: *Circle one:* gray or white) matter is composed of bundles of longer, myelinated axons that carry messages back and forth to and from the brain.

**OBJ. 9:**  There are numerous ways of studying the brain. The (62) _____lograph records the electrical activity of the brain. In computerized (63) _____ _____, a narrow X–ray beam is passed through the head; measurements of the amount of radiation that passes through permits the computer to generate a three–dimensional image of the brain. Positron (64) _____ _____ translates the glucose metabolized by parts of the brain into an image. In magnetic (65) _____ imaging, radio waves cause parts of the brain to emit signals that are integrated into an image of the brain.

**OBJ. 10 and OBJ. 11:**  The hindbrain includes the (66) m_____, which is vital in heartbeat, blood pressure, and respiration; the pons, which transmits information concerning movement and is also involved in attention and respiration; and the (67) _____lum, which is involved in maintaining balance and controlling motor behavior.

The (68) _____ar activating system (RAS) begins in the hindbrain and continues through the midbrain into the forebrain and is vital in the functions of attention, sleep, and arousal.

Important structures of the forebrain include the thalamus, hypothalamus, limbic system, basal ganglia, and cerebrum. The (69) _____mus serves as a relay station for sensory stimulation. The (70) _____us is vital in the control of body temperature, motivation, and emotion. The (71) _____ic system is involved in memory and in the drives of hunger, sex, and aggression. The basal (72) _____ are involved in posture and muscle coordination, and their deterioration is linked to Parkinson's disease. The surface of the cerebrum is called the (73) _____tex. The cortex is (74) _____luted in shape. Valleys in the cortex are called (75)_____sures. The hemispheres of the cerebral cortex are connected by the (76) _____ _____sum.

**OBJ. 12:**  The (77) _____ic nervous system (ANS) regulates the glands and involuntary activities such as heartbeat, digestion, and (78) d_____ of the pupils. The (79) _____tic division of the ANS dominates in activities that expend the body's resources, such as experiencing anxiety or fleeing a predator. The (80) _____tic division dominates during processes that build the body's reserves, such as eating.

## SECTION 3: The Cerebral Cortex

**OBJ. 13:** The ancient Egyptians attributed control of the person to a (81) hom_____, who they believed dwelled within the skull. The cerebral cortex is divided into the frontal, parietal, temporal, and (82) _____al lobes. The visual cortex is in the (83) _____al lobe, and the auditory cortex is in the (84) _____al lobe. The sensory cortex lies behind the central fissure in the (85) _____al lobe. The motor cortex lies in the (86) _____al lobe, across the (87) _____al fissure from the sensory cortex.

(88) A_____ areas of the cortex are involved in learning, thought, memory, and language. The (89) l_____ areas of the cortex lie near the intersection of the frontal, temporal, and parietal lobes in the dominant hemisphere. For the great majority of right-handed people, the (90: *Circle one:*left or right) hemisphere of the cortex is dominant; for 70 percent of left-handed people, the left hemisphere is also dominant. In (91) _____'s aphasia, people speak slowly and laboriously, in simple sentences. In (92) _____'s aphasia, the ability to understand language is impaired. The (93: *Circle one:*left or right) hemisphere of the cortex seems to play a special role in understanding and producing language. The (94: *Circle one:* left or right) hemisphere of the cortex seems to play a special role in aesthetic and emotional response.

**OBJ. 14:** Split-brain operations are sometimes carried out in an effort to control (95) _____sy. In such operations, the (96) _____ _____um is severed. Split-brain patients may be able to verbally describe a screened-off object like a pencil that is held in the hand connected to the (97) d_____ hemisphere, but cannot do so when the object is held in the other hand.

**OBJ. 15:** José Delgado caused a brave bull to cease its charge by sending electrical impulses into the animal's (98) _____ _____tem. Olds and Milner's research suggests that a "pleasure center" exists in the (99) _____mus of the rat.

## SECTION 4: The Endocrine System
**OBJ. 16 and OBJ. 17:**The endocrine system consists of (100) _____less glands that secrete hormones. The (101) _____mus secretes a number of hormones that regulate the functions of other glands. The pituitary gland secretes (102) _____ hormone, which regulates the growth of muscles, bones, and glands. An excess of growth hormone can lead to (103) _____ly. Another pituitary hormone, (104) _____in, regulates maternal behavior in lower animals and stimulates production of (105) m_____ in women. ADH increases the reabsorption of (106) _____e to conserve fluid. (107) _____in stimulates labor in pregnant women.

The (108) p_____ secretes insulin, which enables the body to metabolize (109) _____. Diabetes melitis is caused by excess sugar in the blood—a condition known as (110) _____mia. (111) Hypo_____ is caused by too little sugar in the blood, and is characterized by shakiness and dizziness.

The thyroid hormone (112) _____in affects the body's metabolism. (113) Hypo_____ results from abnormally low levels of thyroxin. Hypothyroidism is characterized by excess weight in adulthood, and it can cause (114) _____ism in children, which is characterized by stunted growth and mental (115) _____tion.

The adrenal cortex produces (116) cortico_____s, which promote development of muscle mass and increase resistance to stress and activity level. The adrenal medulla secretes (117) _____ine (also called epinephrine), which increases the metabolic rate and is involved in general emotional arousal.

Sex hormones secreted by the testes and (118) _____es are responsible for prenatal sexual differentiation. Female sex hormones also regulate the (119) _____al cycle. The female hormone (120) _____one helps maintain pregnancy. Premenstrual syndrome (PMS) is usually mild, but (121) _____ins, which cause uterine contractions, can also cause painful cramping.

## SECTION 5: Heredity

**OBJ. 18:** The biological science that is concerned with the transmission of traits from generation to generation is called (122) _____s. The specialty that is concerned with the transmission of traits that give rise to behavior is called (123) _____ genetics.

　　(124) _____s are the basic building blocks of heredity. Genes consist of (125) _____ _____, which is abbreviated DNA. A large number of genes make up each (126) _____e. People normally have (127) _____ chromo-somes. People receive (128) _____ chromosomes from the father and 23 from the mother. In DNA, adenine is always combined with (129) _____ine, and cytosine is always combined with (130) _____ine.

**OBJ. 19:** Psychologists conduct (131) k_____ studies to help determine the role of genetic factors in behavior patterns and mental processes. The more closely people are related, the more (132) g_____ they have in common. Parents and children have a (133) _____ percent overlap in their genetic endowments, and so do (134) _____lings (brothers and sisters).

　　A fertilized egg cell is called a (135) _____e. Identical twins are formed from (136: *Circle one:* one or two) zygote(s), and are termed (137) _____zy-gotic. Fraternal twins are formed from (138: *Circle one:* one or two) zygote(s), and are termed (139) _____zygotic. Monozygotic twins are important in the study of the relative influences of heredity and the (140) _____ment.

　　Adoptee studies, in which children are separated from their parents at an early age (or in which identical twins are separated at an early age) and then reared apart provide special opportunities for sorting out the effects of (141) n_____ and nurture.

**OBJ. 20:** Traits are determined by pairs of (142) _____s. When dominant traits combine with recessive traits, the (143) _____ traits are shown. Recessive traits are shown only if a recessive gene from one parent combines with a (144) _____ gene from the other. People with recessive genes for illnesses are said to be (145) _____iers of those illnesses.

**OBJ. 21:** Experiments show that animals can be selectively bred to heighten the influence of many (146) _____s. Rats, for example, can be selectively bred for (147) _____ learning ability. However, we cannot assume that maze-learning ability in rats corresponds directly to human (148) _____gence.

**OBJ. 22:** In the future, genetic (149) _____ing may lead to the development of new vaccines; new methods of prenatal screening; and to the direct modification of the genetic codes of unborn children, so that inherited diseases are prevented.

### Answer Key to *Chapter Review*

1. nervous
2. neurotransmitters
3. Glial
4. soma
5. dendrites
6. axons
7. synapses
8. sheath
9. Ranvier
10. axons
11. node
12. afferent
13. efferent
14. electrochemical
15. sodium
16. resting
17. action
18. firing
19. fire
20. hundreds
21. absolute
22. relative
23. terminal
24. dendrite
25. cleft
26. Excitatory
27. Inhibitory

28. vesicles
29. terminals
30. receptor
31. Acetylcholine
32. curare
33. hippocampus
34. Alzheimer's
35. Dopamine
36. Parkinson's
37. overutilize
38. sites
39. norepinephrine
40. dopamine (or norepinephrine)
41. norepinephrine (or dopamine)
42. serotonin
43. LSD
44. endorphins
45. inhibitory
46. axons
47. nuclei
48. ganglia
49. peripheral
50. spinal cord
51. somatic (or autonomic)
52. autonomic (or somatic)
53. central
54. muscular
55. parasympathetic
56. reflex
57. afferent
58. efferent
59. interneuron
60. gray
61. White
62. electroencephalograph
63. axial tomography
64. emission tomography
65. resonance
66. medulla
67. cerebellum
68. reticular
69. thalamus

70. hypothalamus
71. limbic
72. ganglia
73. cerebral cortex
74. convoluted
75. fissures
76. corpus callosum
77. autonomic
78. dilation
79. sympathetic
80. parasympathetic
81. homunculus
82. occipital
83. occipital
84. temporal
85. parietal
86. frontal
87. central
88. Association
89. language
90. left
91. Broca's
92. Wernicke's
93. left
94. right
95. epilepsy
96. corpus callosum
97. dominant
98. limbic system
99. hypothalamus
100. ductless
101. hypothalamus
102. growth
103. acromegaly
104. prolactin
105. milk
106. urine
107. oxytocin
108. pancreas
109. sugar
110. hyperglycemia
111. Hypoglycemia

112. thyroxin
113. Hypothyroidism
114. cretinism
115. retardation
116. Corticosteroids
117. adrenaline
118. ovaries
119. menstrual
120. progesterone
121. prostaglandins
122. genetics
123. behavior
124. Genes
125. deoxyribonucleic acid
126. chromosome
127. 46
128. 23
129. thymine
130. guanine
131. kinship
132. genes
133. 50
134. siblings
135. zygote
136. one
137. monozygotic
138. two
139. dizygotic
140. environment
141. nature
142. genes
143. dominant
144. recessive
145. carriers
146. traits
147. maze
148. intelligence
149. engineering

# ESL–BRIDGING THE GAP

| | Idioms | Explanation |
|---|---|---|
| 83 | cast off | sent; thrown |
| 84 | stems from | originates from |
| 84 | lose control | cannot control |
| 84 | speeds up | increases |
| 84 | play a role | have a part in; contribute to |
| 84 | switched on | turned on; activated |
| 84 | winding up with | acquiring |
| 84 | catch up | equal, having been behind or below |
| 84 | go bald | lose their hair |
| 84 | builds up | accumulates |

| | Cultural Reference | Explanation |
|---|---|---|
| 79 | Pablo Picasso | Spanish artist born in 1881, and lived in France after 1900 |
| 81 | way to prepare frog's legs | frog's legs are a delicacy (expensive and special food); |
| 81 | system of "checks and balances" | refers to the system of the U.S. government which balances the powers of the three branches (parts) of government |
| 81 | mortgage payment | monthly payment made to pay off a loan to a bank for house |
| 81 | crossed fingers | to cross the middle finger over the index finger (first finger after the thumb) |
| 81 | pump iron | exercise strenuously |
| 81 | body-building contests | contests of body muscle and strength |
| 81 | finishing school | a kind of school in the U.S. that teaches and emphasizes good manners |
| 81 | tastes good/good taste | tastes" in the first sentence is a verb; "taste" in the second sentence is a noun. |
| 81 | a potential Shakespeare | a person who has the ability to become a great writer. He wrote many plays, including Hamlet, which is considered to be the greatest play in the English language. |
| 81 | ruling houses of Europe | the kings and queens of the European countries |
| 81 | patents appending | a patent application has been filed, but the U.S. Patent Office has not been given. |

| | Phrases and Expressions (Different Usage) | |
|---|---|---|
| 78 | swear in court | insist; be completely positive; refers to testifying in a court of law under oath |
| 78 | winking out | disappearing |
| 78 | in flux | always changing |
| 78 | fossil records | fossils are the calcified bones of animals that existed and died millions of years ago |
| 78 | without a trace | nothing remains to indicate that the creatures (people or animals) were here |
| 78 | now being cracked | now being deciphered and understood |
| 78 | unlocking the mysteries of | investigating and discovering what has not been understood |
| 79 | thicket of trees | group of trees close together |
| 79 | lie end to end | the end of one touches the end of the next one |
| 79 | waste products | products that are not needed and must be removed |
| 79 | occupy center stage | are the most important; do the most important activity |
| 81 | fabulous forest | a dense and beautiful group of trees |
| 81 | trunk-like | like the trunk of a tree |
| 81 | be buffeted about | moved and hit each other and other neurons |
| 81 | entertain some rather nasty thoughts | think unpleasant thoughts |
| 81 | withdraw it | take it away from the place; remove it |
| 81 | lightning rods | a metal wire designed to conduct lightning (redirect it) away and down into the ground where it will do less harm |
| 82 | in a resting state | when a neuron is not active |
| 83 | created anew | made again |
| 83 | into a specifically tailored harbor | a site, or place, which is chemically unique for that neurotransmitter |
| 83 | highlight | accentuate; emphasize |
| 84 | overutilize | use too much |
| 84 | block the action | stop the action |
| 84 | "runner's high " | high" refers to a very good feeling experienced by people while running longer distances |
| 84 | There you have it | now you understand it |
| 86 | piece of business | item of information |
| 86 | make us proud | at will cause us, as people, to feel good about ourselves; we are better than animals |

Chapter 3   Biology and Behavior    87

| Phrases and Expressions (Different Usage) | | Additional Terms from the Text | | |
|---|---|---|---|---|
| 87 | capable of "local government" | capable of responding to; refers to a localized response | | |
| 88 | knee-jerk reflex | quick and sudden movement up of the leg in response to it having been hit just under the kneecap | | |
| 88 | Every show has a star | every performance has one performer who is the most important | | |
| 89 | work our way forward | move in a forward direction, studying the brain as we move | | |
| 90 | to play a filtering role | to filter; to select | | |
| 90 | screening others out | ignoring others | | |
| 90 | egg- orfootball-shaped | shaped like an egg or football | | |
| 90 | day in and day out | every day | | |
| 90 | perpetually reintroduced | introduced to the same person many times | | |
| 90 | as a result | the result of this is that | | |
| 91 | In novel approaches | in some new and different treatments | | |
| 91 | the crowning glory | the most beautiful and magnificent part | | |
| 93 | spending of body energy from stored reserves | the body is using energy from what has been saved (reserved) | | |
| 93 | flight or flight response | fight the predator or flee (go away from quickly) | | |
| 93 | pitch black | completely dark, with no light | | |
| 95 | a devil of a time | a very difficult time; a lot of trouble | | |
| 95 | screened off | hidden | | |
| 106 | breathe a sigh of relief | make a sound to indicate that an unpleasant situation has been **corrected** | | |
| 107 | a twisting ladder | steps that turn as they go up | | |
| 107 | set the stage | prepare for the event | | |
| 110 | look alike | look the same | | |
| 111 | maze-learning ability | ability to learn how to travel a maze in order to locate the exit | | |
| 111 | maze-bright | intelligent about figuring out a maze | | |
| 111 | maze-dull | unintelligent about figuring out a maze and not successful at it | | |
| 112 | to find a food goal | to find the food by finding the route to the food | | |
| 112 | blind-alley entrance | an entrance in a maze which stops and does not lead to the goal or to the exit | | |

1. Neurons
   (a) transmit neural impulses.
   (b) support and nourish glial cells.
   (c) manufacture myelin.
   (d) are one kind of neurotransmitter.

2. Axons end in smaller, branching structures called
   (a) synapses.
   (b) dendrites.
   (c) terminals.
   (d) myelin sheaths.

3. When the neuron is in a resting state, _____ ions are more common inside than in the body fluid outside the neuron.
   (a) sodium
   (b) chlorine
   (c) fluorine
   (d) radon

4. Motor neurons are otherwise known as
   (a) afferent neurons.
   (b) efferent neurons.
   (c) glial cells.
   (d) reflex arcs.

5. The small fluid–filled gap between neurons, across which neurotransmitters travel, is called the
   (a) synapse.
   (b) axon terminal.
   (c) dendrite.
   (d) synaptic cleft.

6. A person you know begins to show symptoms such as hallucinations, delusions, and jumbling or confusion of thoughts. According to the research reported in the text, it is most likely that these symptoms are linked to _____ of dopamine.
   (a) excess production
   (b) overutilization
   (c) scarcity
   (d) cyclical secretion

7. Which of the following is a neuropeptide?
   (a) adrenaline
   (b) dopamine
   (c) myelin
   (d) enkephalin

8. In the brain and spinal cord, the cell bodies of neurons are gathered into clumps called
   (a) soma.
   (b) ganglia.
   (c) nuclei.
   (d) gray matter.

9. Which of the following structures is found in the hindbrain?
   (a) pons
   (b) hypothalamus
   (c) limbic system
   (d) basal ganglia

10. An elderly person you know is showing awkward movements and a shuffling gait. According to information presented in the text, this behavior pattern is most likely to reflect the death of a group of neurons that regulate the
    (a) cerebellum.
    (b) motor cortex.
    (c) medulla.
    (d) basal ganglia.

11. When we are afraid, the _____ division of the ANS accelerates the heart rate.
    (a) somatic
    (b) peripheral
    (c) sympathetic
    (d) parasympathetic

12. The motor cortex lies in the _____ lobe.
    (a) frontal
    (b) parietal
    (c) temporal
    (d) occipital

13. A student participating in psychological research reports visual sensations although her eyes are closed and covered with dark material. She is probably receiving direct artificial stimulation of the _____ lobe.
    (a) frontal
    (b) parietal
    (c) temporal
    (d) occipital

14. The right hemisphere of the cerebral cortex is usually relatively more involved with
    (a) understanding syntax.
    (b) decoding visual information.
    (c) problem solving.
    (d) associating written words with their sounds.

15. If you wanted to be able to reward a rat with a burst of electricity for engaging in a certain behavior, it would probably be most useful to implant the electrode into a section of the rat's
    (a) reticular activating system.
    (b) parietal lobe.
    (c) hypothalamus.
    (d) spinal cord.

16. Who is known for implanting a radio–controlled electrode in the limbic system of a "brave bull"?
    (a) Delgado
    (b) Gazzaniga
    (c) Milner
    (d) Olds

17. According to the text, _____ promotes growth of female reproductive tissues and maintains pregnancy.
    (a) estrogen
    (b) prolactin
    (c) growth hormone
    (d) progesterone

18. Which of the following is NOT known to contribute to the regulation of levels of testosterone?
    (a) hypothalamus
    (b) adrenal medulla
    (c) pituitary gland
    (d) testes

19. In the rebuilding of strands of DNA, cytosine combines with
    (a) adenine.
    (b) cytosine.
    (c) guanine.
    (d) thymine.

20. People with Alzheimer's disease have reduced levels of _____ in their brains.
    (a) neuropeptides
    (b) acetycholine
    (c) adrenalin
    (d) norepinephrine

**Answer Key to *Posttest***

1. A
2. C
3. B
4. B
5. D
6. B
7. D
8. C
9. A
10. D
11. C
12. A
13. D
14. B
15. C
16. A
17. D
18. B
19. C
20. B

| | |
|---|---|
| Neuron | Knobs |
| Neurotransmitters | Myelin sheath |
| Glial cells | Node of Ranvier |
| Soma | Afferent neurons |
| Dendrites | Efferent neurons |
| Axon | Mnemonic |
| Terminals | Neural impulse |

| | |
|---|---|
| Swellings at the ends of terminals. Also referred to as bulbs or buttons. | A nerve cell. |
| A fatty substance that encases and insulates axons, facilitating transmission of neural impulses. | Chemical substances involved in the transmission of neural impulses from one neuron to another. |
| A noninsulated segment of a myelinated axon. | Cells that nourish and insulate neurons, direct their growth, and remove waste products from the nervous system. |
| Neurons that transmit messages from sensory receptors to the spinal cord and brain. Also called sensory neurons. | A cell body. |
| Neurons that transmit messages from the brain or spinal cord to muscles and glands. Also called motor neurons. | Rootlike structures, attached to the soma of a neuron, that receive impulses from other neurons |
| Aiding memory, usually by linking chunks of new information to well-known schemes. | A long, thin part of a neuron that transmits impulses to other neurons from branching structures called terminals. |
| The electrochemical discharge of a nerve cell, or neuron. | Small structures at the tips of axons. |

| | |
|---|---|
| Polarize | Absolute refractory period |
| Resting potential | Relative refractory period |
| Permeability | Synapse |
| Depolarize | Hippocampus |
| Action potential | Dopamine |
| Threshold | Noradrenaline |
| All-or-none principle | Serotonin |

Chapter 3 Biology and Behavior

| | |
|---|---|
| A phase following firing during which a neuron's action potential cannot be triggered. | To ready a neuron for firing by creating an internal negative charge in relation to the body fluid outside the cell membrane. |
| A phase following the absolute refractory period during which a neuron will fire in response to stronger-than-usual messages. | The electrical potential across the neural membrane when it is not responding to other neurons. |
| A junction between the axon terminals of one neuron and the dendrites or soma of another neuron. | The degree to which a membrane allows a substance to pass through it. |
| A part of the limbic system of the brain that is involved in memory formation. | To reduce the resting potential of a cell membrane from about -70 millivolts toward zero. |
| A neurotransmitter that is involved in Parkinson's disease and that appears to play a role in schizophrenia. | The electrical impulse that provides the basis for the conduction of a neural impulse along an axon of a neuron. |
| A neurotransmitter whose action is similar to that of the hormone adrenaline and that may play a role in depression. | The point at which a stimulus is just strong enough to produce a response. |
| A neurotransmitter, deficiencies of which have been linked to affective disorders, anxiety, and insomnia. | The fact that a neuron fires an impulse of the same strength whenever its action potential is triggered. |

| | |
|---|---|
| Endorphins | Spinal reflex |
| Nerve | Interneuron |
| Nuclei | Gray matter |
| Ganglia | White matter |
| Central nervous system | Medulla |
| Peripheral nervous system | Pons |
| Spinal cord | Cerebellum |

Chapter 3  Biology and Behavior

| | |
|---|---|
| A simple, unlearned response to a stimulus that may involve only two neurons. | Neurotransmitters that are composed of amino acids and that are functionally similar to morphine. |
| A neuron that transmits a neural impulse from a sensory neuron to a motor neuron. | A bundle of axons and dendrites from many neurons. |
| In the spinal cord, the grayish neurons and neural segments that are involved in spinal reflexes. | Plural of nucleus. A group of neural cell bodies found in the brain or spinal cord. |
| In the spinal cord, axon bundles that carry messages from and to the brain. | Plural of ganglion. A group of neural cell bodies found elsewhere in the body (other than the brain or spinal cord). |
| An oblong area of the hindbrain involved in regulation of heartbeat and respiration. | The brain and spinal cord. |
| A structure of the hindbrain involved in respiration, attention, and sleep and dreaming. | The part of the nervous system consisting of the somatic nervous system and the autonomic nervous system. |
| A part of the hindbrain involved in muscle coordination and balance. | A column of nerves within the spine that transmits messages from sensory receptors to the brain and from the brain to muscles and glands throughout the body. |

| | |
|---|---|
| Reticular activating system | Basal ganglia |
| Comatose | Cerebrum |
| Thalamus | Cerebral cortex |
| Hypothalamus | Corpus callosum |
| Limbic system | Somatic nervous system |
| Amygdala | Autonomic nervous system |
| Septum | Sympathetic nervous system |

| | |
|---|---|
| Ganglia located between the thalamus and cerebrum that are involved in motor coordination. | A part of the brain involved in attention, sleep, and arousal. |
| The large mass of the forebrain, which consists of two hemispheres. | In a coma, a state resembling sleep from which it is difficult to be aroused. |
| The wrinkled surface area (gray matter) of the cerebrum. | An area near the center of the brain involved in the relay of sensory information to the cortex and in the functions of sleep and attention. |
| A thick fiber bundle that connects the hemispheres of the cortex. | A bundle of nuclei below the thalamus involved in body temperature, motivation, and emotion. |
| The division of the peripheral nervous system that connects the central nervous system with sensory receptors, skeletal muscles, and the surface of the body. | A group of structures involved in memory, motivation, and emotion that forms a fringe along the inner edge of the cerebrum. |
| The division of the peripheral nervous system that regulates glands and activities such as heartbeat, respiration, digestion, and dilation of the pupils. (ANS) | A part of the limbic system that apparently facilitates stereotypical aggressive responses. |
| The branch of the ANS that is most active during emotional response, such as fear and anxiety that spend the body's reserves of energy. | A part of the limbic system that apparently restrains stereotypical aggressive responses. |

| | |
|---|---|
| Parasympathetic | Association areas |
| Frontal lobe | Aphasia |
| Parietal lobe | Wernicke's aphasia |
| Temporal lobe | Broca's aphasia |
| Occipital lobe | Epilepsy |
| Somatosensory cortex | Split-brain operation |
| Motor cortex | Tactile |

| | |
|---|---|
| Areas of the cortex involved in learning, thought, memory, and language. | The branch of the ANS that is most active during processes such as digestion that restore the body's reserves of energy. |
| Impaired ability to comprehend or express oneself through language. | The lobe of the cerebral cortex that lies to the front of the central fissure. |
| A language disorder characterized by difficulty comprehending the meaning of spoken language. | The lobe that lies just behind the central fissure. |
| A language disorder characterized by slow, laborious speech. | The lobe that lies below the lateral fissure, near the temples of the head. |
| Temporary disturbances of brain functions that involve sudden neural discharges. | The lobe that lies behind and below the parietal lobe and behind the temporal lobe. |
| An operation in which the corpus callosum is severed, usually in an effort to control epileptic seizures. | The section of cortex in which sensory stimulation is projected. It lies just behind the central fissure in the parietal lobe. |
| Of the sense of touch. | The section of cortex that lies in the frontal lobe, just across the central fissure from the sensory cortex. Neural impulses in the motor cortex are linked to muscular responses throughout the body. |

# Chapter 4

# Sensation and Perception

Directions: This *PRETEST* will give you feedback about how well you understand Chapter 4. In order to enhance your mastery of Chapter 4, complete all the sections of this chapter of the Study Guide. Then you can take the *POSTTEST* and compare your results.

1. Of the following, _____ have the shortest wavelengths of the spectrum of electromagnetic energy.
   (a) cosmic rays
   (b) X-rays
   (c) sound waves
   (d) visible colors

2. Weber's constant for the pitch of a tone is
   (a) 1/7th.
   (b) 1/53rd.
   (c) 1/333rd.
   (d) 1/20,000th.

3. You look at a lamp ten feet away and it is in focus. As you walk toward it, the lamp remains in focus because the _____ of your eyes are accommodating to the image of the lamp by changing their thickness.
   (a) corneas
   (b) irises
   (c) lenses
   (d) pupils

4. Cones reach their maximum adaptation to darkness in about _____ minutes.
   (a) 5
   (b) 10
   (c) 30
   (d) 45

5. Colors across from one another on the color wheel are labeled
   (a) primary.
   (b) afterimages.
   (c) analogous.
   (d) complementary.

6. _____ suggested that the eye must have three different types of cones, some sensitive to red, some to green, and some to blue.
   (a) Thomas Young
   (b) Sir Isaac Newton
   (c) Hermann von Helmholtz
   (d) Ewald Hering

7. The Necker cube is used by psychologists to demonstrate the concept of
   (a) perceptual shifts.
   (b) motion parallax.
   (c) analogous colors.
   (d) strabismus.

8. You attend a motion picture, and it seems to you as if the people and objects being projected onto the screen are moving. Actually, your impression that the people and objects are moving is made possible by
   (a) the phi phenomenon.
   (b) stroboscopic motion.
   (c) the autokinetic effect.
   (d) motion parallax.

9. When we are driving along a dark road at night, the Moon may appear to move along with us. This is an example of
   (a) the autokinetic effect.
   (b) perspective.
   (c) motion parallax.
   (d) the phi phenomenon.

10. The unit for expressing the loudness of a sound is named after
(a) Bell.
(b) Hertz.
(c) Helmholtz.
(d) Newton.

11. A combination of dissonant sounds is referred to as
(a) timbre.
(b) overtones.
(c) noise.
(d) white noise.

12. Hairlike receptor cells on the organ of Corti bend in response to vibrations of the
(a) eardrum.
(b) oval window.
(c) stirrup.
(d) basilar membrane.

13. Within the ears are found organs for
(a) vision.
(b) kinesthesis.
c) the vestibular sense.
(d) extrasensory perception.

14. We have about _____ taste buds.
(a) 10
(b) 100
(c) 10,000
(d) 10,000,000

15. _____ is sensed along the sides of the tongue.
(a) Sweetness
(b) Bitterness
(c) Saltiness
(d) Sourness

16. Sensory receptors located _____ appear to fire in response to touching the surface of the skin.
(a) on the surface of the skin
(b) around the roots of hair cells
(c) at the tips of hair cells
(d) in tendons, joints, and muscles

17. The view that pain messages may not get through to the brain when the "switchboard" that transmits pain messages become "flooded" is termed
(a) gate theory.
(b) opponent–process theory.
(c) volley principle.
(d) acupuncture.

18. Organs in the _____ alert you as to whether your body is changing speeds.
(a) joints
(b) tendons
(c) ears
(d) olfactory membrane

19. A spinal–injured man was taught to walk by being provided electronic feedback about the working of the leg muscles. The nature of this feedback was
(a) kinesthetic.
(b) vestibular.
(c) visual.
(d) extrasensory.

20. Through your _____ sense, you can tell when an elevator begins to move, whether it is going up or down, and when it stops.
(a) trichromatic
(b) kinesthetic
(c) olfactory
(d) vestibular

**Answer Key to *Pretest***

| 1. | A | 11. | C |
|----|---|-----|---|
| 2. | C | 12. | D |
| 3. | C | 13. | C |
| 4. | B | 14. | C |
| 5. | D | 15. | D |
| 6. | C | 16. | B |
| 7. | A | 17. | A |
| 8. | B | 18. | C |
| 9. | C | 19. | A |
| 10. | A | 20. | D |

## Sensation and Perception

Chapter 4 concerns sensation (the mechanical processes by which sensory receptors are stimulated and sensory information is transmitted to the central nervous system) and perception (the process by which sensory information is organized and interpreted). There is discussion of basic concepts in sensation and perception, including absolute and difference thresholds, signal–detection theory, and sensory adaptation.

## Visible Light

Visible light constitutes one band of the spectrum of electromagnetic energy. The wavelength of light determines its hue, and the amplitude of the waves determines their brightness. The structures and functions of the eye, including the retina's photoreceptors (rods and cones), are described. Dark adaptation and visual acuity are discussed.

## Color

The psychological dimensions of color–hue, brightness, and saturation—are explored. Bending colors of the spectrum into a "color wheel" allows meaningful discussion of "warm" versus "cool" colors; and of complementary versus analogous colors. The trichromatic and opponent-process theories of color vision are explained. Color blindness is defined and described.

## Visual Perception

Several aspects of visual perception are described, including Gestalt rules for perceptual organization; the perception of movement (and apparent movement); the monocular and binocular cues that give rise to depth perception; the perceptual constancies (size, shape, color, and brightness), and how these constancies may give rise to visual illusions.

## Sound Waves

The nature of sound waves (for example, frequency and amplitude) is explored in the section on hearing, as are the structures and functions of the ear—including the "command post" of hearing, the organ of Corti. The place and frequency theories of pitch perception are explained.

## Smell and Taste

Then the chemical senses of smell and taste are examined. "Basic" odors and basic tastes are listed, as are the receptors for smell (in the olfactory membrane) and for taste (in taste buds). The concept of taste is differentiated from that of flavor. Research concerning menstrual synchrony and pheromones is explored.

## Skin

The skin senses of touch, pressure, warmth, cold, and pain are touched upon. There is emphasis on the ways in which we perceive intense heat and on the subject of pain. The gate theory of pain is explored, including ways in which endorphins, acupuncture, and SPA may act to reduce pain.

## Kinesthesis and Vestibular sense

Kinesthesis and the vestibular sense are defined, and there is mention of the bodily locations of these senses (joints, tendons, and muscles for kinesthesis; the semicircular canals of the ears for the vestibular sense).

# LEARNING OBJECTIVES

| | |
|---|---|
| 1. Define and contrast the terms *sensation* and *perception*. | **Sensation & Perception: Your Ticket of Admission to the World Outside** |
| 2. Define *psychophysics*, and explain the historical contribution of Ernst Weber. | |
| 3. Define and distinguish between *absolute thresholds* and *difference thresholds* for stimuli. | |
| 4. Define *signal–detection theory* and explain the factors that influence the perception of signals. | |
| 5. Explain what is meant by *sensory adaptation*, and distinguish between *sensitization* and *desensitization* to stimuli. | |
| 6. Explain the electromagnetic nature of light. | **Vision: Letting the Sun Shine In** |
| 7. List the parts of the eye, and describe functions. | |
| 8. Describe the functions of *rods* and *cones*, and explain how they differ in dark adaptation. | |
| 9. Define the color concepts of *hue*, *brightness*, and *saturation*. | |
| 10. Define *warm* and *cool colors*, and explain how artists use warm and cool colors to achieve certain effects. | |

11. Define *complementary colors* and *analogous colors*, and explain how artists use complementary and analogous colors to achieve certain effects.

12. Explain the *trichromatic* and *opponent-process theories* of color vision.

13. Describe different kinds of *color blindness*.

## Visual Perception

14. Explain the Gestalt rules of *perceptual organization*.

15. Explain the ways in which we perceive actual movement, and explain what is meant by illusions of movement such as the *autokinetic effect* and *stroboscopic motion*.

16. List and explain several *monocular* and *binocular cues* for depth.

17. Describe the visual disorders discussed in the text.

18. Explain the perceptual constancies: *size, color, brightness*, and *shape constancy*. Show how they can give rise to visual illusions.

## Hearing

19. Explain the transmission and structure of sound waves, including *pitch* and *loudness*.

20. List the parts of the ear and describe their functions.

21. Explain the theories of *pitch perception*.

22. Describe three kinds of deafness.

Smell, Taste, Skin, Kinesthesis, Vestibular Sense

23. Explain how people sense odors.

24. List the four basic tastes, and explain how people sense them.

25. List the skin senses and explain how people perceive hotness and pain.

26. Describe *kinesthesis*.

27. Describe the *vestibular sense*.

**Additional Notes**

## Sensation and Perception: Your Ticket of Admission to the World Outside

1. Absolute Threshold

2. Difference Threshold

3. Signal-Detection Theory

4. Feature Detectors

5. Binding in the Brain

6. Sensory Adaptation

## Vision: Letting the Sun Shine In

1. Light: What Is This Stuff?

2. The Eye: The Better to See You With

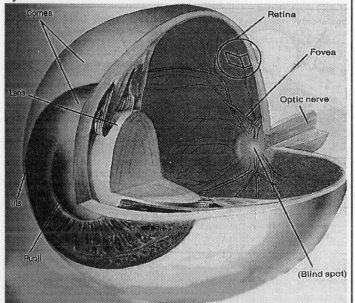

3. Color Vision

4. Psychological Dimensions of Color

5. Theories of Color Vision

6. Color Blindness

## Visual Perception

   1. Perceptual Organization

   2. Perception of Movement

   3. Depth Perception

   4. Problems in Visual Perception

   5. Perceptual Constancies

   6. Visual Illusions

## Hearing

   1. Pitch and Loudness

   2. The Ear

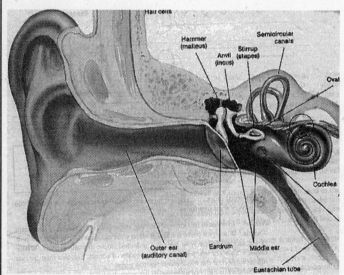

   3. Locating Sounds

   4. Perception of Loudness and Pitch

   5. Deafness

| | |
|---|---|
| **Smell** | |
| **Taste** | |
| **The Skin Senses** | |
| 1.  Touch and Pressure | |
| 2.  Temperature | |
| 3.  Pain: The Often Unwanted Message | |
| **Kinesthesis** | |
| **The Vestibular Sense: On Being Upright** | |

## Reading for Remembering

**1. Skim**
Skim the entire chapter.

**2. Outline**
Read the outline at the front of the chapter in the text.

**3. Questions**
Write out several questions that come to your mind that you think will be answered in the chapter.

**4. Read the material**

**5. Highlight**
While reading, highlight the most important information (no more than 10%).

**6. Answers**
As you read, get the answers to your questions.

**7. Recite**
When you finish reading an assignment, make a speech about it. Recite the key points.

**8. Review**
Plan your first review within 24 hours.

**9. Review again**
Weekly reviews are important–perhaps only four or five minutes per assignment. Go over your notes. Read the highlighted parts of your text. Recite the more complicated points.

### More About Review

You can do short reviews anytime, anywhere, if you are prepared. Take your text, study guide, or flash cards to the dentist's office, and if you don't have time to read a whole assignment, review last week's assignment. Conduct five-minute reviews whenever and wherever you can. Three-by-five cards work well for review. Write ideas on cards or make up cards from the cut-out sections of this Study Guide and carry them with you. These short review periods require only a little effort and can be fun!

## Try Your Own Mental Images

Most memory experts agree that mental images are very powerful tools. Here are some additional pointers so you can make up your own.

1. Turn information into mental pictures. We remember pictures better than words, and the funnier or more unusual, the better.

2. Make things meaningful to **you**.

3. Connect the information to what you already know.

*Example:*
To remember how much information short-term and long-term memory can hold, picture a huge group of people standing on the grass in a park. The seven people standing closest to you have unusually short legs and all the rest of the people have unusually long legs. (Remember, we said funny is good.) The short legged people represent the fact that we are able to hold an average of 7 items in short-term memory. The many long legged people represent that long term memory is practically unlimited.

Now think of one of your own mental images and write or draw it below.

# KEY TERMS AND CONCEPTS

1. Acupuncture _____

2. Sensation _____

3. Perception _____

### Sensation and Perception: Your ticket of Admission to the World Outside

4. Absolute threshold _____

5. Psychophysicist _____

6. Method of constant stimuli _____

7. Psychophysical _____

8. Pitch _____

9. Difference threshold _____

10. Weber's constant _____

11. Just noticeable difference (jnd) _____

12. Signal–detection theory _____

13. Noise _____

14. Feature detectors _____

15. Binding _____

16. Synchrony theory _____

17. Convergence zones _____

18. Sensory adaptation _____

19. Sensitization _____

20. Desensitization _____

### Vision

21. Light _____

22. Visible light _____

23. Prism _____

24. Hue _____

25. Cornea _____

26. Pupil _____

27. Lens _____

28. Retina _____

29. Photoreceptors _____

30. Bipolar cells _____

31. Ganglion cells _____

32. Optic nerve _____

33. Fovea _____

34. Blind spot _____

35. Rods _____

36. Cones _____

37. Dark adaptation _____

### Creating an Inner World of Color: Color Vision

38. Saturation _____

39. Complementary hues _____

40. Primary colors _____

41. Secondary colors _____

42. Tertiary colors _____

43. Afterimage _____

44. Analogous _____

45. Trichromatic theory _____

46. Opponent–process theory _____

47. Microspectrophotometry _____

48. Trichromat _____

49. Monochromat _____

50. Dichromat _____

## Visual Perception

51. Closure _____

52. Perceptual organization _____

53. Ambiguous figure _____

54. Proximity _____

55. Similarity _____

56. Continuity _____

57. Common fate _____

58. Top-down processing _____

59. Bottom-up processing _____

60. Illusions _____

61. Autokinetic effect _____

62. Stroboscopic motion _____

63. Phi phenomenon _____

64. Monocular cues _____

65. Binocular cues _____

66. Perspective _____

67. Interposition _____

68. Shadowing _____

69. Texture gradient _____

70. Motion parallax _____

71. Binocular cues _____

72. Retinal disparity _____

73. Convergence _____

74. Visual acuity _____

75. Nearsighted _____

76. Farsighted _____

77. Presbyopia _____

78. Strabismus _____

79. Astigmatism _____

80. Size constancy _____

81. Color constancy _____

82. Brightness constancy _____

83. Shape constancy _____

## Hearing

84. Auditory _____

85. Hertz _____

86. Amplitude _____

87. Decibel (dB) _____

88. Consonant _____

89. Dissonant _____

90. Overtones _____

91. Timbre _____

92. White noise _____

93. Eardrum _____

94. Oval window _____

95. Cochlea _____

96. Basilar membrane _____

97. Organ of Corti _____

98. Auditory nerve _____

99. Place theory _____

100. Frequency theory _____

101. Duplicity theory _____

102. Conductive deafness _____

103. Sensorineural deafness _____

## Smell

104. Odor _____

105. Olfactory _____

106. Olfactory nerve _____

**Taste**

107. Taste cells _____

108 Taste buds _____

**The Skin Senses**

109. Two-point threshold _____

110. Analgesic _____

111. Placebo _____

**Kinesthesis**

112. Kinesthesis _____

113. Vestibular sense _____

114. Semicircular canals _____

**Additional Terms**

_____

_____

_____

_____

_____

_____

_____

_____

_____

_____

_____

_____

_____

_____

_____

_____

# CHAPTER REVIEW

**OBJ. 1:** Sensation refers to mechanical processes that involve the stimulation of (1) s_____ receptors (neurons) and the transmission of sensory information to the (2) c_____ nervous system. Perception is not mechanical. (3) P_____ is the active organization of sensations into a representation of the world. (4) P_____ reflects learning and expectations, as well as sensations.

## SECTION 1:  Sensation and Perception: Your Ticket of Admission to the World Outside

**OBJ. 2 and OBJ. 3:** The (5) _____ threshold for a stimulus, such as light, is the lowest intensity at which it can be detected. A person's absolute threshold for light is the lowest (6) _____ty of light that he or she can see 50 percent of the time, according to the method of (7) _____nt stimuli. The minimum difference in intensity that can be discriminated is the (8) _____ threshold. Difference thresholds are expressed in fractions called (9) _____'s constants. Weber's (9) co_____ for light is 1/60th.

**OBJ. 4:** According to (10) _____al–detection theory, several factors determine whether a person will perceive a stimulus. The detection of a signal is determined by the sensory stimuli themselves, the biological (11) s_____ system of the person, and (12) psy_____ factors, such as motivation and attention.

**OBJ. 5:** Sensory (13) _____tion refers to the processes by which we become more sensitive to stimuli of low magnitude and less sensitive to stimuli relatively constant in magnitude. The process of becoming more sensitive to stimulation is referred to as (14) _____tion, or positive adaptation. The process of becoming less sensitive to stimulation is referred to as (15) de_____, or (16) _____tive adaptation.

## SECTION 2:  Vision: Letting the Sun Shine In

(17) V_____ is our dominant sense.

**OBJ. 6:** Visible light triggers visual (18)_____s. Visible light is one part of a spectrum of (19) _____netic energy. Electromagnetic energy is described in terms of (20) _____s. The wavelength of visible light determines its color, or (21) h_____.

**OBJ. 7:** The eye senses and transmits visual stimulation to the (22) _____tal lobe of the (23) ce_____ cortex. Light enters the eye through the transparent (24) c_____. The amount of light allowed in is determined by the size of the opening of the muscle called the (25) _____s. The opening in the iris is called the (26) p_____. Once past the iris, light passes through the (27) _____s, which accommodates to the image by changing its thickness. Accommodation of the lens focuses light so that a clear image is projected onto the (28) r_____. The retina is composed of (29) photo_____ called rods and (30) _____s. The rods and cones send neural messages through the (31) _____ar cells to ganglion cells. The axons of the ganglion cells constitute the (32) _____ic nerve, which conducts the sensory input to the brain.

The (33) _____a is the most sensitive part of the retina. The blind spot is the part of the retina where the axons of (34) _____n cells congregate to form the optic nerve.

**OBJ. 8:** The fovea is populated almost exclusively by (35) _____s, which permit perception of color. Rods are spaced most densely near the (36) _____s, and they transmit sensations of light and (37) d_____ only. Rods are more (38) s_____ than cones to light. Rods continue to (39) a_____ to darkness once cones have reached peak adaptation.

## SECTION 3: Color Vision

**OBJ. 9 :**  White light or sunlight can be broken down into the colors of the visible (40) _____m by using a triangular glass solid called a (41) _____ m. The wavelength of light determines its color or (42)h_____. The brightness of a color is its degree of lightness or (43) _____ness. Brighter colors are (44: *Circle one:* lighter or darker). The saturation of a color is its (45) _____ness. Pure hues have the greatest intensity or (46) b_____.

**OBJ. 10:** Yellows, oranges, and reds are considered (47) w_____ colors. Blues and (48) _____s are considered cool. In works of art, (49) _____ colors seem to advance toward the viewer. (50) C_____ colors seem to recede.

**OBJ. 11:** Colors across from one another on the color (51) w_____ are termed complementary. (52) Red–_____ and blue-yellow are the major complementary pairs. The mixture of lights is an (53) _____tive process. When we mix lights of complementary colors, they dissolve into (54) _____. In works of art, complementary colors clash when they are placed next to one another, and there seem to be (55) _____tions where they meet. The (56) _____image of a color is its complement.

The primary colors of red, blue, and (57) _____ cannot be produced by mixing pigments of other hues. Secondary and (58) _____ary colors are produced by mixing other colors. (59)A_____ colors lie next to one another on the color wheel. The color combinations of works of art using analogous colors are (60) _____ious.

**OBJ. 12:** According to the (61) _____ theory of color vision, there are three types of cones. Some cones are sensitive to red, some to blue, and some to (62) _____ light. Opponent–process theory proposes three types of color receptors: red–green, (63) _____, and (64) _____. (65) _____ theory better accounts for afterimages; however, both theories seem to have some validity.

**OBJ. 13:** People with normal color vision are called (66) _____mats. Color–blind people who can see light and dark only are called (67) _____mats. Dichromats are more common, and they can discrimi-nate only two colors: red and (68) _____, or blue and (69) _____. Partial color blindness is a sex–linked trait that strikes mostly (70: *Circle one:* males or females).

## SECTION 4: Visual Perception

**OBJ. 14 :** Gestalt rules of (71) _____ _____tion influence our grouping of bits of sensory stimulation into meaningful wholes. Rules of perceptual organization concern (72) _____– ground relationships, proximity, similarity, continuity, common fate, and closure. Our perceptions seem to be unstablewhen figure–ground relationships are (73) _____ous. The Rubin (74) _____ and the Necker (75) _____ are examples of ambiguous figures.

**OBJ. 15:** Explain the ways in which we perceive actual movement, and explain what is meant by illusions of movement such as the autokinetic effect and stroboscopic motion. We perceive real movement by sensing (76) m_____ across the retina, and by sensing change of (77) p_____ of an object in relation to other objects. The (78) _____tic effect is the tendency to perceive a point of light in a darkened room as moving. (79) _____opic motion, used in films, is the perception of a rapidly presented series of still pictures as moving.

**OBJ. 16:** Depth perception involves monocular and (80) _____lar cues. Monocular cues include perspective, in which we tend to perceive (81) p_____ lines as converging as they recede from us; clearness—(82: *Circle one:* nearby or distant) objects are perceived as clearer; interposition, shadowing, texture gradient, motion (83) p_____, and accommodation. According to motion parallax, distant objects appear to move more (84: *Circle one:* rapidly or slowly) than nearby objects. Binocular cues include retinal (85) _____ and convergence of the eyes. Closer objects have (86: *Circle one:* greater or lesser) retinal disparity and require (87: *Circle one:* greater or lesser) convergence.

**OBJ. 17:** Visual (88) _____y is sharpness of vision. People who must be abnormally close to objects to discriminate their details are termed (89) _____ed. People who must stand farther back than normal from objects in order to visually discriminate their details are termed (90) _____ed. As people age, the lens becomes relatively (91) b_____. This brittle-ness causes a condition called (92) _____pia, which is similar in effect to (93)_____ – sightedness. (94) _____mus is a visual disorder in which the eye muscles do not work to-gether, so that people seem to be looking at an object with one eye only. (95) Ast_____ is a visual disorder where vertical and horizontal contours cannot be focused upon simultaneously.

**OBJ. 18:** Through experience we develop a number of perceptual constancies. For example, we learn to assume that objects retain their size, (96)s_____, (97) b_____, and (98) c_____ despite their distance, their position, or changes in lighting conditions. In the case of size constancy, we tend to perceive an object as remaining the same size, although the size of the image on the (99) r_____ varies as a function of the object's (100) d_____ from the viewer.

Visual illusions use (101) p_____ cues as well as twists on rules for organization to deceive the eye. The effects of the Müller-Lyer and Ponzo illusions can probably be explained by using the principle of (102) _____ constancy.

## SECTION 5: Hearing
**OBJ. 19:** (103) A_____ stimulation, or sound waves, require a medium such as air or water for transmission. Sound waves alternately (104) _____ress and expand molecules of the medium, creating (105) _____s.

The human ear can hear sounds varying in fre-quency from 20 to (106) _____ cycles per second. The greater the frequency of the sound (107) _____s, the higher the (108) p_____ of a sound.

The loudness of a sound is measured in (109) _____els, which are abbreviated *dB*. We can suffer hearing loss if exposed to protracted sounds of (110) _____ dB or more. In addition to producing specified notes, instruments may produce tones that are greater in frequency and referred to as (111) _____s. Such overtones contribute to the richness or (112) t_____ of a sound. A combination of (113) _____nt sounds is referred to as noise.

**OBJ. 20:** The ear consists of an outer, (114) m_____, and (115) _____ ear. A thin membrane in the outer ear, called the (116) _____, vibrates in response to sound waves, and transmits them to the middle and (117) _____ ears. The middle ear contains the three bones, the "hammer," (118) _____, and (119) _____, which also vibrate and transmit sound waves to another membrane called the (120) _____ window. The oval window then transmits sound waves to the bony tube of the inner ear called the (121) _____a. Within the cochlea are fluids that vibrate against the (122) b_____ membrane. The "command post of hearing," or organ of (123) C_____, is attached to the basilar membrane. Sound waves travel from the organ of Corti to the brain by the (124)_____ry nerve. Sounds are perceived as louder when more of the sensory neurons on the organ of (125) _____ fire.

**OBJ. 21:** Two of the major theories that have been advanced to account for the perception of pitch are place theory and (126) _____ theory. According to place theory, the pitch of a sound is determined by the segment of the (127) _____ _____ne that vibrates in response to it. According to frequency theory, the frequency with which sensory neurons fire corresponds to the (128) _____ of the sound. So–called (129) _____ity theory advances the view that pitch perception depends both on the place and frequency of neural response.

**OBJ. 22:** (130) _____tive deafness occurs because of damage to the structures of the middle ear that conduct and amplify sound waves from the outer ear to the inner ear. (131) Sensori_____ deafness stems from damage to the structures of the inner ear or to the auditory frequency of neural response. (132) _____tion deafness stems from exposure to very loud sounds.

## SECTION 6: Smell
**OBJ. 23:** An odor is a sample of a number of (133) _____ules of the substance being smelled. Odors are detected by the (134) _____ membrane in each nostril. The sense of smell adapts rapidly to odors, even unpleasant ones.

## SECTION 7: Taste
**OBJ. 24:** There are four primary taste qualities: sweet, sour, (135) _____, and (136) _____. Flavor involves not only the taste of food, but also its (137) _____, texture, and temperature. The receptor neurons for taste are called (138) _____ cells. Taste cells are located in (139) _____ _____s on the tongue.

The "taste loss" found among the elderly is probably due to a decline in the sense of (140) _____.

## SECTION 8: The Skin Senses
**OBJ. 25:** There are five skin senses: touch, pressure, warmth, (141) _____, and (142) _____. The (143) _____–_____nt threshold method allows psychophysicists to assess sensitivity to pressure by determining the distance by which two rods touching the skin must be separated before the subject will report that there are two rods, not one. Sensations of (144) _____ture are relative; when we are feverish, another person's skin may seem cool to the touch. The perception of hotness relies on the simultaneous firing of receptors for cold and (145) _____.

Pain originates at the point of contact and is transmitted to the brain by various chemicals, including prostaglandins, (146) br_____, and substance P. According to (147) _____ theory, rubbing and scratching painful areas may reduce pain by sending competing messages to the brain. Naturally occurring (148) _____ins also help relieve pain.

## SECTION 9: Kinesthesis
**OBJ. 26:** Kinesthesis is the sensing of bodily (149) p_____ and movement. Kinesthesis relies on sensory organs in the joints, (150) t_____, and (151) _____s.

## SECTION 10: The Vestibular Sense
**OBJ. 27:** The vestibular sense informs us as to whether we are in an (152) _____ position or changing speeds. The vestibular sense is housed primarily in the (153) s_____ _____ of the ears.

### Answer Key to *Chaper Review*

1. sensory
2. central
3. Perception
4. Perception
5. absolute
6. intensity
7. constant
8. difference
9. Weber's; constant
10. signal
11. sensory
12. psychological
13. adaptation
14. sensitization
15. desensitization
16. negative
17. Vision
18. sensations
19. electromagnetic
20. wavelengths
21. hue
22. occipital
23. cerebral
24. cornea
25. iris
26. pupil
27. lens

28. retina
29. photoreceptors
30. cones
31. bipolar
32. optic
33. fovea
34. ganglion
35. cones
36. lens
37. dark
38. sensitive
39. adapt
40. spectrum
41. prism
42. hue
43. darkness
44. lighter
45. pureness
46. brightness
47. warm
48. greens
49. warm
50. Cool
51. wheel
52. green
53. additive
54. gray
55. vibrations
56. afterimage
57. yellow
58. tertiary
59. Analogous
60. harmonious
61. trichromatic
62. green
63. blue–yellow (or light–dark)
64. light–dark (or blue–yellow)
65. Opponent–process
66. trichromats
67. monochromats
68. green
69. yellow

70. males
71. perceptual organization
72. figure
73. ambiguous
74. vase
75. cube
76. movement
77. position
78. autokinetic
79. Stroboscopic
80. binocular
81. parallel
82. nearby
83. parallax
84. slowly
85. disparity
86. greater
87. greater
88. acuity
89. nearsighted
90. farsighted
91. brittle
92. presbyopia
93. farsightedness
94. Strabismus
95. Astigmatism
96. shape
97. brightness
98. color
99. retina
100. distance
101. perceptual
102. size
103. Auditory
104. compress
105. vibrations
106. 20,000
107. waves
108. pitch
109. decibels
110. 85–90
111. overtones

112. timbre
113. dissonant
114. middle
115. inner
116. eardrum
117. inner
118. anvil (or stirrup)
119. stirrup (or anvil)
120. oval
121. cochlea
122. basilar
123. Corti
124. auditory
125. Corti
126. frequency
127. basilar membrane
128. frequency
129. duplicity
130. Conductive
131. Sensorineural
132. Stimulation
133. molecules
134. olfactory
135. salty (or bitter)
136. bitter (or salty)
137. odor (or aroma)
138. taste
139. taste buds
140. smell
141. cold (or pain)
142. pain (or cold)
143. two–point
144. temperature
145. warmth
146. bradykinin
147. gate
148. endorphins
149. position
150. tendons
151. muscles
152. upright
153. semicircular canal

| | Idioms | Explanation |
|---|---|---|
| 122 | make sense | organize and understand |
| 125 | told apart from | distinguished between |
| 125 | in keeping with | accurate in relation to |
| 126 | suited to | appropriate to |
| 134 | leaps out | noticeable suddenly |
| 138 | far apart | great distance between |
| 142 | slowed down | decreased in speed |
| 149 | make perfect sense | is perfect in its logic |
| 159 | leave off | end |
| 159 | make a living | earning money for bills |
| 160 | fall in love | being to love |
| 161 | "get them | attack them |

| | Cultural Reference | |
|---|---|---|
| 133 | rhododendron and hibiscus | plants with large bright flowers |
| 135 | Rothko & d'Arcangelo | modern 20th century American artists |
| 136 | Seurat | 19th century French painter |
| 136 | Old Glory | affectionate work for U.S. flag |
| 139 | junkyard | place for large trash |
| 139 | birds in the bush | It is better to take what you are sure of. |
| 139 | Escher | 20th century American artist |
| 141 | Birds that flock together seem to be of a feather | people who are similar like to be together |
| 142 | scoreboard in baseball stadium | large sign where score is kept |
| 142 | hometeam scores | team in a person's own town gets points |
| 142 | fireworks | explosives that are ignited for light and noise |
| 150 | arrowheads | stones shaped to a point by American Indians and tied to a stick |
| 153 | do not hear the roar of the ocean | it is a tradition for children to be told that the noise they hear in a large seashell is the sound of the ocean. |
| 153 | a stereo set | an electronic device to play music from records or tapes |
| 165 | James Reston | a famous writer and an editor of the *New York Times* |
| 165 | stock market reports | reports on the sale prices of important stocks |

| | Phrases and Expressions (Different Usage) | |
|---|---|---|
| 122 | foot-long doll | a doll 12 inches long |
| 122 | full-grown person | an adult |
| 122 | ticket of admission | ticket to get into a theater |
| 124 | literally..., watch every step you take | a person needs to be very careful |
| 124 | dim the lights | slowly turn lights down |
| 124 | near darkness | until it is almost dark |
| 124 | randomized | not in any order |
| 124 | it bridges | one affects the other |
| 125 | from day to day | changes every day |
| 125 | from occasion to occasion | changes according to the occasion |
| 125 | glow in the dark | shine in the dark |
| 125 | tell them apart | to tell the difference between them |
| 125 | consider weight lifting | think about lifting weights |
| 125 | round it off | change it to the nearest whole number |
| 125 | barbell | a type of weight for exercising |
| 125 | dumbbell | a type of weight for exercising |
| 125 | readily apparent | very noticeable |
| 125 | threefold | three times |
| 126 | so far | from the beginning of the chapter until now |
| 126 | background noise | noise that is not the focus of our attention |
| 126 | advanced years | old age |
| 126 | abuzz with signals | a lot of background noise |
| 126 | hanging in the air | noticeable |
| 126 | backdrop of your consciousness | present, but not noticeable |
| 128 | a lay person | a person who is not a professional artist |
| 128 | only thing that remains constant is change | change always occurs and we can expect that |
| 128 | On the other hand | however, there is another way to think about it |
| 128 | lapping of the waves | the sound of the waves |
| 129 | stuff called light | the material they called light |
| 129 | a backward student | not a good student |
| 130 | a lasting impression | a permanent impression |
| 130 | in a similar fashion | in the same manner |
| 131 | a camera buff | a person who knows a lot about cameras |
| 131 | therefore | because this occurs |
| 133 | a featureless blaze | it is hard to see objects because the sun is bright |
| 133 | the brighter the color, the lighter it is | as color gets brighter, it also gets lighter |
| 134 | in contrast | the opposite occurs |

Chapter 4  Sensation and Perception  119

| | Phrases and Expressions (Different Usage) | |
|---|---|---|
| 134 | But wait? You say. | does not seem right |
| 134 | True enough | this is true |
| 135 | is working properly | is operating correctly |
| 136 | miscolored flag | flag with wrong colors |
| 137 | the families intermarry | the colors that are related mix with other colors |
| 137 | partly overlapped | a piece of the color was over a piece of another |
| 137 | theoretical updates | recent research has changed the theory |
| 138 | shards of information | pieces of information |
| 138 | meaningful whole | a complete concept which has meaning |
| 138 | as the saying goes | as we know the expression to be |
| 138 | in other words | another way to say this is the following |
| 142 | jumpy | not smooth |
| 142 | rapidly wrap around | move fast around building |
| 143 | stop and go traffic | many cars on a busy street |
| 144 | perceptions are mocked | perceptions are deceived |
| 144 | roadside markers | mark the edge of road |
| 146 | a cross-eyed look | when both eyes look toward nose |
| 146 | confusion would reign | there would be great confusion |
| 146 | As we neared it | As we became closer to it |
| 146 | wall-eyed | only one eye looks at object |
| 147 | muttered to himself | talk to self softly |
| 147 | in fear | he was afraid |
| 147 | wind their way | move slowly towad |
| 147 | fiercely difficult | extremely difficult |
| 147 | stand ready to | be ready to argue |
| 149 | seen from above | look down from the top |
| 149 | to play tricks on | what we see fools us |
| 149 | endless staircase | stairs that do not end |
| 150 | lifelong | all of life, to the end |
| 150 | take some bets | wager money |
| 151 | advertising slogan | an expression to sell |
| 151 | in so doing | when it does this |
| 153 | lull us to sleep | make us sleepy |
| 153 | in this way | this ids how it occurs |
| 155 | when it comes to the sense of smell | think about sense of smell |
| 160 | pecking orders | the order of importance |
| 160 | made quite a stink | caused great disruption |
| 160 | do pushups | do exercises |
| 160 | unparalleled commitment | unmatched commitment |
| 160 | mindless | with no thoughts or ideas |
| 160 | dirty drones | lazy workers |
| 161 | golden opportunity | wonderful opportunity |
| 161 | taste cells are the rabbits of the sense | rabbits reproduce often |
| 162 | nerve endings | the end of nerves |
| 162 | per se | by itself; that and no other |

| | Phrases and Expressions (Different Usage) | |
|---|---|---|
| 162 | all in all | when we consider all |
| 162 | spaced throughout | in different place all through the body |
| 163 | whole platoon | a great many groups |
| 163 | unexpected twists | not what we expect |
| 165 | in the mood | do you want to |

**Additional Terms from the Text**

120    Chapter 4    Sensation and Perception

1. Perception is defined as the
   (a) stimulation of sensory receptors by forms of physical energy.
   (b) organization of sensations into an inner map of the world.
   (c) transmission of sensory information to the brain.
   (d) formation of mental images.

2. Which of the following colors is longest in wavelength?
   (a) red
   (b) yellow
   (c) indigo
   (d) green

3. The difference threshold for light is defined as the
   (a) difference in wavelengths between analogous hues.
   (b) amplitude divided by the wavelength.
   (c) smallest difference in intensity required to perceive a difference in intensity.
   (d) weakest amount of light the average person can perceive.

4. The amount of light that enters the eye is determined by the size of the
   (a) cornea.
   (b) lens.
   (c) retina.
   (d) pupil.

5. Rods and cones are both
   (a) bipolar cells.
   (b) ganglion cells.
   (c) photoreceptors.
   (d) color receptors.

6. You have normal color vision. You look at a sheet of paper that is colored yellow for about 30 seconds. Then you shift your gaze to a sheet of paper that is white. On this paper, you perceive the color
   (a) green.
   (b) blue.
   (c) white.
   (d) red.

7. The Ponzo illusion can probably be explained by the
   (a) volley principle.
   (b) autokinetic effect.
   (c) phi phenomenon.
   (d) principle of size constancy.

8. The cue for depth perception that involves both eyes is
   (a) retinal disparity.
   (b) motion parallax.
   (c) perspective.
   (d) shape constancy.

9. The Rubin vase is used by psychologists to illustrate the principle of
   (a) shape constancy.
   (b) size constancy.
   (c) retinal disparity.
   (d) an ambiguous figure.

10. You look at a work of art that contains many colors. Some of these colors seem to leap out at you, while others seem to recede. The colors that appear to advance toward you are most likely to be _____ colors.
    (a) complementary
    (b) analogous
    (c) warm
    (d) cool

11. The _____ is a structure of the inner ear.
    (a) eardrum
    (b) basilar membrane
    (c) hammer
    (d) stirrup

12. You see several birds flying in the same direction. It occurs to you that you assume these birds are going to the same place for the same reason. Your assumption illustrates the Gestalt principle of
    (a) shape constancy.
    (b) continuity.
    (c) similarity.
    (d) common fate.

13. The frequency of a sound is expressed in the unit
    (a) waves.
    (b) dB.
    (c) Hz.
    (d) pitch.

14. Duplicity theory is used to explain perception of
    (a) color.
    (b) body position.
    (c) taste.
    (d) sound.

15. Which of the following is a chemical sense?
    (a) smell
    (b) vision
    (c) the vestibular sense
    (d) kinesthesis

16. Research with pheromones suggests that
    (a) there is really no such thing as a pheromone.
    (b) only lower animals are responsive to them.
    (c) they regulate sexual behavior in all animals.
    (d) most people are not responsive to them.

17. _____ women rated their husbands' body odors as more noxious than their own.
    (a) Japanese
    (b) West German
    (c) Italian
    (d) U.S.

18. Receptors for _____ lie toward the back of the tongue.
    (a) sweetness
    (b) bitterness
    (c) saltiness
    (d) sourness

19. All of the following are involved in the perception of pain, **EXCEPT**
    (a) prostaglandins,
    (b) bradykinin,
    (c) amacrine cells,
    (d) P.

20. Kinesthetic sensory organs are found in all of the following, **EXCEPT**
    (a) joints.
    (b) tendons.
    (c) muscles.
    (d) bones.

**Answer Key to *Posttest***

1.  B
2.  A
3.  C
4.  D
5.  C
6.  B
7.  D
8.  A
9.  D
10. C
11. B
12. D
13. C
14. D
15. A
16. D
17. A
18. B
19. C
20. D

| | |
|---|---|
| Sensation | Hue |
| Perception | Cornea |
| Absolute threshold | Iris |
| Pitch | Pupil |
| Difference threshold | Lens |
| Signal-detection theory | Retina |
| Light | Photoreceptors |

| | |
|---|---|
| The color of light, as determined by its wavelength. | The stimulation of sensory receptors and the transmission of sensory information to the central nervous system. |
| Transparent tissue forming the outer surface of the eyeball. | The process by which sensations are organized into an inner representation of the world. |
| A muscular membrane whose dilation regulates the amount of light that enters the eye. | The minimal amount of energy that can produce a sensation. |
| The apparently black opening in the center of the iris, through which light enters the eye. | The highness or lowness of a sound, as determined by the frequency of the sound waves. |
| A transparent body behind the iris that focuses an image on the retina. | The minimal difference in intensity required between two sources of energy so that they will be perceived as being different. |
| The area of the inner surface of the eye that contains rods and cones. | The view that the perception of sensory stimuli involves the interaction of physical, biological, and psychological factors. |
| Cells that respond to light. | The part of the electromagnetic spectrum that stimulates the eye and produces visual sensations. |

| | |
|---|---|
| Optic nerve | Trichromatic theory |
| Fovea | Opponent-process theory |
| Blind spot | Perceptual organization |
| Rods | Ambiguous |
| Cones | Monocular cues |
| Dark adaptation | Perspective |
| Afterimage | Motion parallax |

The theory that color vision is made possible by three types of cones, some of which respond to red light, some to green, and some to blue.

The nerve that transmits sensory information from the eye to the brain.

The theory that color vision is made possible by three type of cones, some of which respond to red or green light, some to blue or yellow, and some only to the intensity of light.

An area near the center of the retina that is dense with cones and where vision is consequently most acute.

The tendency to integrate perceptual elements into meaningful patterns.

The area of the retina where axons from ganglion cells meet to form the optic nerve.

Having two or more possible meanings.

Rod-shaped photoreceptors that are sensitive only to the intensity of light.

Stimuli suggestive of depth that can be perceived with only one eye.

Cone-shaped photoreceptors that transmit sensation of color.

A monocular cue for depth based on the convergence (coming together) of parallel lines as they recede into the distance.

The process of adjusting to conditions of lower lighting by increasing the sensitivity of rods and cones.

A monocular cue for depth based on the perception that nearby objects appear to move more rapidly in relation to our own motion.

The lingering visual impression made by a stimulus that has been removed.

| | |
|---|---|
| Retinal disparity | Oval window |
| Convergence | Cochlea |
| Visual acuity | Basilar membrane |
| Auditory | Organ of Corti |
| Hertz | Auditory nerve |
| Amplitude | Place theory |
| Eardrum | Frequency theory |

| | |
|---|---|
| A membrane that transmits vibrations from the stirrup of the middle ear to the cochlea within the inner ear. | A binocular cue for depth based on the difference in the image cast by an object on the retinas of the eyes as the object moves closer or farther away. |
| The inner ear; the bony tube that contains the basilar membrane and the organ of Corti. | A binocular cue for depth based on the inward movement of the eyes as they attempt to focus on an object that is drawing nearer. |
| A membrane that lies coiled within the cochlea. | Sharpness of vision. |
| The receptor for hearing that lies on the basilar membrane in the cochlea. | Having to do with hearing. |
| The axon bundle that transmits neural impulses from the organ of Corti to the brain. | A unit expressing frequency of sound waves. One Hertz, or 1 Hz, equals one cycle per second. |
| The theory that the pitch of a sound is determined by the section of the basilar membrane that vibrates in response to the sound. | Height of sound wave which is related to loudness. |
| The theory that the pitch of a sound is reflected in the frequency of the neural impulses that are generated in response to the sound. | A thin membrane that vibrates in response to sound waves, transmitting the waves to the middle and inner ears. |

Directions: This *PRETEST* will give you feedback about how well you understand Chapter 5. In order to enhance your mastery of Chapter 5, complete all the sections of this chapter of the Study Guide. Then you can take the *POSTTEST* and compare your results.

1. Brain waves are measured by means of the
   (a) electrocardiogram.
   (b) electroencephalograph.
   (c) electromyograph.
   (d) thermistor.

2. During stage 4 sleep, the brain emits _____ waves.
   (a) alpha
   (b) beta
   (c) delta
   (d) theta

3. Sleep terrors tend to occur during
   (a) REM sleep.
   (b) sleep spindles.
   (c) the hypnagogic state.
   (d) deep sleep.

4. You decide that you will begin an exercise program in order to trim off some excess weight. According to the text, you may also expect to spend a greater proportion of the time you are asleep in
   (a) REM sleep.
   (b) NREM sleep.
   (c) the hypnagogic state.
   (d) paradoxical sleep.

5. According to Hartmann, long sleepers spend proportionately more time in _____ than short sleepers.
   (a) REM sleep
   (b) sleep spindles
   (c) deep sleep
   (d) the hypnagogic state

6. According to the activation–synthesis model, dreams largely reflect
   (a) unconscious urges.
   (b) wish fulfillment.
   (c) protective imagery.
   (d) biological activity.

7. Anxiety and tension are thought to be causes of
   (a) insomnia.
   (b) narcolepsy.
   (c) apnea.
   (d) the hypnagogic state.

8. _____ may be caused by a thick palate or a defect in the breathing centers of the brain.
   (a) Apnea
   (b) Narcolepsy
   (c) Bed–wetting
   (d) Sleep terrors

9. You are surprised to find that a physician has prescribed an antidepressant drug for a neighbor's child who has been having some sleeping problems. Then you remember that, according to your psychology textbook, the antidepressant drug *imipramine* has been found helpful in cases of
   (a) sleep terrors.
   (b) narcolepsy.
   (c) bed–wetting.
   (d) sleepwalking.

10. Which of the following is **NOT** one of the American Psychiatric Association's criteria for substance abuse?
(a) causing or compounding a social, occupational, psychological, or physical problem
(b) physiological dependence
(c) duration of the problem for at least one month
(d) a pattern of use that interferes with other areas of life

11. When they drink, the college–age children of alcoholics _____ than the children of nonalcoholics.
(a) show lower tolerance
(b) develop withdrawal symptoms more rapidly
(c) show better visual–motor coordination
(d) are more likely to become physically ill

12. In terms of its action on the body, cocaine is correctly categorized as a
(a) depressant.
(b) hallucinogenic.
(c) narcotic.
(d) stimulant.

13. The most widely used drug on college campuses is
(a) cocaine.
(b) marijuana.
(c) LSD.
(d) alcohol.

14. _____ was once known as "God's own medicine."
(a) Heroin
(b) Alcohol
(c) Cocaine
(d) Nicotine

15. According to the text, _____ prevents users from becoming "high" if they take heroin afterward.
(a) antabuse
(b) naloxone
(c) methadone
(d) imipramine

16. Hyperactivity in children is thought to be caused by
(a) immaturity of the cerebral cortex.
(b) overactivity of the pons.
(c) overactivity of the reticular activating system.
(d) damage in the limbic system.

17. In TM, one practices meditation by
(a) whirling.
(b) concentrating on one's body movements.
(c) repeating a Far–Eastern mantra.
(d) repeating the word "One."

18. A friend tells you that he has learned how to raise the temperature in a finger through biofeedback training. Your friend probably acquired this skill in order to
(a) relax the muscles of the forehead.
(b) control headaches.
(c) lower acid secretion in the gastrointestinal tract.
(d) emit alpha waves.

19. A friend says to you, "Aren't meditation and hypnosis really the same thing?" You are taking a psychology course, and you correctly say that they are not, but you do point out that they have at least one similarity: meditation and hypnosis both involve
(a) going into a trance.
(b) entering a transcendental state.
(c) heightening awareness of a bodily function.
(d) narrowing of attention.

20. According to neodissociation theory,
(a) hypnotized subjects are aware of many things going on around them, even though they are focusing primarily on the hypnotist.
(b) the trance state is induced by age regression.
(c) only subjects who are highly motivated to be hypnotized can be hypnotized.
(d) one cannot enter a hypnotic trance unless one is suggestible.

**Answer Key to *Pretest***

| | | | |
|---|---|---|---|
| 1. B | 6. D | 11. C | 16. A |
| 2. C | 7. A | 12. D | 17. C |
| 3. D | 8. A | 13. D | 18. B |
| 4. B | 9. C | 14. A | 19. D |
| 5. A | 10. B | 15. B | 20. A |

# OVERVIEW

Chapter 5 explores states of consciousness, including the "normal" waking state and altered states, including those induced by sleep, drugs, meditation, biofeedback, and hypnosis. Consciousness is a controversial topic in that it deals with private events. Earlier in the century, consciousness was practically banned from scientific psychology. Definitions of consciousness include sensory awareness, direct inner awareness, personal unity, and the waking state.

There are several stages of sleep, and we undergo about five sleep cycles in a typical eight-hour night. Most dreams occur in REM (rapid–eye–movement) sleep. Evidence concerning the functions of sleep and dreams is reviewed. Sleep appears to serve a restorative function, and dreams may reflect the integration (synthesis) of biological activity in the brain. Sleep disorders such as insomnia, narcolepsy, apnea, bed–wetting, sleepwalking, and sleep terrors are discussed.

Substance abuse and substance dependence are defined. The consciousness–altering (psychoactive) effects of depressants, stimulants, and hallucinogenics are discussed. The physical effects and the potential of these drugs for inducing dependence are explored.

Meditation is discussed as a method for altering consciousness and inducing a "relaxation response." Biofeedback is explained as a method of feeding back information about bodily functions to organisms, and its capacity to teach people to control involuntary functions is explored. The history of hypnotism is outlined, as are the changes in consciousness brought about by hypnosis. It is shown that we need not resort to the notion of a hypnotic "trance" to explain the effects of hypnosis. Contemporary theories of hypnosis focus on role playing and on the selective deployment of attention.

# LEARNING OBJECTIVES

| | A Minor Question: What *Is* Consciousness? |
|---|---|
| 1. Discuss the controversy concerning the inclusion of *consciousness* as a topic in the science of psychology. | |
| 2. Explain the following definitions of *consciousness*: consciousness as sensory awareness, direct inner awareness, personal unity, and the waking state. | |
| | **Sleep and Dreams** |
| 3. List the four stages of *NREM sleep*, and discuss the features of each. Make reference to *brain waves* in your discussion. | |
| 4. Describe *REM sleep*, and explain why it is also referred to as paradoxical sleep. | |

5. Summarize research concerning the functions of sleep, focusing on the effects of sleep deprivation, and on long versus short sleepers.

6. Discuss *dreams*, including theories of dream content, and distinguish between *nightmares* and *sleep terrors*.

7. Describe the sleep disorders *insomnia, narcolepsy, apnea, bed–wetting*, and *sleepwalking*.

## Altering Consciousness through Drugs

8. Define *substance abuse* and *substance dependence*.

## Depressants

9. Summarize research concerning the psychological and physical effects of alcohol.

10. Discuss the effects of *opiates* and *opioids*, and explain how *methadone* is used to treat heroin dependence.

11. Discuss the effects of *barbiturates* and *methaqualone*.

## Stimulants

12. Discuss the effects of *amphetamines*.

13. Discuss the effects of *cocaine*.

14. Discuss the effects of the ingredients in cigarette smoke, and explain how stress influences the desire for smokers to increase their usage of cigarettes.

| | **Hallucinogenics** |
|---|---|
| 15. Discuss the effects of *marijuana*. | |
| 16. Discuss the effects of LSD, and summarize research concerning the flashback controversy. | |
| | **Altering Consciousness through Meditation** |
| 17. Summarize research concerning the effects of *meditation*. | |
| | **Altering Consciousness through Biofeedback** |
| 18. Summarize research concerning the effects of *biofeedback training*. | |
| | **Altering Consciousness through Hypnosis** |
| 19. Describe the history of *hypnosis*. | |
| 20. Discuss the changes in consciousness that can be brought about by hypnosis. | |
| 21. Explain the *role* and *neodissociation theories* of hypnosis. | |
| | **Additional Notes** |
| | |
| | |
| | |

### A Minor Question:  What *Is* Consciousness?

## Sleep and Dreams

1. The Stages of Sleep

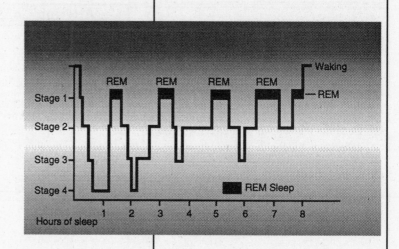

2.  Functions of Sleep

3.  Dreams: "Such Stuff as Dreams Are Made On"

4.  Sleep Disorders

   • Insomnia

   • Narcolepsy

   • Apnea

   • Deep-Sleep Disorders:
     Sleep Terrors, Bed-Wetting, & Sleepwalking

| | |
|---|---|
| **Altering Consciousness through Drugs** <br><br>   1. Substance Abuse and Dependence <br><br><br>   2. Causal Factors in Substance Abuse and <br>      Dependence | |
| **Depressants** <br><br>   1. Alcohol <br><br><br><br>   2. Opioids <br><br><br>   3. Barbiturates and Methaqualone <br><br><br><br> **Stimulants** <br><br>   1. Amphetamines <br><br><br>   2. Cocaine <br><br><br>   3. Cigarettes (Nicotine) | |

## Hallucinogenics

    1. Marijuana

    2. LSD

    3. Other Hallucinogenics

## Altering Consciousness through Meditation: When Eastern Gods Meet Western Technology

    1. Transcendental Meditation

    2. How to Meditate

## Altering Consciousness through Biofeedback: Getting in Touch with the Untouchable

    1. Electromyograph

    2. Heart Rate

    3. Blood Pressure

    4. Amount of Sweat on Palms

## Altering Consciousness through Hypnosis: On Being Entranced

    1. Hypnotic Induction

    2. Changes in Consciousness Brought About by Hypnosis

    3. Theories of Hypnosis

## Psychology and Modern Life

    1. Coping with Insomnia: How to Get to Sleep at Night

    2. Quitting and Cutting Down on Smoking

This is a mind-map review sheet for the section in Chapter 5 on *Altering Consciousness through Drugs*. Some students prefer to review using a drawing like this, others prefer regular notes or outlines. Try doing mind-maps of your own in many different colors and see if you enjoy using them for chapter reviews. You can then decide which note taking technique works best for you.

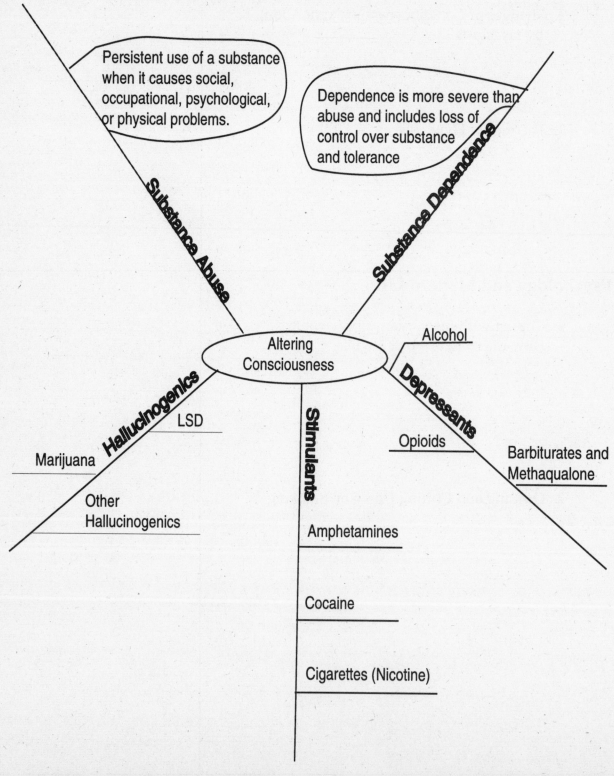

Persistent use of a substance when it causes social, occupational, psychological, or physical problems.

Dependence is more severe than abuse and includes loss of control over substance and tolerance

Substance Abuse

Substance Dependence

Altering Consciousness

Hallucinogenics

LSD

Marijuana

Other Hallucinogenics

Stimulants

Amphetamines

Cocaine

Cigarettes (Nicotine)

Alcohol

Depressants

Opioids

Barbiturates and Methaqualone

# KEY TERMS AND CONCEPTS

## The Minor Question: What Is Consciousness?

1. Sensory awareness _____

2. Selective attention _____

3. Direct inner awareness _____

4. Preconscious _____

5. Unconscious _____

6. Repression _____

7. Suppression _____

8. Nonconscious _____

9. Self _____

10. Altered states of consciousness _____

## Sleep and Dreams

11. Circadian rhythm _____

12. Electroencephalograph (EEG) _____

13. Volt _____

14. Non–rapid–eye–movement (NREM) sleep _____

15. Rapid–eye–movement (REM) sleep _____

16. Alpha waves _____

17. Theta waves _____

18. Hypnagogic state _____

19. Sleep spindles _____

20. K complex _____

21. Delta waves _____

22. Dreams _____

23. Activation–synthesis model _____

24. Incubus _____

25. Succubus _____

26. Insomnia _____

27. Narcolepsy _____

28. Apnea _____

29. Sleep terrors _____

30. Tranquilizers _____

## Altering Consciousness Through Drugs

31. Psychoactive _____

32. Depressants _____

33. Stimulants _____

34. Substance abuse _____

35. Tolerance (for a drug) _____

36. Abstinence syndrome _____

37. Delirium tremens (DT's) _____

38. Disorientation _____

39. Hallucinations _____

## Depressants

40. Sedative _____

41. Euphoria _____

42. Cirrhosis of the liver _____

43. Wernicke–Korsakoff syndrome _____

_____

44. Opioids _____

45. Narcotics _____

46. Analgesia _____

47. Morphine _____

48. Heroin _____

49. Methadone _____

50. Barbiturate _____

51. Methaqualone _____

## Stimulants

52. Amphetamines _____

53. Attention-deficit/hyperactivity disorder _____

_____

54. Cocaine _____

55. Hydrocarbons _____

56. Passive smoking _____

57. Nicotine _____

**Hallucinogenics**

58. Hallucinogenic _____

59. Marijuana _____

60. Psychedelic _____

61. Delta–9–tetrahydrocannabinol (THC) _____

_____

62. Hashish ("hash") _____

63. Lysergic diethylamide acid (LSD) _____

_____

64. Flashbacks _____

65. Mescaline _____

66. Phencyclidine (PCP) _____

**Altering Consciousness Through Meditation**

67. Meditation _____

68. Transcendental Meditation (TM) _____

_____

69. Mantra _____

70 Relaxation response _____

**Altering Consciousness Through Biofeedback**

71. Biofeedback training _____

72. Electromyograph (EMG) _____

**Altering Consciousness Through Hypnosis**

73. Hypnosis _____

74. Pseudomemories _____

75. Hypermnesia _____

76. Age regression _____

77. Regression _____

78. Role theory _____

79. Neodissociation theory _____

**Additional Terms**

## SECTION 1: A Minor Question: What *Is* Consciousness?

**OBJ. 1:** In 1904, William (1) _____ wrote an article, "Does Consciousness Exist?" John (2) _____, the father of modern behaviorism, argued that only observable (3) b_____ should be studied by psychologists. However, (4) cog_____ psychologists believe that we cannot discuss meaningful human behavior without referring to consciousness.

**OBJ. 2:** Consciousness has several meanings, including sensory awareness; direct (5) _____r awareness of cognitive processes; personal (6) _____y, or the sense of self; and the waking state. Sensory (7) _____ness refers to consciousness of the environment. (8) D_____ inner awareness refers to consciousness of thoughts, images, emotions, and memories.

Sigmund Freud differentiated among ideas that are conscious; (9) _____scious, that is, available to awareness by focusing on them; and (10) _____scious, that is, unavailable to awareness under ordinary circumstances.

## SECTION 2: Sleep and Dreams

**OB. 3:** (11) Elec_____ (EEG) records show different stages of sleep. Different stages of sleep characterized by different (12) b_____ waves. We have four stages of (13) non_____ (NREM) sleep. Stage (14) _____ sleep is lightest, and stage (15) _____ sleep is deepest.

The strength of brain waves is measured in the unit (16) _____s. When we close our eyes and relax, before going to sleep, our brains emit (17) _____a waves. As we enter stage 1 sleep, we enter a pattern of (18) _____a waves. The transition from alpha to theta waves may be accompanied by brief hallucinatory, dreamlike images referred to as the (19) _____gic state. During stage 2 sleep, sleep (20) _____les appear. We emit slow,

strong (21) _____a waves during stages 3 and 4 sleep.

**OBJ. 4:** After a half hour or so of stage (22) _____ sleep, we journey upward through the stages until we enter REM sleep. REM sleep is characterized by rapid (23) _____ movements beneath closed lids, and by the emission of brain waves that resemble those of light stage (24) _____ sleep. Because EEG patterns during REM sleep resemble those of the waking state, REM sleep is also referred to as (25) _____ical sleep. During REM sleep we dream about (26) _____ percent of the time. We dream about (27) _____ percent of the time during NREM sleep.

During a typical eight-hour night, we undergo about (28) _____ trips through the different stages of sleep. Our first journey through stage 4 sleep is usually (29: *Circle one:* longest or shortest). Sleep tends to become (30: *Circle one:* lighter or deeper) as the night wears on. Periods of REM sleep tend to become (31: *Circle one:* longer or shorter) toward morning.

**OBJ. 5:** Sleep apparently helps restore a tired body, but we do not know exactly how sleep restores us, or how much sleep we need. People who sleep nine or more hours a day are called long sleepers. Long sleepers are more concerned about (32) _____ment than short sleepers are. Long sleepers are more creative than short sleepers, but also more anxious and (33) _____ed. Long sleepers spend proportionately more time in (34: *Circle one:* REM or NREM) sleep than short sleepers do.

People who are sleep-deprived show temporary problems in (35) _____tion, which may reflect episodes of (36) _____line sleep. People deprived of REM sleep show REM– (37) _____nd during subsequent sleep periods.

**OBJ. 6:** Dreams are most vivid during (38: *Circle one:* REM or NREM) sleep. Freud theorized that dreams reflect (39) _____scious wishes and serve the function of protecting sleep. According to the activation–synthesis model, dreams reflect activation by the (40) _____s, and automatic integration of resultant neural activity by the cerebral (41) co_____. The content of most dreams is an extension of the events or concerns of the day.

Nightmares are kinds of dreams that occur during (42) _____ sleep. Sleep (43) _____rs are more frightening and occur during deep sleep.

**OBJ. 7:** Difficulty falling asleep is called (44) _____–_____et insomnia. Insomnia sufferers show higher levels of (45) _____tic activity than nonsufferers as they try to get to sleep. In narcolepsy, otherwise referred to as a sleep (46) _____ck, a person falls suddenly, irresistibly asleep. In (47) _____a, the person stops breathing periodically during the night. Apnea sufferers usually start breathing again because of build–up of (48) _____ _____de. Bed–wetting has been seen as reflective of parental harshness, but this problem may also reflect immaturity of the (49) _____ system. The antidepressant drug *imipramine* sometimes helps by increasing (50) _____der capacity. Sleepwalking, like bed–wetting, is a (51) _____p sleep disorder. Bed–wetting and sleepwalking are problems of child-hood that usually end when the child matures.

## SECTION 3: Altering Consciousness through Drugs

**OBJ. 8:** Substance use is considered abuse when it is continued for at least one (52) _____ despite the fact that it is causing or compounding a social, (53) oc_____, psychological, or (54) ph_____ problem. The (55) am_____ of the substance used is not the crucial factor. Substance dependence is characterized by (56: *Circle one:* increased or decreased) use despite efforts to cut down and by (57) _____cal dependence.

Physiological dependence is evidenced by tolerance or by an (58) ab_____ syndrome upon withdrawal.

People usually first try drugs because of (59) _____ity, but usage can be reinforced by anxiety reduction, feelings of euphoria, and other sensations. People are also motivated to avoid (60) _____wal symptoms once they become physiologically dependent. Some people may have genetic predispositions to become physiologically dependent on certain substances.

## SECTION 4: Depressants

**OBJ. 9:** The group of substances called depressants acts by slowing the activity of the (61) _____ nervous system.

Alcohol is an intoxicating depressant that leads to (62) phy_____ dependence. Alcohol impairs (63) cog_____ functioning, slurs the (64) s_____, and reduces (65) m_____ coordination. Alcohol provides people with an excuse for (66) _____re or for (67) anti_____ behavior, but alcohol has not been shown to induce antisocial behavior directly. As a depressant, alcohol also (68: *Circle one:* increases or decreases) sexual response, although many people expect alcohol to have the opposite effect.

(69) De_____tion, or helping a physiologi-cally dependent alcoholic safely through the abstinence syndrome, is a straightforward medical procedure. The greater problem is assisting alcoholics to cope with life's (70) _____s through measures other than drinking.

**OBJ. 10:** Opiates are a group of (71) _____cs derived from the opium poppy. (72) _____ds are similar to opiates in chemical structure, but are synthe-sized in the laboratory. The opiates (73) mor_____ and (74) h_____ are depressants that reduce pain, but they are also bought on the street because of the euphoric rush they provide. Opiates and opioids can lead to (75) ph_____ dependence and distressing (76) ab_____ syndromes. The synthetic narcotic (77) _____done has been used to treat heroin dependence. The drug (78) _____ one blocks the "high" of heroin.

**OBJ. 11:** Barbiturates are (79) _____ nts with many medical uses. These uses include treatment of (80) ep _____, of high (81) _____ pressure, and of anxiety and insomnia. Barbiturates lead rapidly to (82) ph _____ dependence.

## SECTION 5: Stimulants

**OBJ. 12:** Stimulants act by (83:*Circle one:* increasing or decreasing) the activity of the nervous system.

(84) _____ ines are stimulants that produce feelings of euphoria when taken in high doses. But high doses of amphetamines may also cause restlessness, insomnia, psychotic symptoms, and a "crash" upon (85) _____ al. Amphetamines and a related stimulant, (86) R _____, are commonly used to treat hyperactive children.

**OBJ. 13:** The stimulant (87) c _____ was used in Coca–Cola prior to 1906. Now it is an illegal drug that provides feelings of (88) _____ ia and bolsters self–confidence. As with the amphetamines, overdoses can lead to (89) _____ ness, (90) in _____, and psychotic reactions. There is controversy as to whether stimulants lead to (91) _____ cal dependence, although it is generally agreed that any drug can lead to (92) _____ cal dependence.

**OBJ. 14:** Cigarette smoke contains carbon (93) _____ ide, hydrocarbons, and the stimulant (94) _____ ine. Regular smokers adjust their smoking to maintain a consistent blood level of nicotine, suggestive of (95) _____ cal dependence. Cigarette smoking has been linked to death from heart disease, cancer, and many other disorders.

Stress tends to (96: *Circle one:* increase or decrease) cigarette consumption among smokers. It appears that stress increases the acidity of the (97) u _____. (98) N _____ is excreted more rapidly when the urine is highly acidic. For this reason, smokers under stress may have to smoke (99: *Circle one:* more or less) to maintain the same (100) b _____ level of nicotine.

## SECTION 6: Hallucinogenics

**OBJ. 15:** Hallucinogenic substances produce (101) _____ tions, or sensations and perceptions in the absence of external stimulation that become confused with reality.

Marijuana is a (102) _____ genic drug. Marijuana's psychoactive ingredients including (103) delta _____ inol, or THC. THC often produces heightened and distorted (104) _____ tions, relaxation, feelings of (105) em _____, and reports of new insights. Hallucinations are possible. Marijuana has also been accused of causing (106) _____ tional syndrome, or loss of ambition. However, evidence concerning amotivational syndrome is (107) _____ tional, not experimental. The long-term (108) cog _____ and physical effects of marijuana usage are not fully known, although it appears clear that marijuana smoke is physically harmful.

**OBJ. 16:** LSD is a hallucinogenic drug that produces vivid (109) _____ tions. So–called LSD (110) _____ cks may reflect psychological rather than physiological factors. Persons prone to flashbacks are more oriented toward (111) _____ sy and toward allowing their thoughts to (112) _____ der. Regular use of hallucinogenics may lead to psychological (113) _____ dence and to (114) tol _____. However, hallucinogenics are not known to lead to (115) _____ cal dependence.

## SECTION 7: Altering Consciousness through Meditation

**OBJ. 17:** In meditation, one focuses "passively" on an object or a (116) m _____ in order to alter the normal person–environment relationship. In this way consciousness (that is, the normal focuses of attention) is altered and a (117) re _____ _____ is often induced. (118) Tr _____ Meditation (TM) and other forms of meditation appear to reduce high blood pressure along with producing relaxation. There is controversy as to whether meditation is more relaxing or effective in reducing (119) b _____ pressure than is simple quiet sitting or resting.

## SECTION 8: Altering Consciousness through Biofeedback

**OBJ. 18:** Biofeedback is a system that (120) _____s back information about a bodily function to an organism. Neal Miller taught rats to increase or decrease their (121) _____ _____s by giving them electric shock in their "pleasure centers" when they performed the targeted response. Through biofeedback training, people and lower animals have learned to consciously control a number of (122) _____tary or autonomic functions. The (123) _____graph (EMG) monitors (124) m_____ tension and helps people become more aware of muscle tension in the forehead and elsewhere.

## SECTION 9: Altering Consciousness through Hypnosis

**OBJ. 19:** Hypnosis in its modern form was originated by Franz (125) M_____. Mesmer explained the hypnotic "trance" through his concept of animal (126) _____ism. In the second half of the Nineteenth Century, hypnotism contributed to the development of (127) _____tic theory. By means of hypnosis, Charcot and Janet found that so-called (128) _____ical disorders had psychological roots. Freud suggested that hypnosis was one avenue to the (129) _____scious mind.

Today hypnotism is used in night club acts and thus has its sensationalistic aspects. However, psychologists responsibly use hypnosis to help clients relax, to help them (130) _____ine vivid imagery, and to help them cope with (131) p_____. Police use hypnosis to prompt the (132) m_____ of witnesses.

**OBJ. 20:** People who are readily hypnotized are said to have hypnotic (133) _____lity. Suggestible people have (134) _____tive attitudes toward hypnosis, and are highly (135) _____ed to become hypnotized.

Hypnosis typically brings about the following changes in consciousness: passivity, narrowed (136) _____tion, (137) _____sia (heightened memory), suggestibility, assumption of unusual roles, perceptual distortions, (138) post_____ amnesia, and posthypnotic suggestion.

**OBJ. 21:** According to Freud's psychoanalytic theory, the hypnotic trance represents (139) _____sion.

Current theories of hypnosis do not rely on the existence of a special (140) t_____ state. According to role theory, hypnotized subjects enact the (141) _____ of being in a hypnotic trance. In order to enact this role, they must be aware of the (142) _____iors that constitute the trance, and motivated to imitate these behaviors.

According to (143) neo_____tion theory, hypnosis involves the selective deployment of attention. Subjects attend mainly to the hypnotist, but also perceive other events (144) _____ly, as though they had "hidden (145) _____s."

### Answer Key to *Chapter Review*

| | |
|---|---|
| 1. James | 19. Hypnagogic |
| 2. Watson | 20. Spindles |
| 3. behavior | 21. Delta |
| 4. cognitive | 22. 4 |
| 5. inner | 23. Eye |
| 6. unity | 24. 1 |
| 7. awareness | 25. Paradoxical |
| 8. Direct | 26. 80 |
| 9. preconscious | 27. 20 |
| 10. unconscious | 28. Five |
| 11. Electroencephalograph | 29. Longest |
| 12. Bbrain | 30. Lighter |
| 13. non-rapid eye movement | 31. Longer |
| 14. 1 | 32. Achievement |
| 15. 4 | 33. Depressed |
| 16. volts | 34. REM |
| 17. Alpha | 35. Attention |
| 18. Theta | 36. Borderline |

37. rebound
38. REM
39. unconscious
40. pons
41. cortex
42. REM
43. terrors
44. sleep-onset
45. autonomic (or sympathetic)
46. attack
47. apnea
48. carbon dioxide
49. nervous
50. bladder
51. deep
52. month
53. occupational
54. physical
55. amount
56. increased
57. physiological
58. abstinence
59. curiosity
60. withdrawal
61. central
62. physiological
63. cognitive
64. speech
65. motor
66. failure
67. antisocial
68. decreases
69. Detoxification
70. stresses
71. narcotics
72. Opioids
73. morphine

74. heroin
75. physiological
76. abstinence
77. methadone
78. naloxone
79. depressants
80. epilepsy
81. blood
82. physiological
83. increasing
84. Amphetamines
85. withdrawal
86. Ritalin
87. cocaine
88. euphoria
89. restlessness
90. insomnia
91. physiological
92. psychological
93. monoxide
94. nicotine
95. physiological
96. increase
97. urine
98. Nicotine
99. more
100. blood
101. hallucinations
102. hallucinogenic
103. delta-9–tetrahydro cannabinol
104. perceptions
105. empathy
106. amotivational
107. correlational
108. cognitive
109. hallucinations
110. flashbacks

111. fantasy
112. wander
113. dependence
114. tolerance
115. physiological
116. mantra
117. relaxation response
118. Transcendental
119. blood
120. feeds
121. heart rates
122. involuntary
123. electromyograph
124. muscle
125. mesmer
126. magnetism
127. psychodynamic (or psychoanalytic)
128. hysterical
129. unconscious
130. imagine
131. pain
132. memory
133. suggestibility
134. positive
135. motivated
136. attention
137. hypermnesia
138. posthypnotic
139. regression
140. trance
141. role
142. behaviors
143. neodissociation
144. subconsciously
145. observers

| | Idioms | Explanation |
|---|---|---|
| 174 | fade away | indicate that you were absolutely positive |
| 174 | bear witness | indicate that you were absolutely positive |
| 202 | gives way | changes and becomes |
| 202 | wears off | the effects are not apparent anymore |

| | Cultural References | Explanation |
|---|---|---|
| 180 | Marc Chagall | a Russian artist born in 1887 who became a French citizen in 1922 and painted in France |
| 184 | supermarket | a large indoor market where customers choose from a great amount of items |
| 184 | Karl Marx | a German socialist and political economist who lived in London; author of **Communist** Manifesto and Das Kapital |
| 187 | Civil War | The American Civil War, or War Between the States, was a tragic war between **the northern states** and the southern states |
| 187 | Franco-Prussian War | a war between France and Prussia (Germany) in which the Germans were the **victors.** |
| 201 | nightclub act | entertainment in a restaurant |
| 201 | lie-detector test | a mechanism that measures blood pressure and other physiological responses to **determine if a** person who is being questioned is telling the truth |

| | Phrases and Expressions (Different Usage) | |
|---|---|---|
| 174 | the scoop | the answer |
| 174 | venerable guru | old and very wise intellectual and spiritual leader |
| 174 | life and limb and bank account | emotional and physical existence and also money |
| 174 | tackle the $64,000 question | study and discuss the biggest question there is |
| 174 | a proper area | a correct area; an appropriate area |
| 174 | the proper province | the correct or appropriate area for the study of psychology to have control |
| 174 | further cemented | increased and made permanent |
| 175 | readily available | easily received |

| | Phrases and Expressions (Different Usage) | |
|---|---|---|
| 175 | summon up | remember; look for and get |
| 175 | afterall | when you think about it |
| 175 | essence of | basis; the basic or most important element |
| 175 | bring them about | cause them |
| 178 | some scrawls | movements of pencil or pen |
| 178 | printout | prints or pages that have printing on them from a computer |
| 178 | a rather steep descent | extreme decline |
| 178 | brief bursts | short small explosions |
| 179 | outdated theory | a theory that does not have support now |
| 179 | power isn't switched off | a reference to turning off the electric current |
| 179 | contest the view | argue against |
| 179 | "wrecked" the following day | feeling very bad or terrible the next day |
| 179 | "catch up on our sleep" | get the sleep which we did not get before |
| 179 | long versus short sleepers | people who sleep many hours are different from people who sleep few hours |
| 179 | happy-go-lucky | an attitude of happiness without concern for problems which may occur later; |
| 179 | self-satisfied | happy with oneself |
| 179 | closed the gap | there was not any difference |
| 179 | horror stories | terrible incidents |
| 179 | droopy eyelids | eyelids that are closing slowly over the eyeballs |
| 181 | dream theater | the way that you dream; dream arena |
| 181 | unlikely candidates | probably not good means or methods |
| 181 | time-triggered mechanism | a mechanism which acts at a specific time |
| 181 | thrash about | move with energy |
| 181 | wear and tear | a little physical damage |
| 181 | gain your footing | become balanced |
| 181 | that is | this means that |
| 181 | a novel method | new and unusual method |
| 181 | Along what dream paths would you wander if | how and what you would dream if |
| 181 | get things going my way | have my dreams in my control |
| 182 | All too familiar | everybody knows about and it is unfortunate that so many people experience it |
| 182 | sleep-onset | the point at which sleep begins |

Chapter 5   States of Consciousness

| | | |
|---|---|---|
| 182 | set the stage | prepare |
| 182 | to run infamies | to occur frequently in families |
| 183 | buildup | accumulation |
| 183 | no one need be to blame | no one is responsible for |
| 183 | "outgrow" the disorder | grow older and more mature, and so do not do it anymore |
| 183 | befall them | happen to them |
| 183 | Contrary to myth | different from what most people think is true |
| 184 | take you up | make you feel good |
| 184 | let you down | make you feel calm and sometimes depressed |
| 184 | toy of the well-to-do | plaything of the wealthy |
| 184 | price breaks | the cost has greatly decreased |
| 185 | "sleeping it off" | sleeping along time after having had a lot of **alcohol** |
| 185 | a handful | a few, not all |
| 185 | in effect | in reality; what actually happens but is not planned |
| 186 | meant so much to so many | the most important for a large number of people |
| 186 | drug of choice | the drug which most adolescents prefer |
| 187 | short-term use | use for a brief period of time |
| 187 | slurs the speech | speech is not clear; words are not pronounced carefully |
| 187 | the following highlight | in the following essay, which we emphasize |
| 187 | heavy drinking | drinking a lot of alcohol |
| 187 | light to moderate | drinking small amounts of alcohol occasionally |
| 188 | chronic drinkers | people drinking large amounts of alcohol regularly |
| 188 | heart of the problem | the real problem to be solved |
| 188 | remain in treatment | remain in a therapy program |
| 188 | drop out | leave, stop the treatment |
| 188 | handful of meetings | a very few meetings |
| 190 | street drugs | drugs sold illegally on the street |
| 190 | poor judgment | bad judgment |
| 190 | from drug to drug | the effects of drugs differ from one another |
| 190 | all-night cram sessions | remaining awake all night in order to study for an exam |
| 190 | are different opinions | opinion is mixed there |
| 191 | deadens pain | get rid of pain |
| 191 | quickening of the heart | the rate of the beat of the |
| 191 | | heart increases suddenly |
| 192 | came to the attention | was noticed by |
| 192 | habit forming | a person might acquire a habit for it |
| 192 | novice smoker | new smoker |
| 192 | mental "kick" | a sudden good feeling |
| 192 | light headedness | to feel dizzy |
| 192 | grows wild | grows without anyone planting or caring for it |

| | | |
|---|---|---|
| 194 | short-term memory | memory of recent events |
| 194 | rise in workload | increase in the work that the heart will have to do |
| 195 | melt away | gradually disappears |
| 195 | underlie | be the cause of |
| 195 | opens new worlds | makes new experience available |
| 195 | LSD "trips " | fantasies and of the mind caused by LSD |
| 195 | swear off | make a positive decision to not use it or do it anymore |
| 195 | thoughts... wander | uncontrolled thoughts |
| 195 | replay of the experience | repeat the experience |
| 195 | for the sake of | deprive oneself of one experience for another |
| 195 | peak experiences | experiences of euphoria |
| 195 | similar psychological threads | they are connected |
| 198 | normal person-environment relationship | the normal relationship of the person to the environment |
| 198 | just taking this time out | doing nothing except to change activities, or relax |
| 198 | final word on meditation is not yet in | there are no conclusive research findings on meditation gather |
| 198 | firsthand knowledge | some acquire some knowledge by doing it yourself |
| 198 | try it out | attempt it |
| 198 | outbreath | a breath that you breathe out of your mouth |
| 198 | wrapped in | completely involved |
| 198 | to squelch them | to eliminate them |
| 198 | above all | the important thing is |
| 200 | can take for granted | assume, accept |
| 200 | Once in a while | it happens, but not often |
| 200 | to be sure | it is true |
| 200 | hair stands literally on end | the hair on the head stands straight up from fear |
| 202 | not to be far from the mark | it may be almost accurate |
| 202 | avenue to the unconscious | way to reach the unconscious |
| 202 | to narrow attention | to focus |
| 202 | a track record | has had success in the past |
| 203 | nonetheless | nevertheless, opposite manner |
| 203 | to take... with a grain of salt | to consider not very important or believable |
| 206 | popping pills | taking pills frequently |
| 206 | "go with" fantasies | allow the fantasies to occur |
| 206 | with mind trips | with fantasy |
| 207 | would-be-reducers | cigarette smokers who reduce the amount they smoke |
| 207 | just one hitch | only one problem |
| 207 | side effects | effects which result from the activity |
| 207 | in curbing overeating | in reducing overeating |

148    Chapter 5    States of Consciousness

1. Sigmund Freud labeled mental events that are unavailable to awareness under most circumstances as
   (a) preconscious.
   (b) unconscious.
   (c) repressed.
   (d) dissociated.

2. According to the text, the least controversial meaning of the word "consciousness" refers to
   (a) direct inner awareness.
   (b) sensory awareness.
   (c) the normal waking state.
   (d) the sense of self.

3. The strength of brain waves is expressed in the unit
   (a) decibels.
   (b) Hertz.
   (c) amperes.
   (d) volts.

4. Sleep spindles appear during stage _____ sleep.
   (a) 1
   (b) 2
   (c) 3
   (d) 4

5. Beth feels well-rested after sleeping only about six hours each night, but Jane seems to require nine to ten hours of sleep a night in order to feel well–rested. According to Hartmann's research, Beth is more likely than Jane to be
   (a) happy–go–lucky.
   (b) creative.
   (c) lazy.
   (d) anxious.

6. Jim usually sleeps eight hours a night. About how many dreams is he likely to have during the night?
   (a) none
   (b) one
   (c) five
   (d) twenty–five or more

7. Freud believed that dreams "protected sleep" by
   (a) causing us to emit alpha waves.
   (b) inhibiting the reticular activating system.
   (c) producing rapid eye movements.
   (d) keeping disturbing ideas out of awareness.

8. According to the activation-synthesis model, stimulation by the _____ generally inhibits motor activity.
   (a) cerebral cortex
   (b) thalamus
   (c) pons
   (d) reticular activating system

9. Which of the following is also known as a "sleep attack"?
   (a) narcolepsy
   (b) sleep terrors
   (c) apnea
   (d) K complex

10. Which of the following is **NOT** part of the abstinence syndrome for alcohol?
    (a) rapid pulse
    (b) low blood pressure
    (c) anxiety
    (d) tremors

11. Methaqualone is a(n) _____ drug.
    (a) depressant
    (b) stimulant
    (c) antidepressant
    (d) hallucinogenic

12. Which of the following is **LEAST** likely to cause physiological dependence?
    (a) barbiturates
    (b) LSD
    (c) methaqualone
    (d) methadone

13. The stimulant nicotine is found in
    (a) Dexedrine.
    (b) Benzedrine.
    (c) Ritalin.
    (d) cigarettes.

14. Physiological dependence on _____ was once known as the "soldier's disease."
    (a) heroin
    (b) morphine
    (c) Valium
    (d) alcohol

15. Benson found that people who meditate twice daily
    (a) show lower blood pressure.
    (b) show normalized blood pressure.
    (c) produce more frequent delta waves.
    (d) show higher respiration rates.

16. TM was introduced by
    (a) Maharishi Mahesh Yogi.
    (b) Franz Mesmer.
    (c) Herbert Benson.
    (d) Neal Miller.

17. Biofeedback is defined as a system that feeds back information about _____ to an organism.
    (a) autonomic functions
    (b) heart rate
    (c) voluntary functions
    (d) a bodily function

18. Hypnosis is derived from the Greek word for
    (a) trance.
    (b) role-playing.
    (c) sleep.
    (d) suggestibility.

19. Who first encouraged a patient to talk and express her feelings freely while she was hypnotized?
    (a) Sigmund Freud
    (b) Pierre Janet
    (c) Josef Breuer
    (d) Jean Martin Charcot

20. Arnold knows that you are taking a psychology course and asks you if you think he would be a "good subject" for hypnosis. You point out that research suggests that hypnosis is most successful with people who
    (a) understand what is expected of them during the "trance state".
    (b) are seeking the approval of the hypnotist.
    (c) are unfamiliar with hypnosis.
    (d) are below average in intelligence.

**Answer Key to *Posttest***

1. B
2. A
3. D
4. B
5. A
6. C
7. D
8. C
9. A
10. B
11. A
12. B
13. D
14. B
15. B
16. A
17. D
18. C
19. C
20. A

| | |
|---|---|
| Sensory awareness | Nonconscious |
| Selective attention | Self |
| Direct inner awareness | Altered states of consciousness |
| Preconscious | Circadian rhythm |
| Unconscious | Electroencephalograph |
| Repress | Volt |
| Suppression | Non-rapid-eye-movement sleep |

| | |
|---|---|
| Descriptive of bodily processes such as the growing of hair, of which we cannot become conscious. We may recognize that our hair is growing but cannot directly experience the biological process. | Knowledge of the environment through perception of sensory stimulation–one definition of consciousness. |
| The totality of impressions, thoughts, and feelings. The sense of self is another definition of consciousness. | The focus of one's consciousness on a particular stimulus. |
| States other than the normal waking state, including sleep, meditation, the hypnotic trance, and the distorted perceptions produced by use of some drugs. | Knowledge of one's own thoughts, feelings, and memories without use of sensory organs–another definition of consciousness. |
| Referring to cycles that are connected with the 24-hour period of the earth's rotation. | In psychodynamic theory, descriptive of material that is not in awareness but can be brought into awareness by focusing one's attention. |
| An instrument that measure electrical activity of the brain. EEG. | In psychodynamic theory, descriptive of ideas and feelings that are not available to awareness. |
| A unit of electrical potential. | In psychodynamic theory, to eject anxiety-provoking ideas, impulses, or images from awareness, without knowing that one is doing so. |
| Stages of sleep 1 through 4   NREM. | The deliberate, or conscious, placing of certain ideas, impulses, or images out of awareness. |

| | |
|---|---|
| Rapid-eye-movement sleep | Insomnia |
| Alpha waves | Narcolepsy |
| Theta waves | Apnea |
| Hypnagogic state | Sleep terrors |
| Delta waves | Tranquilizers |
| Dreams | Depressant |
| Activation-synthesis model | Stimulant |

| | |
|---|---|
| A term for three types of sleeping problems: (1) difficulty falling asleep, (2) difficulty remaining asleep, and (3) waking early. | A stage of sleep characterized by rapid eye movements, which have been linked to dreaming. REM. |
| A sleep disorder characterized by uncontrollable seizures of sleep during the waking state. | Rapid, low-amplitude brain waves that have been linked to feelings of relaxation. |
| A temporary cessation of breathing while asleep. | Slow brain waves produced during the hypnagogic state. |
| Frightening dreamlike experiences that occur during the deepest stage of NREM sleep. Nightmares, in contrast, occur during REM sleep. | The drowsy interval between waking and sleeping, characterized by brief, hallucinatory, dreamlike experience. |
| Drugs used to reduce anxiety and tension. | Strong, slow brain waves usually emitted during stage 4 sleep. |
| A drug that lowers the rate of activity of the nervous system. | A sequence of images or thoughts that occur during sleep. Dreams may be vague and loosely plotted or vivid and intricate. |
| A drug that increases activity of the nervous system. | The view that dreams reflect activation of cognitive activity by the reticular activating system and synthesis of this activity into a pattern by the cerebral cortex. |

| Substance abuse | Euphoria |
| --- | --- |
| Tolerance | Cirrhosis of the liver |
| Abstinence syndrome | Wernicke-Korsakoff syndrome |
| Delirium tremens | Opioids |
| Disorientation | Narcotics |
| Hallucinations | Analgesia |
| Sedative | Morphine |

| | |
|---|---|
| Feelings of well-being, elation. | Persistent use of a substance even though it is causing or compounding problems in meeting the demands of life. |
| A disease caused by protein deficiency in which connective fibers replace active liver cells, impeding circulation of the blood. Persons who drink excessively may be prone to this disease. | Habituation to a drug, with the result that increasingly higher doses of the drug are needed to achieve similar effects. |
| A cluster of symptoms associated with chronic alcohol abuse and characterized by confusion, memory impairment, and filling in gaps in memory with false information. | A characteristic cluster of symptoms that results from sudden decrease in an addictive drug's level of usage. |
| A group of narcotics derived from the opium poppy, or similar in chemical structure, that provides a euphoric rush and depresses the nervous system. | A condition characterized by sweating, restlessness, disorientation, and hallucination. The "DTs" occur in some chronic alcohol users when there is a sudden decrease in usage. |
| Drugs used to relieve pain and induce sleep. The term is usually reserved for opioids. | Gross confusion. Loss of sense of time, place, and the identity of people. |
| A state of not feeling pain although fully conscious. | Perceptions in the absence of sensation. |
| An opioid introduced at about the time of the U.S. Civil War. | A drug that soothes or quiets restlessness or agitation. |

| | |
|---|---|
| Heroin | Passive smoking |
| Methadone | Nicotine |
| Barbiturate | Hallucinogenic |
| Methaqualone | Marijuana |
| Amphetamines | Psychedelic |
| Attention-deficit disorder | THC |
| Cocaine | LSD |

| | |
|---|---|
| Inhaling of smoke from the tobacco products and exhalations of other people; also called second-hand smoking. | An opioid. Heroin, ironically, was used as a "cure" for morphine addiction when first introduced. |
| A stimulant found in tobacco smoke. | An artificial narcotic that is slower acting than, and does not provide the rush of, heroin. Methadone use allows heroin addicts to abstain from heroin. |
| Giving rise to hallucinations. | An addictive depressant used to relieve anxiety or induce sleep. |
| The dried vegetable matter of the *Cannabis sativa* plant. | An addictive depressant; often called "ludes". |
| Causing hallucinations, delusions, or heightened perceptions. | Stimulants consisting of colorless liquid. |
| The major active ingredient in marijuana. | A disorder that begins in childhood and is characterized by a persistent pattern of lack of attention, with or without hyperactivity and impulsive behavior. |
| A hallucinogenic drug. | A powerful stimulant. |

| | |
|---|---|
| Flashbacks | Electromyograph |
| Mescaline | Hypnosis |
| Meditation | Pseudomemories |
| Transcendental meditation | Hypermnesia |
| Mantra | Age regression |
| Relaxation response | Regression |
| Biofeedback training | Neodissociation theory |

Chapter 5 States of Consciousness   159

| | |
|---|---|
| An instrument that measures muscle tension. EMG. | Distorted perceptions or hallucinations that occur days or weeks after LSD usage, but mimic the LSD experience. |
| A condition in which people appear to be highly suggestible and behave as though they are in a trance. | A hallucinogenic drug derived from the mescal (peyote) cactus. |
| Hypnotically-induced false memories. | As a method for coping with stress, a systematic narrowing of attention that slows the metabolism and helps produce feelings of relaxation. |
| Greatly enhanced or heightened memory. | The simplified form of meditation brought to the United States by the Maharishi Mahesh Yogi. TM. |
| In hypnosis, taking on the role of childhood, commonly accompanied by vivid recollections of one's past. | A word or sound that is repeated in TM. |
| Return to a form of behavior characteristic of an earlier stage of development. | Benson's term for a group of responses that can be brought about by meditation. They involve lowered activity of the sympathetic branch of the autonomic nervous system. |
| A theory that explains hypnotic events in terms of the splitting of consciousness. | The systematic feeding back to an organism information about a bodily function so that the organism can gain control of that function. |

Directions: This *PRETEST* will give you feedback about how well you understand Chapter 6. In order to enhance your mastery of Chapter 6, complete all the sections of this chapter of the Study Guide. Then you can take the *POSTTEST* and compare your results.

1. In the conditioning of a taste aversion, which of the following would correspond to the flavor of the food that acquires noxious properties?
   (a) CR
   (b) CS
   (c) UR
   (d) US

2. A conditioned response is a(n)
   (a) associated reflex.
   (b) fear reaction to a neutral stimulus.
   (c) previously neutral stimulus that elicits a response.
   (d) learned reaction to a previously neutral stimulus.

3. In classical conditioning, the CR is
   (a) reinforced.
   (b) identical to the UR.
   (c) similar to the UR.
   (d) elicited by a neutral stimulus.

4. When an extinguished response has recovered spontaneously, it
   (a) was not actually extinguished in the first place.
   (b) is easier to extinguish a second time.
   (c) is more difficult to extinguish a second time.
   (d) can be suppressed, but not extinguished.

5. In operant conditioning, it usually takes longest for an initial correct response to be emitted by means of
   (a) trial and error.
   (b) physical guiding.
   (c) verbal instruction.
   (d) modeling.

6. Negative reinforcers are defined as stimuli that
   (a) increase the frequency of a response when they are applied.
   (b) decrease the frequency of a response when they are applied.
   (c) increase the frequency of a response when they are removed.
   (d) decrease the frequency of a response when they are removed.

7. A child disrupts the class in order to earn the teacher's disapproval. Teacher disapproval is apparently a _____ reinforcer.
   (a) primary positive
   (b) primary negative
   (c) conditioned positive
   (d) conditioned negative

8. In backward conditioning, the _____ is presented first.
   (a) US
   (b) CS
   (c) UR
   (d) CR

9. A rat presses a lever only when a buzzer is sounding. We may assume that the buzzer
   (a) is an unconditioned stimulus.
   (b) has been paired repeatedly with the neutral stimulus.
   (c) has instinctive meaning to the rat.
   (d) is a discriminative stimulus.

10. Kecia's usual route to work is blocked. She quickly chooses a second route on which she expects light traffic. Her behavior suggests that
    (a) she has a cognitive map of the area.
    (b) she is engaging in trial–and–error behavior.
    (c) the alternate route is a successive approximation.
    (d) conditioning teaches where reinforcement is available.

11. E. C. Tolman's research suggests that in order for rats to learn the routes through mazes, the rats must
    (a) be reinforced for reaching the ends of the mazes.
    (b) be allowed to explore the mazes.
    (c) run through the mazes when they are highly motivated.
    (d) make the appropriate conditioned responses.

12. According to contingency theory, organisms learn to associate stimuli when
    (a) they are presented contiguously.
    (b) they are combined into a compound stimulus.
    (c) their operants are reinforced.
    (d) one stimulus provides information about the other.

13. According to the text, behavior modification has helped manage classroom behavior chiefly because of
    (a) use of punishments.
    (b) consistent application of principles of learning.
    (c) widespread acceptance by school districts.
    (d) teachers' beliefs that behavior modification works.

14. New operants are acquired most quickly through a _____ schedule of reinforcement.
    (a) fixed–interval
    (b) fixed–ratio
    (c) continuous
    (d) variable

15. Bismarck's ability to reach a food reward is taken as evidence of _____ learning.
    (a) insight
    (b) latent
    (c) observational
    (d) trial–and–error

16. Who asserts that classical conditioning works by changing the ways in which organisms represent the environment?
    (a) Ivan Pavlov
    (b) John Watson
    (c) Robert Rescorla
    (d) B. F. Skinner

17. In _____ conditioning, the CS is presented and then removed prior to presentation of the US.
    (a) delayed
    (b) trace
    (c) simultaneous
    (d) backward

18. In the two types of interval schedules, "interval" refers to
    (a) distance.
    (b) speed.
    (c) time.
    (d) any or all of the above choices.

19. In the bell–and–pad method, children are taught to
    (a) substitute a CR for a CS.
    (b) discriminate a bell from a pad.
    (c) fear a bell.
    (d) wake up in response to bladder tension.

20. The behavior–therapy method of flooding is based on the principle of
    (a) discrimination training.
    (b) systematic desensitization.
    (c) extinction.
    (d) counterconditioning.

**Answer Key to *Pretest***

| | | | |
|---|---|---|---|
| 1. B | 6. C | 11. B | 16. C |
| 2. D | 7. C | 12. D | 17. B |
| 3. C | 8. A | 13. B | 18. C |
| 4. B | 9. D | 14. C | 19. D |
| 5. A | 10. A | 15. A | 20. C |

Chapter 6 focuses on various types of learning. Learning is defined in different ways by behaviorists and cognitive psychologists.

Pavlov's experiments in teaching dogs to salivate in response to previously neutral stimuli, such as bells, are important events in the history of the scientific study of learning—and classical conditioning, in particular. In classical conditioning, a previously neutral stimulus (called the conditioned stimulus, or CS) comes to elicit the response usually brought forth by another stimulus (the unconditioned stimulus, or US) by being paired repeatedly with the other stimulus. According to traditional classical–conditioning theory, learning occurs because stimuli are contiguous. According to the cognitive contingency theory of conditioning, however, learning occurs because one stimulus provided information about another.

In operant conditioning, reinforcement increases the frequency of the behavior it follows. The concepts of generalization, discrimination, extinction, and spontaneous recovery apply both to classical and operant conditioning. Reinforcers can be positive or negative, primary or secondary (conditioned). There are four basic kinds of reinforcement schedules: fixed–interval, variable–interval, fixed–ratio, and variable–ratio.

In addition to conditioning, the chapter discusses insight learning, latent learning, observational learning, and concept learning. In insight learning there is a sudden reorganization of the perceptual elements in a problem, permitting a solution. Research in latent learning shows that organisms can learn in the absence of reinforcement, and that a distinction must be made between learning and performance. In observational learning, organisms learn by observing others; emission of a response and reinforcement are unessential to the learning process.

## LEARNING OBJECTIVES

1. Define *learning* from the behavioral and the cognitive perspectives.

2. Describe the role of Ivan Pavlov in the history of the psychology of learning.

3. Describe the process of *classical conditioning*, referring to the roles of the US, CS, UR, and CR.

**Classical Conditioning**

4. Describe various types of classical conditioning.

5. Explain how *contingency theory* poses a challenge to the traditional explanation for classical conditioning.

6. Define the processes of *extinction* and *spontaneous recovery* in classical conditioning.

7. Explain what is meant by *generalization* and *discrimination* in classical conditioning.

8. Discuss applications of classical conditioning.

## Operant Conditioning

9. Describe the roles of Edward Thorndike and B. F. Skinner in the history of the psychology of learning.

10. Explain what happens during *operant conditioning*.

11. Distinguish between various kinds of *reinforcers*.

12. Describe the processes of *extinction* and *spontaneous recovery* in operant conditioning.

13. Explain the difference between *reinforcers* and *rewards* and *punishments*, and explain why psychologists advise against using punishments.

14. Explain what a *discriminative stimulus* is.

15. Define various schedules of reinforcement and explain their effects on behavior.

16. Describe the process of *shaping*.

17. Discuss applications of operant conditioning.

## Cognitive Factors in Learning

18. Define *latent learning* and describe evidence that supports this kind of learning.

19. Describe *observational learning*.

## Psychology and Modern Life

20. Summarize research findings concerning the effects of media violence and ways in which these effects can be mitigated.

## Additional Notes

## Classical Conditioning

1. Ivan Pavlov Rings a Bell

2. Stimuli and Responses in Classical Conditioning
   - US
   - CS
   - UR
   - CR

3. Types of Classical Conditioning

4. Taste Aversion

5. Extinction and Spontaneous Recovery

6. Generalization and Discrimination

7. Higher-Order Conditioning

8. Applications of Classical Conditioning

## Operant Conditioning

1. Thorndike and the Law of Effect

2. Skinner and Reinforcement

3. Types of Reinforcers

4. Extinction and Spontaneous Recovery

5. Reinforcers versus Rewards and Punishments

6. Discriminative Stimuli

7. Schedules of Reinforcement

8. Applications of Operant Conditioning

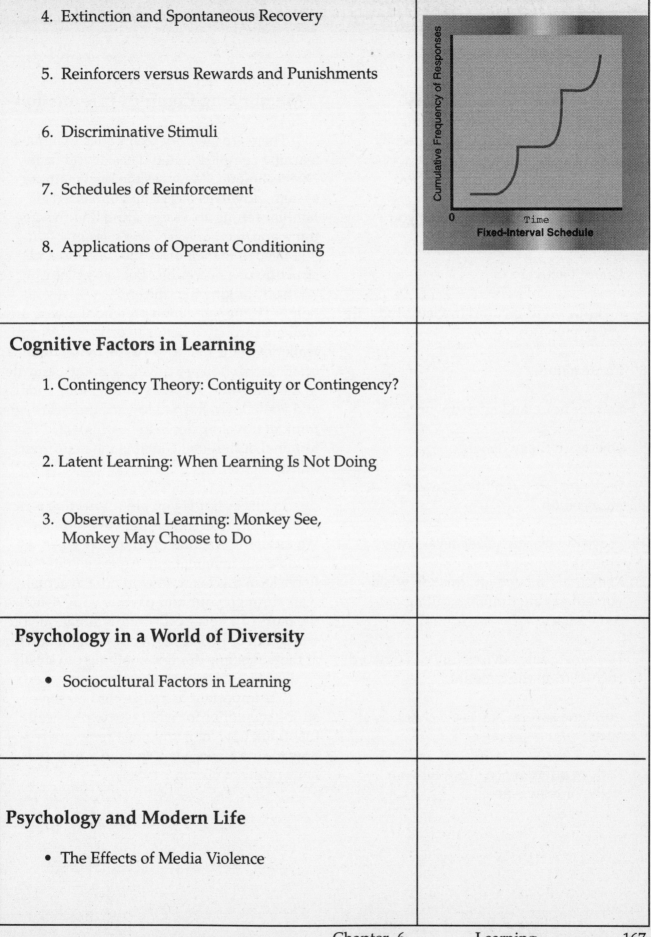

**Fixed-Interval Schedule**

## Cognitive Factors in Learning

1. Contingency Theory: Contiguity or Contingency?

2. Latent Learning: When Learning Is Not Doing

3. Observational Learning: Monkey See, Monkey May Choose to Do

## Psychology in a World of Diversity

- Sociocultural Factors in Learning

## Psychology and Modern Life

- The Effects of Media Violence

## Improving Memory

1. Learn general first and then specific.

2. Make material meaningful to you.

3. Create associations with what you already know.

4. Learn it actively.

5. Imagine vivid pictures (review Study Tip in Chapter 4).

6. Recite aloud.

7. Reduce noise and interruptions.

8. Overlearn the material.

9. Be aware of your attitude toward information.

10. Space out learning over several days.

11. Remember related information when you are having trouble recalling something.

12. Use mnemonic devices (rhymes or words created from the material).

13. Combine several of these techniques at once.

14. Reduce interference. Turn off your stereo or television.

## Memorizing Complex Information

There are memory techniques that make learning complex material easier and faster. One technique, known as the "loci memory system," involves picturing yourself in a familiar setting and associating it with something you need to learn. Let's assume that you needed to memorize the function and structure of a nerve cell. Begin by picturing yourself walking into the entry hall of your home. At the same time pretend that you are walking through a dendrite of a cell. As you walk down the hall toward the living room, imagine that you are traveling in the dendrite to the cell body. As you exit the living room and walk down the hall toward the bedrooms, think of traveling down an axon toward the terminal button that contains the neurotransmitter.

In this example you are connecting new information with something very familiar. We recall information much better when we involve our imagination. An even better way to perform this exercise would be to actually walk through your home while you visualize the parts of a nerve cell. In this situation you would not only be using your imagination but at the same time doing something physically.

It is important to realize that we have strong memories for what we do physically. Just think how long you have remembered how to ride a bike, even though you may not have ridden a bike in years.

# KEY TERMS AND CONCEPTS

1. Taste aversion _____

2. Learning _____

### Classical Conditioning

3. Reflex _____

4. Stimulus _____

5. Conditioned response (CR) _____

6. Classical Conditioning _____

7. Contiguous _____

8. Unconditioned stimulus (US) _____

9. Unconditioned response (UR) _____

10. Orienting reflex _____

11. Conditioned stimulus (CS) _____

12. Simultaneous conditioning _____

13. Delayed conditioning _____

14. Trace conditioning _____

15. Backward conditioning _____

16. Extinction _____

17. Acquisition trial _____

18. Extinction trial _____

19. Spontaneous recovery _____

20. Generalization _____

21. Discrimination training _____

22. Discrimination _____

23. Higher–order conditioning _____

24. Flooding _____

25. Systematic desensitization _____

26. Counterconditioning _____

### Operant Conditioning

27. Instrumental conditioning _____

28. Random trial-and-error behavior _____

29. Law of effect _____

30. Reinforcement _____

31. Operant behavior _____

32. Operants _____

33. Cumulative recorder _____

34. Positive reinforcer _____

35. Negative reinforcer _____

36. Primary reinforcer _____

37. Secondary reinforcer _____

38. Conditioned reinforcer _____

39. Reward _____

40. Empirically _____

41. Punishment _____

42. Model _____

43. Time out _____

44. Discriminative stimulus _____

45. Continuous reinforcement _____

46. Partial reinforcement _____

47. Pathological gambler _____

48. Fixed–interval schedule _____

49. Variable–interval schedule _____

50. Fixed–ratio schedule _____

51. Variable–ratio schedule _____

52. Shaping _____

53. Successive approximations _____

54. Socialization _____

55. Token economy _____

56. Programmed learning _____

### Cognitive Factors in Learning

57. Contingency _____

58. Latent _____

59. Observational learning _____

**OBJ. 1:** From the behaviorist perspective, learning is defined as a relatively permanent change in behavior that arises from (1) _____ ence. From the cognitive perspective, learning involves processes by which experience contributes to relatively permanent changes in the way organisms mentally (2) _____ sent the environment.

## SECTION 1: Classical Conditioning

**OBJ. 2:** Classical conditioning is defined as a simple form of learning in which an originally (3) _____ al stimulus comes to bring forth, or (4) e _____, the response usually brought forth by another stimulus by being paired repeatedly with that stimulus.

When Pavlov discovered conditioning, he was attempting to identify neural receptors in the mouth that triggered a response from the (5) _____ ary glands. Salivation in response to meat is unlearned, a (6) _____ ex. Reflexes are elicited by (7) _____ li. A stimulus may be defined as an (8) _____ mental condition that evokes a response from an organism. Pavlov discovered that reflexes can also be learned, or conditioned, through (9) _____ tion. Pavlov called learned reflexes (10) _____ nal reflexes. Today conditional reflexes are termed (11) _____ _____ ses.

**OBJ. 3:** In classical conditioning, a previously neutral stimulus, called the (12) _____ ned stimulus (or CS) comes to elicit the response evoked by a second stimulus, called the (13) _____ ned stimulus (or US) by being paired repeatedly with the second stimulus. A response to a US is called an (14) _____ ned response (UR), and a response to a CS is termed a (15) _____ ned response (CR).

**OBJ. 4:** Classical conditioning occurs efficiently when the (16) _____ ned stimulus (CS) is presented about 0.5 seconds before the (17) _____ ned stimulus (US). In (18) _____ neous conditioning, the CS is presented at the same time as the US and is left on until the response occurs. In (19) _____ ed conditioning, the CS is presented before the US and is left on until the response is shown. In trace conditioning, the CS is presented and removed (20: *Circle one*: prior to or after) presentation of the US. In (21) _____ ard conditioning, the US is presented prior to the CS.

**OBJ. 5:** According to contingency theory, the (22) con _____ presentation of stimuli—that is, the coappearance of the US and the CS—does not explain classical conditioning. Instead, learning occurs only when the CS provides (23) _____ tion about the US. According to (24) con _____ theory, learning occurs because a CS indicates that the US is likely to ensue.

Taste aversions differ from other kinds of classical conditioning in a couple of ways: First, (25: *Circle one*: only one or several) associations may be required. Second, the US and CS need not be presented (26) _____ uously; the US (nausea) can occur hours after the CS (flavor of food). Research in taste aversion also challenges the (27) _____ rist view that organisms learn to associate any stimuli that are contiguous. Instead, it seems that organisms are biologically predisposed to develop aversions that are (28) _____ tive in their environmental settings.

**OBJ. 6:** After a US–CS association has been learned, repeated presentation of the (29) _____ ned stimulus (for example, a bell) without the US (meat) will extinguish the CR (salivation). But extinguished responses may show (30) _____ neous recovery as a function of time that has elapsed since the end of the extinction process.

**OBJ. 7:** In stimulus (31) _____ ation, organisms show a CR in response to a range of stimuli similar to the CS. In stimulus (32) _____ ation, organisms learn to show a CR in response to a more limited range of stimuli by pairing only the limited stimulus with the US.

In higher–order conditioning, a previously neutral stimulus comes to serve as a (33) _____ned stimulus after being paired repeatedly with a stimulus that has already been established as a CS.

**OBJ. 8:** Classical conditioning involves ways in which (34) _____uli come to serve as signals for other stimuli.

In the (35) bell–and–_____ method for teaching children to stop bedwetting, a (36) b_____ is sounded when the child urinates in bed, waking the child. Urine is detected by a (37) _____ placed beneath the sheets and then the bell is sounded. The bell is paired repeatedly with fullness in the child's (38) bl_____. In this way, sensations of a full bladder (the conditioned stimulus) gain the capacity to wake the child just as the bell (the [39] _____ned stimulus) did.

In the case of Little (40) _____, a young boy was taught to fear rats. In this case study, John (41) _____ and Rosalie (42) _____ clanged steel bars behind Albert's head as Albert played with a rat.

The behavior–therapy fear–reduction methods of flooding and systematic desensitization are based on the principle of (43) _____tion. In (44) _____ding, the client is exposed to the fear-evoking stimulus until fear responses are extinguished. In systematic (45) _____zation, the client is exposed gradually to fear–evoking stimuli under circumstances in which he or she remains relaxed. In the fear–reduction method of (46) _____tioning, a pleasant stimulus is paired repeatedly with a fear–evoking object, in this way counteracting the fear response.

## SECTION 2: Operant Conditioning

**OBJ. 9:** Edward L. Thorndike used so–called (47) p_____ boxes to study learning in cats. Thorndike also originated the law of (48) _____ct, which holds that responses are "stamped in" by re-wards and "stamped out" by (49) _____ments. B. F. Skinner introduced the concept of (50) _____ment. Skinner also devised a kind of cage, which has since become dubbed the (51) S_____ _____, which could be used to study discrete operant behaviors in animals. Skinner's use of the (52) _____tive recorder also permitted precise measurement of operant behavior, even in the absence of the researcher.

**OBJ. 10:** In operant conditioning, behaviors that manipulate the environment in order to attain reinforc-ers are termed (53) _____ts. In operant condi-tioning, an organism learns to emit an operant because it is (54) _____ed. Initial "correct" responses may be performed by random trial and (55) _____r, or by physical or verbal guiding. A reinforcement is a stimulus that increases the (56) _____cy of an operant.

**OBJ. 11:** Positive reinforcers increase the probability that operants will occur when they are (57: *Circle one*: applied or removed). Negative reinforcers (58: *Circle one*: increase or decrease) the probability that operants will occur when they are (59: *Circle one*: applied or removed). (60) _____ary reinforcers have their value because of the biological makeup of the organ-ism. (61) _____ary reinforcers, such as money and approval, acquire their value through association with established reinforcers. Secondary reinforcers are also referred to as (62) _____ned reinforcers.

**OBJ. 12:** In operant conditioning, (63) _____tion results from repeated performance of operant behavior in the absence of reinforcement. In operant condition-ing, the (64) _____nt is extinguished. (65) Sp_____ recovery of learned responses can occur as a function of the passage of time following extinction.

**OBJ. 13:** Rewards, like reinforcers, are (66) _____li that increase the frequency of behavior. But rewards differ from reinforcers in that rewards are considered (67) pl_____ stimuli. Punishments are defined as (68) _____sive stimuli that suppress the fre-quency of behavior. Skinner preferred to use the term reinforcer because reinforcement is defined in terms of its effects on observable (69) _____ior.

Many learning theorists prefer treating children's

misbehavior by ignoring it or using time out from (70) _____ment rather than by using punishment. Strong punishment (71: *Circle one*: will or will not) suppress undesired behavior. However, punishment also has some "side effects." One is that punishment (72: *Circle one*: does or does not) teach acceptable, alternative behavior. Punishment (73) sup_____ undesired behavior only when its delivery is guaranteed. Punishment also may cause the organism to (74) w_____ from the situation, as in the child's running away from home, cutting classes, or dropping out of school. Moreover, punishment can create anger and hostility, can lead to overgeneralization, and can serve as a (75) m_____ for aggression. Finally, children (76) l_____ punished responses, whether or not they perform them.

**OBJ. 14:** A (77) _____ative stimulus indicates when an operant will be reinforced.

**OBJ. 15:** A (78) co_____–reinforcement schedule leads to most rapid acquisition of new responses, but operants are maintained most economically through (79) _____tial reinforcement. Partial reinforcement also makes responses more resistant to (80) _____tion.

There are four basic schedules of reinforcement. In a (81) _____–_____ schedule, a specific amount of time must elapse since a previous correct response before reinforcement again becomes available. In a variable–interval schedule, the amount of (82) _____ is allowed to vary. With a (83) _____–interval schedule, an organism's response rate falls off after each reinforcement, then picks up as it nears the time when reinforcement will be dispensed. The resultant record on the cumulative recorder shows a series of characteristic upward-moving waves, which are referred to as fixed–interval (84) _____lops. In a (85) _____–_____ schedule, a fixed number of correct responses must be performed before one is reinforced. In a variable-ratio schedule, the (86) _____ of correct responses that must be performed before reinforcement becomes available is allowed to vary.

Payment for piecework is an example of a (87) _____–_____ schedule. The unpredictability of (88: *Circle one*: fixed or variable) schedules maintains a high response rate. Slot machines tend to pay off on (89) _____–ratio schedules.

**OBJ. 16:** In shaping, we at first (90) r_____ small steps toward behavioral goals. We reinforce (91) _____sive approximations to the goal. Eventually we reinforce organisms for performing complex behavioral (92) _____s, with each link performed in proper sequence.

**OBJ. 17:** Parents and peers socialize children into acquiring (93) "sex–_____iate" behavior patterns through the elaborate use of rewards and punishments. Parents and peers also tend to (94: *Circle one*: reward or punish) their children for sharing with others and to (95: *Circle one*: reward or punish) them for being too aggressive.

In (96) _____back training (BFT), people and lower animals learn to control bodily functions in order to attain reinforcement. When people receive BFT, the reinforcement is usually (97) _____tion.

In (98) t_____ economies, psychologists give mental patients or prison inmates tokens, such as poker chips, for desired behavior. The tokens (99) re_____ desired behavior because they can be exchanged for television time, desserts, and other desired commodities. Lang and Melamed used (100) _____ance learning to save the life of a baby that repeatedly threw up after eating. When the child tensed prior to vomiting, a tone was sounded and followed by a painful but (presumably) harmless electric shock. We can explain this procedure through Mowrer's (101) _____–factor learning. Through (102) _____cal conditioning, the tone (CS) came to elicit expectation of electric shock (US), so that the shock could be used sparingly. But the shock and, after classical conditioning, the tone were aversive stimuli. Through (103) _____nt conditioning, the infant learned to suppress the behaviors (muscle tensions) that were followed with aversive stimulation. By so doing, the aversive stimuli were removed. And so, the aversive stimuli served as (104: *Circle one*: positive or negative) reinforcers.

In using behavior (105) _____tion in the classroom, teachers usually reinforce desired behavior and attempt to (106) ex_____ undesired behavior by ignoring it. (107) _____med learning is based on the assumption that learning tasks can be broken down into a number of small steps. Correct performance of each small step is (108) _____ced.

## SECTION 3: Cognitive Learning

**OBJ. 18:** Tolman's work in (109) l_____ learning also found that organisms learn in the absence of reinforcement. Tolman also distinguished between learning and (110) _____ance, and found that organisms do not necessarily perform all the behaviors that they have learned.

**OBJ. 19:** Albert (111) B_____ and other social–learning theorists have shown that people can also learn by observing others. In observational learning, it is not necessary that people emit (112) _____nses of their own, nor that their behavior be (113) _____orced, in order for learning to take place. Learners may then choose to (114) p_____ the behaviors they have observed when "the time is ripe"—that is, when they believe that they will be rewarded.

## SECTION 4: Psychology and Modern Life

**OBJ. 20:** People may (115) im_____ aggressive models if they believe that aggression is appropriate for them under a specific set of conditions. Media violence may contribute to aggressive behavior by increasing the level of (116) ar_____ of viewers, by (117) dis_____ of aggressive impulses, by providing models for development of aggressive skills, and (118) hab_____ of viewers to violence.

**Answer Key to *Chapter Review***

1. experience
2. represent
3. neutral
4. elicit (or evoke)
5. salivary
6. reflex
7. stimuli
8. environmental
9. association
10. conditional
11. conditioned responses
12. conditioned
13. unconditioned
14. unconditioned
15. conditioned
16. conditioned
17. unconditioned
18. simultaneous
19. delayed
20. prior to
21. backward
22. contiguous
23. information
24. contingency
25. only one
26. contiguously
27. behaviorist
28. adaptive
29. conditioned
30. spontaneous
31. generalization
32. discrimination
33. conditioned
34. stimuli
35. pad
36. bell
37. pad
38. bladder
39. unconditioned

40. Albert
41. Watson
42. Rayner
43. extinction
44. flooding
45. desensitization
46. counterconditioning
47. puzzle
48. effect
49. punishments
50. reinforcement
51. Skinner box
52. cumulative
53. operants
54. reinforced
55. error
56. frequency
57. applied
58. increase
59. removed
60. Primary
61. Secondary
62. conditioned
63. extinction
64. pperant
65. spontaneous
66. stimuli
67. pleasant
68. aversive
69. behavior
70. reinforcement
71. will
72. does not
73. suppresses
74. withdraw
75. model

76. learn
77. discriminative
78. continuous
79. partial
80. extinction
81. fixed-interval
82. time
83. fixed-interval
84. scallops
85. fixed–ratio
86. number
87. fixed–ratio
88. variable
89. variable-ratio
90. reinforce
91. successive
92. chains
93. sex-appropriate
94. reward
95. punish
96. biofeedback
97. information
98. token
99. reinforce
100. avoidance
101. two
102. classical
103. operant
104. negative
105. modification
106. extinguish
107. Programmed
108. reinforced
109. latent
110. performance
111. Bandura

112. responses
113. reinforced
114. Pperform
115. imitate
116. arousal
117. disinhibition
118. habituation

| | Idioms | Explanation |
|---|---|---|
| 213 | By the way | incidentally; not important or relevant, but interesting |
| 213 | drop off | decrease |
| 213 | falls off | decreases |
| 231 | picks up | increases |
| 232 | on the tight track | performing very well and learning fast |
| 232 | caught (catch) up | equaled (equal) the standard after having been behind it |
| 239 | touched (touch) on | mentioned (mention); referred (refer) to |

| | Cultural References | |
|---|---|---|
| 212 | Rocketman | an adventure movie about a rocket which was man; a chapter was shown at the theater every week |
| 212 | buttered popcorn | a popular food sold at movie theaters; made from corn |
| 230 | one armed bandits" | slot machines operated by pulling a lever; bandits are robbers or thieves |
| 230 | the racetrack or casino or in the lottery | a lot of money won from betting (wagering) on racehorses, gambling houses, and from choosing winning number |
| 231 | rebates | a refund (money returned after having been delivered) |
| 232 | break dancing; moon walk | popular and current dance steps |
| 232 | fox trot | a dance step which was popular before 1950; the music required slow dancing |
| 232 | standard shift | in old cars, a person operated a lever by hand in order to change the ratio of the gears that connected the motor and the transmission |
| 232 | shifting without stalling | see "standard shift" it used to be difficult to change the gears |
| 232 | frequent-flyer | a person who flies in a commercial airplane often |
| 232 | poker chips | tokens used in poker games that have value according to their color |
| 232 | Brave New World | a book by Aldous Huxley, a British writer of the 20th century, which postulates a world where people are controlled by the government |

| | Phrases and Expressions (Different Usage) | |
|---|---|---|
| 239 | sky dive | jump from the top of a mountain or from an airplane and "fly" with the aid of a a parachute |
| 239 | surfboard | stand on boards at the edge of the ocean and move on the waves (surf) |
| 239 | dust for finger prints | spread a white powder which will reveal the fingerprints this is done in order to discover the identity of a person |
| 240 | good groan | when a joke is hear person often groans |
| 212 | dared me | said, "We dare you"; tried to persuade me to do something that I did not want to do |
| 212 | rose to the challenge | agreed |
| 212 | Down it slowly | ate with difficulty |
| 212 | head spun | felt sick |
| 212 | do not face | not look at; not eat |
| 212 | on a gut level | on an emotional level; from strong feeling |
| 212 | queasy | nauseous |
| 212 | get into the habit | become accustomed to; do the same thing at the same time |
| 212 | socially acceptable | thought to be the right ones by most people |
| 213 | stick to the straight and narrow | behave correctly; be good |
| 213 | likelihood | probability |
| 213 | traffic citations | tickets to indicate that a fine (money) must be paid for violating rule |
| 213 | triggered | caused |
| 213 | hampered by | hindered by; made difficult by |
| 213 | biological makeup | biological composition |
| 213 | paired repeatedly | accompanied many times |
| 213 | faced with novel events | confronted with "new" event |
| 213 | concrete goals | specific goals want uncalled-for |
| 213 | not worth looking into | not asked for; not important enough to investigate |
| 214 | target response | the response which we are looking for, or expecting |
| 218 | not take place at all | may not occur or happen |
| 218 | purely random | completely random; completely by chance |
| 218 | in a couple of ways | in two ways |
| 218 | Sad to say | unfortunately |
| 218 | further impair | damage more |
| 218 | dietary staples | necessary foods for health |
| 218 | scheme of things | plan of events |
| 218 | fits | corresponds to |

Chapter 6   Learning

| | | |
|---|---|---|
| 218 | updating | causing their expectation to change according to the current environment |
| 218 | whiffs the scent | smells the scent |
| 218 | pull into the driveway | drive into the driveway |
| 218 | squeal with delight | make a happy noise |
| 218 | times can change | the old rules and concerns do not apply now |
| 218 | homecoming | arrival home |
| 219 | led to | caused; resulted in |
| 219 | leveled off at | stopped at |
| 219 | Where would you place your, money? | What do you think? Which do you think would happen? |
| 219 | a bit misleading | difficult to understand; it appears to have one meaning, but actually has another |
| 220 | In the wilds | in the forest or desert; in the natural area |
| 220 | circular paths | go around in a circle |
| 220 | Rustling sounds in the undergrowth | noise in the forest |
| 220 | a narrow range | limited range |
| 221 | After a while | after time passes |
| 221 | an infantile show | acted like a baby |
| 221 | snapped at | tried to bite |
| 221 | errs | makes a mistake |
| 221 | there goes the meat | does not receive the meat |
| 221 | tell our spouses apart | recognize our spouse |
| 222 | land in divorce court | our spouse would divorce us |
| 222 | come to serve | act as |
| 222 | characteristic knock | the person knocks with his or her style, or his or her personality, and we recognize that |
| 222 | bed-wetter... wet their beds | children... urinate in their beds at night |
| 222 | training pants... toilet training | underwear that is thicker than usual in order to absorb urine; it is worn by one to three-year old children while they are learning how to use the toilet |
| 222 | not given to ready displays of emotion | who did not reveal, or let people see, how he felt |
| 223 | undo | correct; make something right that has been wrong |
| 223 | to do just that | to do that, specifically |
| 223 | not a holiday | not a happy experience |
| 223 | munching merrily away | eating without paying attention to what is occurring |
| 223 | not plopped in Peter's lap | not suddenly dropped in Peter's lap without gradual introduction |

| | | |
|---|---|---|
| 223 | castaway eye | looked at so that he could defend himself if he had to |
| 224 | consume the treat | eat the candy and cookies |
| 224 | stray cats | cats that have no homes and live on the street |
| 224 | so-called puzzle boxes | the box is called this because it is a "puzzle" to the cat; |
| 224 | few will top that of | few people have a more unusual story about the war |
| 224 | were scrapped | were not continued or practiced |
| 224 | for the birds | was useless |
| 225 | found wide applications | been applied by many people |
| 225 | brought forth by | created by |
| 225 | routinely ignored | ignored regularly |
| 225 | sniffed its way around | walked around in the cage and sniffing (smelling) at the same time as he walked |
| 226 | and far between | not often came |
| 226 | fast and furious | was very frequent |
| 226 | it mattered little | it is not important |
| 226 | comes to be made | occurs |
| 226 | backside | haunches |
| 226 | age significantly in the process | get a lot older |
| 227 | while it happens in ahead | to plan what to do in the future (sooner or later) |
| 227 | inside the head of an | think like an |
| 228 | away with murder | do a negative act and not be corrected |
| 228 | withdraw from | leave |
| 228 | run away | leave home without telling parents and not returning |
| 228 | cut class | not attend class |
| 228 | drop out of school | stop attending school |
| 228 | at what cost | the other results might be worse later on |
| 228 | draws their attention to | causes them to pay attention to |
| 228 | take ... for granted | accept it but ignore it |
| 228 | slippery dining room floors | the ice cream would melt and cause the floor to be "slippery" |
| 231 | get smoochy | become romantic |
| 231 | chugalugging a bottle of antacid tables | eating pills which are for indigestion |
| 231 | body language | movements of the body which communicate |
| 231 | "hooked" on gambling | addicted to gambling |
| 231 | by tapering off | by reducing gradually |
| 231 | cram the night before | study a lot the night before a test |
| 231 | state of reasonable readiness | a condition of always being ready |
| 231 | muster up the courage | acquires courage |
| 232 | out on the dance floor | to start dancing |
| 234 | to no avail | did not correct the problem |

1. Ivan Pavlov is known for his contribution to the understanding of
   (a) learning to engage in voluntary behavior.
   (b) observational learning.
   (c) classical conditioning.
   (d) contingency theory.

2. Which school of psychologists would define learning as a change in behavior that results from experience?
   (a) behaviorists
   (b) cognitive psychologists
   (c) Gestalt psychologists
   (d) psychoanalysts

3. In Pavlov's experiments, salivation in response to meat was a
   (a) CR.
   (b) CS.
   (c) UR.
   (d) US.

4. In using the bell–and–pad method for overcoming bedwetting, the sensations of a full bladder are the
   (a) CR.
   (b) CS.
   (c) UR.
   (d) US.

5. Extinction in classical conditioning occurs because of repeated presentation of the
   (a) CR in the absence of the CS.
   (b) UR in the absence of the US.
   (c) CS in the absence of the US.
   (d) US in the absence of the CS.

6. In higher–order conditioning, a previously neutral stimulus comes to serve as a CS after being paired with a
   (a) CR.
   (b) CS.
   (c) UR.
   (d) US.

7. Little Albert learned to fear rats as a result of
   (a) clanging of steel bars in the presence of a rat.
   (b) observing a rat attack another animal.
   (c) being informed that rats carry certain harmful diseases.
   (d) being personally bitten by a rat.

8. Who originated the use of puzzle boxes?
   (a) Ivan Pavlov
   (b) John Watson
   (c) B. F. Skinner
   (d) Edward Thorndike

9. According to the law of effect, _____ has the effect of stamping out stimulus–response connections.
   (a) forgetting
   (b) negative reinforcement
   (c) extinction
   (d) punishment

10. Pain is an example of a _____ reinforcer.
    (a) primary positive
    (b) primary negative
    (c) secondary positive
    (d) secondary negative

11. Which of the following statements about punishment is **FALSE**?
    (a) Children learn responses that are punished.
    (b) Punishment increases the frequency of undesired behavior.
    (c) Punished children may withdraw from the situation.
    (d) Punishment may be modeled as a way of solving problems.

12. With a _____ – _____ schedule, an organism's response rate falls off after each reinforcement.
    (a) fixed–interval
    (b) fixed–ratio
    (c) variable–interval
    (d) variable–ratio

13. According to the text, the best way for teachers to use behavior modification in the classroom is to
(a) pay attention to children when they are misbehaving.
(b) pay attention to children when they are behaving correctly.
(c) punish children when they are misbehaving.
(d) reward children when they are misbehaving.

14. Bandura showed that we can acquire operants
(a) only through practice.
(b) by observation alone.
(c) most effectively through shaping.
(d) without paying full attention.

15. In order for observational learning to take place,
(a) stimuli must be paired repeatedly.
(b) a stimulus must elicit a response.
(c) an organism must be reinforced.
(d) an organism must observe another.

16. The text defines a stimulus as
(a) a change in the environment.
(b) a condition that evokes a response from an organism.
(c) any change that is learned.
(d) an environmental condition that evokes a response from an organism.

17. A parent encourages a reluctant child to enter the water of a swimming pool by hugging and petting the child and murmuring "It's really nice. You'll love it." This method is most similar to the behavior–therapy technique of
(a) extinction.
(b) systematic desensitization.
(c) counterconditioning.
(d) flooding.

18. According to contingency theory, learning occurs because
(a) a conditioned stimulus indicates that the unconditioned stimulus is likely to ensue.
(b) stimuli are contiguous.
(c) of repeated trial and error.
(d) organisms observe the outcomes of the behaviors of others and act when they expect that the contingencies will be rewarding.

19. In what way does systematic desensitization differ from flooding? Systematic desensitization is
(a) based on principles of operant conditioning.
(b) less upsetting.
(c) used to reduce fear.
(d) a more rapid process.

20. An important way in which the learning of taste aversions differs from other kinds of classical conditioning is that
(a) often only one pairing of the stimuli is required.
(b) learning rapidly decays.
(c) taste aversions are arbitrary, whereas other kinds of conditioning are adaptive.
(d) there is no reward for learning.

**Answer Key to *Posttest***

1. C
2. A
3. C
4. B
5. C
6. B
7. A
8. D
9. D
10. B
11. B
12. A
13. B
14. C
15. D
16. D
17. C
18. B
19. B
20. A

| | |
|---|---|
| Taste aversion | Unconditioned stimulus (US) |
| Learning | Unconditioned response (UR) |
| Reflex | Conditioned stimulus (CS) |
| Stimulus | Extinction |
| Conditioned response (CR) | Spontaneous recovery |
| Classical conditioning | Generalization |
| Contiguous | Discrimination |

A stimulus that elicits a response from an organism prior to conditioning.

A kind of classical conditioning in which a previously desirable or neutral food becomes repugnant because it is associated with aversive stimulation.

An unlearned response to an unconditioned stimulus.

According to behaviorists, a relatively permanent change in behavior that results from experience.

A previously neutral stimulus that elicits a conditioned response because it has been paired repeatedly with a stimulus that already elicited that response.

A simple unlearned response to a stimulus.

An experimental procedure in which stimuli lose their ability to evoke learned responses because the events that had followed the stimuli no longer occur.

An environmental condition that elicits a response.

The recurrence of an extinguished response as a function of the passage of time.

In classical conditioning, a learned response to a conditioned stimulus.

In conditioning, the tendency for a conditioned response to be evoked by stimuli that are similar to the stimulus to which the response was conditioned.

According to behaviorists, a form of learning in which one stimulus comes to evoke the response usually evoked by the second stimulus by being paired repeatedly with the second stimulus.

In conditioning, the tendency for an organism to distinguish between a conditioned stimulus and similar stimuli that do not forecast an unconditioned stimulus.

Next to one another.

| | |
|---|---|
| Flooding | Positive reinforcer |
| Systematic desensitization | Negative reinforcer |
| Counter-conditioning | Primary reinforcer |
| Operant conditioning | Secondary reinforcer |
| Instrumental conditioning | Reward |
| Law of Effect | Empirically |
| Reinforce | Punishment |

Chapter 6     Learning

| | |
|---|---|
| A reinforcer that when presented increases the frequency of a response. | A behavioral fear-reduction technique based on principles of classical conditioning. Fear-evoking stimuli (CSs) are presented continuously in the absence of actual harm so that fear responses (CRs) are extinguished. |
| A reinforcer that when removed increases the frequency of a response. | A behavioral fear-reduction technique in which a hierarchy of fear-evoking stimuli are presented while the person remains relaxed. |
| An unlearned reinforcer. | A fear-reduction technique in which pleasant stimuli are associated with fear-evoking stimuli so that the fear-evoking stimuli lose their aversive qualities. |
| A stimulus that gains reinforcement value through association with established reinforcers. | A simple form of learning in which an organism learns to engage in behavior because it is reinforced. |
| A pleasant stimulus that increases the frequency of the behavior it follows. | A term similar to operant conditioning, reflecting the fact that the learned behavior is *instrumental* in achieving certain effects. |
| By trial, or experiment, rather than by logical deduction. | Thorndike's principle that responses are "stamped in" by rewards and "stamped out" by punishments. |
| An unpleasant stimulus that suppresses the behavior it follows. | To follow a response with a stimulus that increases the frequency of the response. |

| | |
|---|---|
| Model | Variable-ratio schedule |
| Time out | Shaping |
| Continuous reinforcement | Successive approximations |
| Partial reinforcement | Socialization |
| Fixed-interval schedule | Token economy |
| Variable-interval schedule | Programmed learning |
| Fixed-ratio schedule | Observational learning |

Chapter 6    Learning

| A schedule in which reinforcement is provided after a variable number of correct responses. | An organism that engages in a response that is then imitated by another organism. |
| A procedure for teaching complex behaviors that at first reinforces approximations of the target behavior. | Removal of an organism from a situation in which reinforcement is available when unwanted behavior is shown. |
| Behaviors that are progressively closer to a target behavior. | A schedule of reinforcement in which every correct response is reinforced. |
| Guidance of people into socially desirable behavior by means of verbal messages, the systematic use of rewards and punishments, and other methods of teaching. | One of several reinforcement schedules in which not every correct response is reinforced. |
| An environmental setting that fosters desired behavior by reinforcing it with tokens that can be exchanged for other reinforcers. | A schedule in which a fixed amount of time must elapse between the previous and subsequent times that reinforcement is available. |
| A method of learning in which complex tasks are broken down into simple steps, each of which is reinforced. Errors are not reinforced. | A schedule in which a variable amount of time must elapse between the previous and subsequent times that reinforcement is available. |
| The acquisition of knowledge and skills through the observation of others. | A schedule in which reinforcement is provided after a fixed number of correct responses. |

Directions: This *PRETEST* will give you feedback about how well you understand Chapter 7. In order to enhance your mastery of Chapter 7, complete all the sections of this chapter of the Study Guide. Then you can take the *POSTTEST* and compare your results.

1.  Procedural memory is the same as
    (a) rote memory.
    (b) episodic memory.
    (c) skill memory.
    (d) semantic memory.

2.  Metamemory refers to
    (a) the processes of memory.
    (b) personal knowledge of the processes and functions of one's memory.
    (c) strategies for solving problems.
    (d) the hierarchical organization of long–term memory.

3.  Loftus has found that memories
    (a) tend to be reconstructive.
    (b) are stored photographically in the hippocampus.
    (c) are repressed when we encounter stress.
    (d) for important events are precise.

4.  Which of the following structures has been shown to be involved in the formation of verbal memories?
    (a) the hypothalamus
    (b) the occipital lobe of the cerebral cortex
    (c) Korsakoff's area of the brain
    (d) the thalamus

5.  When H.M.'s uncle died, H.M.
    (a) could not recall who his uncle was.
    (b) showed grief but later asked why his uncle did not visit.
    (c) seemed to understand the loss, but did not show grief.
    (d) could verbally express grief but did not show any emotional response.

6.  Craik and Lockhart assert that
    (a) there are three stages of memory.
    (b) icons are more enduring than echoes.
    (c) memories endure when information is processed deeply.
    (d) maintenance rehearsal rather than retrieval cues are needed to find long–term memories.

7.  Iconic memory makes possible
    (a) a smooth and continuous flow of visual information.
    (b) saccadic eye movements.
    (c) transfer of echoes from the sensory register to short–term memory.
    (d) recall of symbolic information.

8.  According to the serial–position effect,
    (a) items are easiest to remember when they are placed in a series.
    (b) the most important items in a series are most likely to be remembered.
    (c) we usually have a feeling of knowing things that happen to us when we are emotionally aroused.
    (d) we best remember the first and last items in a list.

9.  According to the text, children learn the alphabet by means of
    (a) semantic coding.
    (b) rote repetition.
    (c) rewards and punishments.
    (d) metamemory.

10. Which of the following is an example of proactive interference?
    (a) having difficulty remembering a French word because you have more recently taken Spanish
    (b) not being able to recall a phrase because you have been given the task of counting backward by 3's
    (c) failure to recall relatives' names because of disintegration of cells in hippocampus
    (d) difficulty learning to drive a car with a five–speed standard transmission because you had previously learned to drive a car with a four–speed standard transmission

11. A schema is a
    (a) long–term memory.
    (b) strategy for retrieving information.
    (c) way of mentally representing the world.
    (d) memory molecule.

12. According to the text, the whole–report procedure was used by
    (a) McDougall.
    (b) Brown and McNeill.
    (c) Sperling.
    (d) Loftus.

13. Studies of the tip–of–the–tongue phenomenon suggest that people tend to store information in LTM according to
    (a) semantic and visual codes.
    (b) acoustic and semantic codes.
    (c) acoustic and visual codes.
    (d) mnemonic devices.

14. According to the curve of forgetting,
    (a) memory loss is gradual and even.
    (b) memory loss is steep for several minutes after learning occurs and then levels off.
    (c) memory loss is gradual for several minutes after learning occurs and then falls steeply.
    (d) patterns of memory loss differ so mark-edly from person to person that no generalizations are possible.

15. Elaborative rehearsal is defined as the
    (a) construction of an acoustic code for a visual stimulus.
    (b) relating of new information to known material.
    (c) condensing of information into about seven chunks.
    (d) construction of an acronym, jingle, or phrase.

16. The method of savings is used to investigate
    (a) recall.
    (b) retention.
    (c) recognition.
    (d) relearning.

17. A man cannot recall events for two minutes prior to an automobile accident in which he was involved. This is an example of
    (a) psychogenic amnesia.
    (b) anterograde amnesia.
    (c) retrograde amnesia.
    (d) retroactive interference.

18. Who pioneered the use of nonsense syllables in the study of memory?
    (a) Sperling
    (b) Peterson
    (c) Ebbinghaus
    (d) Loftus

19. In LTM, proper classification of an item
    (a) prevents the trace from decaying.
    (b) assigns it to a permanent category.
    (c) prevents retroactive or proactive interference.
    (d) aids retrieval of accurate information.

20. So–called "memory molecules" are composed of
    (a) ribonucleic acid.
    (b) antidiuretic hormone.
    (c) acetylcholine.
    (d) adrenaline.

**Answer Key to *Pretest***

| | | | |
|---|---|---|---|
| 1. C | 6. C | 11. C | 16. D |
| 2. B | 7. A | 12. A | 17. C |
| 3. A | 8. D | 13. B | 18. C |
| 4. D | 9. B | 14. B | 19. D |
| 5. B | 10. D | 15. B | 20. A |

Chapter 7 begins by distinguishing three kinds of memory—episodic memory (memory of personal events), semantic memory (general knowledge), and procedural (skill) memory. Then there is a description of the three processes of memory: encoding, storing, and retrieving information.

Most psychologists structure memory into sensory memory, short–term memory (STM), and long–term memory (LTM). Sensory memory holds impressions briefly, but long enough so they appear connected. Stimuli in sensory memory decay unless they are attended to. The visual sensory register holds icons, and the auditory sensory register holds echoes. STM holds information for a minute or so. The average person can hold about seven chunks of information in STM. Material in STM that is rehearsed may enter LTM; otherwise it may decay or be displaced by new material. Long-term memories tend to be lost by failure to use the proper retrieval cues, rather than by decay or displacement. Long–term memories

are organized hierarchically. Long–term memories are not perfectly accurate; instead they are reconstructed on the basis of our schemas.

The levels–of–processing model views memory in terms of depth of processing rather than stages.

Ebbinghaus originated the use of nonsense syllables in the study of memory and forgetting. Three types of memory tasks are discussed: recognition, recall, and savings. The possible roles of the following factors in forgetting are explored: interference, repression, and anterograde and retrograde amnesia.

The biology of memory is discussed, including the "false starts" involving engrams and "memory molecules." Contemporary views of the biology of memory involve changes at the neural level (e.g., development of dendrites and synapses and the roles of neurotransmitters and hormones) and changes at the structural level (e.g., in the hippocampus and thalamus).

## LEARNING OBJECTIVES

| | Three Kinds of Memory |
|---|---|
| 1.  Describe the three kinds of memory. | |
| | **Three Processes of Memory** |
| 2.  Describe the three processes of memory. | |
| 3.  Define *memory*. | |

| | **Three Stages of Memory** |
|---|---|
| 4. List what many psychologists refer to as the three stages of memory. | |
| 5. Describe the functioning of *sensory memory*. | |
| 6. Describe the functioning of *short–term memory*. | |
| 7. Describe the functioning of *long–term memory*. | |
| 8. Describe the *levels–of–processing model* of memory. | **The Levels-of-Processing Model of Memory** |
| 9. Explain the origin of the use of *nonsense syllables* in the study of memory and forgetting. | **Forgetting** |
| 10. Explain the types of memory tasks that are used in measuring forgetting. | |
| 11. Explain the role of *interference theory* in forgetting. | |
| 12. Explain the possible role of *repression* in forgetting. | |
| 13. Explain the roles of *anterograde* and *retrograde amnesia* in forgetting. | |

| | **The Biology of Memory: From Engrams to Adrenaline** |
|---|---|
| 14. Describe some "false starts" in the study of the biology of memory. | |
| 15. Describe some current views of the biology of memory. | |
| 16. Discuss methods for improving memory. | |
| | **Additional Notes** |
| | |
| | |
| | |
| | |
| | |

**Five Challenges to Memory**

**Three Kinds of Memory**

1. Episodic Memory

2. Semantic Memory

3. Procedural Memory

**Three Processes of Memory**

1. Encoding

2. Storage

3. Retrieval

**Three Stages of Memory**

1. Sensory Memory

2. Short-Term Memory

3. Long-Term Memory

**The Levels-of-Processing Model of Memory**

# Forgetting

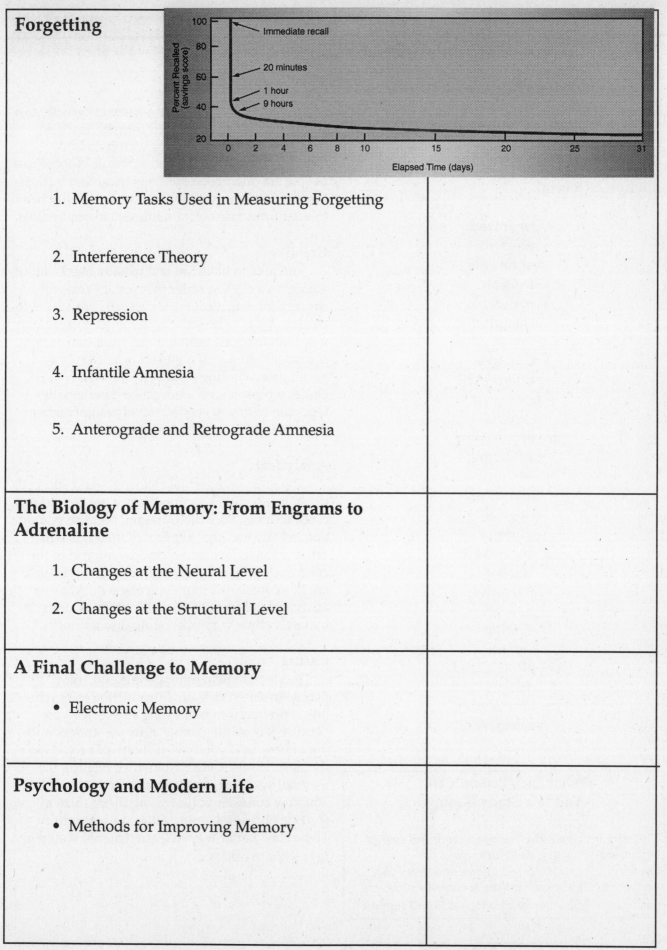

1. Memory Tasks Used in Measuring Forgetting

2. Interference Theory

3. Repression

4. Infantile Amnesia

5. Anterograde and Retrograde Amnesia

# The Biology of Memory: From Engrams to Adrenaline

1. Changes at the Neural Level

2. Changes at the Structural Level

# A Final Challenge to Memory

• Electronic Memory

# Psychology and Modern Life

• Methods for Improving Memory

## Learning Styles

We all learn best in different ways, and we have different priorities. Pick which set of terms best describes you. You may be a mixture of several.

### Organized
efficient
responsible
sensible
dependable
structured

### Creative
spontaneous
fast-paced
skillful
adventuresome
fun-loving

### Analytical
logical
curious
independent
global
innovative

### Caring
warm
people-oriented
feeling
communicative
peacemaker

---

### What Each Person Can Add to a Study Group

**Diversity:** more collective intelligence and energy
**Organized:** structure and efficiency
**Creative:** fun, creative solutions, and faster pace
**Analytical:** figure out systems & complex problems
**Caring:** good communication skills and support

---

### Organized

You prefer to have your course information in an organized and structured format. You also prefer your instructors to be well-prepared, organized, punctual, and on schedule. Organized people are often good students because organization helps memory skills, and dependability helps to keep from missing valuable assignment points.

### Creative

You love to have fun and usually need a lot of variety in a class in order to enjoy it. You will connect more to a course if you can come up with creative ways to be actively involved and make it more fun for you. Sitting in the front half of the classroom offers you a greater opportunity to participate. Finding a study group which includes a person with an organized personality type can help you stay on top of assignments in the course so you never lose points.

### Analytical

You enjoy intellectual challenges and succeeding in intellectual ventures. If you get behind in a class, it can be very discouraging because you do not feel you are "up to speed". Often this will cause an analytical person to lose interest in the course. Usually the more mentally involved you are in a course, the more you enjoy it. Another analytical personality type as a study partner can make for some very interesting discussions!

### Caring

You love to help other people and enjoy people-oriented classes. Introduction to psychology is probably an interesting subject for you because it is about gaining a deeper understanding of people. If you have a choice of projects in the class, choose ones that involve relating the material you are learning to people you know. You may consider volunteering to organize a study group and helping other students study. There is no better way to learn material well than to teach it to others.

# KEY TERMS AND CONCEPTS

## Three Kinds of Memory

1. Episodic memory _____

2. Semantic memory _____

3. Procedural memory _____

4. Mnemonic devices _____

5. Acronym _____

## Three Processes of Memory

6. Encoding _____

7. Visual code _____

8. Acoustic code _____

9. Semantic code _____

10. Storage _____

11. Maintenance rehearsal _____

12. Metamemory _____

13. Retrieval _____

14. Memory _____

## Three Stages of Memory

15. Saccadic eye movement _____

_____

16. Sensory memory _____

17. Memory trace _____

18. Sensory register _____

19. Icon _____

20. Iconic memory _____

21. Eidetic imagery _____

22. Echo _____

23. Echoic memory _____

24. Short-term memory _____

25. Working memory _____

26. Serial–position effect _____

27. Primacy effect _____

28. Recency effect _____

29. Chunk (of information) _____

30. Rote _____

31. Displace _____

32. Long-term memory _____

33. Repression _____

34. Schema _____

35. Elaborative rehearsal _____

36. Superordinate _____

37. Subordinate _____

38. The tip–of–the–tongue phenomenon _____

_____

39. Feeling-of-knowing experience _____

_____

## Forgetting

40. Nonsense syllables _____

41. Recognition _____

42. Recall _____

43. Paired associates _____

44. Posthypnotic amnesia _____

45. Relearning _____

46. Method of savings _____

47. Savings _____

48. Interference theory _____

49. Retroactive interference _____

50. Proactive interference _____

51. Dissociative amnesia _____

52. Infantile amnesia _____

53. Hippocampus _____

54. Anterograde amnesia _____

55. Retrograde amnesia _____

56. Consolidation

## The Biology of Memory: From Engrams to Adrenaline

57. Engram

## Additional Terms

# CHAPTER REVIEW

## SECTION 1: Three Kinds of Memory

**OBJ. 1:** Memories of the events that happen to a person or take place in the person's presence are referred to as (1) _____dic memory. Generalized knowledge is referred to as (2) _____tic memory. We tend to use the phrase "I remember . . ." when we are referring to (3) _____dic memories, but we are more likely to say "I know . . ." in reference to (4) _____tic memories. (5) Pro_____ memory involves knowledge of how to do things. Procedural memory is also referred to as (6) _____ memory.

## SECTION 2: Three Processes of Memory

**OBJ. 2:** The first stage of (7) _____ation processing, or changing information so that we can place it in memory, is called (8) _____ding. When we (9) en_____ information, we convert it into psychological formats that can be mentally represented. To do so, we commonly use (10) _____ual, (11) _____stic, and (12) _____tic codes. A visual code mentally (13) _____sents information as a picture. An acoustic code represents information as a sequence of (14) _____nds. Semantic codes represent stimuli in terms of their (15) _____ing.

The second process of memory is (16) s_____, or the maintaining of information over time. One way of storing information is by (17) _____nance rehearsal, or by mentally repeating it ("saying it to yourself").

The third memory process is (18) _____val, or locating stored information and returning it to consciousness. Retrieval of information from memory requires knowledge of the proper (19) _____es.

**OBJ. 3:** Memory is defined as the processes by which information is (20) _____ded, stored, and (21) _____ved.

## SECTION 3: Three Stages of Memory

**OBJ. 4:** The three stages of memory proposed by Atkinson and Shiffrin are (22) _____sory memory, (23) _____–_____ memory (STM), and (24) _____–_____ (LTM).

**OBJ. 5:** Sensory memory is the stage of memory first encountered by a (25) _____lus. It holds impressions briefly, but long enough so that series of (26) _____tions seem connected. The memory (27) t_____ of a stimulus lasts for only a fraction of a second. Memory traces are "held" in sensory (28) _____ters. Sensory (29) m_____ consists of registers that can briefly hold information that is entered by means of our senses.

Sperling used the (30) _____–report procedure to show that there is a difference between what people can see and what they can report in the visual sensory register. Sperling concluded that the memory trace of visual stimuli (31) d_____ within a second in the visual sensory register.

The mental representations of visual stimuli are referred to as (32) _____ns. The sensory register which holds icons is labeled (33) _____ _____ory. Iconic memories are accurate, (34) _____aphic memories. The ability to retain exact mental representations of visual stimuli over long amounts of time is referred to by psychologists as (35) _____tic imagery. The mental representations of (36) _____stic stimuli are called echoes. The sensory register which holds echoes is referred to as acoustic memory. The memory (37) _____ces of echoes can last for several seconds, many times longer than the traces of icons.

**OBJ. 6:** By focusing attention on a stimulus in the sensory register, you will retain it in (38) _____–_____ memory for a minute or so after the trace of the stimulus decays. Short-term memory is also referred to as (39) _____ing memory. Most of us know that a way of retaining information in short–term memory—and possibly storing it permanently—is to (40) re_____ it. Rote repetition is referred to as (41) _____ance rehearsal.

According to the (42) _____–position effect, we are most likely to recall the first and last items in the series. First items are likely to be rehearsed (43: *Circle one:* more or less) frequently than other items. Last items are likely to have been rehearsed (44: *Circle one:* most or least) recently. The tendency to recall the initial items in a list is referred to as the (45) _____cy effect. The tendency to recall the last items in a list is referred to as the (46)_____cy effect.

Miller noted that the average person can maintain about (47) _____ chunks of information in short–term memory at a time. Children learn the alphabet by (48) r_____—that is, by mechanical associative learning that requires time and (49) re_____.

The Petersons showed that information can be displaced from short–term memory by means of (50) _____ence.

**OBJ. 7:** Long–term memory is the third stage of processing of (51) _____tion.

Sigmund (52) F_____ believed that nearly all of our perceptions and ideas were stored permanently, but memories are not complete. Moreover, our memories are distorted by our (53) _____as, or ways of conceptualizing our worlds. That is, we (54) re_____ our recollections according to our schemas.

There (55: *Circle one:* is or is not) evidence for a limit to the amount of information that can be stored in long-term memory. New information may displace older information in (56: *Circle one:* long or short) – term memory, but there is no evidence that memories in long-term memory are lost by displacement. However, we need the proper (57) c_____s to help us retrieve information in long–term memory.

Information may be transferred from short–term to long–term memory by several means, including rote repetition—also referred to as (58) _____ance

rehearsal. In (59) _____tive rehearsal, new information is related to what is already known.

Psychologists have learned that we tend better to remember the events that occur under (60: *Circle one:* usual or unusual) emotionally arousing circumstances. We retain such detailed memories of events like these that they are referred to as (61) "fl_____ memories." One explanation for flashbulb memory is the (62) dis_____ of the memory. But major events, such as the assassination of a president or the loss of a close relative also have important impacts on our lives. And so we are likely to form networks of associations to other pieces of information—that is, to rehearse them (63) _____tively.

We tend to organize information in long–term memory according to a (64) _____cal structure.

The (65) _____–of–the– (66) _____ phenomenon—also referred to as the feeling–of–knowing experience—seems to reflect incomplete or imperfect learning. The classic "TOT" experiment by Brown and McNeill also suggests that our storage systems are indexed according to cues that include both the sounds and the meanings of words—that is, according to both (67) _____tic and (68) _____tic codes.

(69) C_____–dependent memory refers to information that is better retrieved under the circumstances in which it was encoded and stored, or learned. State–dependent memory is an extension of (70) _____–dependent memory and refers to the finding that we sometimes retrieve information better when we are in a (71) phys_____ or emotional state that is similar to the one in which we encoded and stored the information.

**SECTION 4: The Levels–of–Processing Model of Memory**

**OBJ. 8:** Craik and Lockhart suggest that we (72: *Circle one:* do or do not) "have" a sensory memory, a short–term memory, and a long–term memory per se. They view our ability to remember in terms of a single stage or dimension—the degree to which we (73) pr_____ information. Put it another way: according to the

(74) _____–of–processing model, memories tend to endure when information is processed deeply—when it is attended to, encoded carefully, pondered, and rehearsed elaboratively or related to things we already know well.

## SECTION 5: Forgetting

**OBJ. 9:** German psychologist Hermann (75) _____aus originated the use of nonsense syllable in the study of memory and forgetting. Nonsense syllables are (76: *Circle one:* meaningful or meaningless). Thus their retention is based on (77) ac_____ coding and maintenance (78) _____sal.

**OBJ. 10:** The three memory tasks listed in the text are (79) _____ition, (80) _____ll, and relearning. (81) Re_____ is the easiest type of memory task. In his own studies of recall, Ebbinghaus would read lists of (82) _____ _____bles aloud to the beat of a metronome and then see how many he could produce from memory. Psychologists also often use lists of pairs of nonsense syllables, called (83) _____ed _____ates, to measure recall. People who show posthypnotic (84) _____a cannot recall previously learned word lists following hypnosis. Spanos and his colleagues hypothesize that posthypnotic amnesia occurs when hypnotized subjects interpret the suggestion not to recall information as an "invitation" to refrain from attending to (85) re_____ cues.

Ebbinghaus devised the method of (86) _____ings to study the efficiency of relearning. First he would record the number of repetition required to learn a list of (87) n_____ syllables or words. Then he would record the number of repetitions required to (88) re_____ the list after a certain amount of time had elapsed. He would compute the difference between the numbers of (89) _____tions required to arrive at the savings. According to Ebbinghaus's classic curve of (90) _____ting, there is no loss of memory as measured by savings immediately after a list has been learned. Recollection drops (91: *Circle one:* gradually or precipitously) during the first hour after learning a list. Losses of learning then become more (92: *Circle one:* gradual or precipitous).

**OBJ. 11:** According to (93) _____ence theory, we forget material in short-term and long-term memory because newly learned material interferes with it. In (94) _____tive interference, new learning interferes with the retrieval of old learning. In (95) _____tive interference, older learning interferes with the capacity to retrieve more recently learned material.

**OBJ. 12:** According to Sigmund Freud, we repress many painful memories and unacceptable ideas because they produce (96) an_____, guilt, and shame. Psychoanalysts believe that repression is at the heart of disorders such as (97) _____ive amnesia.

Freud discovered that we usually cannot remember events that took place prior to the age of (98) _____. Freud labeled this phenomenon infantile (99) am_____, and attributed it to (100) re_____. However, the text suggests that infantile amnesia probably reflects the interaction of physiological and (101) _____tive factors. For example, the (102) hip_____, which is involved in memory formation, does not mature until about the age of 2. Moreover, infants' lack of language impairs their ability to (103) en_____ information.

**OBJ. 13:** In (104) _____rade amnesia, there are memory lapses for the period following a traumatic event, such as a blow to the head, electric shock, or an operation. In (105) _____rade amnesia, the source of trauma prevents people from remembering events that took place beforehand.

## SECTION 6: The Biology of Memory: From Engrams to Adrenaline

**OBJ. 14:** Engrams were hypothesized electrical circuits in the brain that were assumed to correspond to (106) m_____ _____ces. Biological psychologists such as (107) L_____ spent fruitless years searching for engrams. During the 1950s and 1960s, research groups headed by McConnell believed that they had found the engram in

(108) ri_____ acid (RNA). But research with RNA could not be (109) _____cated.

**OBJ. 15:** The storage of experience apparently requires that the number of avenues of communication among brain cells be increased by means of development of (110) _____ites and (111) _____pses. Research with sea snails has shown that more of the (112) _____mitter serotonin is released at certain synapses when they are conditioned. As a result, transmission at these synapses becomes (113: *Circle one*: more or less) efficient as trials (learning) progress.

The hormone (114) _____line generally stimulates bodily arousal and activity. Adrenaline and (115) _____uretic hormone (ADH) strengthen memory when they are released following learning.

Alzheimer's disease is associated with the degeneration of cells in an area of the (116) _____pus that normally produces large amounts of (117) _____choline (ACh).

The hippocampus is involved in relaying incoming sensory information to parts of the (118) cor_____. Therefore, it appears vital to the storage of (119: *Circle one:* new or old) information, even if (120: *Circle one:* new or old) information can be retrieved without it. Persons with hippocampal damage can form new (121) _____ral memories, even though they cannot form new (122) _____ic memories.

The (123) _____mus, a structure near the center of the brain, seems involved in the formation of verbal memories.

### Answer Key to *Chapter Review*

1. episodic
2. semantic
3. episodic
4. semantic
5. Procedural
6. skill
7. information
8. encoding
9. encode
10. visual
11. acoustic
12. semantic
13. represents
14. sounds
15. meaning
16. storage
17. maintenance
18. retrieval
19. cues
20. encoded
21. retrieved
22. sensory
23. short–term
24. long–term
25. stimulus
26. perceptions
27. trace
28. registers
29. memory
30. partial-report
31. Decays
32. Icons
33. Iconic memory
34. Photographic
35. Eidetic
36. acoustic
37. traces
38. short–term
39. working
40. rehearse (or repeat)
41. maintenance
42. serial-position
43. more
44. most
45. primacy
46. recency
47. seven
48. rote
49. repetition
50. interference
51. information
52. Freud
53. schemas
54. reconstruct
55. is not
56. short
57. cues
58. maintenance
59. elaborative
60. unusual
61. flashbulb
62. distinctness
63. elaboratively
64. hierarchical
65. tip
66. tongue
67. acoustic
68. semantic
69. Context-dependent
70. context-dependent
71. physiological
72. do not
73. process
74. levels
75. Ebbinghaus
76. meaningless
77. acoustic
78. rehearsal
79. recognition
80. recall
81. Recognition
82. nonsense syllables
83. paired associates
84. amnesia
85. retrieval
86. savings
87. nonsense
88. relearn
89. repetitions
90. forgetting
91. precipitously
92. gradual
93. interference
94. retroactive
95. proactive
96. anxiety
97. dissociative
98. three
99. amnesia
100. repression
101. cognitive
102. hippocampus
103. encode
104. anterograde
105. retrograde
106. memory traces
107. Lashley
108. ribonucleic
109. replicated
110. dendrites
111. synapses
112. neurotransmitter
113. more
114. adrenaline
115. antidiuretic
116. hippocampus
117. acetylcholine
118. cortex
119. new
120. old
121. procedural
122. episodic
123. thalamus

| Cultural References | Explanation |
|---|---|
| 251 bride's apparel | a tradition exists which indicates that a bride should always wear something old, something new, something borrowed and something blue for future happiness |
| 251 blizzard of 1988 | extremely heavy (strong winds and a lot of snow) snowstorm occurred in 1988 in the northeast part of the U.S. |
| 254 elementary school | all children in the U.S. must attend school from age 6 to 16 or grade 1 to grade 8. Elementary school is from grade I1 to 6 or grade 1 to 5. |
| 259 zip code | number at the end of an address which indicates the postal region a person lives |
| 259 bank cash card | a plastic credit card which allows you to take out money from a bank machine |
| 259 GM | General Motors |
| 259 CBS | Columbia Broadcasting System |
| 259 IBM | International Business Machines |
| 259 AT&T | American Telephone and Telegraph |
| 259 CIA | Central Intelligence Agency (government agency) |
| 259 FBI | Federal Bureau of Investigation (government agency) |
| 262 cocktail parties | late afternoon or evening parties where many people gather to talk and drink alcohol and meet people. |
| 266 peanut butter<br>266 sandwich | a peanut butter sandwich is probably the most common lunch food for U.S. children. |
| 267 Public Broadcasting System documentary | PBS is a TV channel which has no advertising and specializes in educational programs and documentaries |
| 269 out of the ballpark | the rules that everybody agrees upon; (a reference to baseball, ball that goes out of the ballpark is out of bounds, or has broken a rule |
| 282 kiss your partner | a custom in the U.S. is to kiss the person you love at midnight on New Year's Eve |

| Phrases and Expressions (Different Usage) | |
|---|---|
| 284 Great Lakes | all school children learn the names and locations of this group of five lakes located together in the north part of the U.S. |
| 250 not to be outdone | did not want to have anyone tell better stories than she could |
| 250 ears perked up | listened intently and suddenly |
| 250 not to be faulted | no one could argue with her; she was right |
| 250 wee hours | early morning hours, but still night |
| 250 wove a wonderful<br>250    patchwork quilt | told a wonderful intricate story; refers to bed covers that are made by hand and have intricate patterns |
| 250 much less those | not even those (an emphatic statement) |
| 250 take a back seat | become not important |
| 250 cheating! | I don't want you to cheat (be unfair) |
| 251 not looking over Shakespeare's shoulder | not standing next to Shakespeare and watching him |
| 251 Put it another way | say it another way; in different words |
| 252 grisly surgery | to dismantle your computer; remove the mechanism |
| 252 take a minute | please, stop reading for a minute and do what I say |
| 252 come back | return to reading |
| 252 so doing | by doing this |
| 252 well into | become involved in |
| 254 No apologies | I am not apologizing |
| 254 Let us have a try | let us try; make an attempt |
| 254 in a lifetime | the complete life of a person |
| 254 going in one ear and out the other | not retaining the information |
| 254 stream of thought, or of consciousness | continuous thought without thinking about the thought |
| 254 streamlike | like a stream or river, a continuous flow |
| 254 impressions briefly | maintains impressions for a short time |
| 255 flashed on a screen | put quickly on a screen and then removed |
| 255 remarkably long periods | unusually long periods; longer than expected |
| 255 turn away | stop looking at it |
| 258 declines with age, all but disappearing | as the child gets older, the ability decreases and almost disappears |

   Chapter 7    Memory

| | | |
|---|---|---|
| 258 | being seamless | continuous |
| 258 | fallen into | become (in a negative manner) |
| 258 | frantically searching | looking in a busy and upset manner |
| 259 | tried to get back to it | tried to do it again |
| 259 | first impressions tend to last | what we notice or feel about a person the first time we meet is the way we tend to continue to think and feel |
| 259 | easier on the digestion | easier to undertake, or do |
| | upper limit | the maximum |
| 259 | Fact of the matter | actually |
| 259 | hefty premiums | a lot of extra money |
| 259 | toll-free | no money (toll) is required to make the call |
| 259 | nature of the business | what kind of business it is |
| 260 | against myself | be came angry with myself |
| 260 | mental dressing down | telling myself how terrible I am and that I should change |
| 260 | self-reproach | reproach myself |
| 260 | falls between the cracks | is not retained; it is lost |
| 260 | wreak havoc | greatly disrupt |
| 260 | long-term | over a long period of time |
| 260 | shoved on | put on carelessly |
| 261 | dredging up | remembering |
| 261 | with a vengeance | emphatically, definitely; strongly |
| 261 | your new acquaintance's name | trying to retain your new acquaintance's name |
| 261 | vast storehouse | a very large storage area |
| 262 | evidence is far from compelling | there is no substantial evidence |
| 262 | a quirk | a particular habit that was different from other people's habits |
| 262 | in for it | had to suffer because of it |
| 262 | color our memories | have an effect on our memories |
| 262 | indeed distorted by | definitely distorted by |
| 263 | less than wholly reliable | not completely reliable |
| 263 | testimony | an explanation of an occurrence by someone who saw |
| 263 | cause for concern | a reason to be concerned |
| 263 | line-ups | a line of innocent individuals and suspected individuals to determine if witnesses can identify suspect as guilty |
| 263 | On the other hand | however |
| 263 | In sum | in summary; I will summarize what I have said so far |
| 263 | to date | |
| 265 | Not exactly | this is not exactly true |
| 265 | the vibrancy in your step | how vibrant you felt; how wonderful you felt, which make you walk happily |

| | | |
|---|---|---|
| 266 | them out | to choose them |
| 269 | not on the mark | in the correct general area, but not completely accurate |
| 269 | high and dry | out of the water; (a slang expression to mean without help when you need it) |
| 269 | ashore | on land; the edge of the water |
| 269 | under the influence | while the drug is in the body and affecting functions |
| 269 | grip of anger | the feel of strong anger |
| 270 | feed on happiness | cause and also be the result of happiness |
| 271 | a vicious cycle | occurs when the result of one act produces a bad result which again produces another bad result and so on |
| 271 | pushed in | influenced in |
| | fell into | could be organized into |
| 272 | sandwiched in between | put in between |
| 273 | CEG-arette | cigarette" is spelled "cig... ", however the pronunciation is similar so the association is appropriate |
| 273 | pop in | enter the mind without trying to retrieve it |
| 275 | stall | cause the engine to stop because the car is in the wrong gear |
| 275 | very cloudy | very unclear; not very clear |
| 275 | not weighted in the direction of | does not support |
| 275 | too broad | too wide |
| 275 | to hold water | to be true |
| 275 | often-cited | the incident is told often |
| 277 | uncle's passing | uncle's death |
| 277 | was rapidly unfolding | was quickly occurring |
| 278 | turn our attention to | attend |
| 278 | be housed | have a place to live |
| 279 | to scrunch up | to make the middle of the back rise, thus making the length shorter |
| 280 | the evolutionary ladder | a reference to Charles Darwin's theory of evolution |
| 280 | beleaguered humans | humans that are surrounded with problems |
| 281 | the flip side | on the other side |
| 283 | flapping about | moving around |
| 383 | a throbbing toe | a toe that hurts |
| 384 | some choice words | appropriately negative, or angry, words |
| 384 | meaty application | interesting application |
| 384 | laid eyes on the word | looked at the word |
| 384 | Broadly speaking | generally speaking; not specifically |
| 384 | fall under the heading of | are under the topic |

1. Tim remembers that Shakespeare wrote *Hamlet*. This type of memory is referred to as
   (a) episodic memory.
   (b) metamemory.
   (c) procedural memory.
   (d) semantic memory.

2. George Sperling used the _____ method in his studies of sensory memory.
   (a) partial–report
   (b) savings
   (c) paired–associates
   (d) whole–report

3. Visual impressions last for _____ in the sensory memory.
   (a) up to a second
   (b) about 2–5 seconds
   (c) about half a minute
   (d) several minutes or longer

4. Only about 5 percent of children show
   (a) metamemory.
   (b) iconic memory.
   (c) photographic memory.
   (d) eidetic imagery.

5. Echoic memory is defined as
   (a) an acoustic code.
   (b) the pathways between the thalamus and the auditory cortex.
   (c) the sensory register that holds auditory stimuli.
   (d) a type of procedural memory.

6. Working memory is another term for
   (a) iconic memory.
   (c) semantic memory.
   (c) elaborative rehearsal.
   (d) short–term memory.

7. You are given the task of remembering the written phrase, "Every good boy does fine." You say the phrase mentally, or "to yourself," and then you repeat it to yourself ten times. Which of the following methods have you employed?
   (a) visual encoding and elaborative rehearsal
   (b) acoustic encoding and maintenance rehearsal
   (c) semantic encoding and maintenance rehearsal
   (d) episodic memory and procedural memory

8. You are asked to memorize this list of letters: TBJKZMGXTR. You repeat the list several times. Which letters are you most likely to recall?
   (a) the sequence JKM
   (b) the sequence ZM
   (c) the Z and the X
   (d) the first T and the R

9. A student studies for a test in the room in which the test will be administered. The student is apparently hoping that performance will be facilitated by _____ memory.
   (a) context–dependent
   (b) state–dependent
   (c) photographic
   (d) iconic

10. Information is **LEAST** likely to be lost through decay in
    (a) iconic memory.
    (b) echoic memory.
    (c) short–term memory.
    (d) long–term memory.

11. Which of the following has been compared to a shelf or workbench so that once it is full, some things fall off when new items are shoved on?
    (a) episodic memory
    (b) sensory memory
    (c) short–term memory
    (d) long–term memory

12. Which of the following is most likely to remain firmly "embedded" in your memory over the decades?
    (a) the name of your second–grade teacher
    (b) a sonnet you memorized in high school
    (c) how you celebrated your 11th birthday
    (d) how to ride a bicycle

13. John forgets a dentist appointment about which he had been extremely anxious. Freud would probably attribute his forgetting to
    (a) repression.
    (b) anterograde amnesia.
    (c) proactive interference.
    (d) decay of the memory trace.

14. Loftus and Palmer showed subjects a film of a car crash and then asked them to fill out questionnaires that included a question about how fast the cars were going at the time. Subjects who reported that the cars were going "fastest" had been asked to estimate how fast the cars were going when they _____ one another.
    (a) "hit"
    (b) "smashed"
    (c) "bumped"
    (d) "touched"

15. Which of the following does the text state is the most effective way of transferring information from STM into LTM?
    (a) eidetic imagery
    (b) maintenance rehearsal
    (c) elaborative rehearsal
    (d) becoming emotionally aroused

16. According to the text, the feeling–of–knowing experience seems to reflect
    (a) lack of visual retrieval cues.
    (b) incomplete or imperfect learning.
    (c) skill memory rather than semantic memory.
    (d) STM displacement by anxiety–evoking information.

17. A parent knows that you are taking a psychology course and asks how he can teach his young child the alphabet. You note that children usually learn the alphabet by
    (a) mechanical associative learning.
    (b) use of elaborative rehearsal.
    (c) semantic coding.
    (d) chunking.

18. Information in short–term memory tends to be forgotten by means of
    (a) dissociative amnesia.
    (b) failure to use appropriate retrieval cues.
    (c) displacement.
    (d) retrograde amnesia.

19. The easiest type of memory task is
    (a) recall.
    (b) recognition.
    (c) relearning.
    (d) savings.

20. When sea snails are conditioned, more of the neurotransmitter _____ is released at certain synapses. As a result, transmission at these synapses becomes more efficient as trials (learning) progress.
    (a) acetylcholine
    (b) dopamine
    (c) norepinephrine
    (d) serotonin

Answer Key to *Posttest*

| | |
|---|---|
| 1. D | 11. C |
| 2. A | 12. D |
| 3. A | 13. A |
| 4. D | 14. B |
| 5. C | 15. C |
| 6. D | 16. B |
| 7. B | 17. A |
| 8. D | 18. C |
| 9. A | 19. B |
| 10. D | 20. D |

| | |
|---|---|
| Episodic memory | Acoustic code |
| Semantic memory | Semantic code |
| Procedural memory | Storage |
| Mnemonic | Maintenance rehearsal |
| Acronym | Metamemory |
| Encoding | Retrieval |
| Visual code | Memory |

| | |
|---|---|
| Mental representation of information as a sequence of sounds. | Memories of events experienced by a person or that take place in the person's presence. |
| Mental representation of information according to its meaning. | General knowledge as opposed to episodic memory. |
| The maintenance of information over time. The second stage of information processing. | Knowledge of ways of doing things; skill memory. |
| Mental repetition of information order to keep it in memory. | Systems for remembering in which items are related to easily recalled sets of symbols, such as acronyms, phrases, or jingles. |
| Self-awareness of the ways in which memory functions, allowing the person to encode, store, and retrieve information effectively. | A word that is composed of the first letters of the elements of a phrase. |
| The location of stored information and its return to consciousness. The third stage of information processing. | Modifying information so that it can be placed in memory. The first stage of information processing. |
| The processes by which information is encoded, stored, and retrieved. | Mental representation of information as a picture. |

| Sensory memory | Serial-position effect |
|---|---|
| Memory trace | Primacy effect |
| Sensory register | Recency effect |
| Icon | Chunk |
| Eidetic imagery | Rote |
| Short-term memory | Displace |
| Working memory | Long-term memory |

Chapter 7    Memory

| | |
|---|---|
| The tendency to recall more accurately the first and last items in a series. | The type or stage of memory first encountered by a stimulus. Sensory memory holds impressions briefly, but long enough so that series of perceptions are psychologically continuous. |
| The tendency to recall the initial items in a series of items. | An assumed change in the nervous system that reflects the impression made by a stimulus. Memory traces are said to be "held" in sensory registers. |
| The tendency to recall the last items in a series of items. | A system of memory that holds information briefly, but long enough so that it can be processed further. There may be a sensory register for every sense. |
| A stimulus or group of stimuli that are perceived as a discrete piece of information. | A mental representation of a visual stimulus that is held briefly in sensory memory. |
| Mechanical associative learning that is based on repetition. | The maintenance of detailed visual memories over several minutes. |
| In memory theory, to cause chunks of information to be lost from short-term memory by adding new items. | The type or stage of memory that can hold information for up to a minute or so after the trace of the stimulus decays. Also called working memory. |
| The type or stage of memory capable of relatively permanent storage. | Same as short-term memory. |

| | |
|---|---|
| Repression | Recall |
| Schema | Relearning |
| Elaborative rehearsal | Interference theory |
| Tip-of-the-tongue phenomenon | Retroactive interference |
| Context-dependent memory | Proactive interference |
| State-dependent memory | Dissociative amnesia |
| Recognition | Infantile amnesia |

Chapter 7   Memory

| | |
|---|---|
| Retrieval or reconstruction of learned material. | In Freud's psychodynamic theory, the ejection of anxiety-evoking ideas from conscious awareness. |
| A measure of retention. Material is usually relearned more quickly than it is learned initially. | A way of mentally representing the world, such as a belief or an expectation that can influence perception of persons, objects, and situations. |
| The view that we may forget stored material because other learning interferes with it. | A method for increasing retention of new information by relating it to information that is well known. |
| The interference of new learning with the ability to retrieve material learned previously. | The feeling that information is stored in memory although it cannot be readily retrieved. |
| The interference by old learning with the ability to retrieve material learned recently. | Information that is better retrieved in the context in which it was encoded and stored, or learned. |
| Amnesia thought to stem from psychological conflict or trauma. | Information that is better retrieved in the physiological or emotional state in which it was encoded and stored, or learned. |
| Inability to recall events that occur prior to the age of 2 or 3. Also called childhood amnesia. | In information processing, the easiest memory task, involving identification of objects or events encountered before. |

Directions: This *PRETEST* will give you feedback about how well you understand Chapter 8. In order to enhance your mastery of Chapter 8, complete all the sections of this chapter of the Study Guide. Then you can take the *POSTTEST* and compare your results.

1. The bus driver problem indicates the importance of
   (a) rote repetition of mental representation of the elements of a problem.
   (b) prototypes.
   (c) the availability heuristic.
   (d) paying attention to relevant information.

2. According to the text, all of the following are examples of thinking, **EXCEPT**
   (a) mentally representing information.
   (b) daydreaming.
   (c) deductive reasoning.
   (d) making decisions.

3. The water–jar problems indicate the role of _____ in problem solving.
   (a) heuristic devices
   (b) functional fixedness
   (c) incubation
   (d) mental sets

4. Which of the following is closest in meaning to constructing a coherent mental representation of a problem?
   (a) making inferences about premises
   (b) understanding a problem
   (c) selecting the most efficient heuristic devices
   (d) using prototypes as exemplars

5. A mathematical formula for solving a problem is an example of a(n)
   (a) mental set.
   (b) analogy.
   (c) algorithm.
   (d) heuristic device.

6. Means–end analysis is an example of a(n)
   (a) mental set.
   (b) analogy.
   (c) algorithm.
   (d) heuristic device.

7. All of the following help individuals solve problems, **EXCEPT**
   (a) insight.
   (b) incubation.
   (c) heuristic devices.
   (d) functional fixedness.

8. Köhler's research with Sultan was an important historic event in the psychological study of
   (a) problem solving by insight.
   (b) creativity.
   (c) the incubation effect.
   (d) judgment and decision making.

9. According to Guilford, creativity involves
   (a) deductive reasoning.
   (b) inductive reasoning.
   (c) convergent thinking.
   (d) divergent thinking.

10. Which of the following enhances creativity?
    (a) being offered a reward for creativity
    (b) being watched while one is working
    (c) competing for prizes
    (d) flexibility

11. In inductive reasoning,
    (a) we reason from individual cases or particular facts to a general conclusion.
    (b) the conclusion must be true if the premises are true.
    (c) thought is limited to present facts.
    (d) the individual associates fluently and freely to the elements of the problem.

12. Consider the following two problems:
    (1) 8 x 7 x 6 x 5 x 4 x 3 x 2 x 1
    (2) 1 x 2 x 3 x 4 x 5 x 6 x 7 x 8
    People shown problem one tend to estimate the answer to be higher than people estimating the answer to problem two because of
    (a) representativeness heuristic.
    (b) anchoring and adjustment heuristic.
    (c) availability heuristic.
    (d) framing effect.

13. The fact that people often tend to focus on examples that confirm their judgments and ignore events that do not lead to
    (a) overconfidence.
    (b) the framing effect.
    (c) divergent thinking.
    (d) the availability heuristic.

14. The language characteristic of *semanticity* means that
    (a) words can mean whatever we want.
    (b) sentences have surface & deep structures.
    (c) words serve as symbols.
    (d) children intuitively grasp meaning.

15. _____ change the forms of words in order to indicate grammatical relationships such as number and tense.
    (a) Inflections
    (b) Morphemes
    (c) Phonemes
    (d) Semantics

16. Which of the following is true of two–word utterances?
    (a) The order of appearance is the same for diverse languages as Russian and Turkish.
    (b) The order of appearance is the same for different European languages only.
    (c) The appearance of two–word utterances shows that conditioning does not play a role in language development.
    (d) The word order tends to be haphazard.

17. A 3–year–old says, "Mommy goed away." This statement is an example of
    (a) failure to understand grammar.
    (b) overregularization.
    (c) overextension.
    (d) understanding of deep structure, but not surface structure.

18. Who is credited with originating the lingustic–relativity hypothesis?
    (a) Chomsky
    (b) Whorf
    (c) Wechsler
    (d) Slobin

19. According to Pinker, Black dialect
    (a) is less complex than standard English.
    (b) is more complex than standard English.
    (c) has grammatical rules that are the same as those of standard English.
    (d) follows consistent rules.

20. Evidence for the nativist theory of language development is found in
    (a) the invariant sequences of language development.
    (b) the fact that language development is made possible by cognitive analytical abilities.
    (c) children's motivation to express the meanings that conceptual development makes available to them.
    (d) the fact that parents reinforce children for the grammatical correctness of their utterances.

**Answer Key to** *Pretest*

| | |
|---|---|
| 1. D | 11. A |
| 2. B | 12. B |
| 3. D | 13. A |
| 4. B | 14. C |
| 5. C | 15. A |
| 6. D | 16. A |
| 7. D | 17. B |
| 8. B | 18. B |
| 9. D | 19. D |
| 10. D | 20. A |

# OVERVIEW

Chapter 8 discusses two key cognitive topics in psychology: thinking and language.

Topics covered in thinking include concepts and prototypes, problem solving, creativity, reasoning, and judgment and decision making. The roles of prototypes, exemplars, and positive and negative instances in concept formation are outlined. Discussion of problem solving includes the roles of algorithms and heuristic devices ("rules of thumb"), and factors such as incubation, mental sets, and functional fixedness. It is shown that creativity helps us find novel solutions to problems, and that intelligence and creativity are moderately related. Types of reasoning include deductive and inductive reasoning. Heuristic devices are involved in judgments and decision making as they are in problem solving. A number of factors affect judgment and decision making, including the framing effect and overconfidence.

The basics of language consist of phonology (units of sound), morphology (units of meaning), syntax (word order), and semantics (communication of meaning). Language development is traced from prelinguistic events, such as cooing and babbling, to telegraphic speech and more complex language. It is shown how children's language "errors" (as in overregularizations) actually provide evidence for an intuitive understanding of grammar. Learning, nativist, and cognitive theories of language acquisition are outlined. While learning plays an important role in language development, the capacity to acquire language also depends on some kind of neural "prewiring."

Thought is possible without language, but language facilitates thought. In contrast to the linguistic–relativity hypothesis, language may merely show what concepts a culture considers important, but not greatly limit the ability of members of that culture to think about other concepts.

# LEARNING OBJECTIVES

| | |
|---|---|
| 1. Define *concepts* and *prototypes*, and explain how they function as building blocks of thought. | **Concepts and Prototypes: Building Blocks of Thought** |
| 2. Describe various approaches to problem solving. | **Problem Solving** |

3. Discuss factors that affect problem solving.

4. Discuss the relationships between *problem solving, creativity,* and *intelligence.*

### Creativity

5. Discuss personality and situational factors that affect creativity.

### Reasoning

6. Describe various types of reasoning.

### Judgment and Decision Making

7. Discuss the role of *heuristics* in decision making.

8. Describe the *framing effect.*

9. Discuss factors that lead to overconfidence in judgment and decision making.

### Language

10. Define *language.*

11. Explain the three properties of language.

12. Discuss the basics of language: *phonology, morphology, syntax,* and *semantics.*

| | **Language Development** |
|---|---|
| 13. Trace the development of language in human beings. | |
| 14. Discuss *Black dialect*. | |
| 15. Explain the learning, nativist, and cognitive views of language | |
| | **Language and Thought** |
| 16. Discuss the relationships between language and thought. | |
| | **Additional Terms** |
| | |
| | |
| | |
| | |
| | |

## Concepts and Prototypes: Building Blocks of Thought

## Problem Solving

1. Approaches to Problem Solving: Getting from Here to There

2. Factors that Affect Problem Solving

## Creativity

1. Creativity and Intelligence: Was Picasso Smart?

2. Factors that Affect Creativity: Are Starving Artists More Creative?

## Reasoning

- Types of Reasoning

## Judgment and Decision Making

1. Heuristics in Decision Making: If It Works, Must It Be Logical?

2. The Framing Effect: Say That Again?

3. Overconfidence: Is Your Hindsight 20-20?

# Language

- Basic Concepts of Language

# Language Development

1. Development of Vocabulary

2. Development of Syntax

3. Toward More Complex Language

4. Theories of Language Development

# Language and Thought

- The Linguistic-Relativity Hypothesis

# Psychology and Modern Life

- Bilingualism and Bilingual Education

# Creating Useful Notes

## Be Prepared

1. **Complete outside assignments before class.** Most instructors assume that students complete assignments, and they develop their lectures accordingly. It is more difficult to take notes when you have little understanding about what is being said in class.

2. **Bring to class pen, paper, notebook**, and any other materials that could be useful. Consider bringing your textbook to class, especially if the lectures relate closely to the text.

3. **Sit close to the front and center.** Students who get as close as possible to the front of the class often do better on tests for several reasons. The closer you sit to the instructor, the less likely you are to fall asleep or daydream. There are also fewer people to watch, and the board will be easier to read. A professor who sounds boring from the back of the room might sound more interesting if you're closer (at least it is worth a try). Sitting in back can signal a lack of commitment.

4. **Arrive early and review**. Review your notes from the previous class. Scan your reading assignment. Look at the sections you have underlined. Note questions you intend to ask.

## Stay Focused

5. **Accept your mind wandering**, and then bring your attention back to the class. If an important (but unrelated to the class) issue comes to mind, write it down, and then refocus on the class. It helps if you notice how your pen feels in your hand. Paying attention to the act of writing can bring you back to the lecture.

6. **Imagine yourself right in front of the instructor.** Imagine that you and the instructor are the only ones in the room and the lecture is a personal talk with you. Pay attention to the instructor's body language and facial expressions. Look the instructor in the eye.

7. **Pay attention to the room.** When you start daydreaming, bring yourself back to the lecture by paying attention to the temperature in the room, the feel of your chair, or the amount of light in the room. Experiencing the room will help keep you mentally in it.

8. **Avoid judgments about the lecture or the lecturer.** When you hear something you disagree with, write it down and let it go. Internal debates can prevent you from learning new information. Don't let your attitude about an instructor's lecture style, habits, or appearance get in the way of your learning.

9. **Participate in class whenever possible.** Ask questions. Chances are, the question you think is "dumb" is also on the minds of several of your classmates. Volunteer for demonstrations. Join in class discussions. This helps to not only keep your interest in the class, but it also makes the class more fun for everyone.

## Stay Alert for Clues

10. **Repetition** is a signal that the instructor thinks the information is important.

11. **Lecture structure** is given by such phrases as: "The three factors involved are..."; "On the other hand..."; "The most important consideration...". You can use these phrases to organize your notes.

12. **Information written** by instructors on the board, overhead projector, or computer projection indicate key points that they are trying to convey.

13. **Watch the instructor's eyes.** If instructors glance at their notes and then make a point, the information is probably important (and a potential test question).

14. **Instructor's enthusiasm** often indicates what he or she feels is more important and therefore test-worthy. Create a special symbol for your notes when the instructor states that something will be on the test.

# KEY TERMS AND CONCEPTS

1. Thinking _____

### Concepts and Prototypes: Building Blocks of Thought

2. Concept _____

3. Prototype _____

4. Exemplar _____

5. Positive instance _____

6. Negative instance _____

### Problem Solving

7. Understanding _____

8. Algorithm _____

9. Systematic random search _____

10. Heuristics _____

11. Means–end analysis _____

12. Mental set _____

13. Insight _____

14. Cognitive map _____

15. Incubation _____

16. Functional fixedness _____

17. Well–defined problem _____

18. Ill–defined problem _____

### Creativity

19. Creativity _____

20. Convergent thinking _____

21. Divergent thinking _____

22. Brainstorming _____

### Reasoning

23. Reasoning _____

24. Deductive reasoning _____

25. Premise _____

26. Inductive Reasoning _____

### Judgment and Decision Making

27. Representativeness heuristic _____

28. Availability heuristic _____

29. Anchoring and adjustment heuristic _____

30. Framing effect _____

### Language

31. Symbol _____

32. Language _____

33. Semanticity _____

34. Infinite creativity _____

35. Syntax _____

36. Displacement _____

37. Phonology _____

38. Phoneme _____

39. Morpheme _____

40. Inflections _____

41. Semantics _____

42. Surface structure _____

43. Deep structure _____

### Language Development

44. Prelinguistic _____

45. Cooing _____

46. Babbling _____

47. Overextension _____

48. Holophrase _____

49. Overregularization _____

50. Models _____

51. Psycholinguistic theory _____

52. Language acquisition device _____

53. Sensitive period _____

### Language and Thought

54. Linguistic–relativity hypothesis _____

Items numbered 1 through 20 represent concepts discussed in the chapter on Thinking and Language. Items lettered A through T represent examples of these concepts. Indicate which example matches each concept by writing the letter that represents the example in the blank space to the left of the concept.

___ 1. Algorithm

___ 2. Systematic random search

___ 3. Means–end analysis

___ 4. Mental set

___ 5. Insight

___ 6. Cognitive map

___ 7. Incubation

___ 8. Functional fixedness

___ 9. Creativity

___10. Divergent thinking

___11. Brainstorming

___12. Deductive reasoning

___13. Premise

___14. Inductive reasoning

___15. Representativeness heuristic

___16. Availability heuristic

___17. Framing effect

___18. Overextension

___19. Holophrase

___20. Overregularization

A. Because of sensationalistic newscasts, you assume that New York City is a terrible place to live.

B. A child says, "Doggy!" but means "I want you to give me that dog right now!"

C. A child refers to a horse as a "big doggy."

D. You generate lists of all the meanings you can think of for the verbs "see" and "pull."

E. You use the formula that helped you solve one problem with problems that seem to be similar.

F. You try to figure out how to get to a certain address by picturing where you are now and attempting to reduce the discrepancy (in this case, the distance between the two locations).

G. The solution to a problem comes to you in a flash.

H. The Duncker candle problem.

I. A child says, "I seed it" instead of "I saw it."

J. An attempt to solve an anagram by trying every possible letter combination.

K. You bring together a group of people to generate as many solutions as they can think of for a particular problem.

L. The statement "People are mortal" serves as this in the syllogism about Socrates.

M. Because a couple already has five daughters, you assume that their sixth child is likely to be a son.

N. You conclude that Socrates is mortal because Socrates is a person and people are mortal.

O. A politician sees that you are unwilling to consider decreasing social security benefits and therefore begins to argue with you about the importance of balancing the budget instead.

P. The Pythagorean theorem.

Q. You put aside a difficult problem for a while, hoping that an effective way of approaching it will come to you later on.

R. A person assumes that a greeting that was effective with one person will be effective with another.

S. A psychological concept that involves the ability to make many associations, some of them remote, to a concept.

T. A mental image of a maze, which aids a rat in reaching a food goal.

## Answer Key to *Matching Exercise*

| | | | |
|---|---|---|---|
| 1. P | 5. G | 9. S (or D) | 13. L | 17. O |
| 2. J | 6. T | 10. D (or S) | 14. R | 18. C |
| 3. F | 7. Q | 11. K | 15. M | 19. B |
| 4. E | 8. H | 12. N | 16. A | 20. I |

The bus driver problem illustrates that one of the requirements of problem solving is paying attention to relevant (1) _____tion. (2) _____ing may be defined as mental activity that is involved in understanding, processing, and communicating information. Thinking entails attending to information, mentally (3) _____ting it, reasoning about it, and making judgments and (4)_____sions about it. Language allows us to (5) _____icate our thoughts and record them for posterity.

## SECTION 1: Concepts and Prototypes: Building Blocks of Thought

**OBJ. 1:** Concepts are mental (6) _____ories used to class together objects, relations, events, abstractions, or qualities that have common properties. Much of thinking has to do with (7)cat_____ing new objects and events and with (8) man_____ting the relationships among concepts.

We tend to organize concepts in (9) hi_____. Examples that best match the essential features of categories are termed (10) _____types. Prototypes are good (11) _____ples of concepts. Many simple prototypes such as *dog* and *red* are taught by (12) _____plars. Dogs are (13) _____tive instances of the dog concept. Cats are (14) _____tive instances of the dog concept. In language development, the overinclusion of instances in a category (reference to horses as dogs) is labeled (15) over_____.

## SECTION 2: Problem Solving

**OBJ. 2:** Problem solving begins with attempting to (16) _____and the problem. Understanding a problem requires focusing on the key

(17) inf_____. Understanding a problem means constructing a coherent (18) m_____ (19) rep_____ of the problem. Successful understanding of a problem generally requires three features: First, The parts or elements of our (20)_____tal representation of the problem relate to one another in a meaningful way. Second, the elements of our mental representation of the problem should (21) cor_____ to the elements of the problem in the outer world. Third, we need a storehouse of background (22) _____edge that we can apply to the problem.

An (23) _____thm is a specific procedure for solving a type of problem. In solving anagram problems, the algorithm termed the (24) sys_____ random search involves listing every possible letter combination, using from one to all letters.

(25) H_____ics are rules of thumb that help us simplify and solve problems. Heuristics are shortcuts that allow for more rapid (26) _____tions. In the type of heuristic device called the (27) means–_____ analysis, we assess the difference between our current situation and our goals and then do what we can to reduce this discrepancy.

An (28) _____gy is a partial similarity among things that are different in other ways. The analogy (29) he_____ applies the solution of an earlier problem to the solution of a new one.

**OBJ. 3:** (30) E_____s solve problems more efficiently and rapidly than novices do. Experts at solving a certain kind of problem have a more extensive (31) kn_____ base in the area, have better memories for the elements in the problems, form mental images or (32) rep_____tions that facilitate problem solving, relate the problem to other problems that are similar in structure, and have more efficient methods for problem solving.

A (33) m_____ set is the tendency to respond to a new problem with the same approach that helped solve earlier, similar-looking problems. Some problems are solved by rapid "perception of relationships" among the elements of the problem, or (34) _____ght. Standing back from a difficult problem for a while sometimes allows the (35) _____tion of insight. When standing back from the problem is helpful, it may be because it provides us with some distance from unprofitable but persistent (36) _____tal sets.

(37) Fu_____ _____ness is the tendency to think of an object in terms of its name or its familiar usage. Functional fixedness can be similar to a (38) m_____ set in that it can make it difficult for you to use familiar objects to solve problems in novel ways.

Problems can be well–defined or (39) _____–defined. In a (40) _____–defined problem, the original state, the goal, and the rules for reaching the goal are all clearly spelled out. In an ill–defined problem, the original state, the goal, or the rules are less than clear.

## SECTION 3: Creativity

**OBJ. 4:** A (41) _____tive person may be more capable of solving problems to which there are no preexisting solutions, no tried and tested formulas. We tend to perceive creative people as (42: *Circle one:* willing or unwilling to take chances, unaccepting of limitations, appreciating art and music, capable of using the materials around them to make unique things, (43: *Circle one:* challenging or accepting) social norms and assumptions, willing to take an unpopular stand, and inquisitive. Many psychologists view creativity as the ability to make unusual, sometimes remote, associations to the elements of a problem to generate new (44) _____tions that meet the goals.

Creativity demands (45) _____gent thinking rather than convergent thinking. In (46)_____gent thinking, thought is limited to present facts as the problem–solver tries to narrow thinking to find the best solution. In (47) _____gent thinking, the problem–solver associates more fluently and freely to the various elements of the problem.

Creative people (48: *Circle one:* do or do not) tend to be intelligent. Intelligence (49: *Circle one:* is or is not) a guarantee of creativity.

**OBJ. 5:** Research evidence shows that concern about evaluation by other people (50: *Circle one:* enhances or reduces) creativity. Being watched while one is working (51: *Circle one:* enhances or reduces) creativity. Being offered a reward for creativity (52: *Circle one:* enhances or reduces) creativity.

(53) Br_____ing is a group process that encourages creativity by stimulating a great number of ideas—even wild ideas—and suspending judgment until the process is completed.

## SECTION 4: Reasoning

**OBJ. 6:** The text defines reasoning as the (54) _____ming of information to reach conclusions. (55)_____ive reasoning is a form of reasoning in which the conclusion must be true if the premises are true. (56) _____ses provide the assumptions or basic information that allows people to draw conclusions. In (57) _____ive reasoning, we reason from individual cases or particular facts to a general conclusion. Inductive reasoning (58: *Circle one:* does or does not) permit us to draw absolute conclusions.

## SECTION 5: Judgment and Decision Making

**OBJ. 7:** People make most run–of–the–mill, daily decisions on the basis of (59: *Circle one:* complete or limited) information. People use rules of thumb—(60) _____tic devices—in their judgments and decision making, just as they do in problem solving.

According to the (61) rep_____ness heuristic, people make judgments about events (samples) according to the populations of events that they appear to represent. According to the (62)_____ity heuristic, our estimates of frequency or probability are based on how easy it is to find examples of relevant events.

The anchoring and (63) _____ment heuristic suggests that there can be a good deal of inertia to our judgments. In forming opinions or making estimates, we have an initial view, or presumption, that serves as the (64) a_____. As we receive additional (65) inf_____, we make adjustments.

**OBJ. 8:** The (66) fr_____ effect refers to the way in which wording, or the context in which information is presented, can influence decision making.

**OBJ. 9:** Most of us tend (67: *Circle one:* to have or not to have) overconfidence in our decisions. One reason we tend (68: *Circle one:* to be or not to be) confident is that we tend to focus on examples that confirm our judgments and to ignore events that do not.

## SECTION 6: Language

**OBJ. 10:** Language is the communication of thoughts and feelings through (69) s_____. These symbols are arranged according to rules of (70) _____ar.

**Obj. 11:** Language has the properties of (71) sem_____ity, infinite creativity, and (72) _____ment. Semanticity means that words serve as (73) _____ls for actions, objects, and relational concepts. Infinite creativity refers to the capacity to combine (74) _____s into original sentences. Displacement is the capacity to communicate (75) in_____ about objects or events in another time or place.

**OBJ. 12:** The basic components of language include phonology, (76) mor_____, (77) _____ax, and semantics. Phonology is the study of the basic (78) _____s of a language. A basic sound is labeled a (79) _____me.

Morphemes are the smallest units of (80) _____ing in a language. Morphemes consist of one or more (81) ph_____ pronounced in a particular order. Morphemes such as *s* and *ed* tacked on to the ends of nouns and verbs are examples of (82) _____cal markers or (83)_____tions. Inflections change the forms of words to indicate grammatical relationships such as (84) n_____ (singular or plural) and (85) t_____ (e.g., present or past).

Syntax is the system of rules that determines how words are strung together to make up phrases and (86) _____ces. The rules for (87) _____rd order are the *grammar* of a language.

Semantics is the study of (88) _____ing— of the relationship between language and the objects or events language depicts. The (89) s_____structure of a sentence refers to its superficial construction—the location of words. A sentence's (90) _____p structure refers to its underlying meaning.

## SECTION 7: Language Development

**OBJ. 13:** Children cry at birth and begin to (91) c_____ by about two months. (92) _____s are frequently vowel-like and may resemble repeated "oohs" and "ahs." Cooing appears associated with feelings of (93) _____sure.

(94) _____ling is the first kind of vocalization that has the sound of speech. Babbling appears at about six months and contains (95) _____emes found in many languages. Babbling is innate, although it can be modified by learning. Crying, cooing, and babbling are all (96) pre_____ events. They are prelinguistic because they lack (97) _____city.

Children's (98) _____ive vocabularies consist of the words that they can understand, as demonstrated, for example, by following directions. Children's (99) _____ive vocabulary consists of the words that they use in their speech. Receptive vocabulary growth (100: *Circle one:* lags or outpaces) expressive vocabulary growth.

Children speak their first words at about the age of (101) _____. Children try to talk about more objects than they have words for, and so they often (102) <u>over</u>_____ the meaning of one word to refer to things and actions for which they do not have words.

Children first use (103) _____-word utterances. These utterances express the meanings found in complete sentences and are referred to as (104) _____phic speech. One–word utterances are also called (105) _____ases. Two-word telegraphic utterances appear toward the end of the (106) _____d year. Children also use (107) <u>over</u>_____<u>izations</u>, as in "I seed it" and "Mommy sitted down." The "errors" made in overregularizing indicate a grasp of the rules of (108) _____ar.

Girls are slightly (109: *Circle one:* inferior or superior) to boys in their language development. Children from families of lower socioeconomic status have (110: *Circle one:* poorer or richer) vocabularies than children from middle– or upper–class families.

**OBJ. 14:** Black dialect is a (111) <u>dia</u>_____ of standard English. The major difference between Black dialect and standard English lies in the use of (112) _____bs. Black dialect has (113: *Circle one:* consistent or inconsistent) rules and allows for the expression of thoughts that are as complex as those permitted by standard English.

**OBJ. 15:** From a social–cognitive perspective, parents serve as (114) _____els of language usage. Children learn language, at least in part, by (115) <u>obs</u>_____ and (116) <u>imi</u>_____. Many vocabulary words, including irregular verbs, are learned by (117) <u>imi</u>_____. But social learning cannot account for children's (118) _____larization of regular nouns and verbs. B. F. Skinner outlined his view of the role of (119) _____ment in language development as follows: "A child acquires (120) <u>v</u>_____ behavior when relatively unpatterned vocalizations, selectively reinforced, assume forms which produce appropriate consequences in a given verbal community."

The (121) _____st view of language development holds that innate factors cause children to attend to and acquire language in certain ways. According to (122) _____istic theory, language acquisition involves an interaction between environmental influences, such as exposure to parental speech and reinforcement, and an inborn tendency to acquire language. This inborn tendency has been labeled the (123)_____ _____tion Device (LAD). Chomsky argues that the LAD allows children to understand a (124) "<u>un</u>_____ grammar," an underlying deep structure that involves rules as to how phonemes and morphemes are combined to symbolize events and yield meaning. Lenneberg proposes that there is a (125) _____tive period for learning language that begins at about 18 to 24 months and lasts until puberty. This sensitive period is based on (126) _____city of the brain.

Cognitive views of language development focus on the relationships between (127)_____ive development and language development. Jean Piaget believed that cognitive development (128: *Circle one:* follows or precedes) language development. The opposing point of view holds that children create (129) _____ive classes to understand things that are labeled by words.

**SECTION 8: Language and Thought**
**OBJ. 16:** Thought is possible without (130)_____age, but language facilitates thought. According to the (131) _____–relativity hypoth-

esis, language structures (and limits) the way in which we perceive the world. Critics argue that a (132) _____ lary may suggest the concepts deemed important by the users of a language; however, vocabulary limits do not necessarily prevent language users from making distinctions for which there are no (133) _____ ds.

## ADDITIONAL NOTES:

_____

_____

_____

_____

_____

_____

_____

_____

_____

_____

_____

_____

_____

_____

_____

_____

_____

_____

_____

_____

_____

_____

_____

**Answer Key to *Chapter Review***

1. information
2. Thinking
3. representing
4. decisions
5. communicate
6. categories
7. categorizing
8. manipulating
9. hierarchies
10. prototypes
11. examples
12. exemplars
13. positive
14. negative
15. overextension
16. understand
17. information
18. mental
19. representation
20. mental
21. correspond
22. knowledge
23. algorithm
24. systematic
25. Heuristics
26. solutions
27. means–end
28. analogy
29. heuristic
30. Experts
31. knowledge
32. representations
33. mental
34. insight
35. incubation
36. mental
37. Functional fixedness
38. mental
39. ill–defined

40. well–defined
41. creative
42. willing
43. challenging
44. combinations
45. divergent
46. convergent
47. divergent
48. do
49. is not
50. reduces
51. reduces
52. reduces
53. Brainstorming
54. transforming
55. Deductive
56. Premises
57. inductive
58. does not
59. limited
60. heuristic
61. representativeness
62. availability
63. adjustment
64. anchor
65. information
66. framing
67. to have
68. to be
69. symbols
70. grammar
71. semanticity
72. displacement
73. labels
74. words
75. information
76. morphology
77. syntax
78. sounds

79. phoneme
80. meaning
81. phonemes
82. grammatical
83. inflections
84. number
85. tense
86. sentences
87. word
88. meaning
89. durface
90. deep
91. coo
92. Coos
93. pleasure
94. Babbling
95. phonemes
96. prelinguistic
97. semanticity
98. receptive
99. expressive
100. outpaces
101. one (12 months)
102. overextend
103. one
104. telegraphic
105. holophrases
106. second
107. overgeneralizations
108. grammar
109. superior
110. poorer
111. dialect
112. verbs
113. consistent
114. models
115. observation
116. imitation
117. imitation

118. overregularization
119. reinforcement
120. verbal
121. nativist
122. psycholinguistic
123. Language Acquisition
124. universal
125. sensitive
126. plasticity
127. cognitive
128. precedes
129. cognitive
130. language
131. linguistic
132. vocabulary
133. words

| | Idioms | Explanation |
|---|---|---|
| 290 | hit me with | brought to me |
| 290 | kinds of torture | difficult experiences |
| 293 | in a flash | quickly |
| 294 | beat a horse to death | go over a point again and again |
| 294 | storehouse | large amount |
| 295 | scanning | reviewing |
| 297 | unscramble | figure out |
| 297 | riddled me | told me a puzzle |
| 298 | (drat?) | expression of disappointment |
| 299 | just desserts | earned reward |
| 302 | limitless course | goes on for a very long time |
| 303 | nipped in the bud | stopped at a young age |

| | Cultural Reference | Explanation |
|---|---|---|
| 296 | domino theory | a game where one piece falls and hits over other pieces one by one |
| 300 | pair of pliers | a tool for grasping (holding) |
| 305 | ice breaker | action to begin a relationship |
| 311 | "lie fallow" | not active |
| 313 | "upset the apple cart" | change things against the wishes of others |
| 313 | raise the ante | make the goal higher |
| 314 | What a milestone! | originally a milestone was a stone that marked off each mile on a road. Now it is used to mean reaching an important higher level of development |
| 316 | now-oriented | do not understand anything but what is going on right now |
| 324 | waves | waves are formed in the ocean when the water rises up at certain points. It is used here to mean a sudden increase |
| 290 | inkling | idea, feeling |
| 290 | superfluous | of no value |
| 290 | vast | great |
| 290 | deliberate | on purpose |
| 290 | entwined | mixed in with |
| 290 | theorems | an idea thought to be true |
| 290 | philosophical treatise | formal written ideas |
| 291 | cognition | thinking |
| 291 | hierarchies | organized systems |
| 292 | coincide | match; are similar |
| 292 | peek | look |
| 293 | complicated | complex, a lot of details |
| 294 | averting | avoiding |
| 294 | provocations | make someone angry |
| 294 | generate | create; make up |
| 294 | irrelevant | not important |

| | Phrases and Expressions (Different Usage) | |
|---|---|---|
| 294 | coherent | understandable |
| 294 | inferences | statements |
| 294 | familiarizing | getting to know better |
| 295 | invariably | always |
| 295 | appropriate | correct |
| 295 | substantive | important; real |
| 295 | discrepancy | difference |
| 296 | ultimate goal | goal in the end |
| 296 | Precedents | past legal decisions |
| 296 | retrieving | finding |
| 296 | relevant | important and related |
| 297 | novices | people who are new at something |
| 297 | parallelogram | a box with opposite sides that are at the same angle |
| 297 | intricacies | small details |
| 297 | vastly | largely |
| 298 | was stranded | could not leave |
| 298 | delectable | very good tasting |
| 298 | elusive | hard to catch |
| 298 | regathered | brought together again |
| 299 | sniffed | smell |
| 299 | fiddle | to touch all over |
| 301 | savor | enjoy slowly |
| 301 | a bluff | a hill that is flat on top |
| 301 | a bay | an inlet of water |
| 301 | sketching | drawing |
| 301 | enigmatic | very difficult to understand |
| 302 | novel | new |
| 302 | concur | agree |
| 302 | essential | important |
| 302 | fluently | easily and with skill |
| 302 | designated | chosen |
| 302 | modest connection | small connection |
| 302 | reside within | are within |
| 303 | nonconformist | do not go along with what other people do |
| 303 | exaggeration | say something is bigger than it really is |
| 304 | plummets | falls quickly and a long ways |
| 304 | wildly | very |
| 304 | skeptical | questioning |
| 304 | Ponder | Think about |
| 304 | preposterous | silly |
| 305 | bamboozled | fooled, confused |
| 305 | toying with | playing with |
| 306 | catch a few extra winks | sleep a little longer |
| 306 | jingling | making noise |
| 306 | route | road |
| 306 | pluses and minuses | good and bad points |
| 306 | run-of-the-mill | normal |

| Phrases and Expressions (Different Usage) | |
|---|---|
| 306 | serious hot water | big trouble |
| 307 | well-publicized | heard a lot about |
| 307 | begrudgingly | not wanting to |
| 308 | excursion | trip |
| 308 | overconfidence | believe in them too much |
| 308 | alter | change |
| 308 | in the face | when shown |
| 309 | 20-20 hindsight | know something but only after it has happened |
| 309 | hamstring muscle | tendon at the back of the knee |
| 309 | blustery | very hot |
| 309 | flimsy | weak |
| 309 | toss | throw |
| 309 | exclusive claim | say only we can do it |
| 310 | skrieks | screams, loud noises |
| 310 | "on the map" | famous; people notice it |
| 310 | chronically | continuously |
| 310 | prominence | important position |
| 311 | math map | location of countries and well their children do in math |
| 311 | avert | prevent |
| 311 | deterioration | break down |
| 311 | facilitate | help |
| 311 | simmer idly | get into trouble because of too much free time |
| 311 | arbitrary | not fair |
| 311 | punitive | punishing |
| 313 | depicts | shows |
| 313 | hull of a boat | bottom portion of a boat |
| 313 | master grammar | learn grammar well |
| 313 | chronicle | list and explain in order |
| 314 | resemble | sound like |
| 314 | coincidental | by chance |
| 315 | utterances | sounds |
| 315 | expands | increase |
| 316 | faulty | incorrect, wrong |
| 316 | facility | ability |
| 316 | entertained | enjoy |
| 316 | recast | say again in a different way |
| 317 | haphazardly | not in an organized way |
| 317 | negation | make negative |
| 318 | commendable | very good |
| 318 | equivalent | the same as |
| 318 | pampered | cared for extremely well |
| 319 | crucial | important; critical |
| 319 | utter | speak |
| 319 | steadfastly | firmly; will not give in |
| 319 | unpatterned | no structure |
| 319 | prelinguistic | before actually talking |
| 319 | intrinsically | inside themselves |
| 319 | refusal | will not do |
| 319 | universality | same throughout the world |
| 319 | inborn | born with |
| 320 | plasticity | ability to change |
| 320 | facilitates | make it happen |
| 320 | mere handmaiden | servant |
| 320 | polished off her plate | eaten it all |

| Phrases and Expressions (Different Usage) | |
|---|---|
| 322 | arises | happens |
| 322 | reared | brought up in |
| 325 | per se | itself |
| 325 | erroneously | falsely |
| 325 | intertwined | mixed together |
| 325 | Painstaking research | carefully done research |
| 325 | anecdotal | personal histories |
| 326 | incumbent upon them | put upon them |

| Additional Terms | |
|---|---|

1. According to the text, the incubation effect may be explained by
   (a) breakthrough of unconscious ideas into the conscious.
   (b) distancing problem–solvers from persistent but unprofitable mental sets.
   (c) conscious searching for heuristic devices.
   (d) spontaneous means–end analysis.

2. Each of the following contributes to creativity, **EXCEPT** for
   (a) flexibility.
   (b) fluent thinking.
   (c) divergent thinking.
   (d) convergent thinking.

3. Prototypes are defined as _____ that best match the essential features of categories.
   (a) positive instances
   (b) negative instances
   (c) examples
   (d) concepts

4. In the text, the series of letters OTTFFSSE represents
   (a) the first letters of the names of psychologist.
   (b) the first letters of numbers.
   (c) a random series of letters.
   (d) an example of the availability heuristic.

5. According to the text, _____ a problem is defined as constructing a coherent mental representation of the problem
   (a) understanding
   (b) incubating
   (c) solving
   (d) defining

6. "Rules of thumb" are more technically termed
   (a) algorithms.
   (b) semantics.
   (c) prototypes.
   (d) heuristics.

7. The domino theory is presented in the text as an example of a(n)
   (a) analogy.
   (b) algorithm.
   (c) heuristic.
   (d) mental set.

8. According to the text, a person whose native language is English would be more efficient at solving the anagram RCWDO than a person whose native language is Spanish because of
   (a) selection of appropriate linguistic heuristic devices.
   (b) divergent thinking ability.
   (c) lack of functional fixedness.
   (d) expertise.

9. Consider this problem: "A farmer had 17 sheep. All but 9 died. How many sheep did he have left?" If a person who is good at math arrives at the wrong answer, it is probably because of
   (a) creativity.
   (b) a mental set.
   (c) functional fixedness.
   (d) overconfidence.

10. According to the text, Bismarck showed evidence of
    (a) semanticity.
    (b) insight.
    (c) overconfidence.
    (d) infinite creativity.

11. People who are experts at solving a certain kind of problem have all of the following, **EXCEPT**
    (a) a more extensive knowledge base in the area.
    (b) better memories for the elements in the problems.
    (c) greater creativity.
    (d) more efficient methods for problem solving.

12. The text defines language as the communication of thoughts and feelings through _____ that are arranged according to rules of grammar.
    (a) words
    (b) sentences
    (c) concepts
    (d) symbols

13. The smallest unit of meaning in a language is the
    (a) morpheme.
    (b) phoneme.
    (c) word.
    (d) concept.

14. The word "cats" consists of _____ morpheme(s).
    (a) no
    (b) one
    (c) two
    (d) four

15. The meaning of the phrase "an English-speaking home" reflects the _____ of the phrase.
    (a) surface structure
    (b) deep structure
    (c) syntax
    (d) inflections

16. Which of the following is **NOT** a prelinguistic event?
    (a) the holophrase
    (b) cooing
    (c) babbling
    (d) crying

17. A parent knows that you are taking a psychology course and expresses concern to you that his 24–month–old child refers to the "gooses" and "sheeps" she saw on the farm. As an expert on language development, you state that the child's formation of the plural in this way probably suggests that
    (a) the language–acquisition device has not yet been activated.
    (b) parents or other children in the family speak this way.
    (c) learning does not play an important role in language acquisition.
    (d) language development is proceeding normally.

18. A weakness of the learning theory of language development is that
    (a) parents reinforce their children for the grammatical correctness of utterances.
    (b) crying and cooing is innate.
    (c) two–word utterances develop in an invariant sequence around the world.
    (d) children imitate the speech patterns of their peers as well as their parents.

19. Lenneberg hypothesizes that there is a sensitive period for language development that is made possible by
    (a) plasticity of the brain.
    (b) the advent of puberty.
    (c) emergence of preoperational thought.
    (d) the onset of linguistic vocalizations.

20. The Dani and the Bassa peoples have only two words for colors. According to the text, this limited color vocabulary probably suggests that
    (a) it has not been necessary for them to make further distinctions.
    (b) they are partially or fully colorblind.
    (c) their environments are relatively colorless.
    (d) they would not be able to think about different kinds of colors without first learning words for them.

**Answer Key to *Posttest***

| | |
|---|---|
| 1. B | 11. C |
| 2. D | 12. D |
| 3. C | 13. A |
| 4. B | 14. C |
| 5. A | 15. B |
| 6. D | 16. A |
| 7. A | 17. D |
| 8. D | 18. C |
| 9. B | 19. A |
| 10. B | 20. A |

| | |
|---|---|
| Thinking | Algorithm |
| Concept | Systematic random search |
| Prototype | Heuristics |
| Exemplar | Means-end analysis |
| Positive instance | Mental set |
| Negative instance | Insight |
| Understanding | Cognitive map |

| | |
|---|---|
| A systematic procedure for solving a problem that works invariably when it is correctly applied. | Mental activity that is involved in understanding and communicating about information. Thinking entails paying attention to information, mentally representing it, reasoning and making decisions about it. |
| An algorithm for solving problems in which each possible solution is tested according to a particular set of rules. | A mental category that is used to class together objects, relations, events, abstractions, or qualities that have common properties. |
| Rules of thumb that help us simplify and solve problems. | A concept of a category of objects or events that serves as a good example of the category. |
| A heuristic device in which we try to solve a problem by evaluating the difference between the current situation and the goal. | A specific example. |
| The tendency to respond to a new problem with an approach that was successfully used with similar problems. | An example of a concept. |
| In Gestalt psychology, a sudden perception of relationships among elements of the "perceptual field," permitting the solution of a problem. | An idea, event, or object that is not an example of a concept. Concept formation is aided by presentation of positive and negative instances. |
| A mental representation or picture of the elements in a learning situation, such as a maze. | Constructing a coherent mental representation of a problem. |

| | |
|---|---|
| Incubation | Deductive reasoning |
| Functional fixedness | Premise |
| Creativity | Inductive reasoning |
| Convergent thinking | Representativeness heuristic |
| Divergent thinking | Availability heuristic |
| Brainstorming | Framing effect |
| Reasoning | Symbol |

| | |
|---|---|
| A form of reasoning about arguments in which conclusions are deduced from premises. The conclusions are true if the premises are true. | In problem solving, a hypothetical process that sometimes occurs when we stand back from a frustrating problem for a while and the solution "suddenly" appears. |
| A statement or assertion that serves as the basis for an argument. | The tendency to view an object in terms of its name or familiar usage. |
| A form of reasoning in which we reason from individual cases or particular facts to a general conclusion. | The ability to generate novel solutions to problems. |
| A decision-making heuristic in which people make judgments about samples according to the populations they appear to represent. | A thought process that attempts to narrow in on the single best solution to a problem. |
| A decision-making heuristic in which our estimates of frequency or probability of events are based on how easy it is to find examples. | A thought process that attempts to generate multiple solutions to problems. |
| The influence of wording, or the context in which information is presented, on decision making. | A group process that encourages creativity by stimulating a large number of ideas and suspending judgment until the process is completed. |
| Something that stands for or represents another object, event, or idea. | The transforming of information to reach conclusions. |

| | |
|---|---|
| Language | Surface structure |
| Syntax | Deep structure |
| Phonology | Cooing |
| Phoneme | Babbling |
| Morpheme | Overextension |
| Inflections | Holophrase |
| Semantics | Overregularization |

| | |
|---|---|
| The superficial grammatical construction of a sentence. | The communication of information by means of symbols arranged according to rules of grammar. |
| The underlying meaning of a sentence. | The rules in a language for placing words in proper order to form meaningful sentences. |
| Prelinguistic, articulated, vowel-like sounds that appear to reflect feelings of positive excitement. | The study of the basic sounds in a language. |
| The child's first vocalizations that have the sounds of speech. | A basic sound in a language. |
| Overgeneralizing the use of words to objects and situations to which they do not apply–a normal characteristic of the speech of young children. | The smallest unit of meaning in a language. |
| A single word used to express complex meanings. | Grammatical markers that change the forms of words to indicate grammatical relationships such as number and tense. |
| The application of regular grammatical rules for forming inflection (e.g., past tense and plurals) to irregular verbs and nouns. | The study of the meanings of a language–the relationships between language and objects and events. |

# Chapter 9  Intelligence

Directions: This *PRETEST* will give you feedback about how well you understand Chapter 9. In order to enhance your mastery of Chapter 9, complete all the sections of this chapter of the Study Guide. Then you can take the *POSTTEST* and compare your results.

1. The term *intelligence* is most similar in meaning to
   (a) academic achievement.
   (b) musical talent.
   (c) language ability.
   (d) underlying competence.

2. Binet's test was developed further in the United States by
   (a) Sternberg.
   (b) Stern.
   (c) Terman.
   (d) Thurstone.

3. Whose data suggested that intelligence consists of "primary mental abilities"?
   (a) Wechsler
   (b) Thurstone
   (c) Spearman
   (d) Sternberg

4. Who suggested that awareness of one's own inner feelings is a kind of intelligence?
   (a) Wechsler
   (b) Binet
   (c) Sternberg
   (d) Gardner

5. Reshaping the environment is an example of functioning on the _____ level of intelligence.
   (a) primary
   (b) contextual
   (c) componential
   (d) experiential

6. Which of the following is **NOT** part of the componential level of intelligence?
   (a) language components
   (b) metacomponents
   (c) performance components
   (d) knowledge–acquisition components

7. Who defined intelligence as the "capacity of an individual to understand the world [and the] resourcefulness to cope with its challenges"?
   (a) Sternberg
   (b) Wechsler
   (c) Binet
   (d) Gardner

8. At the age of 2, children show counting and spatial skills along with visual–motor coordination by building a tower of four blocks to match a model. This is an example of an item similar to those found on a test created by
   (a) Goodenough.
   (b) Cattell.
   (c) Wechsler.
   (d) Binet.

9. A child has an MA of 12. From this information we can conclude that she
   (a) is more intelligent than most of her peers.
   (b) is less intelligent than most of her peers.
   (c) has an IQ within the broad average range.
   (d) is about as intelligent as the typical 12–year–old.

10. The concept of the deviation IQ was introduced by
    (a) Wechsler.
    (b) Stern.
    (c) Gardner.
    (d) Simon.

11. _____ attempted to construct a culture–free intelligence test.
    (a) Gardner
    (b) Simon
    (c) Wechsler
    (d) Goodenough

12. The symbol *g* was used by Spearman to signify
    (a) general intelligence.
    (b) primary mental abilities.
    (c) the ability to do well on intelligence tests.
    (d) IQ, but not intelligence.

13. According to Sternberg, deciding what problem to solve and selecting appropriate strategies and formulas are examples of the _____ of intellectual functioning.
    (a) performance components
    (b) experiential level
    (c) metacomponents
    (d) contextual level

14. Wechsler distributed IQ scores so that _____ percent of them fall within the range of 90 to 110.
    (a) 2
    (b) 16
    (c) 32
    (d) 50

15. Which of the following groups scores highest on intelligence tests?
    (a) Caucasian Britishers
    (b) Japanese
    (c) Hispanic Americans
    (d) Native Americans

16. Stern suggested that IQ be computed by the formula:
    (a) (CA/MA) x 100
    (b) (CA-MA) x 100
    (c) (MA/CA) x 100
    (d) (MA-CA) x 100

17. Approximately _____ percent of the population obtains IQ scores suggestive of intellectual deficiency on the Wechsler scales.
    (a) 2
    (b) 7
    (c) 16
    (d) 25

18. The IQ scores of _____ twins reared _____ show the highest correlations.
    (a) identical;  together
    (b) fraternal;  together
    (c) identical;  apart
    (d) fraternal;  apart

19. You are visiting your old high school, and a former teacher says to you, "You're taking psychology. Does it matter how children are treated while they are taking intelligence tests?" You clear your throat and say, "In a study by Zigler and his colleagues, children were made as comfortable as possible during intelligence testing. The results showed that
    (a) test scores decreased for children made most comfortable."
    (b) test scores were 15 points higher than those for a control group."
    (c) middle–class children made relatively greater gains from this procedure."
    (d) disadvantaged children made relatively greater gains from this procedure."

20. The largest group of psychologists and educational specialists voice the opinion that
    (a) intelligence reflects the interaction of heredity and environmental influences.
    (b) only heredity really influences intelligence.
    (c) only environmental influences really affect the development of intelligence.
    (d) neither heredity nor the environment has a meaningful influence on intelligence.

**Answers to *Pretest***

| 1. D | 6. A | 11. D | 16. C |
|------|------|-------|-------|
| 2. C | 7. B | 12. A | 17. A |
| 3. B | 8. D | 13. C | 18. A |
| 4. D | 9. D | 14. D | 19. D |
| 5. B | 10. A | 15. B | 20. A |

Intelligence is a controversial topic with racial and political overtones. Factor theories and cognitive theories of intelligence are explored. The difference in meaning between the terms *intelligence* (a hypothetical trait) and *IQ* (a score on an intelligence test) is specified. Various individual and group tests for measuring intelligence are described, as are socioeconomic and racial differences in intelligence.

The "testing controversy"—that is, the issue as to whether intelligence tests are culturally biased—is examined, and the effort to construct culture–fair intelligence tests is discussed. Evidence concerning the genetic and environmental determinants of intelligence is described in detail. Most psychologists conclude that heredity and environment interact to contribute to IQ scores.

# LEARNING OBJECTIVES

| | |
|---|---|
| 1. Define *intelligence*. | |
| | **Theories of Intelligence** |
| 2. Discuss various factor theories of intelligence. | |
| 3. Discuss Gardner's theory of multiple intelligences. | |
| 4. Discuss Sternberg's triarchic theory of intelligence. | |
| 5. Describe the development and features of the major individual intelligence tests. | |
| | **Measurement of Intelligence** |
| 6. Discuss socioeconomic and ethnic differences in intelligence. | |

| | |
|---|---|
| 7. Discuss the issue of whether or not intelligence tests contain cultural biases against ethnic minority groups and immigrants. | **The Testing Controversy: Just What Do Intelligence Tests Measure?** |
| 8. Discuss the effort to develop culture–free intelligence tests. | |
| 9. Discuss research concerning genetic influences on intelligence. | **The Determinants of Intelligence: Where Does Intelligence Come From?** |
| 10. Discuss research concerning environmental influences on intelligence. | |
| | **Additional Notes** |
| | |
| | |
| | |
| | |
| | |

## Theories of Intelligence

1. Factor Theories

2. Gardner's Theory of Multiple Intelligences

3. Sternberg's Triarchic Theory

## Measurement of Intelligence

1. Individual Intelligence Tests

2. Group Tests

## The Testing Controversy: Just What Do Intelligence Tests Measure?

- Is It Possible to Develop Culture-Free Intelligence Tests?

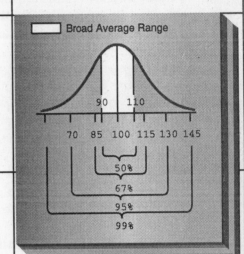

## The Determinants of Intelligence: Where Does Intelligence Come From?

1. Genetic Influences on Intelligence

2. Environmental Influences on Intelligence

3. On Ethnicity and Intelligence: A Concluding Note

## Psychology and Modern Life
- Mental Retardation and Giftedness

## Anxiety Interferes with Performance

Do you freeze up on exams, worried that you won't do well? We can turn one exam into a "do or die" catastrophic situation. Yes, we should try our best, but we are not doomed for life if we fail at something. Perhaps the following examples will help you see a failure for what it is, just one more step in the process of life.

- **Einstein**'s parents thought he was retarded. He spoke haltingly until age 9. He was advised by a teacher to drop out of high school: "You'll never amount to anything, Einstein."
- **Isaac Newton** did poorly in grade school.
- **Beethoven**'s music teacher once said of him, "as a composer he is hopeless".
- When **Thomas Edison** was a boy, his teachers told him he was too stupid to learn anything.
- **Woolworth** got a job in a dry goods store when he was 21, but his employers would not let him wait on a customer because he "didn't have enough sense."
- A newspaper editor fired **Walt Disney** because he had "no good ideas."
- **Leo Tolstoy** flunked out of college.
- **Louis Pasteur** was rated as "mediocre" in chemistry when he attended college.
- **Abraham Lincoln** entered the Black Hawk War as a captain and came out as a private.
- **Winston Churchill** failed the sixth grade.
- **Henry Ford** barely made it through high school.
- **Charles Goodyear** bungled an experiment and discovered vulcanized rubber.
- **Paul Gauguin** was a failed stockbroker before becoming a world famous painter.

> Failures mean very little
> in the big picture of our life.
> It is just important
> that we keep trying.

## Keeping Your Motivation in School

1. Be clear about your goals. Say that you want to start a study group. Then commit yourself to inviting people and setting a time and place to meet. Promise your classmates that you'll do this.

2. Commit to your goals, and ask a friend to hold you accountable. Focus on the importance of keeping your word.

3. Reassess your goals if your actions do not match your goals. Ask for help if your lack of skills or your bad habits are getting in the way.

4. Set up a reward system for yourself. This works as well for adults as it does for children. In fact, stop right now and think of some rewards you would enjoy (and can afford).

5. Positive self-talk can make a real difference. Replace "I can't stand this" with "I'll feel great when this is done" or "Doing this will help me get something I want".

6. Put on the pressure by pretending that the due date for your project has been moved up two weeks. Raising the stress level slightly can move you into action. Then the question of motivation is not the issue; your meeting the project date is.

7. Finding a role model can help you do the things a successful student must do. You can "try on" this person's actions and attitudes, looking for tools that feel right for you. Acting "as if" for a time can really make transformational changes in our lives.

# KEY TERMS AND CONCEPTS

1. Intelligence _____

2. Trait _____

3. Achievement _____

**Theories of Intelligence**

4. Factor _____

5. g _____

6. s _____

7. Factor analysis _____

8. Primary mental abilities _____

9. Triarchic _____

10. Contextual level _____

11. Experiential level _____

12. Componential level _____

13. Metacomponents _____

14. Performance components _____

15. Knowledge–acquisition components _____

**Measurement of Intelligence**

16. Mental age _____

17. Intelligence quotient (IQ) _____

**The Testing Controversy: Just What Do Intelligence Tests Measure?**

18. Cultural bias _____

19. Culture–free _____

**The Determinants of Intelligence: Where Does Intelligence Come From?**

21. Determinants _____

22. Heritability _____

# EXERCISES: MISSING INFORMATION

Fill in the missing information in each of the following tables. Check your answers on the next page.

**Table 1:     Louis Thurstone's (1) P_____ Mental Abilities**

| ABILITY | DESCRIPTION |
|---|---|
| Visual and spatial abilities | Visualizing forms and spatial relationships |
| (2) P_____ speed | Grasping perceptual details rapidly, perceiving similarities and differences between stimuli |
| Numerical ability | Computing numbers |
| (3) V_____ meaning | Knowing the meanings of words |
| Memory | Recalling information (words, sentences, etc.) |
| (4) W_____ fluency | Thinking of words quickly (rhyming, doing crossword puzzles, etc.) |
| Deductive reasoning | Deriving examples from general rules |
| (5) I_____ reasoning | Deriving general rules from examples |

## Table 2:  Subtests from the Wechsler Adult Intelligence Scale

| VERBAL SUBTESTS | (6) P_____ SUBTESTS |
|---|---|
| 1.  (7) I_____: "What is the capital of the United States?" "Who was Shakespeare?" | 7.  (10) D_____ Symbol: Learning and drawing meaningless figures that are associated with numbers. |
| 2.  Comprehension: "Why do we have zip codes?" "What does 'A stitch in time saves 9' mean?" | 8.  (11) P_____ Completion: Pointing to the missing part of a picture. |
| 3.  Arithmetic: "If 3 candy bars cost 25 cents, how much will 18 candy bars cost?" | 9.  (12) B_____ Design: Copying pictures of geometric designs using multicolored blocks. |
| 4.  (8) S_____: "How are good and bad alike?" "How are peanut butter and jelly alike?" | 10.  (13) P_____ Arrangement: Arranging cartoon pictures in sequence so that they tell a meaningful story. |
| 5.  Digit (9) S_____: Repeating a series of numbers forwards and backwards. | 11.  (14) O_____ Assembly: Putting pieces of a puzzle together so that they form a meaningful object. |
| 6.  Vocabulary: "What does canal mean?" | |

Items for verbal subtests 1, 2, 3, 4, and 6 are similar, but not identical, to actual test items on the WAIS.

## Table 3:  Variations in IQ Scores

| RANGE OF SCORES | PERCENT OF POPULATION | BRIEF DESCRIPTION |
|---|---|---|
| 130 and above | (15) _____ | Very (16)s_____ |
| 120–129 | (17) _____ | Superior |
| 110–119 | 16 | Above (18) a_____ |
| 100–109 | 25 | High average |
| 90–99 | (19) _____ | (20) L_____ average |
| 80–89 | 16 | Slow learner |
| 70–79 | 7 | Borderline |
| Below 70 | 2 | Intellectually deficient |

## Answer Key to *Exercises*

**Table 1**
1. Primary
2. Perceptual
3. Verbal
4. Word
5. Inductive

**Table 2**
6. Performance
7. Information
8. Similarities
9. Span
10. Digit
11. Picture
12. Block
13. Picture
14. Object

**Table 3**
15. 2
16. superior
17. 7
18. average
19. 25
20. Low

**SECTION 1: Theories of Intelligence**

**OBJ. 1:** (1) Ach_____ refers to knowledge and skills gained from experience.
(2) _____ence somehow provides the cognitive basis for academic achievement. Intelligence is usually perceived as underlying competence, or (3) _____ing ability, whereas achievement involves acquired competencies or performance.

**OBJ. 2:** Many investigators view intelligence as consisting of one or more mental abilities, or (4) f_____s. The Frenchman Alfred (5) _____t developed modern intelligence–testing methods about 100 years ago.

Charles (6) S_____ suggested that the behaviors we consider to be intelligent have a common underlying factor. Spearman labeled this factor (7) _____, for "general intelligence." Spearman also noted that even people are relatively superior in some areas and suggested that (8)s_____, or s, factors account for specific abilities. To test his views, Spearman developed a statistical method called (9) f_____ _____s.

Louis Thurstone suggested the presence of nine specific factors, which he labeled (10)_____ary mental abilities. One primary mental ability, (11) w_____ fluency, enables us to rapidly develop lists of words that rhyme.

**OBJ. 3:** Howard Gardner proposes the existence of (12) _____ kinds of intelligence. He believes that each kind of intelligence has its neurological base in a different area of the (13)b_____.
Gardner's "intelligences" include (14) l_____ ability, logical–mathematical ability, (15) bodily–_____ talents, musical talent, (16) spatial–_____ skills, awareness of one's own inner feelings, and sensitivity to other people's feelings. Gardner's critics question whether such special talents are equivalent in

meaning to what they see as a broader concept of (17) int_____.

**OBJ. 4:** Robert Sternberg views intelligence in terms of (18) _____tion processing. Sternberg constructed a three–level, or (19) _____ic, model of intelligence. The levels are contextual, experiential, and (20) co_____. The contextual level permits people to adapt to the demands of their (21) _____ments. On the (22) _____tial level, intelligent behavior is defined by the abilities to cope with novel situations and to process information automatically.

The componential level of intelligence consists of three processes: (23) meta_____, performance components, and (24) knowledge–_____ components. Metacomponents concern our awareness of our own (25) _____al processes. (26) P_____ components are the mental operations or skills used in solving problems or processing information. (27) _____–aquisition components are used in gaining new knowledge.

David (28) W_____ described intelligence as the "capacity of an individual to understand the world [and the] resourcefulness to cope with its challenges."

**SECTION 2: Measurement of Intelligence**

**OBJ. 5:** Binet devised an early scale for measuring intelligence because the (29) F_____ public school system sought an instrument that could identify children who were likely to be in need of special attention. The first version was termed the (30) Binet–_____ scale. The Binet–Simon scale yielded a score called a (31) m_____ age, or MA.

Louis (32) T_____ adapted the Binet–Simon scale for use with children in the United

States. The current version is the (33) _____ = Binet Intelligence Scale (SBIS). The SBIS yields an (34) int_____ q_____ (IQ).

The IQ reflects the relationship between a child's mental age and actual age, or (35)_____cal age (CA). The IQ was first computed by the formula IQ = ([36] M_____ Age/Chronological Age) x 100.

The (37) _____ler scales group test questions into a number of separate subtests. Wechsler described some of his scales as measuring (38) v_____ tasks and others as assessing (39) _____ance tasks.

Wechsler introduced the concept of the (40) _____tion IQ. The average test result at any age level is defined as an IQ score of (41) _____. Wechsler distributed IQ scores so that the middle 50% of them fall within the "broad (42) _____age range" of 90 to 110.

**OBJ. 6:** Lower–class U.S. children attain IQ scores some 10 to 15 points (43: *Circle one:* higher or lower) than those of middle– and upper–class children. African American children tend to attain IQ scores some 15–20 points (44: *Circle one:* higher or lower) than their White agemates. Hispanic American and Native American children score significantly (45: *Circle one:* above or below) the norms of White children.

Asian Americans frequently obtain (46: *Circle one:* higher or lower) scores on the math portion of the Scholastic Aptitude Test than White Americans. Students in China and Japan obtain (47: *Circle one:* higher or lower) scores than Americans on standardized achievement tests in math and science. According to Sue and Okazaki, the higher scores of Asian students may reflect different values in the home, the school, or the culture at large rather than differences in underlying (48) _____ence or competence. They argue that Asian Americans place relatively greater emphasis on the value of (49)_____tion.

## SECTION 3: The Testing Controversy: Just What Do Intelligence Tests Measure?

**OBJ. 7:** A survey of psychologists and educational specialists found that most (50: *Circle one:* do or do not) consider intelligence tests somewhat biased against African Americans and members of the lower classes. During the 1920s, intelligence tests were misused to prevent the (51) im_____ion of many Europeans and others into the United States. Scores on (52) _____ence tests may reflect cultural familiarity with the concepts required to answer test questions correctly, instead of underlying intellectual competence.

**OBJ. 8:** If scoring well on intelligence tests requires a certain type of cultural experience, the tests are said to have a (53) _____al bias. Psychologists such as Raymond B. (54) C_____ and Florence (55) G_____ have tried to construct culture–free intelligence tests. Middle-class White children (56: *Circle one:* do or do not) outperform African American children on Cattell's and Goodenough's tests.

Motivation to do well may also be a cultural factor. Highly motivated children (57: *Circle one:* do or do not) attain higher scores on intelligence tests than less–well–motivated children do.

## SECTION 4: The Determinants of Intelligence: Where Does Intelligence Come From?

**OBJ. 9:** Psychologists examine the IQ scores of closely and distantly related people who have been reared together or (58) a_____. If heredity is involved in human intelligence, closely related people ought to have (59: *Circle one:* more or less) similar IQs than distantly related or unrelated people, even when they are reared separately. The IQ scores of identical (MZ) twins are (60: *Circle one:* more or less) alike than the scores for any other pairs, even when the twins have been reared apart. Correlations between children and their foster parents and between cousins are (61: *Circle one:* strong or weak).

Studies generally suggest that the (62) _____ility of intelligence is between 40% and 60%. In other words, about half of the variations in IQ scores among people can be accounted for by (63) h_____.

Genetic pairs (such as MZ twins) reared together show (64: *Circle one:* higher or lower) correlations between IQ scores than similar genetic pairs (such as other MZ twins) who were reared apart. For this reason, the same group of studies suggests that the environment (65: *Circle one:* does or does not) play a role in IQ scores.

Another strategy for exploring genetic influences on intelligence is to compare the correlations between adopted children and their biological and (66) _____ive parents. When children are separated from their biological parents at early ages, one can argue that strong relationships between their IQs and those of their natural parents reflect (67) _____ic influences. Strong relationships between their IQs and those of their adoptive parents are (68: *Circle one:* more or less) likely to reflect environmental influences. Several studies have found a (69: *Circle one:* stronger or weaker) relationship between the IQ scores of adopted children and those of their biological parents than with the IQ scores of their adoptive parents.

**OBJ. 10:** The home environment and styles of parenting (70: *Circle one:* do or do not) appear to have an effect on IQ. Children of mothers who are emotionally and verbally responsive, who provide appropriate play materials, who are involved with their children, and who provide varied daily experiences during the early years attain (71: *Circle one:* higher or lower) IQ scores later on.

The child's early environment (72: *Circle one:* is or is not) linked to IQ scores and academic achievement. Good parent–child relationships and maternal encouragement of independence are (73: *Circle one:* positively or negatively) linked to Mexican American children's IQ scores.

(74) H_____ Start programs enhance the IQ scores and academic skills of poor children by exposing them to materials and activities that middle–class children take for granted. During the elementary and high school years, graduates of preschool programs are (75: *Circle one:* more or less) likely to be left back or placed in classes for slow learners.

Older people (76: *Circle one:* do or do not) show some decline in general intellectual ability as measured by scores on intelligence tests. The drop–off is (77: *Circle one:* most or least) acute in processing speed. People of (78: *Circle one:* high or low) SES tend to maintain intellectual functioning more adequately than people (79: *Circle one:* high or low) in SES.

**Answer Key to *Chapter Review***

1. Achievement
2. Intelligence
3. learning
4. factors
5. Binet
6. Spearman
7. *g*
8. specific
9. factor analysis
10. primary
11. word
12. seven
13. brain
14. language
15. bodily–kinesthetic
16. spatial–relations
17. intelligence

18. information
19. triarchic
20. componential
21. environments
22. experiential
23. metacomponents
24. knowledge–acquisition
25. intellectual
26. Performance
27. Knowledge–acquisition
28. Wechsler
29. French
30. Binet–Simon
31. mental
32. Terman
33. Stanford–Binet
34. intelligence quotient
35. chronological
36. Mental
37. Wechsler
38. verbal
39. performance
40. deviation
41. 100
42. average
43. lower
44. lower
45. below
46. higher
47. higher
48. intelligence

49. education
50. do
51. immigration
52. intelligence
53. cultural
54. Cattell
55. Goodenough
56. do
57. do
58. apart
59. more
60. more
61. weak
62. heritability
63. heredity
64. higher
65. does
66. adoptive
67. genetic
68. more
69. stronger
70. do
71. higher
72. is
73. positively
74. Head
75. less
76. do
77. most
78. high
79. low

| | Idioms | Explanation |
|---|---|---|
| 336 | signature human | things usually seen only in people |
| 336 | antlike | something totally focused on a tasks |
| 342 | "feeble-minded" | of low intelligence |
| 347 | narrow the gap | get closer to |

| | Cultural Reference | Explanation |
|---|---|---|
| 336 | mainframes | very large computers |
| 341 | testing casualties | victim of wrong test scores |
| 344 | a rich mine | a large and important amount |
| 346 | preschool | school for children too young for fornal schooling |
| 346 | left back | repeat a grade in school |

| | Additional Terms from the Text | |
|---|---|---|

| | Phrases and Expressions (Different Usage) | |
|---|---|---|
| 330 | adaptive | able to change when needed |
| 330 | unclad | no clothes on |
| 330 | familiarity | previous understanding |
| 331 | rhyme | words that end in the same sound |
| 333 | compose | write musical pieces |
| 334 | promising job | effectively |
| 335 | undergone | gone through |
| 335 | revision | changes |
| 336 | mimicked | copied |
| 336 | attain | achieve |
| 336 | cluster | group |
| 336 | examiner | person given the test |
| 336 | outscore | get higher test scores |
| 341 | extraction | ethnic background |
| 341 | vastly | greatly |
| 341 | underlying | basic |
| 341 | sentiments | feelings |
| 342 | inhibiting social mobility | stop improvement in social group |
| 342 | oppression | keeping someone at a low status |
| 342 | controversy | different opinions |
| 343 | determinants | what makes up |
| 343 | empirical | measurable |
| 344 | ingenious | create, smart |
| 344 | point up | show |
| 344 | shortcomings | problems |
| 344 | selectively bred | mate together for a reason |
| 344 | distantly related | not a close relative |
| 344 | reared separately | brought up apart |
| 344 | reunited | brought together |
| 345 | be too broad | too general |
| 345 | impartial | not caring |
| 345 | verbally responsive | talk back to them a lot |
| 346 | varied | often something different |
| 346 | maternal | mother |
| 346 | enriched | very interesting |
| 347 | attend | go to |
| 347 | extensively | a large amount |
| 347 | doubtlessly | certainly |
| 347 | dignity | worth of respect |
| 347 | endure | experience |
| 353 | abnormalities | damaged |
| 353 | outstanding | unusually good |

Chapter 9     Intelligence

Chapter 9 Intelligence

1. According to the text, critics of Gardner's theory question
(a) his statistical methods.
(b) the effort to expand the numbers of factors that can be identified as aspects of intellectual function.
(c) whether special talents are equivalent in meaning to what they see as a broader concept of intelligence.
(d) whether environmental factors contribute to intellectual functioning.

2. According to the text, _____ percent of the population is at least above average in intelligence.
(a) 2
(b) 7
(c) 16
(d) 25

3. According to the text, several studies on IQ have confused the factors of _____ and ethnicity because disproportionate numbers of African, Hispanic, and Native Americans are found among the lower socioeconomic classes.
(a) race
(b) gender
(c) social class
(d) intelligence

4. Which of the following would **NOT** qualify as a cultural factor that contributes to performance on intelligence tests?
(a) motivation to do well
(b) familiarity with the subjects that test questions are based on
(c) opportunity to play with pencils, paper, and numbers
(d) genetic factors

5. Among older people, the drop–off in general intellectual functioning is most acute in
(a) processing speed.
(b) knowledge of the meanings of words.
(c) categorical thinking.
(d) spatial–relations skills.

6. Who suggested the existence of the greatest number of factors in intellectual functioning?
(a) Guilford
(b) Gardner
(c) Spearman
(d) Thurstone

7. All in all, studies generally suggest that the heritability of intelligence is between _____ percent.
(a) 20 and 40
(b) 40 and 60
(c) 60 and 80
(d) 80 and 100

8. Baumrind and Jackson argue that a strong belief in _____ can undermine parental and educational efforts to enhance children's intellectual development.
(a) musical training
(b) g
(c) the predominance of environmental factors
(d) the predominance of genetic factors

9. Who considers bodily–kinesthetic talent to be a kind of intelligence?
(a) Simon
(b) Williams
(c) Gardner
(d) Terman

10. Research suggests that musical training enhances
(a) spatial reasoning.
(b) vocabulary.
(c) mathematical ability.
(d) general underlying competence.

11. Who developed a statistical method called factor analysis?
(a) Cattell
(b) Spearman
(c) Stern
(d) Terman

12. According to Sternberg, deciding which problem to solve is one of the _____ of intelligence.
    (a) experiential components
    (b) metacomponents
    (c) performance components
    (d) contextual components

13. A friend says, "I keep on hearing all this stuff about IQ's. What is an IQ, anyhow?" You note that your psychology textbook defines an *IQ* as
    (a) a personality trait.
    (b) word fluency.
    (c) the capacity to understand the world and the resourcefulness to cope with its challenges.
    (d) a score on an intelligence test.

14. According to the text, who conceived of intelligence as a group of primary mental abilities?
    (a) Charles Spearman
    (b) Louis Thurstone
    (c) Louis Terman
    (d) Alfred Binet

15. An intelligence test constructed by _____ yields a deviation IQ.
    (a) Raymond Cattell
    (b) Louis Terman
    (c) David Wechsler
    (d) Arthur Jensen

16. Intelligence test scores tend to correlate about _____ with school grades.
    (a) +0.50 to +0.60
    (b) +0.60 to +0.70
    (c) +0.70 to +0.80
    (d) +0.80 to +0.90

17. Culture–fair tests have not lived up to their promise in that
    (a) middle–class White children outperform African American children on them.
    (b) they do not have adequate test–retest reliability.
    (c) it has not been possible to standardize them.
    (d) test results do not correlate with performance on the Stanford–Binet or Wechsler scales.

18. A friend says, "We run experiments to find out everything else, so why can't we run experiments to find out exactly how much of a person's intelligence is due to heredity and how much is due to the environment?" You point out that we do not have experimental evidence concerning the genetic determinants of human intelligence because
    (a) it would be unethical to selectively breed people.
    (b) it is theoretically impossible to separate the effects of heredity and the environment.
    (c) data from kinship and adoptee studies has been faked.
    (d) psychologists have not been able to agree on the definition of intelligence in humans.

19. Which of the following groups tends to attain the highest scores on intelligence tests?
    (a) Caucasians
    (b) Hispanic Americans
    (c) African Americans
    (d) Japanese

20. Test takers learn and draw meaningless figures that are associated with numbers in the _____ subtest of the Wechsler Adult Intelligence Scale.
    (a) Digit Symbol
    (b) Picture Completion
    (c) Block Design
    (d) Picture Arrangement

## Answer Key to *Posttest*

| | |
|---|---|
| 1. C | 11. B |
| 2. D | 12. B |
| 3. C | 13. D |
| 4. D | 14. B |
| 5. A | 15. C |
| 6. A | 16. B |
| 7. B | 17. A |
| 8. D | 18. A |
| 9. D | 19. D |
| 10. A | 20. A |

| | |
|---|---|
| Intelligence | Experiential level |
| Trait | Componential level |
| Achievement | Metacomponents |
| Factor | Performance components |
| Factor analysis | Knowledge-acquisition components |
| Primary mental abilities | Mental age |
| Contextual level | Intelligence quotient (IQ) |

Chapter 9 Intelligence   251

| | |
|---|---|
| Those aspects of intelligence that permit people to cope with novel situations and process information automatically. | A complex and controversial concept. |
| The level of intelligence that consists of metacomponents, performance components, and knowledge-acquisition components. | A distinguishing characteristic that is presumed to account for consistency in behavior. |
| Components of intelligence that are based on self-awareness of our intellectual processes. | That which is attained by one's efforts and made possible by one's abilities. |
| The mental operations used in processing information. | A cluster of related items such as those found on an intelligence test. |
| Components used in gaining knowledge, such as encoding and relating new knowledge to existing knowledge. | A statistical technique that allows researchers to determine the relation-ships among large numbers of items such as test items. |
| The accumulated months of credit that a person earns on the Stanford-Binet Intelligence Scale. | According to Thurstone, the basic abilities that make up intelligence. |
| Originally, a ratio obtained by dividing a child's score (or mental age) on an intelligence test by his or her chronological age. | Those aspects of intelligent behavior that permit people to adapt to their environment. |

# Chapter 10  Motivation and Emotion

Directions: This *PRETEST* will give you feedback about how well you understand Chapter 10. In order to enhance your mastery of Chapter 10, complete all the sections of this chapter of the Study Guide. Then you can take the *POSTTEST* and compare your results.

1. Some _____ are states of physical deprivation.
   (a) primary drives
   (b) stimulus motives
   (c) psychological needs
   (d) physiological needs

2. Jamie has wanted to work as an artist since she was a child. This is an example of a(n)
   (a) need.
   (b) instinct.
   (c) drive.
   (d) motive.

3. According to the text, _____ tend to be species–specific.
   (a) drives
   (b) instincts
   (c) needs
   (d) motives

4. _____ asserted that we have social instincts, such as love and sympathy.
   (a) William James
   (b) Walter Cannon
   (c) Stanley Schachter
   (d) Sigmund Freud

5. We would expect an ethologist to be supportive of _____ theory.
   (a) drive-reduction
   (b) humanistic
   (c) instinct
   (d) cognitive-appraisal

6. A major criticism of on-line, interactive sex is that it
   (a) wastes space on the information super-highway.
   (b) tends to maintain sexist illusions about women.
   (c) is too costly for most to afford.
   (d) it attracts more women than men.

7. According to the text, physiological drives operate largely according to _____ theory.
   (a) instinct
   (b) psychoanalytic
   (c) humanistic
   (d) drive–reduction

8. Learning theory views sexual orientation in terms of
   (a) the sexual orientation of parents.
   (b) genetic factors.
   (c) early reinforcements of sexual behavior.
   (d) levels of testosterone

9. All of the following are activating effects of sex hormones **EXCEPT**
   (a) sex drive.
   (b) sexual response.
   (c) structure of genitals.
   (d) sexual interest.

10. Cognitive-dissonance can best be described as
(a) awareness that two thoughts do not make sense together.
(b) an indicator of affiliation motivation.
(c) aggressive motives.
(d) a force of achievement motivation.

11. According to the text, our optimal levels of arousal
(a) are determined by learning experiences.
(b) are constant throughout the day.
(c) reflect our preferences for leisure activities.
(d) are determined to some degree by innate factors.

12. The opponent-process theory focuses on
(a) reducing primary drives.
(b) learning to associate acquired drives.
(c) how emotions tend to trigger the opposing emotion.
(d) how people seek to reduce rather than increase the amount of stimulation impinging on them.

13. A parent notes that you are taking a psychology course and asks you, "Has anybody done research on how parents instill a desire to get high grades and to go somewhere in life in their children?" You clear your throat and answer that, "Winterbottom found that the mothers of children with high *n* Ach
(a) were, on the average, superior in intelligence."
(b) had fed their children on demand as infants."
(c) encouraged independent thought and action equally in their sons and daughters."
(d) made demands and imposed restrictions on their sons in primary school."

14. Stanley Schachter explains the findings of his research into anxiety and *n* Aff by means of
(a) James–Lange theory.
(b) cognitive dissonance theory.
(c) the theory of social comparison.
(d) the wheel of emotions.

15. Psychoanalysts refer to the venting of aggressive impulses as _____.

(a) dominance
(b) catharsis
(c) aggression
(d) power

16. According to the text, the emotion of _____ involves predominantly parasympathetic arousal.
(a) anxiety
(b) depression
(c) anger
(d) love

17. A friend asks you how people are "hooked up" to lie detectors. You inform him that the polygraph provides information about emotional responses by assessing each of the following, EXCEPT
(a) heart rate.
(b) electrodermal response.
(c) brain waves.
(d) blood pressure.

18. Intrinsic reward is
(a) self-satisfaction.
(b) money.
(c) prestige.
(d) recognition.

19. Who argued that events trigger arousal, action, and the cognitive experiencing of an emotion simultaneously?
(a) Philip Bard
(b) Stanley Schachter
(c) William James
(d) Jerome Singer

20. When compared to people of normal weight, obese people tend to
(a) be less sensitive to the taste of food.
(b) chew more frequently.
(c) eat lower quantities of sweet foods.
(d) eat lower quantities of bitter foods.

### Answer Key to *Pretest*

| | | |
|---|---|---|
| 1. D | 8. C | 15. B |
| 2. D | 9. C | 16. B |
| 3. B | 10. A | 17. C |
| 4. A | 11. D | 18. A |
| 5. C | 12. C | 19. A |
| 6. B | 13. D | 20. D |
| 7. D | 14. C | |

Chapter 10 deals with motivation and emotion. Motives concern the "whys" of behavior. Emotions can motivate behavior, but emotions are also responses to situations.

Distinctions are made between motives, needs, drives, and incentives. Then several theories of motivation are outlined. According to instinct theory, inherited dispositions activate specific behavior patterns, or *FAPs*. According to drive–reduction theory, people learn to engage in behaviors that have the effect of reducing primary and acquired drives. According to humanistic theory, behavior can be motivated by the conscious desire for personal growth. Some cognitive theorists hypothesize that people are born "scientists" who innately strive to understand the world around them so that they can predict and control events. Other cognitive theorists assert that people are motivated to achieve cognitive consistency.

Physiological needs (states of deprivation) give rise to physiological drives (aroused conditions that activate behavior that will satisfy these needs). Physiological drives largely operate according to drive–reduction theory, and that there is a bodily tendency (called homeostasis) to maintain a steady state. The hunger drive is influenced by internal physical factors, such as stomach contractions and the blood sugar level, and by psychological factors, such as the time of day or observing others eating. Thirst is largely regulated by receptors in the kidneys and the hypothalamus.

Stimulus motives, such as sensory stimulation, activity, exploration, and manipulation, are not homeostatic. Rather they act to increase the stimulation impinging upon us. It appears that each of us has optimal levels of arousal at which we function most efficiently. The examples of the needs for achievement, affiliation, and power are explored in depth.

Emotion is defined. Bridges and Izard's views on the development of emotions are described. Ekman's research is described as evidence for the universality of the expression of certain emotions. It is shown how facial feedback may contribute to emotional experience. The James-Lange, Cannon-Bard, and cognitive–appraisal theories of emotional arousal are outlined and evaluated. Romantic love is discussed as an emotion which is found only in cultures that idealize the concept.

The section on *Psychology and Modern Life* explores coping with obesity.

## LEARNING OBJECTIVES

| | Coming to Terms with Motivation |
|---|---|
| 1. Define *motives*, *needs*, *drives*, and *incentives*. | |
| | **Theories of Motivation: The Whys of Why** |
| 2. Explain and evaluate the *instinct*, *drive-reduction*, *opponent-process*, *humanistic*, *cognitive*, and *sociocultural theories* of motivation. | |

3. Explain the concept of *homeostasis*.

### Hunger: Do You Go by "Tummy-Time"?

4. Summarize research concerning the hunger drive.

### Sex: A Sociocultural Perspective

5. Explain the difference between the organizing and the activating effects of sex hormones.

### Stimulus Motives

6. Explain what is meant by *stimulus motives*.

7. Describe the effects of *sensory deprivation*.

### Cognitive Consistency: Making Things Fit

8. Explain the concept of *effort justification*.

### The Three A's of Motivation: Achievement, Affiliation, and Aggression

9. Summarize research on the need for *achievement*.

10. Summarize research on the need for *affiliation*.

11. Summarize research on *aggression*.

### Emotion: Adding Color to Life

12. Define *emotion*, and describe the role of emotions in human behavior.

13. Summarize research concerning the accuracy of lie detectors.

14. Explain the Bridges and Izard theories of the development of emotions.

15. Describe research concerning the universality of the expression of emotions.

16. Explain the *facial–feedback hypothesis* of emotion.

17. Explain and evaluate the James–Lange, Cannon–Bard, and cognitive–appraisal theories of emotion.

18. Summarize research concerning psychological and biological factors in obesity.

### Psychology and Modern Life

### Additional Notes

## Coming to Terms with Motivation

## Theories of Motivation: The Whys of Why

1. Instinct Theory: "Doing What Comes Naturally"?

2. Drive-Reductionism and Homeostasis: "Steady, Steady..."

3. Opponent-Process Theory: From Lambs to Lions

4. Humanistic Theory: " I've Got to Be Me"?

5. Cognitive Theory: "I Think, Therefore I Am Consistent"?

6. Sociocultural Theory

7. Evaluation: Which Whys Rise to the Occasion?

Self-Actualization
Fulfillment of unique potentials

Esteem
Achievement, competence, approval, recognition, prestige, status

Love and Belongingness
Intimate relationships, social groups, friends

Safety
Protection from environment, housing, clothing, crime security

Physiological
Hunger, thirst, elimination, warmth, fatigue, pain avoidance, sexual release

## Hunger: Do You Go by "Tummy-Time"?

## Sex: A Sociocultural Perspective

1. Organizing & Activating Effects of Sex Hormones

2. Sexual Orientation

## Stimulus Motives

1. Sensory Stimulation and Activity

2. Exploration and Manipulation

## Cognitive Consistency: Making Things Fit

1. Balance Theory

2. Cognitive-Dissonance Theory:
   "If I Did It, It Must Be Important"?

## The Three A's of Motivation: Achievement, Affiliation, and Aggression

1. Achievement

2. Affiliation: "People Who Need People"

3. Aggression: Some Facts of Life and Death

## Emotion: Adding Color to Life

1. Arousal, Emotions, and Lie Detection

2. How Many Emotions Are There?
   Where Do They Come From?

3. The Expression of Emotions

4. The Facial-Feedback Hypothesis

5. Theories of Emotion: Is Feeling First?

## Obesity

## Changing a Habit

1. Choose a target behavior. Identify the activity you want to change.

2. Record a baseline. Count the number of desired or undesired responses you make each day.

3. Establish goals. Remember to set realistic and progressive goals for gradual improvement on each successive week. Set daily goals that add up to the weekly goals.

4. Choose reinforcers. Set up daily rewards and weekly rewards that are meaningful to you.

5. Record your progress.

6. Collect and enjoy your rewards.

7. Adjust your plan as needed.

### Behavioral Contract

If you have trouble sticking with the above steps, try a behavioral contract. In the contract you state a specific problem behavior you want to control, or a goal you want to achieve. Also state the rewards you will receive, privileges you will forfeit, or punishments you must accept. The contract should be typed and signed by you and a person you trust.

### Good Ways to Break Bad Habits

1. **Stop reinforcing the habit.**

   Try to discover what is reinforcing a response and remove, avoid, or delay the reinforcement.

2. **Try alternate behaviors.**

   Try to use the same reinforcement with new responses. For example, if you want to stop smoking but you realize your smoking provides you with your only breaks at work, try taking a walk in the fresh air whenever you want a cigarette.

3. **Avoid cues that trigger the habit.**

   Avoid the cues that precede the bad habit you are trying to break. For example, don't walk in the supermarket door by the bakery if you are trying not to eat sweets.

4. **Try incompatible responses.**

   Do something that is incompatible with your bad habit. For example, if you do a jigsaw puzzle while you watch T.V., you can't eat.

1. Cognitive-dissonance theory _____

### Coming to Terms with Motivation

2. Motive _____

3. Need _____

4. Drive _____

5. Physiological drives _____

6. Incentive _____

### Theories of Motivation: The Whys of Why

7. Instinct _____

8. Fixed action pattern (FAP) _____

9. Ethologist _____

10. Releaser _____

11. Pheromones _____

12. Drive-reduction theory _____

13. Primary drives _____

14. Acquired drives _____

15. Homeostasis _____

16. Opponent-process theory _____

17. Self–actualization _____

### Hunger: Do You Go by "Tummy-Time"?

18. Satiety _____

19. Lesion _____

20. Ventromedial nucleus (VMN) _____

21. Hyperphagic _____

22. Lateral hypothalamus _____

23. Aphagic _____

### Sex: A Sociocultural Perspective

24. Organizing effects _____

25. Activating effects _____

26. Testosterone _____

27. Estrus _____

28. Menopause _____

29. Sexual orientation _____

30. Heterosexual _____

31. Gay male _____

32. Lesbian _____

33. Bisexual _____

34. Concordance _____

### Stimulus Motives

35. Stimulus motives _____

36. Sensory deprivation _____

37. Innate _____

38. Novel stimulation _____

39. Copulate _____

### Cognitive Consistency: Making Thinks Fit

40. Balance theory _____

41. Nonbalance _____

42. Imbalance _____

43. Attitude-discrepant behavior _____

44. Effort justification _____

### The Three A's of Motivation: Achievement, Affiliation, and Aggression

45. Thematic Apperception Test _____

46. Affiliation _____

47. Theory of social comparison _____

48. Catharsis _____

### Emotion: Adding Color to Life

49. Emotion _____

50. Sympathetic _____

51. Parasympathetic _____

52. Facial–feedback hypothesis _____

53. Euphoric _____

# CHAPTER REVIEW

## SECTION 1: Coming to Terms with Motivation

**OBJ. 1:** Motives can be defined as hypothetical states within organisms that (1) _____vate behavior and direct organisms toward (2) _____s. Physiological needs generally reflect states of physical (3) _____tion. Psychological needs (4: *Circle one:* are or are not) necessarily based on states of deprivation and may be learned, or acquired through (5) ex_____. Needs give rise to (6) _____s, which are psychological in nature and arouse us to action. An (7) _____tive is an object, person, or situation that is perceived as being capable of satisfying a need.

## SECTION 2: Theories of Motivation: The Whys of Why

**OBJ. 2:** According to the (8) in_____ theory of motivation, animals are born with preprogrammed tendencies to behave in certain ways in certain situations. Within instinct theory, stimuli called (9) _____sers elicit innate fixed (10) _____ patterns, or *FAPs*. William James and William (11) Mc_____ argued that people have various instincts that lead not only to survival, but also to (12) s_____ behavior.

According to Clark (13) _____'s drive–reduction theory of motivation, (14) _____ds are pleasant because they reduce drives. As a consequence, we are motivated to engage in (15) be_____ that leads to rewards. Drive–reduction theorists differentiate between (16) pr_____ (innate) drives and (17) _____red (learned) drives.

(18) _____istic psychologists argue that behavior can be growth–oriented. Humanists believe that people are motivated to consciously strive for personal (19) _____ment. Abraham (20) M_____ hypothesized that people have a hierarchy of needs, including an innate need for self–actualization. Maslow's hierarchy includes physiologi-cal needs, safety needs, love and (21) _____ness needs, esteem needs, and, at the top, the need for (22) self–_____ation.

## SECTION 3: Hunger: Do You Go by "Tummy-Time"?

**OBJ. 3:** Physiological drives are unlearned and thus also referred to as (23) _____ry drives. Physi-ological drives generally function according to the principle of (24) _____sis, which is the body's tendency to maintain a steady state.

**OBJ. 4:** Hunger is regulated by several internal mechanisms, including (25) _____ch contrac-tions, blood (26) s_____ level, receptors in the mouth and liver, and the responses of the hypothala-mus. Chewing and swallowing provide some sensa-tions of (27) _____ty. The (28) _____al nucleus (VMN) of the hypothalamus apparently functions as a stop–eating center. Lesions in this area lead to (29) _____gia in rats, a condition in which the animals grow to several times their normal body weight, but then level off. It is as if lesions in the VMN raise the (30) _____t point of the stop–eating center to be triggered at a much higher level. The (31) _____al hypothalamus apparently functions as a start–eating center. Lesions in the lateral hypothalamus can lead to (32) _____gia in rats.

## SECTION 4: Sex: A Sociocultural Perspective

**OBJ. 5:** The (33)_____ltural perspective of sexuality studies how sexuality is expressed from culture to culture.

The mating behavior of animals has been shown to be controlled by hormonal level; and human sexual response (34: *Circle one:* has also or has not) been shown to be controlled by hormonal levels.

In reference to sexual orientation, (35) _____ual people are sexually attracted to people of the other gender.

## SECTION 5: Stimulus Motives

**OBJ. 6:** Stimulus motives are like physiological needs in that they are also (36)____nate. Physiological needs motivate us to (37: *Circle one:* increase or reduce) the stimulation that impinges upon us. Stimulus motives, by contrast, motivate us to (38: *Circle one:* increase or decrease) the stimulation impinging upon us.

People and many lower animals have needs for stimulation and activity, for exploration and manipulation. Sensation–seekers engage in behavior that results in a high level of (39)_____tion. Four factors appear to be involved in sensation seeking: seeking of thrill and (40)_____ture; tendency to act out on impulses, or (41) dis_____; seeking of experience; and susceptibility to (42)_____dom.

**OBJ. 7:** Studies in sensory (43)_____ation show that lack of stimulation is aversive. After a few hours, subjects in these studies become bored and (44)_____table. As time goes on, some of them report visual (45)_____ations, which tend to be limited to geometric figures. After a few days, subjects find it difficult to (46) co_____ on problems.

## SECTION 6: Cognitive Consistency: Making Things Fit

**OBJ. 8:** Cognitive theorists propose that people want to have realistic views of the world, and (47) ad____ their pictures of the world to reduce discrepancies and accommodate new information. They tend to explain their behavior so that (48: *Circle one:* unpleasant or pleasant) activites seem worthwhile.

## SECTION 7: The Three A's of Motivation: Achievement, Affliliation, and Aggression

**OBJ. 9:** Psychologist David (49) Mc_____ pioneered the assessment of *n* Ach through fantasy. In doing so, McClelland used Murray's Thematic (50)_____tion Test, or TAT.

People with high *n* Ach attain (51: *Circle one:* higher or lower) grades and earn (52: *Circle one:* more or less) money than people of comparable ability with lower *n* Ach. Douglas Bray found that *n* was helpful in getting ahead at AT&T, but two other factors were more important: (53)_____ative skills and (54) inter_____ skills. Mothers with high *n* tend to encourage their children to think and act (55)_____dently.

**OBJ. 10:** The need for (56)_____ation prompts us to join groups and make friends. Stanley Schachter found that anxiety tends to (57: *Circle one:* increase or decrease) the need for affiliation. When anxious, we prefer to affiliate with people who (58:*Circle one:* share or do not share) our predicaments. Schachter explains this preference through the theory of social (59)_____ison. This theory holds that when we are in (60)_____guous situations, we seek to affiliate with people with whom we can compare feelings and behaviors.

**OBJ. 11:** The need for (61) p_____ is the need to control organizations and other people. So-called leadership-motive syndrome is characterized by high needs for power and (62) self–_____, and a low need for (63)_____tion. The need for power is often linked to prolonged activity of the (64)_____tic branch of the autonomic nervous system. Prolonged sympathetic activation can lead to high (65) b_____ pressure and the breaking down of the body's (66)_____une system.

## SECTION 8: Emotion: Adding Color to Life

**OBJ. 12:** An emotion is a state of (67)_____ing. Emotions have physiological, (68)_____al, and cognitive components. Emotions motivate behavior, but can also serve as (69)_____nses to situations and as goals in themselves. The emotion of anxiety involves predominantly (70)_____etic arousal. The emotion of depression involves predominantly (71)_____etic arousal.

**OBJ. 13:** So–called lie detectors are known technically as (72)_____aphs. Polygraphs assess sympathetic (73)_____al rather than lies per se. Polygraphs monitor four bodily functions: heart rate; blood (74)_____e; respiration rate; and

(75) _____ dermal response, which is an index of sweating. Supporters of the polygraph claim that it is successful in over (76) _____ percent of cases. However, subjects can reduce the accuracy rate of polygraphs, as lie detectors, by thinking about disturbing events during the interview, biting their tongues, or creating (77) _____ etic arousal in other ways.

**OBJ. 14:** According to Bridges, we are born with (78) _____ emotion(s). Other emotions become (79) _____ tiated as time passes. According to the theory proposed by Carroll (80) _____ d, all emotions are present and adequately differentiated at birth. However, they are not shown all at once. Instead, emotions emerge in response to the child's developing needs and (81) _____ tional sequences.

**OBJ. 15:** The expression of many emotions appears to be (82) _____ sal. (83) Sm_____ appears to be a universal sign of friendliness and approval. Psychologist Paul (84) E_____ showed subjects throughout the world photographs of people posing emotions, such as anger, disgust, fear, happiness, sadness, and surprise. All groups correctly identified the emotions being portrayed.

**OBJ. 16:** According to the (85) f_____ – f_____ hypothesis, posing intense facial expressions can heighten emotional response. Inducing (86) _____ ing leads subjects to report more positive feelings. Subjects who are induced to frown rate cartoons as more (87) ag_____. It seems that intense expressions heighten (88) _____ al; they may also provide muscular feedback that is characteristic of certain feeling states.

**OBJ. 17:** Psychologists are not agreed as to the relative importance of physiological arousal and (89) co_____ appraisal in activating particular emotions. According to the James–Lange theory, emotions have specific patterns of (90) ar_____ and (91) ac_____ that are triggered by certain external events. Emotions follow, rather than cause, the overt behavioral (92) re_____ s to events.

The Cannon–Bard theory proposes that processing of events by the brain gives rise simultaneously to

(93) _____ nomic activity (arousal), (94) _____ lar activity (action), and cognitive activity (the mental experiencing of the emotion). From this view, emotions (95) ac_____ bodily responses, but are not produced by bodily changes.

According to the theory of cognitive appraisal, emotions have largely similar patterns of (96) _____ al. Emotions essentially vary along a (97) _____ g to weak dimension that is determined by one's level of arousal. The emotion a person will experience in response to an external stimulus reflects that person's (98) ap_____ of the stimulus—that is, the meaning of the stimulus to him or her. A classic study by (99) Sch_____ and Singer suggested that a similar pattern of arousal can be labeled quite differently, depending on a person's situation. However, the Schachter and Singer study has been replicated with different results.

Research seems to suggest that patterns of arousal are more specific than suggested by the theory of (100) _____ itive appraisal, but that cognitive appraisal does play an important role in determining our responses to events.

## SECTION 9: Psychology and Modern Life

**OBJ. 18:** Obesity (101: *Circle one:* runs or does not run) in families. A study of Scandinavian adoptees by Stunkard found that children bear a closer resemblance in weight to their (102: *Circle one:* adoptive or biological) parents than to their (103: *Circle one:* adoptive or biological) parents.

One reason that obese people may desire to eat more than normal-weight is that they have larger numbers of (104) f_____ cells, or adipose tissue. As time passes after eating, the (105) _____ d sugar level drops, causing fat to be drawn off from these cells in order to provide further nourishment. The resultant fat deficiency is signalled to the (106) _____ amus, triggering the hunger drive. Obese people may send (107: *Circle one:* stronger or weaker) signals to the hypothalamus because of the larger number of fat cells.

Fatty tissue metabolizes food more (108: *Circle one:* rapidly or slowly) than muscle. For this reason, a person with a high fat–to–muscle ratio will metabolize food (109: *Circle one:* less or more) slowly than a person of the same weight with a (110: *Circle one:* higher or lower) fat–to–muscle ratio. The average man has a (111: *Circle one:* higher or lower) fat–to–muscle ratio than the average woman.

Keesey notes that people who are dieting and people who have lost significant amounts of weight usually do not eat enough to satisfy the (112) _____t points in their hypothalamuses. As a consequence, compensating metabolic forces are set in motion; that is, (113: *Circle one:* fewer or more) calories are burned. Repeated cycles of dieting and regaining lost weight—referred to as (114) "_____ – _____ dieting"—might be particularly traumatic to one's set point. Brownell points out that yo–yo dieting may teach the body that it will be intermittently deprived of food, thereby (115: *Circle one:* accelerating or slowing down) the metabolism whenever future food intake is restricted.

Many people are highly responsive to (116: *Circle one:* internal or external) cues for hunger, such as the smell of food or seeing other people eat. However, the links between obesity and responsiveness to external cues have recently been brought into question.

Effective diets tend to use combinations of the following elements: improving (117) nu_____al knowledge, decreasing intake of (118) _____ries, exercise, and behavior (119) _____cation.

### Answer Key to *Chapter Review*

1. motivate
2. goals
3. deprivation
4. are not
5. experience
6. drives
7. incentive
8. instinct
9. releasers
10. action
11. McDougall
12. social
13. Hull's
14. rewards
15. behavior
16. primary
17. acquired
18. Humanistic
19. fulfillment
20. Maslow
21. belongingness
22. self–actualization
23. primary
24. homeostasis
25. stomach
26. sugar
27. satiety
28. ventromedial
29. hyperphagia
30. set
31. lateral
32. aphagia
33. sociocultural
34. has not
35. heterosexual
36. innate
37. reduce
38. increase
39. stimulation
40. adventure
41. disinhibition
42. boredom
43. deprivation
44. irritable
45. hallucinations
46. concentrate
47. adjust
48. unpleasant
49. McClelland
50. Apperception

51. higher
52. more
53. administrative
54. interpersonal
55. independently
56. affiliation
57. increase
58. share
59. comparison
60. ambiguous
61. power
62. self-control
63. affiliation
64. sympathetic
65. blood
66. immune
67. feeling
68. situational
69. responses
70. sympathetic
71. parasympathetic
72. polygraphs
73. arousal
74. pressure
75. electrodermal
76. 90
77. sympathetic
78. one
79. differentiated
80. Izard
81. maturational
82. universal
83. Smiling
84. Ekman
85. facial–feedback
86. smiling
87. aggressive
88. arousal
89. cognitive
90. arousal
91. action

92. responses
93. autonomic
94. muscular
95. accompany
96. arousal
97. strong
98. appraisal
99. Schachter
100. cognitive
101. runs
102. biological
103. adoptive
104. fat
105. blood
106. hypothalamus
107. stronger
108. slowly
109. more
110. lower
111. higher
112. set
113. fewer
114. yo–yo
115. slowing down
116. external
117. nutritional
118. calories
119. modification

| Idioms | | Explanation |
|---|---|---|
| 356 | tortuously slowly | irritating and slow |
| 356 | breakneck speed | very fast |
| 357 | propel...toward goals | motivate the organisms to work to achieve goals |
| 360 | well-fed society | fairly rich nation |
| 363 | fog of the anesthesia | not thinking clearly after a strong pain killer |
| 364 | pearl of an island | beautiful island |
| 366 | pulling down the curtains | pull down coverings on windows so no one can see |
| 366 | new wrinkle | new approach |
| 366 | hard on the heels | right afterwards |

| Cultural Reference | | Explanation |
|---|---|---|
| 360 | manifest destiny | clearly their right |
| 366 | frozen on the monitor | figure not moving on computer screen |
| 367 | an old fogy like me | an older person |
| 367 | cuneiform writings | ancient writing |
| 369 | slings and arrows | attacks (slings and arrows are weapons) |
| 369 | allegiance to Christian beliefs | committed to following the teachings of Jesus Christ |
| 371 | couch potato | someone who sits around and does nothing |
| 371 | breakneck speeds | so fast people could get hurt and break their necks |
| 371 | catching the big wave | riding an ocean wave on a board |
| 372 | arms of mazes | tunnels of a group of tunnels |
| 372 | zapping video monsters | killing monsters as part of a video game |
| 375 | bind us together | hold together in a relationship |
| 375 | tear up asunder | break up a relationship |
| 375 | academic tasks | school projects |
| 377 | nonentrepreneurial | not part of their own business |
| 377 | Mortal Kombat | a video game that is very violent |
| 377 | decapitate | to cut off the head |
| 380 | Inquisition | A court established by the Roman Catholic Church to find and punish heretics |
| 381 | to ferret out | to uncover; refers to a rodent which is good at hunting |
| 384 | to flunk | to not get a passing grade |
| 384 | down in the dumps | feeling very low; a dump is where trash is put |
| 386 | confederate | someone who acts like a subject but who is really working secretly with the experimenters. |
| 386 | worked for the Oscars | acting very well; Oscars are awards given to movie stars |

| Phrases and Expressions (Different Usage) | | |
|---|---|---|
| 356 | dutifully | carefully did her duty |
| 356 | momentous | very important |
| 356 | fidgeted | moved nervously |
| 356 | weary | very tired |
| 357 | divergent ways | different from one another |
| 357 | counterparts | are similar to one another |
| 359 | cuddle | hug closely |
| 359 | rebound anxiety | anxiety comes back |
| 359 | in awe of | to admire and look up to |
| 359 | combat | work against |
| 359 | diminish | get smaller |
| 359 | aimed toward | focused on |
| 360 | insurmountable | can't get over |
| 360 | hurdles | problems |
| 360 | prestige | important role |
| 360 | status | high level of recognition |
| 360 | novelty | something new and different |
| 360 | order | things organized in a pleasing way |
| 360 | enable | help |
| 360 | stokes | increases |
| 360 | arousing | leads to sexual excitement |
| 360 | milieu | environment |
| 361 | primping | to dress carefully |
| 361 | gossiping | to pass rumors |
| 361 | circular explanations | explaining something so your argument depends back on itself |
| 361 | maternal instinct | inborn desire to be a mother |
| 361 | incompatible | does not make sense with |
| 361 | shunning | not wanting |
| 361 | tried and true | the familiar |
| 361 | core | basis |
| 363 | deficit | shortage |
| 363 | replenish | raise it again |
| 363 | reviving | awakening |
| 363 | grope | to look for blindly |
| 363 | finicky | picky |
| 363 | in concert | together |
| 364 | deviant | wrong, and not normal |
| 364 | carnal cravings | sexual desires |
| 364 | erroneously | incorrectly |
| 364 | figuratively | symbolic meaning |
| 364 | languidly | slowly |
| 365 | anatomic features | body structure |
| 365 | vastly | greatly |
| 365 | superstition | fears that are not based on facts |
| 365 | predispose | influence |
| 366 | experiential factors | based on past experiences |
| 366 | purveyors | people who watch |
| 366 | erotica | sexual material |
| 366 | sojourn | time |

Chapter 10  Motivation and Emotion  267

| Phrases and Expressions (Different Usage) | | Additional Terms from the Text | | |
| --- | --- | --- | --- | --- |
| 367 | **don** | put on | | |
| 368 | **ample** | a lot | | |
| 368 | **familial** | runs in the family | | |
| 369 | **deferential** | give power to the other | | |
| 370 | **churned** | moved | | |
| 370 | **dawned on me** | I figured out | | |
| 370 | **cubicles** | very small rooms | | |
| 370 | **instigated** | started | | |
| 370 | **disorientation** | don't know where you are | | |
| 371 | **exuberant** | extremely happy | | |
| 372 | **gadgets** | little unimportant items | | |
| 374 | **discrepant** | doesn't make sense | | |
| 374 | **clung** | held onto | | |
| 374 | **lopsided** | most of the votes on one side | | |
| 375 | **despite** | even thought they experienced | | |
| 375 | **vast sums** | large amounts | | |
| 375 | **be acquainted** | know them | | |
| 376 | **tangible rewards** | real reward | | |
| 376 | **enhancing** | improving | | |
| 376 | **extrinsic rewards** | rewards from the outside | | |
| 376 | **prestige** | high status | | |
| 376 | **intrinsic rewards** | rewards we feel inside | | |
| 376 | **intervention** | actions | | |
| 377 | **demise** | ending | | |
| 377 | **offshoot** | theory that is from | | |
| 377 | **ensues** | begins | | |
| 377 | **repress** | put a stop to | | |
| 378 | **roundabout ways** | other ways | | |
| 378 | **sarcasm** | humor that can be hurtful | | |
| 378 | **strike out** | be aggressive | | |
| 378 | **distort** | misunderstand | | |
| 378 | **date rapists** | someone who tries to have sex against the other person's will while they are out together | | |
| 378 | **agile** | flexible | | |
| 378 | **under the circumstances** | in certain situations | | |
| 3779 | **deference** | respecting anothers opinion | | |
| 379 | **differentiation** | to tell the difference between | | |
| 379 | **belligerent** | loud and aggressive | | |
| 379 | **provocateur** | one who starts a fight | | |
| 380 | **not laudable** | cannot be praised | | |
| 381 | **Squiggling** | moving toes around quickly | | |
| 381 | **indictments** | to charge with a crime | | |
| 381 | **identifiable** | can be recognized | | |
| 382 | **maturational sequences** | ordered steps of development | | |
| 382 | **Baring** | showing teeth in anger | | |
| 382 | **depicted** | shown | | |
| 383 | **intertwined** | mixed together | | |
| 384 | **trigger** | starts | | |
| 384 | **override sadness** | overcome sadness | | |
| 385 | **central** | important | | |
| 385 | **irrelevant** | not important | | |

1. Physiological _____ are the psychological counterparts of physiological needs.
   (a) drives
   (b) incentives
   (c) responses
   (d) behaviors

2. Inherited dispositions that activate behavior patterns designed to reach specific goals are referred to as
   (a) motives.
   (b) drives.
   (c) instincts.
   (d) releasers.

3. Drive–reduction theory was framed by
   (a) William James.
   (b) William McDougall.
   (c) Abraham Maslow.
   (d) Clark Hull.

4. Drive–reduction theory has the greatest difficulty explaining
   (a) sensation seeking.
   (b) the thirst drive.
   (c) the hunger drive.
   (d) avoidance of extremes in temperature.

5. When the ventromedial nucleus of a rat's hypothalamus is lesioned, the animal becomes
   (a) hyperglycemic.
   (b) hyperphagic.
   (c) hypoglycemic.
   (d) aphagic.

6. A friend has managed to lose 30 pounds, but now complains that he is hungry "all the time." According to the text, obese and formerly obese people may be hungry more often than people who have always been normal weight because of
   (a) a higher blood sugar level.
   (b) lack of adequate nutritional information.
   (c) a higher level of adipose tissue.
   (d) a lesion in the lateral hypothalamus.

7. What is the highest level in Maslow's hierarchy of needs?
   (a) safety
   (b) self-actualization
   (c) love and belonging
   (d) physiological

8. In a classic experiment, an injection of a(n) _____ solution into a goat's hypothalamus triggered heavy intake of fluids.
   (a) salt
   (b) ADH
   (c) calcium
   (d) angiotensin

9. Participants in sensory–deprivation experiments are reported to have experienced all of the following **EXCEPT**
   (a) boredom.
   (b) irritability.
   (c) hallucinations.
   (d) delusions.

10. High sensation seekers are less tolerant of _____ than other people.
    (a) high–risk activities
    (b) sensory deprivation
    (c) novel experiences
    (d) sexual experiences

11. A person's optimal level of arousal is
    (a) the level of arousal at which that person functions most efficiently.
    (b) equivalent to the greatest amount of stimulation that the person can tolerate.
    (c) equivalent to the smallest amount of stimulation that the person can tolerate.
    (d) the level of arousal that is associated with novel stimulation.

12. David McClelland assessed *n* Ach by using the
    (a) MMPI.
    (b) Rorschach inkblot test.
    (c) TAT.
    (d) California Psychological Inventory.

13. According to LeDoux, as stated in the text, strong emotions trigger
    (a) aggression or flight.
    (b) activity in the autonomic nervous system.
    (c) efforts to mentally represent the environment.
    (d) suppression of the immune system.

14. The Chinese are said to have forced suspected criminals to chew rice powder and spit it out as a way of
    (a) making amends to society.
    (b) stimulating facial feedback.
    (c) detecting lying.
    (d) intimidating them.

15. According to the text, the emotion of _____ involves predominantly sympathetic arousal.
    (a) depression
    (b) anger
    (c) acceptance
    (d) fear

16. It is theorized that the facial–feedback hypothesis may influence the experience of emotions in all of the following ways, **EXCEPT**
    (a) kinesthetic feedback.
    (b) feedback from other people.
    (c) release of neurotransmitters.
    (d) modifying the person's level of arousal.

17. A person tries to get herself out of a state of depression by engaging in behaviors that were once enjoyable. This approach to overcoming depression is most consistent with a theory proposed by
    (a) William James.
    (b) Walter Cannon.
    (c) Henry Murray.
    (d) Stanley Schachter.

18. Which of the following statements contradicts the theory of emotion proposed by Schachter and Singer?
    (a) Strong arousal is associated with stronger emotions.
    (b) Situations influence the experience of emotions.
    (c) In ambiguous situations, we may try to determine how we should feel by observing others in the same situation.
    (d) There are some reasonably distinct patterns of arousal that are not fully exchangeable.

19. Effort justification, as described in the cognitive dissonance theory, is focused on convincing
    (a) ourselves that our unpleasant tasks are worth the effort.
    (b) others that our unpleasant tasks are worth the effort.
    (c) others that their unpleasant tasks are worth the effort.
    (d) none of the above

20. The neurotransmitter _____ appears to induce feelings of satiation.
    (a) serotonin
    (b) adrenalin
    (c) noradrenaline
    (d) GABA

**Answer Key to *Posttest***

| | |
|---|---|
| 1. A | 11. A |
| 2. C | 12. C |
| 3. D | 13. B |
| 4. A | 14. C |
| 5. B | 15. D |
| 6. C | 16. B |
| 7. B | 17. A |
| 8. A | 18. D |
| 9. D | 19. A |
| 10. B | 20. A |

| | |
|---|---|
| Cognitive-dissonance theory | Ethologist |
| Motive | Pheromones |
| Need | Drive-reduction theory |
| Drive | Primary drives |
| Physiological drives | Acquired drives |
| Incentive | Homeostasis |
| Instinct | Opponent-process theory |

| | |
|---|---|
| A scientist who studies the behavior patterns that characterized different species. | The view that we are motivated to make our cognitions or beliefs consistent. |
| Chemical secretions that are detected by other members of the same species and stimulate stereotypical behaviors. | A hypothetical state within an organism that propels the organism toward a goal. |
| The view that organisms learn to engage in behaviors that have the effect of reducing drives. | A state of deprivation. |
| Unlearned, or physiological, drives. | A condition of arousal in an organism that is associated with a need. |
| Drives that are acquired through experience, or learned. | Unlearned drives with a biological basis, such as hunger, thirst, and avoidance of pain. |
| The tendency of the body to maintain a steady state. | An object, person, or situation perceived as being capable of satisfying a need. |
| The view that our emotions trigger opposing emotions. | An inherited disposition to activate specific behavior patterns that are designed to reach certain goals. |

| | |
|---|---|
| Self-actualization | Estrus |
| Satiety | Menopause |
| Lesion | Sexual orientation |
| Hyperphagic | Heterosexual |
| Organizing effects | Gay male |
| Activating effects | Lesbian |
| Testosterone | Bisexual |

| | |
|---|---|
| The periodic sexual excitement of many female mammals, during which they can conceive and are receptive to the sexual advances of males. | According to Maslow and other humanistic psychologists, self-initiated striving to become what one is capable of being. |
| The cessation of menstruation. | The state of being satisfied; fullness. |
| The direction of one's erotic interests (e.g., heterosexual, gay male, lesbian, or bisexual). | An injury that results in impaired behavior or loss of a function. |
| A person whose sexual orientation is characterized by desire for sexual activity and formation of romantic relationships with people of the other gender. | Characterized by excessive eating. |
| A male whose sexual orientation is characterized by desire for sexual activity and the formation of romantic relationships with other males. | The directional effects of sex hormones–for example, along stereotypical masculine or feminine lines. |
| A female whose sexual orientation is characterized by desire for sexual activity and the formation of romantic relationships with other females. | The arousal-producing effects of sex hormones that increase the likelihood of dominant sexual responses. |
| A person whose sexual orientation is characterized by desire for sexual activity and the formation of romantic relationships with both women and men. | A male hormone that promotes development of male sexual characteristics and that has activating effects on sexual arousal. |

| | |
|---|---|
| Concordance | Thematic Apperception Test |
| Sensory deprivation | Affiliation |
| Innate | Theory of social comparison |
| Novel stimulation | Catharsis |
| Balance theory | Emotion |
| Attitude-discrepant behavior | Sympathetic |
| Effort justification | Parasympathetic |

| | |
|---|---|
| A test devised by Henry Murray to measure needs through fantasy production. | Agreement. |
| Association or connection with a group. | A research method for systematically decreasing the amount of stimulation that impinges upon sensory receptors. |
| The view that people look to others for cues about how to behave when they are in confusing or unfamiliar situations. | Inborn, unlearned. |
| Is psychodynamic theory, the purging of strong emotions or the relieving of tensions. | An unusual source of arousal or excitement. |
| A state of feeling that has cognitive, physiological and behavioral components. | The view that people have a need to organize their perceptions, opinions, and beliefs in a harmonious manner. |
| Of the sympathetic division of the autonomic nervous system. | Behavior that is inconsistent with an attitude and may have the effect of denying an attitude. |
| Of the parasympathetic division of the autonomic nervous system. | In cognitive-dissonance theory, the tendency to seek justification for strenuous efforts. |

# Chapter 11

# Developmental Psychology

Directions: This *PRETEST* will give you feedback about how well you understand Chapter 11. In order to enhance your mastery of Chapter 11, complete all the sections of this chapter of the Study Guide. Then you can take the *POSTTEST* and compare your results.

1.  Hormones cause a follicle in the _____ to rupture and release an ovum.
    (a) fallopian tube
    (b) uterus
    (c) ovary
    (d) zygote

2.  According to _____, development is continuous.
    (a) Gesell
    (b) Erikson
    (c) Piaget
    (d) Watson

3.  The heart begins to beat during the _____ week of prenatal development.
    (a) second
    (b) fourth
    (c) eighth
    (d) twelfth

4.  Following the gains of infancy, according to the text, children gain about _____ inches a year until they reach the adolescent growth spurt.
    (a) 1 to 2
    (b) 2 to 3
    (c) 3 to 5
    (d) 6 to 8

5.  Which of the following is true of reflexes?
    (a) They involve higher brain functions.
    (b) They begin at one or two months after birth.
    (c) They vary greatly from child to child.
    (d) They are elicited by specific stimuli.

6.  A new parent is concerned about the amount of time his baby spends sleeping each day. You note that newborn children spend about _____ hours a day sleeping.
    (a) 8
    (b) 12
    (c) 16
    (d) 20

7.  According to the text, research by ethologists has most clearly shown that
    (a) ducks and geese undergo imprinting.
    (b) children undergo imprinting.
    (c) there are critical periods for perceptual development.
    (d) fear of strangers begins during a critical period.

8.  Which of the following is an example of assimilation, according to Piaget?
    (a) object permanence
    (b) the syllogism
    (c) the scheme
    (d) a reflex

9.  A child is asked, "Why do stars twinkle?" He responds, "Because they're happy." This response suggests the type of thinking that Piaget termed
    (a) animistic.
    (b) artificialistic.
    (c) concrete operational.
    (d) egocentric.

10. According to Piaget, conservation requires the ability to
    (a) engage in abstract logic.
    (b) take the viewpoint of another person.
    (c) center on two aspects of a situation at once.
    (d) make objective moral judgments.

11. Information–processing theorists are most critical of Piaget's assertion that
    (a) moral judgments become more complex as children mature.
    (b) experience influences the course of cognitive development.
    (c) conservation tasks require children to focus simultaneously on more than one aspect of a problem.
    (d) children undergo four distinct stages of cognitive development.

12. Kohlberg's approach to moral development is considered
    (a) cognitive–developmental.
    (b) behavioral.
    (c) psychodynamic.
    (d) humanistic–existential.

13. According to Kohlberg, choosing one's own ethical principles and believing that it is wrong to obey unjust laws is characteristic of the_____ orientation.
    (a) naively egotistic
    (b) contractual, legalistic
    (c) conscience
    (d) good–boy

14. At puberty, hormones secreted by the _____ stimulate the testes to increase output of testosterone.
    (a) adrenal glands
    (b) testes
    (c) hypothalamus
    (d) pituitary gland

15. Puberty ends when
    (a) the voice has deepened.
    (b) pubic hair appears.
    (c) the long bones make no further gains in length.
    (d) reproduction is first possible.

16. At age 20 or 21, men stop growing taller because _____ prevents the long bones from making further gains in length.
    (a) estrogen
    (b) testosterone
    (c) growth hormone
    (d) luteinizing hormone

17. According to Erikson, young adulthood is characterized by conflict in the area of
    (a) ego identity vs. role diffusion.
    (b) autonomy vs. doubt.
    (c) intimacy vs. isolation.
    (d) generativity vs. stagnation.

18. Each of the following is a characteristic issue of middle age **EXCEPT**
    (a) coming to terms with the dream.
    (b) the empty–nest syndrome.
    (c) shaping the new generation.
    (d) settling down.

19. According to Kübler–Ross, the first stage of dying is
    (a) anger.
    (b) denial.
    (c) depression.
    (d) anxiety.

20. A new parent must return to work because of financial need, but is concerned about the effects of day care. According to the text, research shows that children placed in day care are more _____ than children cared for in the home.
    (a) intelligent
    (b) aggressive
    (c) attached to parents
    (d) anxious

**Answer Key to *Pretest***

| | | | |
|---|---|---|---|
| 1. C | 6. C | 11. D | 16. B |
| 2. D | 7. A | 12. A | 17. C |
| 3. B | 8. D | 13. C | 18. D |
| 4. B | 9. A | 14. D | 19. B |
| 5. D | 10. C | 15. C | 20. B |

Chapter 11 traces human development throughout the life span, from conception to death. The chapter opens with a vignette which describes the process of conception, which takes place in a fallopian tube following the release of an ovum from an ovary (ovulation). Controversies in developmental psychology are discussed, including the nature–nurture controversy and whether development is continuous or discontinuous.

Three stages of prenatal development are outlined: the germinal stage, or ten days to two weeks following conception; the embryonic period, which ends after two months of prenatal development; and the fetal period, which lasts until birth. It is explained how the major organ systems take shape.

Physical development follows cephalocaudal and proximodistal sequences. Gains in height and weight are most dramatic during early development. Adolescent growth spurts also occur. Several reflexes present in newborn children are described. Perceptual development is explored, focusing on details of visual development, such as initial nearsightedness, preference for complex stimuli, and depth perception.

Ainsworth's views on the development of attachment are outlined. Various theories of attachment are explored and evaluated: the behavioral view, the "contact-comfort" view, and the ethological (imprinting) view. Dimensions of child rearing are described.

Piaget's views on children's cognition are discussed, and the concepts of scheme, assimilation, and accommodation are defined. Next, Piaget's four periods of cognitive development are described: the sensorimotor, preoperational, concrete operational, and formal operational periods. Within these periods, the development of object permanence, centration, and conservation is stressed. Piaget's views are evaluated and contrasted to information–processing views of cognitive development. Then Kohlberg's theory of the levels and stages of moral development is outlined.

Adolescence is described as a period of physical and psychological change. Sex hormones usher in physical changes that make reproduction possible, and there are also yearnings for independence from parents. Erikson characterizes adolescence as a period during which we are challenged to develop ego identity.

Adulthood is divided into young, middle, and late periods, and the theories of adult development of Levinson and Erikson are outlined. Researchers and theorists characterize young adulthood as a period of striving for advancement in the career world and developing intimate relationships. Middle adulthood is characterized as a period of reassessment, of coming to terms with one's mortality and one's achievements, and—according to Erikson—of helping to shape the new generation or "stagnating." Late adulthood is generally characterized by declining physical condition, voluntary or involuntary retirement from the career world, and—according to Erikson—facing the inevitability of death with ego integrity or despair.

The Psychology and Modern Life section deals with the issues of day care and child abuse.

# LEARNING OBJECTIVES

| | |
|---|---|
| 1. Describe the process of conception. | |
| | **Controversies in Developmental Psychology** |
| 2. Discuss the nature–nurture controversy in developmental psychology. | |

3. Discuss the issue as to whether development is continuous or discontinuous.

## Prenatal Development

4. Describe the major events of the stages of prenatal development.

## Physical Development

5. Discuss the sequences of physical development.

6. Describe the major *reflexes* that are present at birth.

7. Describe the processes of perceptual development.

## Social Development

8. Describe Ainsworth's views on the development of attachment.

9. Explain and evaluate various theoretical approaches to the formation of parent–infant attachment.

10. Describe the dimensions of child rearing.

11. Describe various ways in which parents enforce restrictions.

## Cognitive Development

12. Define Piaget's concepts of *scheme*, *assimilation*, and *accommodation*.

13. Outline Piaget's four stages of cognitive development, describing the major characteristics of each.

14. Evaluate Piaget's cognitive–developmental theory.

15. Explain how information–processing theorists look upon cognitive development.

16. Describe Kohlberg's levels and stages of moral development.

**Adolescence**

17. Describe major physical and psychological changes that take place during adolescence.

**Adult Development**

18. Describe the challenges and crises of young adulthood.

19. Describe the challenges and crises of middle adulthood.

20. Describe the challenges and crises of late adulthood.

**Psychology and Modern Life**

21. Summarize research concerning the effects of day care.

22. Summarize research concerning factors that contribute to child abuse.

# LECTURE AND TEXTBOOK OUTLINE

## Controversies in Developmental Psychology

1. Does Development Reflect Nature or Nurture?

2. Is Development Continuous or Discontinuous?

## Prenatal Development

## Physical Development

1. Reflexes

2. Perceptual Development

## Social Development

1. Attachment

2. Dimensions of Child Rearing

## Cognitive Development

1. Jean Piaget's Cognitive-Developmental Theory

2. Information-Processing Approaches to Cognitive Development

3. Kohlberg's Theory of Moral Development

4. Evidence for Gender and Ethnocentric Biases

# Adolescence

1. Physical Development

2. Social and Personality Development

3. Gender and Ethnic Factors in Adolescent Identity Formation

# Adult Development

1. Young Adulthood

2. Middle Adulthood

3. Late Adulthood

# Psychology and Modern Life

1. Day Care

2. Child Abuse

## Become an Effective Learner for a Lifetime

Your need to learn will not stop with this class or even when you complete your academic objectives. Our fast-paced technical society demands that all of us are effective learners for our entire lives. I hope that some of the "Effective Studying Ideas" in this Study Guide have helped you be more successful in this cours, and in your future learning endeavors.

Effective learners usually share many of the following characteristics:

1. **Curious**
Have a basic love for learning about anything.

2. **Focused**
Stay on task even when they don't want to.

3. **Flexible**
Are open to changes in the environment and in themselves.

4. **Organized**
Are able to structure information, time, and life.

5. **Skillful**
Develop learning skills and professional skills.

6. **Joyful**
Happiness can be short-lived, but a deep sense of joy stays with you even when times are rough.

7. **Nonjudgmental**
Listen to opposing viewpoints.

8. **Enthusiastic**
Possess an intensity about learning and life.

9. **Healthy**
Emotional and physical problems interfere with the motivation to learn.

10. **Self-Aware**
Are willing to evaluate themselves and their behavior.

11. **Responsible**
Make a commitment to themselves or others, and DO IT!

12. **Willing to Risk**
Take on challenging projects.

13. **Participate**
People seldom learn anything from the sidelines.

14. **Broad Interests**
Interested in everything around them.

15. **Comfortable with Ambiguity**
Sometimes life doesn't make sense.

16. **Courageous**
Feel the fear and do it any way.

17. **Self-Motivated**
Internal drive to self-actualize.

18. **Hard-working**
Genius and creativity are the result of persistence and hard work.

19. **Focused on the Present**
Life takes place in the present, not the past or the future.

1. Zygote _____

2. Siblings _____

3. Embryo _____

### Controversies in Developmental Psychology

4. Maturation _____

5. Stage _____

6. Puberty _____

### Prenatal Development

7. Fetus _____

8. Germinal stage _____

10. Period of the ovum _____

11. Cephalocaudal _____

12. Proximodistal _____

13. Androgens _____

14. Amniotic sac _____

15. Placenta _____

16. Umbilical cord _____

### Physical Development

17. Neonate _____

18. Reflex _____

19. Rooting _____

20. Sphincter _____

21. Pupillary reflex _____

22. Visual accommodation _____

23. Fixation time _____

### Social Development

24. Attachment _____

25. Secure attachment _____

26. Insecure attachment _____

27. Indiscriminate attachment _____

28. Initial–preattachment phase _____

29. Attachment–in–the–making phase _____

30. Clear–cut–attachment phase _____

31. Contact comfort _____

32. Critical period _____

33. Imprinting _____

34. Authoritative _____

### Cognitive Development

35. Assimilation _____

36. Scheme _____

37. Accommodation _____

38. Object permanence _____

39. Sensorimotor stage _____

40. Preoperational stage _____

41. Egocentric _____

42. Animism _____

43. Artificialism _____

44. Conservation _____

45. Center _____

46. Objective responsibility _____

47. Concrete-operational stage _____

48. Decentration _____

49. Subjective moral judgment _____

50. Reversibility _____

51. Formal operational stage _____

52. Information processing _____

53. Metamemory _____

54. Preconventional level _____

55. Conventional level _____

56. Postconventional level _____

57. Reciprocity _____

### Adolescence

58. Adolescence _____ _____

59. Secondary sex characteristics _____ _____

60. Menarche _____ _____

61. Ego identity _____ _____

62. Role diffusion _____ _____

**Adult Development** _____ _____

63. Intimacy versus isolation _____ _____

64. Trying 20s _____ _____

65. Dream _____ _____

66. Age 30 transition _____ _____

67. Catch 30s _____ _____

68. Generativity versus stagnation _____ _____

69. Midlife transition _____ _____

70. Midlife crisis _____ _____

72. Menopause _____ _____

73. Empty–nest syndrome _____ _____

74. Reaction time _____ _____

75. Longevity _____ _____

76. Ego integrity versus despair _____ _____

**Additional Terms**

_____ _____

_____ _____

_____ _____

_____ _____

_____ _____

_____ _____

_____ _____

_____ _____

_____ _____

_____ _____

_____ _____

# CHAPTER REVIEW

## SECTION 1: Introduction

**OBJ. 1:** It is possible to become pregnant for a day or so following (1) _____tion. Ovulation is defined as the releasing of an (2) _____ from an ovary. A person begins to grow and develop when a sperm cell combines with an ovum to become a (3) z_____. Sperm cells can carry X or (4) _____ sex chromosomes. If a sperm cell with (5: *Circle one:* an X or a Y) sex chromosome fertilizes an ovum, a boy is conceived.

## SECTION 2: Controversies in Developmental Psychology

**OBJ. 2:** Those aspects of behavior that originate in our genes and unfold in the child as long as minimal nutrition and social experience are provided are referred to as our (6) _____ure. Those aspects of behavior that can be largely traced to environmental influences such as nutrition and learning are said to reflect our (7) _____ure. Psychologist Arnold (8) G\_\_\_\_ endorsed natural explanations of development. Gesell argued that development is self-regulated by the unfolding of natural plans and processes, or by (9) _____ation. John Watson and other behaviorists leaned heavily toward (10)_____mental explanations. (11) W_____ focused primarily on adaptive behavior patterns, whereas (12) _____ell focused on including physical and motor growth and development.

**OBJ. 3:** Psychologists argue as to whether developmental changes occur gradually—that is, (13) _____ously, or in major qualitative leaps that dramatically alter the ways in which we are structured and behave—that is, (14) _____ously. Behaviorists view development as a (15) _____ous process in which the effects of learning mount gradually, with no major sudden qualitative changes. (16) _____tional theorists, by contrast, believe that there are periods of life during which development occurs so dramatically that we can speak of its occurring in (17) _____ges.

## SECTION 3: Prenatal Development

**OBJ. 4:** Prenatal development may be divided into (18) _____ stages or periods. These are the (19) _____nal stage (approximately the first two weeks), the (20) em_____ stage (which lasts from two weeks to about two months after conception), and the (21) f_____ stage. During the germinal stage, the zygote divides repeatedly as it travels through the (22) f_____ tube and then within the uterus. Then the zygote becomes implanted in the wall of the (23) u_____.

The (24) _____ic period lasts from implantation until the end of the second month. During the embryonic period, the major (25) o_____ systems of the unborn child undergo rapid development. Development follows two general trends: (26) _____caudal and (27) prox_____. Human features are formed; the nervous system becomes formed; and the heart begins to (28) b_____. Sexual (29) _____iation occurs in response to sex hormones. The (30) _____ta is a mass of tissue that permits the embryo (and later on, the fetus) to exchange (31) _____ents and wastes with the mother.

The fourth through sixth months are characterized by (32) mat_____ of fetal organ systems and dramatic gains in size.

The embryo and fetus develop within the (33) _____ic sac, which contains amniotic fluid. The fetus is connected to the mother by the (34) _____ical cord.

## SECTION 4: Physical Development

**OBJ. 5:** The most dramatic gains in height and weight occur during (35) _____tal development. Babies usually double their birth weight in about

Chapter 11    Developmental Psychology    287

(36) _____ months and triple it by the (37) _____ birthday. Following the gains of infancy, children gain about (38) _____ to three inches a year and (39) _____ to six pounds a year until they reach the adolescent growth spurt.

**OBJ. 6:** Infants are born with a number of reflexes. Reflexes are (40) _____ typical responses elicited by specific stimuli. Reflexes occur automatically; they do not involve higher (41) b_____ functions. The most basic reflex for survival is (42) _____hing. In the (43) _____ing reflex, infants turn their heads toward stimuli that touch the cheek. In the (44) _____ing reflex, infants suck objects that touch the lips. In the (45) s_____, or Moro reflex, infants arch their backs and draw up their legs in response to sudden noises and bumps. In the grasp, or (46) _____r reflex, infants grasp objects pressed against the palms of the hands. In the (47) B_____ reflex, they spread their toes when the soles of the feet are stimulated. Reflexes, like rooting and sucking, promote survival and phase out as neural functioning (48) _____ures and many previously automatic processes come under (49) vol_____ control.

**OBJ. 7:** Newborn children sleep about (50) _____ hours a day. The (51) _____ary reflex is present at birth, so the irises widen automatically to admit more light when it is dark, and vice versa. Neonates do not show visual (52) _____dation; they see as through a fixed–focus camera. Visual acuity makes the most dramatic gains between the ages of birth and (53) _____ months.

Infants appear to have an inborn preference for (54: *Circle one:* simple or complex) visual stimulation. Infants are generally capable of depth perception, as measured by behavior on the visual cliff, by the time they are able to (55) c_____.

Most newborns (56) _____xively turn their heads toward unusual sounds. Three–day–old babies prefer their (57) _____rs' voices to those of other women. Newborns can discriminate different odors, and they breathe (58: *Circle one:* more or less) rapidly and are (59: *Circle one:* more or less) active when presented with powerful odors. Newborns can discriminate sweet tastes. The tongue pressure of neonates sucking on a nipple correlates with the amount of (60) s_____ in their liquid diet. Newborns are sensitive to touch, but relatively insensitive to (61) p_____, which may reflect an adaptive response to the process of birth.

## SECTION 5: Social Development

**OBJ. 8:** Ainsworth defines attachment "as an (62) _____tional tie that one person or animal forms between himself and another specific one—a tie that binds them together in (63) s_____ and endures over time." Securely attached babies cry (64: *Circle one:* more or less) frequently and are (65: *Circle one:* more or less) likely to show affection toward their mothers than insecurely attached babies.

Ainsworth identified three stages of attachment: the (66) _____–_____chment phase, which lasts from birth to about 3 months and is characterized by indiscriminate attachment; the (67) attach-ment–in–the–_____ing phase, which occurs at about 3 or 4 months and is characterized by preference for familiar figures; and the (68) c_____–cut–attachment phase, which occurs at about 6 or 7 months and is characterized by intensified dependence on the primary caregiver.

**OBJ. 9:** Behaviorists argue that children become attached to mothers through (69) _____ning, because their mothers feed them and attend to other primary needs. From this view, mothers serve as conditioned (70) _____ers.

The Harlow studies with rhesus monkeys suggest that an innate motive, referred to as (71) c_____ comfort, is more important than conditioning in the development of attachment. Harlow's infant monkeys spent more time on soft terry–cloth (72) su_____ "mothers" than on wire "mothers," even when their feeding bottles protruded from the wire mothers. His infant monkeys were also more willing to explore the environment in the presence of (73: *Circle one:* terry–cloth or wire) surrogate mothers.

Ethologists argue that attachment occurs during a (74) c_____ period. During this critical period, young animals such as ducks and geese form (75) _____ive attachments to the first moving objects they encounter. The process of forming an attachment in this manner is called (76) _____ing. Attachment in these animals is bounded at the early end by the age at which they first engage in (77) lo_____ and, at the upper end, by the development of (78) _____r of strangers.

**OBJ. 10:** Some psychologists classify approaches to child rearing according to two broad dimensions: (79) w_____–coldness, and (80) _____iveness– permissiveness. These dimensions are (81: *Circle one:* dependent or independent).

## SECTION 7: Cognitive Development

**OBJ. 12:** Jean Piaget has advanced our knowledge of children's (82) c_____ development. Piaget saw children as budding (83) _____ists who actively strive to make sense of the perceptual world. Piaget referred to action patterns and mental structures that are involved in acquiring or organizing knowledge as (84) _____s. He defined intelligence as involving processes of (85) _____tion, or responding to events according to existing schemes; and (86) _____tion, or the changing of schemes to permit effective responses to new events.

**OBJ. 13:** Piaget's view of cognitive development includes (87) _____ stages or periods. First comes the (88) _____or stage, which occurs prior to use of symbols and language. During the sensorimotor period, the child comes to mentally represent objects, and thus develops object (89) per_____. Second is the (90) _____tional stage, which is characterized by egocentric thought (or inability to see the world as it is seen by others); animism; artificialism; inability to (91) _____ter on more than one aspect of a situation at a time; and (92: *Circle one:* objective or subjective) moral judgments. Third is the (93) _____–operational period, which is characterized by conservation; less

egocentrism; reversibility; and (94: *Circle one:* objective or subjective) moral judgments. Fourth is the (95) _____–operational period, which is characterized by capacity for abstract logic.

**OBJ. 14:** Various issues have been raised about Piaget's views. For example, Piaget's methodology led him to (96: *Circle one:* overestimate or underesti- mate) the ages at which children can carry out certain kinds of tasks. Also, cognitive skills such as egocen- trism and conservation may develop (97: *Circle one:* more or less) continuously than Piaget thought—not in general stages. On the positive side, it seems that the sequences of development are indeed (98: *Circle one:* variant or invariant), as Piaget believed.

**OBJ. 15:** Information–processing theorists study the development of children's (99) _____gies for processing information. Case and Pascual–Leone focus on children's capacity for (100) _____ry and their use of cognitive strategies, such as the ways in which they focus their (101) _____ion. They note that some Piagetan tasks require several cogni- tive strategies and that young children frequently fail at them because they cannot hold many pieces of information in their (102) _____–term or working memories at once. Case and Pascual–Leone suggest that children's problem–solving abilities are largely made possible by (103) _____gical developments that expand the working (short–term) memory and increasing (104) au_____ity in applying cognitive strategies.

**OBJ. 16:** Kohlberg's theory of cognitive development focuses on the development of (105) _____al reasoning. Kohlberg hypothesizes that the processes of moral reasoning develop through (106) _____ "levels" and (107) _____ stages within each level. In the (108) _____tional level, judgments are based on expectation of rewards or punishments. Stage 1 is oriented toward obedience and (109) _____ment. In stage 2, good behavior is equated with what will allow people to satisfy (110) _____ds. Conventional–level moral judgments reflect the need to conform to conventional standards of right or wrong. According to the stage 3 (111) "_____ orientation," it is good to meet the needs and expectations of others. In stage 4, moral judgments are based on rules that maintain the social (112) _____ r. The third level in Kohlberg's theory is termed (113) _____ tional, and it consists of stages 5 and 6. In stage 5's (114) co _____, legalistic orientation, it is recognized that laws stem from agreed–upon procedures, and that existing laws cannot bind the individual's behavior in unusual circumstances. In stage 6's conscience or (115) _____ ed orientation, people consider behavior that is consistent with their own ethical standards as right.

Critics suggest that postconventional reasoning, especially stage (116) _____ reasoning, may be more reflective of Kohlberg's philosophical ideals than of a natural stage of cognitive development.

## SECTION 8: Adolescence

**OBJ. 17:** Adolescence begins at (117) p_____ and ends with assumption of adult responsibilities. Puberty begins with the appearance of (118) _____ ary sex characteristics, such as the growth of bodily hair, deepening of the (119) _____ in males, and rounding of the breasts and hips in females. Changes that lead to reproductive capacity and secondary sex characteristics are stimulated by (120) _____ rone in the male and by (121) _____ en and androgens in the female. Testosterone causes the penis and (122) _____ es to grow, and pubic hair appears. Small amounts of (123) _____ gens, along with estrogen, stimulate growth of pubic and axillary hair in the female. First menstruation is termed (124) _____ che.

Gould and other researchers have found that adolescents frequently yearn for (125) _____ ence from parents. Erikson considers ego (126) _____ y, or the defining of a life role, the major challenge of adolescence. Adolescents who do not develop ego identity may encounter role (127) d_____.

## SECTION 9: Adult Development

**OBJ. 18:** Adulthood can be divided into young, middle, and (128) _____ adulthood. According to writers such as Gould and Sheehy, young adulthood is generally characterized by striving to advance in the (129) c_____ world. Men's development during this period is largely guided by needs for (130) ind_____ and (131) au_____, while women are more likely to be guided by shifting patterns of (132) at_____ and caring. Erikson considers the development of (133) _____ te relationships a central task of young adulthood. Erikson labels young adulthood the stage of intimacy vs. (134) i_____. According to Levinson, young adults often adopt a (135) _____, which serves as a tentative blueprint for their lives and is characterized by the drive to "become" someone, to leave their mark on history.

During the late 20s and 30s, many women encounter a crisis involving concerns about nearing the end of the (136) f_____ years, closing opportunities, and heightened responsibilities. Sheehy labels the 30s the (137) _____ 30s, because many adults encounter disillusionment and reassess their lives at this time. According to Levinson and Sheehy, the second half of the 30s is frequently characterized by (138) _____ ing down.

**OBJ. 19:** Many middle–aged people encounter feelings of entrapment and loss of purpose that are termed the (139) mi_____ _____. According to Levinson, at about age 40, some marker event causes men to realize that they are a full (140) _____ ion older than 20– year–olds. Women may undergo a midlife transition about (141) _____ years earlier than men, at about 35 rather than 40.

Erikson labels middle age the stage of (142) _____ vs. stagnation. Middle adulthood is a time when we must come to terms with the discrepancies between our (143) _____ ments and the dreams of youth.

Some middle–aged parents become depressed when the youngest child leaves home; they experience the so–called (144) "e_____–_____ syndrome." However, many women at this time show increased (145) dom_____ and (146) _____iveness. It is as if the children's leaving home has freed them from (147) tr_____ expectations of how women are supposed to behave.

**OBJ. 20:** Late adulthood begins at age (148) _____. One reason psychologists have become more concerned about late adulthood is the (149) _____ic imperative; that is, more of us are joining the ranks of the elderly all the time.

In late adulthood, changes in (150) _____m metabolism lead to increased brittleness in the bones. The senses become (151: *Circle one:* more or less) acute, and so the elderly frequently spice their food more heavily. The time required to respond to stimuli—that is, (152) _____ion time—increases. Presumed cognitive deficits among the elderly may actually reflect declining (153) mot_____ or psychological problems, such as (154) de_____. On the job, years of experience frequently compensate for most kinds of age–related deficits.

Heredity plays a role in having a long life span, or (155) _____ity. According to the (156) _____ar aging theory, the ability to repair DNA within cells decreases as we age. Environmental factors, such as exercise, proper diet, and the maintenance of (157) c_____ over one's life can all apparently delay aging to some degree.

Kübler–Ross identifies five stages of dying among the terminally ill: (158) de_____, anger, bargaining, (159) de_____, and final (160) _____ance. Research by other investigators finds that psychological reactions to approaching death are (161: *Circle one:* more or less) varied than Kübler–Ross suggests.

Erikson terms late adulthood the stage of ego (162) _____ty vs. despair. Ego integrity is the ability to maintain one's sense of identity in spite of progressive physical deterioration. Erikson argues that ego integrity is derived from (163) w_____, and he argues that adjustment in the later years requires the wisdom to be able to let go.

## SECTION 10: Psychology and Modern Life

**OBJ. 21:** There (164:*Circle one:* is evidence or is *no* evidence) that day care impairs parent–child bonds of attachment. Day care appears to foster acceptance by the child's (165) p_____. Day care also appears to foster playing at higher developmental levels and (166) _____ring behavior. However, children placed in day care are also somewhat more impulsive and (167) ag_____ than children cared for in the home.

**OBJ. 22:** A number of factors contribute to child abuse: situational (168) st_____; history of (169) a_____ in the family of at least one parent; acceptance of (170) v_____ as a way of coping with stress; failure to become attached to one's children; and rigid attitudes about child rearing. Child abuse is more likely to run in families for (171: *Circle one:* men or women), although it must be emphasized that the majority of people who have been abused do not abuse their own children.

### Answer Key to *Chapter Review*

1. ovulation
2. ovum
3. zygote
4. Y
5. a Y
6. nature
7. nurture
8. Gesell
9. maturation
10. environmental
11. Watson
12. Gesell
13. continuously
14. discontinuously
15. continuous
16. Maturational
17. stages
18. three
19. germinal
20. embryonic

21. fetal
22. fallopian
23. uterus
24. embryonic
25. organ
26. cephalocaudal
27. proximodistal
28. beat
29. differentiation
30. placenta
31. nutrients
32. maturation
33. amniotic
34. umbilical
35. prenatal
36. five
37. first
38. two
39. four
40. stereotypical
41. brain
42. breathing
43. rooting
44. sucking
45. startle
46. palmar
47. Babinski
48. matures
49. voluntary
50. 16
51. pupillary
52. accommodation
53. six
54. complex
55. crawl
56. reflexively
57. mothers'
58. more
59. more
60. sugar
61. pain
62. affectional
63. space
64. less
65. more
66. initial–preattachment
67. attachment–in–the–making
68. clear–cut– attachment
69. conditioning
70. reinforcers

71. contact
72. surrogate
73. terry-cloth
74. critical
75. instinctive
76. imprinting
77. locomotion
78. fear
79. warmth
80. restrictiveness
81. independent
82. cognitive
83. scientists
84. schemes
85. assimilation
86. accommodation
87. four
88. sensorimotor
89. permanence
90. preoperational
91. center
92. objective
93. concrete
94. subjective
95. formal
96. Underestimate
97. more
98. invariant
99. strategies
100. memory
101. attention
102. short-term
103. neurological
104. automaticity
105. moral
106. three
107. two
108. preconventional
109. punishment
110. needs
111. good–boy
112. order
113. postconventional
114. contractual
115. principled
116. six
117. puberty
118. secondary
119. voice
120. testosterone

121. estrogen
122. testes
123. androgens
124. menarche
125. independence
126. identity
127. diffusion
128. late
129. career
130. individuation
131. autonomy
132. attachment
133. intimate
134. isolation
135. dream
136. fertile
137. catch
138. settling
139. midlife crisis
140. generation
141. five
142. generativity
143. achievements
144. empty–nest
145. dominance
146. assertiveness
147. traditional
148. 65
149. demographic
150. calcium
151. less
152. reaction
153. motivation
154. depression
155. longevity
156. cellular
157. control
158. denial
159. depression
160. acceptance
161. more
162. integrity
163. wisdom
164. is *no* evidence
165. peers
166. sharing
167. aggressive
168. stress
169. abuse
170. violence

171. men

| Idioms | | Explanation |
|---|---|---|
| 428 | reach out | look for |
| 431 | draw to an end | finish |
| 431 | in the face of | even though |

| Cultural References | | Explanation |
|---|---|---|
| 396 | a buyer from a New York department store | a person who is responsible for selecting the items which the store will sell |
| 396 | the spring line | the buyer usually makes the selection of spring clothes for a department store in the December; |
| 423 | French fries and shakes at the fast-food counter... | various and popular foods available at restaurants such as McDonald's and Burger King |
| 424 | eligible for driver's licenses | be of the right age to get a driver's license |
| 424 | R-rated | a rating of movies that indicates that it is not appropriate for children because of the violence or sexual content |
| 425 | "age of consent" | the age when a person is allowed to marry without obtaining permission from a parent |
| 426 | tenure | a term which refers to a position given to a teacher which guarantees the job is permanent |
| 427 | Pepsi Generation | an advertising slogan which emphasizes youth; the slogan advertises Pepsi Cola, a popular drink |
| 427 | play shortstop for the Dodgers | a position on a professional baseball team |
| 427 | Wall Street cubby-hole | a small office in a large building in the financial district of New York City |
| 431 | nursing home | an institution which gives food, shelter, and medical care to the elderly |
| 435 | women's movement | ideas which began in the 1950s and became organized into several organizations, such as NOW: the movement supports equality for women |
| 436 | child abuse hotlines | telephone numbers to report physical or mental mistreatment of children |

| Phrases and Expressions (Different Usage) | | |
|---|---|---|
| 234 | unlike | not like |
| 396 | their timing | the time that they choose |
| 396 | a very different drama was unfolding | an exciting occurrence was happening |
| 396 | psychological well-being | psychological health |
| 396 | should we be concerned | should we worry |
| 397 | different views | different opinions |
| 397 | "Programmed" | biologically planned |
| 397 | be largely traced to | predominantly caused by |
| 397 | leaned heavily toward | believed that |
| 397 | broadly speaking | in a general way |
| 398 | major... leaps | important periods of growth that are separate from each other |
| 398 | literally "out of sight" | cannot be seen |
| 398 | nondescript | lacking distinctive qualities |
| 399 | downy hair | soft, fine hair ("downy" refers to the soft feathers on a goose) |
| 399 | turns somersaults | turns his or her heels over his or her head |
| 404 | buzzing | loud; noisy |
| 405 | face like patterns | designs that look like faces |
| 405 | checkerboard | pattern of black and white squares that alternate |
| 405 | placed face down | placed with the face looking at the surface |
| 405 | when so placed | when they were placed this way |
| 405 | to venture onto | to go onto |
| 405 | beckoned repeatedly | indicated frequently with hand movements to come |
| 407 | pull and tug | pull their arms and clothes |
| 407 | "run over" | stepped on |
| 407 | tracked their attachment | watched and studied their attachment |
| 407 | drew intense | became intense |
| 408 | cuddly terry | terry cloth is "towel" material |
| 408 | path to a monkey's heart | the way to make a monkey happy |
| 408 | a comforting base | comfortable place |
| 408 | oversized | a lot bigger than normal size |
| 408 | unwritten rule | informal and nonscientific rule, but accepted |
| 408 | made public | were publicized; were put in national newspapers |
| 408 | fowl | ducks and geese |
| 408 | dawned on me | it occurred to me; I realized |
| 410 | shrugged them off | not paid attention to them |

Chapter 11   Developmental Psychology   293

| | | |
|---|---|---|
| 410 | methods to his children's madness | reasons for the incorrect answers |
| 411 | Crude turning | inexperienced movement |
| 411 413 | out of sight is literally out of mind | if the baby cannot see the object or person, the baby cannot think about it |
| 414 | squat glass | a short and wide glass |
| 414 | wrongdoers | a person who does something wrong |
| 414 | judge... more strongly | are more judgmental |
| 414 | trying out | experimenting with ways of |
| 414 | caring for themselves | methods of dressing, walking, talking and acting |
| 415 | layoffs | loss of jobs; firing people |
| 416 | or are otherwise linked | are in some other way connected |
| 416 | have fared better | have been proved more |
| 416 | to say | it is reasonable to say |
| 416 | as been rocked | structure has been questioned |
| 416 | dashed to rubble | destroyed |
| 416 | to wear away at | to question and to criticize |
| 417 | focus their attention | attend |
| 417 | advances steadily | increases at a regular rate |
| 417 | turned the tables on | reversed their questions |
| 417 | keeping one's attention focused | maintaining attention |
| 417 | jotted down | wrote on paper |
| 417 | adult offenders | adults who commit crimes |
| 417 | agreed-upon | procedures that everyone (society) agrees to |
| 417 | the thrust of | the direction of |
| 423 | growth spurts | short, separate periods of growing |
| 423 | fighting the battle of the bulge | trying not to gain weight |
| 423 | throw down | eat a lot in a short period |
| 423 | come of age | reach puberty; might be considered almost adult |
| 423 | "fish or fowl" | neither children nor adults; neither one definite group or the other; in between |
| 423 | for their own good | so they do not physically or psychologically hurt themselves |
| 424 | for independence | a great desire to be independent |
| 424 | role in life | a position or way of living which is accepted by the person and society |
| 424 | firm sense | a strong feeling |
| 424 | carry them through | help them through |
| 424 | color their achievements with meaning | give their achievements meaning |
| 424 | spread themselves thin | do too many things |
| 424 | blind alley | an endeavor that does not result in interest |
| 424 | mold for themselves | create for themselves |

| | | |
|---|---|---|
| 424 | central task | the most important action |
| 424 | upon entry | when we enter the adult world |
| 424 | our mark on history | do something that future generations will notice |
| 426 | fueled by ambition | motivated by the desire to succeed |
| 426 | pathways in life | directions in life |
| 426 | for their own support | earning the money themselves for rent and food |
| 426 | swerves and bends | frequently changing direction |
| 426 | lose some of its allure in the next year | to not feel important in the next year |
| 426 | "never get myself together" | would never organize myself and my life |
| 426 | nearing the end of the fertile years | close to the time when a woman cannot get pregnant |
| 426 | closing down | not available anymore |
| 426 | settling down | becoming settled in a job and a family |
| 426 | forge ahead | try to succeed |
| 426 | ridden out the storm | survived the difficult years |
| 426 | to put down roots | to settle in a place, a job and with a family |
| 426 | marking time, treading water | not moving forward; not progressing in a job or career |
| 426 | a dramatic shift | a noticeable and important change |
| 427 | middle-level | middle position (job) |
| 427 | grinding out accounts | engaging in a boring activity |
| 427 | coming apart at the seams | feels very unhappy, depressed |
| 427 | loss of purpose | that there is no goal |
| 427 | extramarital affair | sexual attachments that are not with the spouse |
| 427 | overriding drive | predominant effort |
| 427 | come to terms with | understand that the dream may not be fulfilled |
| 428 | sense of urgency | a feeling that the women must be quick |
| 428 | a "last chance" | something must be accomplished now or never |
| 428 | falling off | decrease |
| 428 | paint more of a mixed and optimistic picture | indicate that the problems can be solved more easily |
| 428 | letting go of one's children | allowing one's children to become independent |
| 429 | cut free from traditional shackles | freed from confinements |
| 429 | timed items | items that have a time limit |
| 430 | so far walked the Earth | lived up to this time- lived before us |
| 430 | fare better | act and feel better |
| 431 | the sweep of history | the many years in the past and in the future |
| 431 | to call for | demand |
| 431 | in her landmark book | in her important book |

1. Conception normally takes place in the
   (a) uterus.
   (b) fallopian tube.
   (c) ovary.
   (d) vagina.

2. Development tends to be continuous, according to the views of
   (a) Sigmund Freud.
   (b) Erik Erikson.
   (c) John Watson.
   (d) Jean Piaget.

3. The embryonic period lasts from _____ until about the eighth week of prenatal development.
   (a) implantation
   (b) conception
   (c) ovulation
   (d) the time the zygote reaches the uterus

4. Sex organs begin to differentiate at about the _____ week of prenatal development.
   (a) first
   (b) third
   (c) seventh
   (d) twelfth

5. There is a sudden noise in the nursery, and a newborn baby draws up his legs and arches his back in response. This response is an example of the _____ reflex.
   (a) Babinski
   (b) palmar
   (c) sphincter
   (d) Moro

6. Which of the following is true of perception in babies?
   (a) They prefer the voices of strange men to those of their fathers.
   (b) They cannot hear until they are 2 to 3 weeks old.
   (c) They can perceive depth within a few days after birth.
   (d) They are born with the pupillary reflex.

7. In Harlow's experiments, infant rhesus monkeys showed preference for surrogate mothers
   (a) of their own species.
   (b) that were made from soft material.
   (c) that fed them.
   (d) that were present when they wanted to explore the environment.

8. Piaget viewed children as
   (a) reacting mechanically to environmental stimuli.
   (b) at the mercy of instinctive impulses.
   (c) budding scientists.
   (d) having a hierarchy of needs.

9. According to Piaget, children first show object permanence during the _____ period.
   (a) sensorimotor
   (b) preoperational
   (c) concrete operational
   (d) formal operational

10. According to Piaget, children first center on the motives of wrongdoers, as well as the amount of damage done, during the _____ period.
    (a) sensorimotor
    (b) preoperational
    (c) concrete operational
    (d) formal operational

11. Which of the following stages of moral development comes earliest, according to Kohlberg?
    (a) good–boy orientation
    (b) vontractual, legalistic orientation
    (c) naively egoistic orientation
    (d) obedience–and–punishment orientation

12. According to Kohlberg, stage _____ moral judgments are characterized by respect for authority and social order.
    (a) 1
    (b) 2
    (c) 3
    (d) 4

13. The period of adolescence is defined by
    (a) biological changes only.
    (b) psychosocial changes only.
    (c) both biological and psychosocial changes.
    (d) neither biological nor psychosocial changes.

14. Which of the following biological events usually occurs *last* in males?
    (a) ejaculatory ability
    (b) presence of mature sperm
    (c) growth of bodily hair
    (d) deepening of the voice

15. Menarche is defined as
    (a) the beginning of puberty in girls.
    (b) the appearance of secondary sex characteristics in girls.
    (c) the complete maturation of secondary sex characteristics in girls.
    (d) first menstruation.

16. According to Erikson, adolescence is characterized by the crisis of
    (a) ego identity vs. role diffusion.
    (b) intimacy vs. isolation.
    (c) autonomy vs. doubt.
    (d) ego integrity vs. despair.

17. Sheehy labels the 30s the "Catch 30s," because
    (a) the long bones make no further gains in length.
    (b) of disillusionments and reassessments.
    (c) women enter midlife at about age 35.
    (d) we reach the halfway point of the typical life span.

18. Research shows that middle–aged women
    (a) frequently show increased dominance and assertiveness.
    (b) most often report decreased marital satisfaction.
    (c) cannot make the transition from motherhood to socially useful occupations.
    (d) come under the influence of the dream.

19. According to the cellular aging theory, the ability to repair _____ decreases as we age.
    (a) the cell wall
    (b) the myelin sheath
    (c) DNA
    (d) RNA

20. A woman is concerned about having children of her own because she was abused as a child and has heard that child abuse "runs in families." Research concerning child abuse shows that
    (a) child abuse is more likely to run in families for men than women.
    (b) child abuse is more likely to run in families for women than men.
    (c) the majority of men who have been abused abuse their own children.
    (d) the majority of women who have been abused abuse their own children.

**Answer Key to *Posttest***

| | |
|---|---|
| 1. B | 11. D |
| 2. C | 12. D |
| 3. A | 13. C |
| 4. C | 14. B |
| 5. D | 15. D |
| 6. D | 16. A |
| 7. B | 17. B |
| 8. C | 18. A |
| 9. A | 19. C |
| 10. C | 20. A |

| | |
|---|---|
| Zygote | Cephalocaudal |
| Siblings | Proximodistal |
| Embryo | Androgens |
| Maturation | Amniotic sac |
| Stage | Placenta |
| Puberty | Umbilical cord |
| Fetus | Neonate |

| | |
|---|---|
| Proceeding from top to bottom. | A fertilized ovum. |
| Proceeding from near to far. | Brothers and sisters. |
| Male sex hormones. | The baby from the third through the eighth weeks following conception, during which time the major organ systems undergo rapid differentiation. |
| A sac within the uterus that contains the embryo or fetus. | The orderly unfolding of traits, as regulated by the genetic code. |
| A membrane that permits the exchange of nutrients and waste products between the mother and her developing child but does not allow the maternal and fetal blood streams to mix. | A distinct period of life that is qualitatively different from other stages. |
| A tube between the mother and her developing child through which nutrients and waste products are conducted. | The period of early adolescence during which hormones spur rapid physical development. |
| A newly born child. | The baby from the third month following conception through childbirth, during which time there is maturation of organ systems and dramatic gains in length and weight. |

| Reflex | Authoritative |
| --- | --- |
| Rooting | Assimilation |
| Attachment | Scheme |
| Secure attachment | Accommodation |
| Contact comfort | Object permanence |
| Critical period | Sensorimotor stage |
| Imprinting | Preoperational stage |

| | |
|---|---|
| The style of parenting characterized by warmth and restrictiveness. | A simple unlearned response to a stimulus. |
| According to Piaget, the inclusion of a new event into an existing scheme. | The turning of an infant's head toward a touch, such as by the mother's nipple. |
| According to Piaget, a hypothetical mental structure that permits the classification and organization of new information. | The enduring, affectionate tie that binds one person to another. |
| According to Piaget, the modification of schemes so that information inconsistent with existing schemes can be integrated or understood. | A type of attachment characterized by positive feelings toward attachment figures and feelings of security. |
| Recognition that objects removed from sight still exist, as demonstrated by young children by continued pursuit. | A hypothesized primary drive to seek physical comfort through contact with another. |
| The first of Piaget's stages of cognitive development, characterized by coordination of sensory information and motor activity, early exploration of the environment, and lack of language. | A period of time when a fixed action pattern can be elicited by a releasing stimulus. |
| The second of Piaget's stages, characterized by illogical use of words and symbols, spotty logic, and egocentrism. | A process occurring during a critical period in the development of an organism, whereas that organism responds to a stimulus in a manner that will afterward be difficult to modify. |

| | |
|---|---|
| Egocentric | Subjective moral judgment |
| Animism | Reversibility |
| Artificialism | Formal-operational stage |
| Conservation | Information processing |
| Center | Metamemory |
| Concrete-operational stage | Preconventional level |
| Decentration | Conventional level |

| | |
|---|---|
| According to Piaget, moral judgments that are based on the motives of the perpetrator. | According to Piaget, assuming that others view the world as one does oneself. |
| According to Piaget, recognition that processes can be undone, that things can be made as they were. | The belief that inanimate objects move because of will or spirit. |
| Piaget's fourth stage, characterized by abstraction and logical thought; deduction from principles. | The belief that natural objects have been created by human beings. |
| An approach to cognitive development that deals with children's advances in the input, storage, retrieval, manipulation, and output of information. | According to Piaget, recognition that basic properties of substance, such as weight and mass, remain the same when superficial features change. |
| Knowledge of the functions and processes in one's own memory, as shown by the use of cognitive strategies to retain information. | According to Piaget, to focus one's attention. |
| According to Kohlberg, a period during which moral judgments are based largely on expectation of rewards or punishments. | Piaget's third stage, characterized by logical thought concerning tangible objects, conservation, and subjective morality. |
| According to Kohlberg, a period during which moral judgments largely reflect social conventions. A "law and order" approach to morality. | Simultaneous focusing on more than one dimension of a problem, so that flexible, reversible thought becomes possible. |

| | |
|---|---|
| Postconventional level | Intimacy versus isolation |
| Reciprocity | Menopause |
| Adolescence | Empty-nest syndrome |
| Secondary sex characteristics | Reaction time |
| Menarche | Longevity |
| Ego identity | Ego integrity versus despair |
| Role diffusion | Midlife crisis |

| | |
|---|---|
| Erikson's life crisis of young adulthood, which is characterized by the task of developing abiding intimate relationships. | According to Kohlberg, a period during which moral judgments are derived from moral principles, and people look to themselves to set moral standards. |
| The cessation of menstruation. | Mutual action. |
| A sense of depression and loss of purpose felt by some parents when the youngest child leaves home. | The period of life bounded by puberty and assumption of adult responsibilities. |
| The amount of time required to respond to a stimulus. | Characteristics that differentiate the sexes, such as distribution of body hair and depth of voice, but that are not directly involved in reproduction. |
| A long span of life. | The beginning of menstruation. |
| Erikson's term for the crisis of late adulthood, characterized by the task of maintaining one's sense of identity despite physical deterioration. | Erikson's term for a firm sense of who one is and what one stands for. |
| A crisis experienced by many people during the midlife transition when they realize that life may be more than halfway over, and they reassess their achievements in terms of their dreams. | Erikson's term for lack of clarity in one's life roles–a function of failure to develop ego identity. |

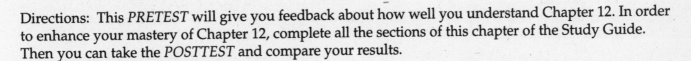

# Chapter 12 — Personality

Directions: This *PRETEST* will give you feedback about how well you understand Chapter 12. In order to enhance your mastery of Chapter 12, complete all the sections of this chapter of the Study Guide. Then you can take the *POSTTEST* and compare your results.

1. A friend cannot remember a disturbing event. According to psychodynamic theory, the automatic ejection of anxiety–evoking ideas from consciousness is termed
   (a) suppression.
   (b) repression.
   (c) amnesia.
   (d) resistance.

2. According to psychodynamic theory, the _____ follows the moral principle.
   (a) id
   (b) ego
   (c) superego
   (d) libido

3. According to psychodynamic theory, the _____ acts as a watchdog, or censor, that screens impulses.
   (a) id
   (b) ego
   (c) superego
   (d) libido

4. As it is conceptualized in psychodynamic theory, the Electra complex is a(n) _____ feature of psychosexual development in
   (a) normal; girls.
   (b) normal; boys.
   (c) abnormal; girls.
   (d) abnormal; boys.

5. According to the text, Alfred Adler and Erich Fromm both criticize Freud for
   (a) theorizing that there are several stages of psychosexual development.
   (b) suggesting that physiological needs are important to people.
   (c) prejudice toward women.
   (d) placing too much emphasis on unconscious motives.

6. According to Carl Jung, archetypes
   (a) are conscious.
   (b) serve the function of instincts.
   (c) render us responsive to cultural themes in stories.
   (d) are learned from stories and motion pictures.

7. Alfred Adler agreed with Carl Jung that
   (a) there is a collective unconscious.
   (b) men have a feminine side, or anima.
   (c) self–awareness plays a major role in personality formation.
   (d) situational variables are as important as person variables in influencing behavior.

8. A man is insecure, shows an excessive need for approval, and "moves toward" others. According to Karen Horney, this man's behavior is probably motivated by
   (a) the theory of social comparison.
   (b) the social instinct.
   (c) the Oedipus complex.
   (d) basic anxiety.

9. Who was the first theorist to distinguish between introverts and extroverts?
   (a) Carl Jung
   (b) Gordon Allport
   (c) Hans J. Eysenck
   (d) Raymond Cattell

Chapter 12     Personality     305

10. The Sixteen Personality Factors Scale was created by
    (a) Hans J. Eysenck.
    (b) Henry Murray.
    (c) Raymond Cattell.
    (d) Gordon Allport.

11. Who is **NOT** a social–learning theorist?
    (a) Albert Bandura
    (b) B. F. Skinner
    (c) Julian Rotter
    (d) Walter Mischel

12. According to B. F. Skinner, adaptation to the environment requires
    (a) surfacing of archetypes that meet the demands of the situation.
    (b) observational learning of behavior.
    (c) flexibility and originality.
    (d) acceptance of behavior patterns that ensure survival.

13. According to the text, which of the following social–learning theory concepts is most similar to a trait?
    (a) a generalized expectation
    (b) a self–regulatory system
    (c) the subjective value of a reward
    (d) a competency

14. Who is **LEAST** likely to be considered humanistic?
    (a) Abraham Maslow
    (b) Albert Bandura
    (c) Sigmund Freud
    (d) Erik Erikson

15. According to Carl Rogers, conditional positive regard may lead children to develop
    (a) unconditional positive regard.
    (b) conditions of worth.
    (c) self–esteem.
    (d) unique frames of reference.

16. Which personality theorist suffered from rickets and pneumonia as a child, and may have developed his theory in part from his own childhood striving to overcome repeated bouts of illness?
    (a) Abraham Maslow
    (b) Carl Jung
    (c) Carl Rogers
    (d) Alfred Adler

17. Which theorist labels stages after traits that might be developed during that stage, rather than after erogenous zones?
    (a) Sigmund Freud
    (b) Gordon Allport
    (c) Erik Erikson
    (d) Raymond Cattell

18. We would **NOT** expect to find a(n) _____ on a projective measure of personality.
    (a) forced–choice format
    (b) inkblot
    (c) ambiguous stimulus
    (d) standardized group of stimuli

19. Which of the following is the most widely used instrument for personality measurement in psychological research?
    (a) Rorschach Inkblot Test
    (b) California Psychological Inventory
    (c) Thematic Apperception Test
    (d) Minnesota Multiphasic Personality Inventory

20. Interpretation of the Minnesota Multiphasic Personality Inventory is clouded by the fact that
    (a) ambiguous stimuli lead to ambiguous responses.
    (b) high validity scale scores do not necessarily invalidate the test for disordered respondents.
    (c) psychologists with a psychodynamic orientation interpret the test differently from psychologists with other orientations.
    (d) whites, African Americans, and other racial groups score similarly.

Answer Key to *Pretest*

| | |
|---|---|
| 1. B | 11. B |
| 2. C | 12. D |
| 3. B | 13. A |
| 4. A | 14. C |
| 5. D | 15. B |
| 6. C | 16. D |
| 7. C | 17. C |
| 8. D | 18. A |
| 9. A | 19. D |
| 10. C | 20. B |

Personality is defined as a reasonably stable pattern of behavior that distinguishes people from one another. The chapter is broken down into two major sections. The first deals with four broad theoretical approaches to personality: psychodynamic theories, trait theories, learning theories, and humanistic–existential theories. The second deals with the psychological measurement of personality.

Sigmund Freud originated psychodynamic theory. There is a description of his mental or psychic structures (the id, ego, and superego), and of his stages of psychosexual development (oral, anal, phallic, latency, and genital). The psychodynamic theories of Carl Jung, Alfred Adler, Karen Horney, and Erik Erikson are then outlined.

Traits are defined as elements of personality that account for behavioral consistency. Gordon Allport's historical contribution is discussed, along with Raymond Cattell's views on surface traits and source traits. Hans Eysenck's personality dimensions of introversion–extroversion and neuroticism are outlined.

Next, learning approaches to personality are outlined. Behaviorism sees behavior patterns as developing largely from environmental influences. Social–learning theory explains behavior in terms of person variables and situational variables.

The humanistic–existential views of Viktor Frankl, Abraham Maslow, and Carl Rogers are discussed. Frankl asserts that people strive for meaning and can make meaningful choices under even the most adverse circumstances. Rogers suggests that people attempt to shape their own personalities ("actualize" themselves) through freedom of choice and action. Each of us has a unique potential and, with unconditional positive regard from others, we shall naturally try to reach our potentials.

Personality tests take samples of behavior, usually by means of self report, to predict future behavior. The following objective tests are stressed: Minnesota Multiphasic Personality Inventory, California Psychological Inventory, and vocational measures. The Rorschach inkblot test and the Thematic Apperception Test are described as the major projective measures of personality.

# LEARNING OBJECTIVES

| | "Why Are They Sad and Glad and Bad?" Introduction to Personality |
|---|---|
| 1. Define *personality*. | |
| | **The Psychodynamic Perspective** |
| 2. Describe the "mental structures" theorized by Sigmund Freud in his *psychodynamic theory*. | |
| 3. List Freud's stages of psychosexual development, and describe the major events that occur during each stage. | |
| 4. Describe the psychodynamic views of Carl Jung. | |

5. Describe the psychodynamic views of Alfred Adler.

6. Describe the psychodynamic views of Karen Horney.

7. Describe the psychodynamic views of Erik Erikson.

8. Evaluate psychodynamic theory.

## The Trait Perspective

9. Define *trait*.

10. Describe the contribution of Gordon Allport to trait theory.

11. Describe the trait–theory views of Raymond Cattell.

12. Describe the trait–theory views of Hans Eysenck.

13. Evaluate trait theory.

## The Learning Perspective

14. Describe the behaviorist approach to understanding personality.

15. Describe the social–cognitive-theory approach to understanding personality, emphasizing the roles of person and situational variables.

16. Evaluate the learning theory of personality.

## The Humanistic-Existential Perspective

17. Describe Abraham Maslow's humanistic–existential views on personality.

18. Describe Carl Rogers' humanistic–existential views on personality.

19. Evaluate humanistic–existential theory.

## Measurement of Personality

20. Differentiate between objective and projective measures of personality.

21. Describe some of the major objective measures of personality.

22. Describe some of the major projective measures of personality.

23. Compare and contrast individuality and relatedness.

24. Discuss sociocultural factors related to one's sense of self, and discuss cognitive gender differences.

## "Why Are They Sad and Glad and Bad?" Introduction to Personality

## The Psychodynamic Perspective

1. Freud's Theory of Psychosexual Development

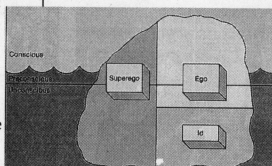

2. Other Psychodynamic Theorists

3. Evaluation of the Psychodynamic Perspective

## The Trait Perspective

1. From Hippocrates to the Present Day

2. Hans Eysenck

3. The Big Five Factor Structure

4. Evaluation of the Trait Perspective

## The Learning Perspective

1. Behaviorism

2. Social-Cognitive Theory

3. Evaluation of the Learning Perspective

# The Humanistic-Existential Perspective

   1. Abraham Maslow and the Challenge of Self-Actualization

   2. Carl Rogers' Self Theory

   3. Evaluation of the Humanistic-Existential Perspective

# Measurement of Personality

   1. Objective Tests

   2. Projective Tests

# Psychology and Modern Life

   1. Gender Differences

   2. The Development of Gender Differences

# Writing "A" Papers

## Preparing Your Paper

### 1. How to Start

Begin by asking the following questions when writing a paper for an instructor: What important questions should I answer in this paper? What are important issues I need to cover in order to demonstrate critical thinking skills?

### 2. Pick Your Topic

Pick a topic you find interesting and that your instructor believes is important. By listening closely in class, you will often detect certain areas that are of high interest to the instructor. Talking with the instructor will also give you ideas.

### 3. Remember Your Audience

Always keep in mind that you are writing to an audience of one person, your instructor. Because your instructor is the person you are writing for, it is very important to take extra time to find out exactly what you need to do in your paper to get a good evaluation. If your instructor is not clear or is unwilling to talk with you about your paper, talk to students who have taken the course.

### 4. Read the Material

Brainstorm a list of important questions you should answer in the paper. To demonstrate critical thinking, come up with questions that examine the subject from more than one view. Acknowledge that there are other significant questions, but that you have chosen to limit yourself to several high-priority questions.

### 5. Go to the Library

Find several books and journals which deal with the questions you have written on your topic. Reference librarians are experts in finding material on very diverse topics. Make copies of any material you think is good for your topic but cannot be checked out of the library. Taking the time to learn to use the library effectively will be time well spent. The library is an incredible resource for your academic career and beyond.

### 6. Develop and Outline

Begin your outline with an introduction. It tells the instructor what important questions you intend to answer. Next, list the questions you will be answering in the order you feel is best to deal with them. The last part of your outline will be the conclusion.

### 7. Show Your Outline to the Instructor

After you have developed the outline, you can ensure you are going the right direction by discussing it with your instructor.

## Writing Your Paper

### 8. Write Your Answers

Collecting the information is probably the most time-consuming part of writing a paper. The next step is to write the answers to your questions as precisely as possible. Be brief. Do not include irrelevant information. Make your point, back it with sufficient examples and data, and leave it at that. Give precise references to your information sources in citations.

### 9. Put Answers in Logical Order

Once you have written your answers, put them in a logical order so that they build upon one another. Your next job is to connect them with written material.

### 10. Rewrite Your Introduction

Now that you have answered your questions and developed the body of your paper, you are ready to rewrite your introduction.

### 11. Write Your Conclusion

In the conclusion, you summarize the major points you have discussed in your paper. You can point out that your paper raises further questions that need to be answered. Your summary shows how all the pieces fit together to prove a point.

### 12. Rewrite Your Paper

After you write your first draft, make an appointment to go over it with your instructor. Writers produce several rough drafts before attempting their final version. Computers are great for this process because there is less rewriting. Allow enough time for this important rewriting, including grammar, spelling, and punctuation.

# KEY TERMS AND CONCEPTS

## Introduction to Personality

1. Personality _____

## The Psychodynamic Perspective

2. Psychodynamic theory _____

3. Conscious _____

4. Preconscious _____

5. Unconscious _____

6. Repression _____

7. Psychoanalysis _____

8. Self–insight _____

9. Resistance _____

10. Psychic structure _____

11. Id _____

12. Pleasure principle _____

13. Ego _____

14. Reality principle _____

15. Defense mechanism _____

16. Superego _____

17. Identification _____

18. Moral principle _____

19. Eros _____

20. Libido _____

21. Erogenous zone _____

22. Psychosexual development _____

23. Oral stage _____

24. Weaning _____

25. Fixation _____

26. Oral fixation _____

27. Anal stage _____

28. Anal fixation _____

29. Anal–retentive _____

30. Anal–expulsive _____

31. Sadism _____

32. Phallic stage _____

33. Clitoris _____

34. Oedipus complex _____

35. Electra complex _____

36. Displaced _____

37. Latency _____

38. Genital stage _____

39. Incest taboo _____

40. Pregenital _____

41. Analytical psychology _____

42. Collective unconscious _____

43. Archetypes _____

44. Self _____

45. Inferiority complex _____

46. Drive for superiority _____

47. Creative self _____

48. Individual psychology _____

49. Basic anxiety _____

50. Basic hostility _____

51. Psychosocial development _____

52. Ego identity _____

## The Trait Perspective

53. Trait _____

54. Lexical hypothesis _____

55. Factor analysis _____

56. Surface traits _____

57. Source traits _____

58. Introversion _____

59. Extroversion _____

60. Neuroticism _____

61. Circular explanation _____

62. Self–consciousness _____

## The Learning Perspective

63. Prosocial _____

64. Social–cognitive theory _____

65. Person variables _____

66. Expectancies _____

67. Subjective value _____

68. Model _____

69. Competencies _____

70. Encode _____

71. Stimulus-outcome relations _____

72. Behavior-outcome relations _____

73. Self–efficacy expectations _____

## The Humanistic–Existential Perspective

74. Phenomenological _____

75. Humanism _____

76. Existentialism _____

77. Authentic _____

78. Self–actualization _____

79. Gestalt _____

80. Frame of reference _____

81. Self–esteem _____

82. Unconditional positive regard _____

83. Conditional positive regard _____

84. Conditions of worth _____

85. Congruence _____

86. Self–ideal _____

## The Sociocultural Perspective

87. Sociocultural perspective _____

88. Individualist _____

89. Collectivist _____

90. Acculturation _____

## Measurement of Personality

91. Phrenology _____

92. Behavior–rating scale _____

93. Aptitude _____

94. Objective tests _____

95. Standardized test _____

96. Forced–choice format _____

97. Validity scales _____

98. Clinical scales _____

99. Response set _____

100. Projective tests _____

101. Ambiguous _____

102. Reality testing _____

## Additional Notes

_____

_____

_____

_____

_____

_____

_____

_____

_____

_____

_____

_____

_____

_____

_____

_____

_____

_____

_____

_____

_____

**SECTION 1: Introduction to Personality**

**OBJ. 1:** Personality can be defined as the reasonably stable patterns of (1) <u>be</u>_____ that distinguish people from one another. Behavior, in this instance, includes thoughts and (2) _____tions. These behavior patterns characterize a person's ways of (3) _____ing to the demands of his or her life.

**SECTION 2: The Psychodynamic Perspective**

**OBJ. 2:** (4) <u>Psycho</u>_____ theories of personality teach that personality is characterized by a struggle between drives, such as sex and aggression on the one hand, and laws, social rules, and moral codes on the other. The laws and social rules become (5) _____lized; that is, we make them parts of ourselves.

Sigmund Freud labeled the clashing forces of personality (6) _____ic structures. Psychodynamic theory assumes that we are driven largely by (7) _____scious motives. Conflict is inevitable as basic instincts of hunger, (8) <u>s</u>_____, and (9) <u>ag</u>_____ come up against social pressures to follow laws, rules, and moral codes. The automatic ejection of anxiety–evoking ideas from awareness is called (10) _____sion. Repression protects us from recognizing many impulses that are in conflict with our moral values.

Freud hypothesized the existence of (11) _____ psychic structures. The unconscious (12) _____ is the psychic structure present at birth. The id represents psychological drives and operates according to the (13) <u>pl</u>_____ principle, seeking instant gratification.

The psychic structure called the (14) _____ is the sense of self, or "I." The ego develops through experience and operates accord-ing to the (15) <u>re</u>_____ principle. The ego takes into account what is practical and possible in gratifying the impulses of the (16) <u>i</u>_____. So–called (17) <u>de</u>_____ mechanisms protect the ego from anxiety by repressing unacceptable ideas or distorting reality.

The third psychic structure is the (18) _____. The superego is the moral sense. It develops throughout early childhood, including the standards of parents and others by means of (19) _____fication. The superego operates according to the (20) <u>m</u>_____ principle. The superego holds forth the example of the (21) <u>i</u>_____ self. It also acts like a (22) <u>co</u>_____, handing out judgments of right and wrong and flooding the ego with (23) <u>g</u>_____ and shame when the verdict is in the negative.

**OBJ. 3:** People undergo psychosexual development as psychosexual energy, or (24) <u>l</u>_____, is transferred from one (25) _____nous zone to another during childhood. There are (26) _____ stages of psychosexual development. They are the oral, (27) _____, phallic, (28) _____, and genital stages.

Freud believed that each stage would bring conflict. During the (29) _____ stage, conflict would center on the nature and extent of oral gratification, and issues such as weaning. Conflict during the anal stage would concern (30) <u>t</u>_____ training and the general issue of (31) <u>s</u>_____–control. (32) <u>Fi</u>_____ in a stage may lead to the development of traits associated with that stage. Fixation in the oral stage, for example, may lead to oral traits such as (33) <u>dep</u>_____ and (34) <u>g</u>_____ility. Anal fixation may result in extremes of (35) <u>cl</u>_____ness versus messiness, or of (36) <u>per</u>_____ism versus carelessness.

The Oedipus and Electra complexes are conflicts of the (37) _____ic stage. In these conflicts, children long to possess the parent of the (38: *Circle one:* same or opposite) gender. and resent the parent of the (39: *Circle one:* same or opposite) gender. Under normal circumstances, these complexes eventually become resolved by identifying with the parent of the (40: *Circle one:* same or opposite) gender.

The (41) _____cy stage is a period of life during which Freud believed sexual feelings remain largely unconscious. Freud believed that we enter the genital stage at (42) p_____. During the genital stage, the (43) i_____ taboo motivates us to displace sexual impulses onto adults or adolescents of the (44: *Circle one:* same or opposite) sex.

Freud believed that it was normal for women to accept the (45) au_____ of their husbands, and to want to bear (46) ch_____. Freud believed that women who compete in the business world had never surrendered the wish to have a (47) p_____ of their own. Neoanalysts and feminists consider Freud's penis–envy hypothesis to be based on ignorance and (48) _____dice.

**OBJ. 4:** Carl Jung's psychodynamic theory is called (49) _____cal psychology. Jung believed that in addition to a personal unconscious mind, we also have a (50) _____tive unconscious, which contains primitive images or (51) _____pes that are reflections of the history of our species. Jung downplayed the importance of the (52) _____ual instinct. He also believed that one of the archetypes was the (53) _____, a conscious, unifying force in personality that provides us with direction and purpose.

**OBJ. 5:** Alfred Adler's psychodynamic theory is called (54) _____ual psychology. Adler believed that people are basically motivated by an (55) _____ity complex, and that this complex gave rise to a compensating drive for (56) _____ity.

**OBJ. 6:** Karen (57) H_____, like Freud, saw parent–child relationships as paramount in importance. When parents treat children indifferently or harshly, the children develop feelings of insecurity that Horney labeled basic (58) _____ty. Children also resent neglectful parents, giving rise to basic (59) _____ty. Later in life, repressed hostility can lead us to relate to others in a (60) _____tic manner.

**OBJ. 7:** Erik Erikson's psychodynamic theory is called the theory of (61) psycho_____ development. Erikson highlights the importance of early (62) _____al relationships rather than the gratification of childhood (63) _____al impulses. Erikson extended Freud's five developmental stages to (64) _____. Erikson's stages are characterized by certain life (65) _____ses. These are the crises of (66) _____ vs. mistrust, (67) _____my vs. shame and doubt, initiative vs. (68) g_____, (69) _____try vs. inferiority, identity vs. (70) _____ diffusion, (71) _____vity vs. stagnation, and integrity vs. (72) de_____.

**OBJ. 8:** Psychodynamic theory (73: *Circle one:* advanced or contradicted) the view that human behavior is subject to scientific analysis. Psychodynamic theory focused attention on the (74: *Circle one:* importance or unimportance) of childhood events. Freud also helped people (75: *Circle one:* deny or recognize) the importance of sexuality and aggressive impulses in their lives.

But Freud has been criticized by followers, like Erik Erikson, Alfred Adler, and Erich Fromm, for placing too much emphasis on sexual urges and (76: *Circle one:* conscious or unconscious) motives. Karl Popper criticizes Freud's psychodynamic theory because:

(a) Freud's theoretical mental processes (77: *Circle one:* can or cannot) be observed;

(b) Freud's theory (78: *Circle one:* does or does not) predict behavior with precision; and

(c) Freud's views are not capable of being disproved.

## SECTION 3: The Trait Perspective

**OBJ. 9:** Traits are personality elements that are inferred from (79) _____ or. Traits are said to endure and to account for behavioral (80) _____ ency.

**OBJ. 10:** Gordon Allport thought of traits as embedded in our (81) _____ us systems. Allport and Odbert catalogued 18,000 human traits from a search through word lists of the sort found in (82) _____ aries.

**OBJ. 11:** According to Raymond Cattell, (83) s_____ traits are characteristic ways of behaving that seem linked in an orderly manner. (84) S_____ traits are underlying traits from which surface traits are derived. Cattell constructed the (85) S_____ Personality Factors Scale, a test that measures source traits.

**OBJ. 12:** Hans J. (86) E_____ has focused on the relationships between two source traits: introversion–extroversion and emotional stability–instability, otherwise known as (87) _____ ism. Eysenck notes that his scheme is reminiscent of that suggested by (88) _____ ates, the Greek physician. Hippocrates suggested that there are (89) _____ basic personality types: (90) _____ ric (quick–tempered), sanguine (warm, cheerful, confident), (91) phl_____ (sluggish, calm, cool), and (92) _____ lic (gloomy, pensive).

**OBJ. 13:** Trait theory has contributed to the development of psychological tests. It has also given rise to theories concerning the (93) _____ t between personality and jobs. It has identified basic traits and pointed out that traits (94: *Circle one:* are or are not) generally stable. On the other hand, trait theories tend to describe rather than (95) ex_____ behavior. Trait–theory explanations of behavior have been criticized as (96) _____ lar. Also, there is somewhat (97: *Circle one:* more or less) situational variability in behavior than trait theorists might allow, especially among people who are (98: *Circle one:* high or low) in private self–consciousness.

## SECTION 4: The Learning Perspective

**OBJ. 14:** Learning theorists of personality place more emphasis on (99) _____ nal variables than on internal, (100) p_____ variables as the shapers of human preferences and behaviors. The behaviorists John B. Watson and B. F. (101) _____ discarded notions of personal freedom, and argued that environmental contingencies can shape people into wanting to do the things that the physical environment and society requires of them.

**OBJ. 15:** Modern social–cognitive theory, in contrast to behaviorism, has a strong (102) cog_____ orientation and focuses on the importance of learning by (103) _____ tion. Rotter argues that behavior depends upon the person's (104) _____ ancies concerning the outcome of that behavior and the perceived or (105) _____ tive values of those outcomes.

Social–learning theorists do not consider only situational rewards and (106) _____ ents important in the prediction of behavior. They also consider the roles of (107) p_____ variables. Person variables include (108) co_____ cies, (109) en_____ ing strategies, expectancies, subjective values, and (110) self–_____ tory systems and plans. Competencies include (111) kn_____ of rules that guide conduct; concepts about ourselves and other people; and

(112) _____ lls. Expectancies are "if–then" statements or personal (113) _____ tions about the outcome (or [114] _____ cement contingencies) of engaging in a response. Bandura refers to beliefs that one can handle a task as (115) self–_____ expectations. We are (116: *Circle one:* more or less) likely to persist at difficult tasks when we believe that we shall succeed at them.

**OBJ. 16:** Learning theories have stimulated us to focus on (117: *Circle one:* observable or unobservable) behavior and on the (118: *Circle one:* internal or situational) determinants of behavior. They have led to innovations in therapy methods and had a (119: *Circle one:* broad or limited) impact on the science of psychology. Behaviorism fails to deal with human (120) cog_____ processes. Social– learning theory has not yet derived satisfying statements about the development of (121) _____ ts and may not pay enough attention to (122) g_____ ic variation.

**SECTION 5: Humanistic–Existential Perspective**

Humanists and (123) _____ lists dwell on the meaning of life. Their awareness of their existence—of their (124) _____ ing in the world—is the hub of the humanistic–existential search for meaning. Because of their focus on conscious, subjective experience, humanistic–existential theories have also been referred to as (125) _____ logical. The European existentialist philosophers Jean–Paul Sartre and Martin Heidegger saw human life as trivial in the grand scheme of things, leading to feelings of (126) _____ ation. Psychological "salvation" requires implanting personal (127) _____ ing on things and making personal (128) ch_____ s.

**OBJ. 17:** Abraham Maslow argued that people also have growth–oriented needs for (129) self–_____ ation. Self–actualization requires taking (130) _____ s.

**OBJ. 18:** Carl Rogers' theory begins with the assumption of the existence of the (131) s_____. According to Carl (132) R_____, the self is an organized and consistent way in which a person perceives his or her "I" to relate to others and the world.

The self is innate and will attempt to become actualized (develop its unique potential) when the person receives (133) _____ ional positive regard. We all have needs for self-esteem and see the world through unique frames of (134) _____ nce. Conditions of (135) w_____ lead to a distorted self–concept, to the disowning of parts of the self, and, often, to anxiety. When we accept our feelings as our own, there is a fit between our self–concepts and our behavior, thoughts, and emotions that Rogers calls psychological (136) _____ ence.

**OBJ. 19:** Phenomenological theories focus on (137) _____ ous experience and grant us the freedom to make choices. But critics point out that conscious experience is private and (138) _____ tive, and thus not ideal subject matter for scientific investigation. Moreover, the concept of (139) self–_____ tion yields circular explanations for behavior.

**SECTION 6: Measurement of Personality**

**OBJ. 20:** In personality measurement, psychologists take a sample of (146) b_____ in order to predict future behavior.

(141) _____ ive tests present test–takers with a standardized set of test items in the form of questionnaires. Respondents are limited to a specific range of answers, as in multiple–choice tests or true–false tests. A (142) fo_____ – _____ format requires respondents to indicate which of two or more statements is true of them, or which of several activities they prefer. Projective tests present (143) _____ uous stimuli and permit the respondent a broad range of answers.

**OBJ. 21:** The (144) M_____ (145) M_____

Personality Inventory (MMPI) is the most widely used psychological test in the clinical setting. The MMPI is an (146) _____ive personality test that uses a true–false format to assess (147) ab_____ behavior. The MMPI contains (148) _____ity scales as well as clinical scales and has been validated empirically.

Other widely used objective personality tests include the (149) C_____ Psychological Inventory, which measures normal behavior patterns, and the (150) S_____/C_____ Interest Inventory, which helps adolescents and adults make occupational choices.

**OBJ. 22:** The foremost projective technique is the (151) R_____ inkblot test, in which test–takers are asked to report what inkblots look like or could be. Rorschach responses are scored according to location, (152) _____nants (e.g., shading, texture, and color), content, and (153) f_____ level.

The (154) T_____ (155) A_____ Test (TAT) consists of ambiguous drawings that test–takers are asked to interpret. The TAT is widely used in research on social motives as well as in clinical practice.

**Answer Key to *Chapter Review***

1. behavior
2. emotions
3. adapting
4. psychodynamic
5. internalized
6. psychic
7. unconscious
8. sex
9. aggression
10. repression
11. three
12. id
13. pleasure
14. ego
15. reality
16. id
17. defense
18. superego
19. identification
20. moral
21. ideal
22. conscience
23. guilt
24. libido
25. erogenous
26. five
27. anal
28. latency
29. oral
30. toilet
31. self-control
32. Fixation
33. dependence (or depression)
34. gullibility
35. cleanliness
36. perfectionism
37. phallic
38. opposite
39. same
40. same
41. latency
42. puberty
43. incest
44. opposite
45. authority
46. children
47. penis
48. prejudice
49. analytical
50. collective
51. archetypes
52. sexual
53. self
54. individual
55. inferiority
56. superiority
57. Horney
58. anxiety
59. hostility
60. neurotic
61. psychosocial
62. social
63. sexual
64. eight
65. crises
66. trust
67. autonomy

68. guilt
69. industry
70. role
71. Ggenerativity
72. despair
73. advanced
74. importance
75. recognize
76. unconscious
77. cannot
78. does not
79. behavior
80. consistency
81. nervous
82. dictionaries
83. surface
84. Source
85. Sixteen
86. Eysenck
87. neuroticism
88. Hippocrates
89. four
90. choleric
91. phlegmatic
92. melancholic
93. fit
94. are
95. explain
96. circular
97. more
98. high
99. situational (or external)
100. person
101. Skinner
102. cognitive
103. observation
104. expectancies
105. subjective
106. punishments
107. person
108. competencies
109. encoding
110. regulatory
111. knowledge
112. Sskills
113. predictions
114. reinforcement

115. self-efficacy
116. more
117. observable
118. situational
119. broad
120. cognitive
121. traits
122. genetic
123. existentialists
124. being
125. phenomenological
126. alienation
127. meaning
128. choices
129. self–actualization
130. risks
131. self
132. Rogers
133. unconditional
134. reference
135. worth
136. congruence
137. conscious
138. subjective
139. self-actualization
140. behavior
141. Objective
142. forced–choice
143. ambiguous
144. Minnesota
145. Multiphasic
146. objective
147. abnormal
148. validity
149. California
150. Strong/Campbell
151. Rorschach
152. determinants
153. form
154. Thematic
155. Apperception

| Idioms | | |
|---|---|---|
| 444 | pick(s) a fight | starts an argument |
| 445 | at worst | the worst |
| 469 | upside down | turned around so that the other side is at the top |

| Cultural References | | |
|---|---|---|
| 446 | Byron | One of the romantic English poets of the 19th century |
| 455 | a date | an invitation to another person to go out socially |
| 456 | her serve | refers to the game of tennis; the serve puts the ball in the game and there is an advantage to the server if she can hit a powerful and accurate serve |
| 456 | any sacks | refers to the game of football; tackle and bring down to the ground the ball carrier of the opposing team |
| 469 | adjusting a carburetor | modifying the mixture between air and gasoline in the engine of a car in order to obtain better operation |
| 469 | golf | a sport requiring accurate hitting of a small ball over a large area of ground and ultimately hitting it into a hole |
| 469 | chess | a game which requires a great amount of skill that is played on a board; a player needs to project future moves in order to capture the opponent's chess pieces |
| 469 | jack-o'-lantern | at Halloween, people often carve faces in pumpkins and then make a lamp (lantern) from it by putting a lighted candle inside |

| Phrases and Expressions (Different Usage) | | |
|---|---|---|
| 441 | So it is that different | this is the way it is; different |
| 441 | Nor do | neither do |
| 441 | After doing so | after we do this |
| 441 | At a given moment | at a specific moment |
| 441 | owes its origin | has its origin, or beginning |
| 440 | shock of dark hair | a lot of dark hair |
| 440 | Forecasting good tidings then doom | predicting good then bad |
| 442 | poked through | went through to |
| 442 | shrouded in mystery | unknown |

| Phrases and Expressions (Different Usage) | | |
|---|---|---|
| 442 | a method of detective work | a method of figuring out answers from evidence and clues |
| 442 | prodded to talk | urged and encouraged to talk |
| 442 | that 'Pops" into their minds | that enters their mind; that they think of |
| 443 | dwell side by side | live or exist next to each other |
| 443 | be met | be gratified |
| 443 | curbs the appetites | restricts the desires |
| 443 | rising into awareness | becoming known |
| 443 | holds forth shining examples | displays excellent examples |
| 443 | hands out judgments | dispenses judgments |
| 443 | floods the ego | overwhelms the ego |
| 443 | stands between | is in between |
| 443 | braving the arrows | risking the criticisms and attacks |
| 443 | have a hard time of it | encounter difficulty |
| 443 | stirred controversy | evoked disagreement |
| 444 | assumed to harbor them | thought to have them |
| 444 | sexual advances | attempts to initiate a physical sexual relationship with the other person |
| 444 | "sickly sweet" manner | so excessively sweet that the manner is offensive |
| 444 | fueled by | caused to operate |
| 444 | clinging | attaching physically and emotionally |
| 445 | "let it all hang out" | display all feelings without any control |
| 445 | to handle | to deal with; to cope with |
| 445 | "ill-equipped" | not equipped with what they needed |
| 445 | staid | established; famous |
| 445 | avenues of fulfillment | methods or ways of having a fulfilled life |
| 445 | inner circle | the friends and colleagues who worked closely with Freud |
| 445 | fell into disfavor | became disliked |
| 446 | render us | cause us to be |
| 446 | shadowy parts | unpleasant aspects |
| 446 | Importance must be attached to fully conscious functions | fully conscious functions must be considered important |
| 446 | spurred him on to | caused him to work harder and achieve |
| 446 | in part | not completely, but enough to be considered |
| 446 | harbor feelings | have feelings and continue to have them |
| 446 | of paramount importance | the most important |
| 446 | driving them away | causing the parents to not care a |

Chapter 12  Personality

| | | |
|---|---|---|
| 446 | overly anxious to please | eager, but with anxiety, to cause the other person to be happy |
| 446 | the price | the negative emotional result |
| 447 | had placed undo emphasis on | had considered much too emphatically the importance of |
| 447 | general climate | general feeling |
| 447 | to a large degree | almost completely |
| 447 | conscious architects | we make our own personalities |
| 447 | grants more power to | gives more powers to |
| 447 | forced upon us by intrapsychic warfare | the compromises that we did not choose which result from the conflicts among the ego, superego and id |
| 447 | polar opposites | extreme opposites; ("polar" refers to the north and south poles) |
| 446 | mar the formation of | obstruct or impede the formation of |
| 447 | short-sighted hedonism | enjoying the moment without thinking about what the negative results might be |
| 447 | strike many psychologists as being | are concepts that many psychologists think are |
| 447 | fought for the idea that | tried to convince people that |
| 447 | grave psychological problems | serious psychological problems |
| 447 | signs of possession by the Devil | caused by the Devil living within the person |
| 448 | far-reaching effects | effects that will continue and also cause problems in the future |
| 448 | saving powers of love | how much love can allow children to recover |
| 450 | is also suspect | is also questionable |
| 450 | address traits | consider traits |
| 450 | "all across the board" | in every situation; all the time |
| 450 | feel at home at gatherings | feel comfortable with groups of people in a social context |
| 453 | that we 'fit" our jobs | that our jobs are appropriate to our abilities |
| 453 | suit us | make us the right person |
| 453 | from situation to situation | behavior may be a particular way in one situation but different in another |
| 454 | hue and cry was | ideas were |
| 454 | largely discard the notions | almost completely dismiss the ideas |
| 454 | as surely as | is the same way as |
| 454 | sidestep rite roles of | ignore the roles |
| 454 | are not so blindly ruled by pleasure and pain | do not allow pleasure and pain to determine their actions |
| 455 | the mercy of | victims of |

| | | |
|---|---|---|
| 455 | calling out | speaking aloud without asking for permission to speak |
| 455 | "unladylike " | not behaving like a lady |
| 455 | codes of conduct | rules for behavior |
| 455 | tossing a football properly | throwing a football in the correct way |
| 456 | "made for each other" | personalities that go together |
| 456 | made themselves miserable | cause themselves to be very unhappy |
| 456 | foster adjustment | encourage behavior that helps adjustment |
| 457 | posits that | states that |
| 457 | keep at a task | continue at one task |
| 458 | the broadest effect | the widest effect; an effect on most of the issues |
| 458 | intellectual forebear | the theories that were before it and influenced it |
| 489 | getting in touch with | becoming aware of |
| 489 | sufficient to say that | it is enough to say that; we do not need to say more |
| 489 | a carrot dangling from a stick | something good which is not close enough to reach |
| 461 | cardinal role | the most important role |
| 461 | victims of circumstance | other situations and the environment affect us and we cannot control that |
| 466 | check off | indicate that it occurred, with a check |
| 466 | forced-choice format | a form that requires that people answer something, even if none of the choices apply to that person |
| 466 | stormy relationships | unstable relationships |
| 467 | for the thrill of it | because I only wanted the exciting sensations |
| 467 | set apart people | identified people |
| 467 | a rich mine | an effective method |
| 467 | unearthing elements | discovering elements |
| 469 | the facts of the matter | the facts |
| 469 | inkblots | large areas of ink on a piece of paper |
| 469 | human torso | human figure without the head or arms or legs |
| 469 | make up stories | create stories |
| 469 | sole criteria | only criteria |
| 469 | for fear of | because we are afraid |

1. Freud labeled the clashing forces of personality
   (a) repression and resistance.
   (b) conscious and unconscious.
   (c) defense mechanisms.
   (d) psychic structures.

2. According to psychodynamic theory, the _____ follows the reality principle.
   (a) id
   (b) ego
   (c) superego
   (d) libido

3. According to psychodynamic theory, the superego usually incorporates the standards of parents through
   (a) identification.
   (b) repression.
   (c) unconditional positive regard.
   (d) classical and operant conditioning.

4. John throws his clothing and books all over the floor, keeps his hair unkempt, and rarely cleans his room. According to psychodynamic theory, John's behavior is suggestive of conflict during the _____ stage of psychosexual development.
   (a) genital
   (b) oral
   (c) phallic
   (d) anal

5. According to psychodynamic theory, the _____ follows the pleasure principle.
   (a) id
   (b) ego
   (c) superego
   (d) libido

6. Alfred Adler believed that people are basically motivated by
   (a) the collective unconscious.
   (b) hostility.
   (c) biological and safety needs.
   (d) an inferiority complex.

7. Karen Horney agreed with Freud that
   (a) some women suffer from penis envy.
   (b) there are eight stages of psychosocial development.
   (c) parent–child relationships are very important.
   (d) sexual impulses are more important than social relationships.

8. According to the text, which of the following theorists believed that a basic element of personality was the Self?
   (a) John B. Watson
   (b) Carl Jung
   (c) Sigmund Freud
   (d) Hans J. Eysenck

9. Gordon Allport looked upon traits as
   (a) archetypes.
   (b) basic instincts.
   (c) generalized expectancies.
   (d) embedded in the nervous system.

10. Raymond Cattell hypothesized the existence of two types of traits: _____ traits and source traits.
    (a) surface
    (b) cardinal
    (c) secondary
    (d) central

11. The outlooks of John B. Watson and B. F. Skinner discarded all of the following notions EXCEPT
    (a) self–direction.
    (b) personal freedom.
    (c) learning.
    (d) choice.

12. _____ has argued for the inclusion of cognitive points of view within the learning perspective.
    (a) Carl Rogers
    (b) Albert Bandura
    (c) John B. Watson
    (d) Carl Jung

13. Which of the following is a situational variable?
    (a) a self–efficacy expectation
    (b) the subjective value of a reward
    (c) a generalized expectancy
    (d) a reward

14. According to Carl Rogers, the sense of self
    (a) is an archetype.
    (b) develops as a result of conditions of worth.
    (c) is innate.
    (d) develops once biological and safety needs have been met.

15. A mother and father tell you that their most important goal for their new child is that she develop a strong sense of self–esteem. According to Carl Rogers, parents are likely to help their children develop self–esteem when they show them
    (a) conditional positive regard.
    (b) conditions of worth.
    (c) unconditional positive regard.
    (d) psychological congruence.

16. Which theorist has focused on the relationships between introversion–extroversion and neuroticism?
    (a) Carl Jung
    (b) Hans J. Eysenck
    (c) Raymond Cattell
    (d) Karen Horney

17. Which theorist explains stable behavior patterns in terms of generalized expectancies?
    (a) Julian Rotter
    (b) John B. Watson
    (c) Raymond Cattell
    (d) Walter Mischel

18. Objective personality tests
    (a) all have forced–choice formats.
    (b) are easier to answer than projective tests.
    (c) limit respondents to a specific range of answers.
    (d) are less valid than projective personality tests.

19. Which of the following tests is used to help diagnose abnormal behavior?
    (a) Minnesota Multiphasic Personality Inventory
    (b) California Psychological Inventory
    (c) Edwards Personal Preference Schedule
    (d) Strong/Campbell Interest Inventory

20. Which of the following is a "determinant" on the Rorschach inkblot test?
    (a) location
    (b) content
    (c) form level
    (d) shading

Answer Key to *Posttest*

1. D
2. B
3. A
4. D
5. A
6. D
7. C
8. B
9. D
10. A
11. C
12. B
13. D
14. C
15. C
16. B
17. A
18. C
19. A
20. D

| | |
|---|---|
| Personality | Self-insight |
| Psychodynamic theory | Resistance |
| Conscious | Psychic structure |
| Preconscious | Id |
| Unconscious | Pleasure principle |
| Repression | Ego |
| Psychoanalysis | Reality principle |

| | |
|---|---|
| Accurate awareness of one's motives and feelings. | The distinct patterns of behavior, thoughts, and feelings that characterize a person's adaptation to life. |
| A blocking of thoughts whose awareness could cause anxiety. | Sigmund Freud's perspective, which emphasizes the importance of unconscious motives and conflicts as forces that determine behavior. |
| In psychodynamic theory, a hypothesized mental structure that helps explain different aspects of behavior. | Self-aware. |
| The psychic structure present at birth, that represents physiological drives and is fully unconscious. | Capable of being brought into awareness by the focusing of attention. |
| The governing principle of the id—the seeking of immediate gratification of instinctive needs. | In psychodynamic theory, not available to awareness by simple focusing of attention. |
| The second psychic structure to develop, characterized by self-awareness, planning, and delay of gratification. | A defense mechanism that protects the person from anxiety by ejecting anxiety-evoking ideas and impulses from awareness. |
| Consideration of what is practical and possible in gratifying needs; the governing principle of the ego. | In this usage, Freud's method of exploring human personality. |

| | |
|---|---|
| Defense mechanism | Psychosexual development |
| Superego | Oral stage |
| Identification | Weaning |
| Moral principle | Fixation |
| Eros | Oral fixation |
| Libido | Anal stage |
| Erogenous zone | Anal fixation |

| | |
|---|---|
| In psychodynamic theory, the process by which libidinal energy is expressed through different erogenous zones during different stages of development. | In psychodynamic theory, an unconscious function of the ego that protects it from anxiety-evoking material by preventing accurate recognition of this material. |
| The first stage of psychosexual development, during which gratification is hypothesized to be attained primarily through oral activities. | The third psychic structure, which functions as a moral guardian and sets forth high standards for behavior. |
| Accustoming a child to not suck the mother's breast or a baby bottle. | In psychodynamic theory, the unconscious assumption of the behavior of another person. |
| In psychodynamic theory, arrested development; attachment to objects of an earlier stage. | The governing principle of the superego, which sets moral standards and enforces adherence to them. |
| Attachment to objects and behaviors characteristic of the oral stage. | In psychodynamic theory, the basic instinct to preserve and perpetuate life. |
| The second stage of psychosexual development, when gratification is attained through anal activities. | (1) In psychodynamic theory, the energy of Eros; the sexual instinct. (2) Generally, sexual interest or drive. |
| Attachment to objects and behaviors characteristic of the anal stage. | An area of the body that is sensitive to sexual sensations. |

| | |
|---|---|
| Anal-retentive | Latency |
| Anal-expulsive | Genital stage |
| Sadism | Analytical psychology |
| Phallic stage | Collective unconscious |
| Oedipus complex | Archetypes |
| Electra complex | Self |
| Displaced | Psychosocial development |

Chapter 12  Personality

| | |
|---|---|
| A phase of psychosexual development characterized by repression of sexual impulses. | Descriptive of behaviors and traits that have to do with "holding in," or self-control. |
| The mature stage of psychosexual development, characterized by preferred expression of libido through intercourse with an adult of the other gender. | Descriptive of behaviors and traits that have to do with unregulated self-expressions, such as messiness. |
| Jung's psychodynamic theory, which emphasizes the collective unconscious and archetypes. | Attaining gratification from inflicting pain upon, or humiliating, others. |
| Jung's hypothesized store of vague racial memories. | The third stage of psychosexual development, characterized by a shift of libido to the phallic region. |
| Basic, primitive images or concepts hypothesized by Jung to reside in the collective unconscious. | A conflict of the phallic stage in which the boy wishes to possess his mother sexually and perceives his father as a rival in love. |
| In analytical psychology, a conscious, unifying force to personality that provides people with direction and purpose. | A conflict of the phallic stage in which the girl longs for her father and resents her mother. |
| Erikson's theory of personality and development, which emphasizes social relationships and eight stages of growth. | Transferred. |

| | |
|---|---|
| Ego identity | Circular explanation |
| Trait | Prosocial |
| Factor analysis | Social-cognitive theory |
| Surface traits | Humanism |
| Source traits | Existentialism |
| Introversion | Authentic |
| Extroversion | Self-actualization |

Chapter 12   Personality

| | |
|---|---|
| An explanation that merely restates its own concepts instead of offering additional information. | A firm sense of who one is and what one stands for. |
| Behavior that is characterized by helping others and making a contribution to society. | A relatively stable aspect of personality that is inferred from behavior and assumed to give rise to consistent behavior. |
| A cognitively-oriented learning theory in which observational learning and person variables, such as values and expectancies, play major roles in individual differences. | A statistical technique that identifies variables or traits that tend to belong together or, as items on a personality test, to be answered in the same direction. |
| The view that people are capable of free choice, self-fulfillment, and ethical behavior. | Cattell's term for characteristic, observable ways of behavior. |
| The view that people are completely free and responsible for their own behavior. | Cattell's term for underlying traits from which surface traits are derived. |
| Genuine; consistent with one's values and beliefs. | A source trait characterized by intense imagination and the tendency to inhibit impulses. |
| In humanistic theory, the innate tendency to strive to realize one's potential. | A source trait characterized by tendencies to be socially outgoing and to express feelings and impulses freely. |

| | |
|---|---|
| Gestalt | Acculturation |
| Unconditional positive regard | Aptitude |
| Conditional positive regard | Objective tests |
| Congruence | Standardized test |
| Sociocultural perspective | Validity scales |
| Individualist | Projective tests |
| Collectivist | Ambiguous |

Chapter 12 Personality

| | |
|---|---|
| The process of adaptation in which immigrants and native groups identify with a new, dominant culture by learning about that culture and making behavioral and attitudinal changes. | A quality of wholeness. |
| A natural ability or talent. | A persistent expression of esteem for the value of a person, but not necessarily an unqualified acceptance of all of the person's behaviors. |
| Tests whose items must be answered in a specified, limited manner. Tests whose items have concrete answers that are considered correct. | Judgment of another person's values on the basis of the acceptability of that person's behaviors. |
| A test that is given to a large number of respondents so that data concerning the typical responses can be accumulated and analyzed. | According to Rogers, a fit between one's self-concept and one's behaviors, thoughts, and feelings. |
| Groups of test items that indicate whether a person's responses accurately reflect that individual's traits. | The view that focuses on the roles of ethnicity, gender, culture, and socioeconomic status in personality formation, behavior, and mental processes. |
| A psychological test that presents ambiguous stimuli onto which the test-taker projects his or her own personality in making a response. | A person who defines herself or himself in terms of personal traits and gives priority to her or his own goals. |
| Having two or more possible meanings. | A person who defines herself or himself in terms of relationships to other people and groups and gives priority to group goals. |

# Chapter 13  Psychological Disorders

Directions: This *PRETEST* will give you feedback about how well you understand Chapter 13. In order to enhance your mastery of Chapter 13, complete all the sections of this chapter of the Study Guide. Then you can take the *POSTTEST* and compare your results.

1. According to the text, the _____ model has been the most prevalent model of psychological disorders throughout history.
   (a) organic
   (b) psychodynamic
   (c) learning
   (d) demonological

2. According to the text, which of the following countries discourages aggression in children?
   (a) The United States
   (b) Ukraine
   (c) Mexico
   (d) Thailand

3. Who first suggested that psychological disorders could be caused by an abnormality of the brain?
   (a) Charcot
   (b) Kraepelin
   (c) Hippocrates
   (d) Freud

4. Some psychologists primarily conceive of schizophrenia as a disorder that impairs the perception, storage, and retrieval of information. These psychologists may be said to be viewing schizophrenic behavior patterns in terms of the _____ model of psychological disorders
   (a) organic
   (b) cognitive
   (c) learning
   (d) psychodynamic

5. A psychologist argues that psychological disorders themselves are the problem, and not any underlying problems. This is the _____ perspective of psychological disorders.
   (a) learning
   (b) organic
   (c) psychodynamic
   (d) demonological

6. The *Diagnostic and Statistical Manual* of the Mental Disorders is published by the
   (a) World Health Organization.
   (b) American Medical Association.
   (c) American Psychiatric Association.
   (d) American Psychological Association.

7. Which of the following literally means "fear of the marketplace"?
   (a) claustrophobia
   (b) agoraphobia
   (c) acrophobia
   (d) ailurophobia

8. The _____ perspective describes psychological disorders as a problem in the chemistry of the brain.
   (a) biological
   (b) cognitive
   (c) learning
   (d) psychodynamic

9. Jim complains that he has an irresistible urge to wash his hands repeatedly, which is a(n)
   (a) obsession.
   (b) compulsion.
   (c) neurosis.
   (d) psychosis.

10. Which of the following is **NOT** a dissociative disorder?
    (a) dissociative identity disorder
    (b) psychogenic amnesia
    (c) retrograde amnesia
    (d) depersonalization

11. Conversion disorder is so named because it appears to convert a
    (a) physical problem into a source of stress.
    (b) source of stress into a physical problem.
    (c) psychological problem into a source of stress.
    (d) social problem into a psychological problem.

12. All of the mood disorders involve
    (a) persistent depression.
    (b) psychotic depression.
    (c) cycles of depression and elation.
    (d) a disturbance in expressed emotions.

13. Persons with _____ are most likely to show delusions of unworthiness.
    (a) paranoid schizophrenia
    (b) disorganized schizophrenia
    (c) antisocial personality disorder
    (d) major depression

14. Depressed persons are **LEAST** likely to make _____ attributions for their failures.
    (a) specific
    (b) stable
    (c) internal
    (d) global

15. Which of the following statements about suicide is most accurate?
    (a) College students make fewer attempts than nonstudents.
    (b) More women than men attempt suicide.
    (c) More women than men succeed at suicide.
    (d) White Americans are more likely than African Americans to commit suicide.

16. The suicide rate is highest among _____ - American teenagers.
    (a) African
    (c) Asian
    (c) Hispanic
    (d) Native

17. The phenothiazines, which are often effective in treating schizophrenia, appear to work by
    (a) increasing utilization of dopamine.
    (b) blocking the action of dopamine receptors.
    (c) increasing the utilization of amphetamines.
    (d) blocking the action of amphetamine receptors.

18. Persons with antisocial personality disorder
    (a) are below average in intelligence.
    (b) tend to show abnormal chromosomal structure.
    (c) were disciplined regularly as children.
    (d) are largely undeterred by punishment.

19. Which of the following is **NOT** a symptom of anorexia nervosa?
    (a) binge eating
    (b) distorted body image
    (c) lack of menstruation
    (d) fear of being overweight

20. According to psychodynamic theory, paraphilias are defenses against
    (a) retribution.
    (b) obsessions and compulsions.
    (c) anxiety.
    (d) dominance by the id.

Answer Key to *Pretest*

| | |
|---|---|
| 1. D | 11. B |
| 2. D | 12. D |
| 3. C | 13. D |
| 4. B | 14. A |
| 5. A | 15. B |
| 6. C | 16. D |
| 7. B | 17. B |
| 8. A | 18. D |
| 9. B | 19. A |
| 10. C | 20. C |

Chapter 13 begins with criteria for determining when behavior is abnormal. Behavior is usually labeled as abnormal when it is unusual or socially unacceptable, when one's perception of reality is faulty, when one is in personal distress, or when one's behavior is self–defeating or dangerous. Historical and contemporary theories, or "models," for explaining and treating abnormal behavior are outlined: the demonological, medical (organic and psychodynamic versions), humanistic–existential, learning, and cognitive models.

Various categories of abnormal behavior are then described, and what is known of their origins is reported. There are five major types of anxiety disorders: phobic, panic, generalized, obsessive–compulsive, and post–traumatic stress disorders. Each is chiefly characterized by anxiety, but they differ in the forms that they take, and also in their origins and their durations.

Four dissociative disorders are presented: psychogenic amnesia, psychogenic fugue, multiple personality, and depersonalization. In each case, there is a sudden change in consciousness or self–identity.

Two somatoform disorders are presented: conversion disorder, in which a source of stress is "converted" into a physical problem; and hypochondriasis, in which the individual complains of serious physical symptoms, although no medical causes can be found.

Mood disorders involve disturbances in the expressed emotions. Two mood disorders are discussed: major depression and bipolar disorder, in which there are mood swings between elation and depression.

Schizophrenic disorders are discussed. They are chiefly characterized by disturbances of thought (for example, loose associations and delusions), although there are also abnormalities in perception and attention (as in hallucinations), motor responses (as in agitation or stupor), and withdrawal and autism. Research concerning the origins of schizophrenia is presented.

Personality disorders are maladaptive and persistent patterns of behavior that disturb the individual or others. Persons with antisocial personality disorder persistently violate the rights of others and show little or no remorse for their misdeeds.

## LEARNING OBJECTIVES

1. Define *psychological disorder.*

2. Explain the following models: demonological, medical (organic and psychodynamic versions), humanistic–existential, learning, and cognitive.

### Classifying Psychological Disorders

3. Discuss the classification of patterns of psychological disorders.

4. Describe the *anxiety disorders* and discuss their origins.

5. Describe the *dissociative disorders* and discuss their origins.

6. Describe the *somatoform disorders* and discuss their origins.

7. Describe the *mood disorders* and discuss their origins.

8. Describe the *schizophrenia* and discuss its origins.

9. Describe the *personality disorders* and discuss their origins.

10. Discuss the different types of *eating disorders*.

11. Describe *sexual disorders* and discuss their origins.

12. Explain who is likely to commit suicide, and discuss the factors that contribute to suicide.

**Additional Notes**

| | |
|---|---|
| **What Are Psychological Disorders?** | |
| **Classifying Psychological Disorders** | |
| **Anxiety Disorders** | |
|     1. Types of Anxiety Disorders | |
|     2. Theoretical Views | |
| **Dissociative Disorders** | |
|     1. Types of Dissociative Disorders | |
|     2. Theoretical Views | |
| **Somatoform Disorders** | |
|     1. Types of Somatoform Disorders | |
|     2. Theoretical Views | |
| **Mood Disorders** | |
|     1. Types of Mood Disorders | |
|     2. Theoretical Views | |

# Schizophrenia

1. Types of Schizophrenia

2. Theoretical Views

# Personality Disorders

1. Types of Personality Disorders

2. Theoretical Views

# Eating Disorders

1. Types of Eating Disorders

2. Theoretical Views

# Sexual Dysfunctions

1. Types of Sexual Dyfunctions

2. Theoretical Views

# Psychology and Modern Life

- Suicide

1. Dissociative identity disorder _____

2. Multiple personality disorder _____

3. Insanity _____

4. Schizophrenia _____

5. Psychological disorders _____

### What Are Psychological Disorders?

6. Hallucinations _____

7. Ideas of persecution _____

### Anxiety Disorders

8. Specific phobia _____

9. Social phobia _____

10. Claustrophobia _____

11. Acrophobia _____

12. Agoraphobia _____

13. Panic disorder _____

14. Generalized anxiety disorder _____
_____

15. Obsession _____

16. Compulsion _____

17. Post-traumatic stress disorder (PTSD) _____
_____

18. Acute stress disorder _____

19. Concordance _____

20. Gamma-aminobutyric acid (GABA) _____
_____

21. Benzodiazepines _____

### Dissociative Disorders

22. Dissociative disorders _____

23. Dissociative amnesia _____

24. Malingering _____

25. Dissociative fugue _____

26. Dissociative identity disorder _____

27. Depersonalization _____

### Somatoform Disorders

28. Somatoform disorders _____

29. Conversion disorder _____

30. La belle indifférence _____

31. Hypochondriasis _____

### Mood Disorders

32. Major depression _____

33. Psychomotor retardation _____

34. Bipolar disorder _____

35. Manic _____

36. Pressured speech _____

37. Rapid flight of ideas _____

38. Learned helplessness _____

39. Attributional style _____

40. Neuroticism _____

### Schizophrenia

41. Delusions _____

42. Stupor _____

43. Paranoid schizophrenia _____

44. Disorganized schizophrenia _____

45. Catatonic schizophrenia _____

46. Waxy flexibility _____

47. Mutism _____

### Personality Disorders

48. Personality disorders _____

49. Paranoid personality disorder _____

50. Schizotypal personality disorder _____

51. Schizoid personality disorder _____

52. Antisocial personality disorder _____

53. Avoidant personality disorder _____

_____

## Eating Disorders

54. Eating disorders _____

55. Anorexia nervosa _____

56. Bulimia nervosa _____

## Sexual Dysfunctions

57. Sexual dysfunctions _____

58. Hypoactive sexual desire disorder _____

_____

59. Female sexual arousal disorder _____

_____

60. Male erectile disorder _____

61. Orgasmic disorder _____

62. Premature ejaculation _____

63. Dyspareunia _____

64. Vaginisimus _____

65. Performance anxiety _____

## Additional Notes

## SECTION 1: What Are Psychological Disorders?

**OBJ. 1:** The text lists (1) _____ criteria for determining whether or not behavior is suggestive of psychological disorders. Behavior tends to be labeled abnormal when it is 1. unusual or (2) _____cally deviant; 2. when it is socially (3) un_____ble; 3. when it involves faulty (4) _____tion of reality; 4. when it is dangerous; 5. when it is (5) self-_____ing; or 6. when it is personally distressing.

## SECTION 2: Models of Psychological Disorders

**OBJ. 2:** There are several models for explaining abnormal behavior. The (6) _____gical model has been the most prevalent model throughout history. According to the demonological model, people behave abnormally when they are (7) _____sed by demons. Possession was believed to stem from (8) _____tion for wrongdoing or from (9) _____craft. Possession was "treated" by means of (10) _____ism.

The medical model has two versions: the (11) o_____ and (12) _____namic versions. The Greek physician (13) _____tes was one of the earliest thinkers to suggest that there was a relationship between abnormal behavior and biological abnormality. Hippocrates believed that abnormal behavior frequently reflected an abnormality of the (14) b_____. In 1883, psychiatrist Emil (15) K_____ argued in his textbook that each form of abnormal behavior has a specific physiological origin—a view which is at the heart of the organic model. Sigmund Freud's (16) psycho_____ model argues that abnormal behavior is symptomatic of an underlying (17) _____gical rather than biological disorder. This psychological disorder is presumed to be (18) _____cious conflict of childhood origins.

According to (19) _____tic–existential theory, psychological problems develop when we fail to recognize our genuine feelings and values, are prevented from making free choices, and do not actualize our unique talents and abilities.

According to learning models, abnormal behavior is not necessarily (20) _____atic of any underlying problem; instead, the abnormal behavior *is* the problem. Abnormal behavior is assumed to be acquired in the same way (21) n_____ behavior is acquired: through processes of (22) _____ning.

(23) _____tive theorists focus on the cognitive events—thoughts, expectations, and attitudes—that accompany or underlie abnormal behavior. (24) In_____–processing theorists view abnormal behavior as disturbance in the cycle of perceiving, storing, and (25) _____ing information. Cognitive theorist Albert Ellis views anxiety problems as reflecting (26) _____nal beliefs and attitudes. Aaron Beck attributes numerous instances of depression to "cognitive (27) _____rs" such as self–devaluation, interpretation of events in a negative light, and general (28: *Circle one:* optimism or pessimism).

## SECTION 3: Classifying Psychological Disorders

**OBJ. 3:** A major system for classifying abnormal behavior is found in the *Diagnostic* and (29) *St_____ Manual* (DSM) of the Mental Disorders. The DSM, which is published by the American (30) Psy_____ Association. The DSM sorts abnormal behavior patterns largely on the basis of (31) _____able commonalities. One result is the downplaying of the concept of the former category of the (32) n_____ses. The current edition of the DSM has greater diagnostic (33) _____ity than earlier editions, as determined by the percentage of diagnosticians who agree on a diagnosis. Some mental–health professionals, like Thomas (34) _____ z, believe that the disorders described in the DSM are really "problems in living," and not disorders in the medical sense of the term. Despite improvements over earlier editions, many psychologists still believe that the DSM still adheres too closely to the (35) _____ al model of abnormal behavior.

## SECTION 4: Anxiety Disorders

OBJ. 4: Anxiety disorders have subjective and (36) _____ cal features. (37) _____ tive features include fear of the worst happening, fear of losing control, nervousness, and inability to relax. Physical features reflect arousal of the (38) _____ tic branch of the autonomic nervous system. The anxiety disorders include irrational fears, or (39) _____ ias; panic disorder, which is characterized by sudden attacks in which people typically fear that they may be losing (40) con_____ or going crazy; free-floating or (41) _____ ized anxiety; (42) obsessive–_____ disorder, in which people are troubled by intrusive thoughts or impulses to repeat some activity; and (43) post–_____ ic stress disorder.

The most widespread phobia among adults is (44) _____ phobia, or fear of being out in open, busy areas. Stage fright and speech anxiety are examples of (45) _____ al phobias, in which people have excessive fear of public scrutiny. Panic disorder differs from other anxiety disorders in part because there is a stronger bodily component to the anxiety, including heavy (46) sw_____ ing and pounding of the (47) h_____. An (48) _____ ion is a recurring thought or image that seems irrational and beyond control. A (49) _____ ion is a seemingly irresistible urge to engage in an act, often repeatedly. Post–traumatic (50) _____ disorder (PTSD) involves intense and persistent

feelings of anxiety and helplessness that are caused by a traumatic experience, such as a physical threat, destruction of one's community, or witnessing a death. The precipitating event is reexperienced, as in the form of intrusive memories, recurrent dreams, and (51) _____ cks, or the sudden feeling that the event is recurring.

Psychodynamic theory explains generalized anxiety as persistent difficulty in maintaining (52) _____ ion of primitive impulses. According to psychodynamic theory, phobias symbolize (53) _____ cious conflicts. From the behaviorist perspective, phobias are (54) _____ ned fears. Susan (55) M_____ suggests that people are genetically predisposed to fear stimuli that may have once posed a threat to their ancestors. (56) _____ nary forces would have favored the survival of individuals who were predisposed toward acquiring fears of large animals, spiders, snakes, heights, entrapment, sharp objects, and strangers. Given the apparent independence of panic attacks from (57: *Circle one:* internal or external) events, researchers are investigating possible organic causes for panic disorder. Psychoanalysts and learning theorists agree that compulsive behavior may be maintained because it reduces (58) _____ ty.

Anxiety disorders (59: *Circle one:* do or do not) tend to run in families. Sandra Scarr and her colleagues tested adolescents and their parents in biologically related and adoptive families and found that the neuroticism scores of parents and (60: *Circle one:* natural or adopted) children correlated more highly than those of parents and (61: *Circle one:* natural or adopted) children. Some people may have a biological predisposition to anxiety in that their receptors to (62) gamma–_____ ric acid (GABA) may not be sensitive enough. GABA is an (63: *Circle one:* excitatory or inhibitory) neurotransmitter that may help quell anxiety reactions.

## SECTION 5: Dissociative Disorders

**OBJ. 5:** Dissociative disorders are characterized by a sudden temporary change in (64) co_____ness or self–identity. The dissociative disorders include (65) _____ive amnesia (motivated forgetting); dissociative fugue (forgetting plus fleeing and adopting a new identity); multiple (66) p_____, in which a person behaves as if distinct personalities occupied the body; and (67) de_____zation disorder, in which people feel as if they are not themselves. One of the best–known cases of multiple personality was depicted in the film *The Three Faces of* (68) _____.

According to psychodynamic theory, dissociative disorders involve massive use of (69) _____sion. According to learning theory, dissociative disorders are conditions in which people learn not to (70) t_____ about disturbing acts or impulses in order to avoid feelings of guilt and shame. Cognitive theorists explain dissociative disorders in terms of where we focus our (71) _____ion at a given time.

## SECTION 6: Somatoform Disorders

**OBJ. 6:** In (72) so_____ disorders, people show or complain of physical problems, such as paralysis, pain, or the persistent belief that they have a serious disease. Evidence of a medical problem (73: *Circle one:* can or cannot) be found.

The somatoform disorders include (74) con_____ disorder and (75) hypo_____is. In a conversion disorder, there is a major change in or loss of (76) p_____ functioning with no organic basis. Some victims of conversion disorder show a remarkable lack of concern over their loss of function, a symptom known as la (77) _____ indifférence. Persons with (78) _____iasis show consistent concern that they are suffering from illnesses, although there are no medical findings.

The (79) _____ic view of conversion disorders is that the symptoms produced by the victim protect the victim from guilt or another source of stress. There is evidence that some hypochondriacs use their complaints as a (80) self-_____ping strategy.

## SECTION 7: Mood Disorders

**OBJ. 7:** Mood disorders are characterized by disturbance in expressed (81) _____ions. Mood disorders include major (82) _____sion, and (83) bi_____ disorder.

Depression is characterized by sadness; lack of (84) _____gy; loss of self–esteem; difficulty in concentrating; loss of (85) in_____ in other people and activities that were enjoyable; (86: *Circle one:* optimism or pessimism); crying; and, sometimes, by thoughts of suicide. (87) M_____ depression can reach psychotic proportions, with grossly impaired reality testing. There may also be poor appetite and severe (88) w_____ loss; agitation or psychomotor (89) _____ation; delusions of (90) un_____ness and guilt; and suicide attempts.

(91) B_____ disorder was formerly known as manic–depression. In bipolar disorder there are mood swings from (92) _____ion to depression and back. Manic people may show pressured speech, have grand, delusional schemes, and jump from topic to topic, a symptom called rapid (93) f_____ of (94) _____s.

Depression is a(n) (95: *Circle one:* normal or abnormal) reaction to a loss or to exposure to unpleasant events. Recent research emphasizes the possible roles of learned helplessness, (96) attri_____al styles, and the roles of (97) neuro_____ters in prolonged depression.

According to psychodynamic theory, prolonged depression may reflect feelings of (98) _____ that are turned inward rather than expressed. Learning theorists have noted similarities between depressed people and ani-

mals who are not (99) _____ced for instrumental behavior. People and animals both show
(100) in_____ty and loss of interest when
they have repeatedly failed to receive reinforcement.

Martin (101) Se_____ and his colleagues
have explored links between depression and
learned helplessness. In experiments on learned
(102) _____ness, animals are eventually
reinforced (by cessation of electric shock) for
doing nothing. For this reason, they may learn to
do nothing as a means of terminating discomfort.
Depressed people are more likely than
nondepressed people to make (103: *Circle one:*
internal or external), (104: *Circle one:* stable or
unstable), and (105: *Circle one:* specific or global)
attributions for failures.

Research suggests that deficiencies in the
neurotransmitter (106) _____in may create a
general predisposition toward affective disorders.
A concurrent deficiency of the neurotransmitter
(107: *Circle one:* adrenaline or noradrenaline) may
then contribute to depression. Concurrent
(108: *Circle one:* excesses or deficiencies) of noradrenaline may contribute to manic behavior. Antidepressant drugs work at least in part by
(109: *Circle one:* elevating or lowering) noradrenaline levels.

**OBJ. 8:** Suicide is more common among
(110: *Circle one:* college students or nonstudents).
Three times as many (111: *Circle one:* men as
women or women as men) attempt suicide.
Suicide is most often linked to feelings of
(112) de_____ and hopelessness. According
to Edwin Shneidman, people who attempt suicide
are usually experiencing unendurable
(113) _____ical pain, and believe that their
range of (114) _____ons is narrowed. People
who threaten suicide are (115: *Circle one:* more or
less) likely to carry out the threat than people who
do not.

# SECTION 8: Schizophrenia

**OBJ. 9:** Schizophrenic disorders are characterized
by disturbances in (116) th_____ and language (as found, for example, in the loosening of
associations and in delusions); in (117) per_____
and attention (as found, for example, in hallucinations); in (118) m_____ activity (as found, for
example, in a stupor or in excited behavior); in
mood (as found, for example, in flat or inappro-
priate emotional responses); and by withdrawal
and autism.

There are (119) _____ major types of
schizophrenia. These include (120) dis_____
schizophrenia; catatonic schizophrenia; and
paranoid schizophrenia. Disorganized schizophrenia is characterized by disorganized
(121) del_____s and vivid, abundant
(122) _____nations. Catatonic schizophrenia
is characterized by impaired motor activity, as in a
catatonic (123) _____or, and by
(124) w_____ flexibility. Paranoid schizophrenia is characterized by paranoid
(125) _____ions.

According to psychodynamic theory, schizophrenic behavior occurs when impulses of the
(126: *Circle one:* id, ego, or superego) overwhelm
the (127: *Circle one:* id, ego, or superego). Social-
learning theorists have accounted for some schizophrenic behaviors by suggesting that inner
(128) f_____ may become more reinforcing
than outer reality when a person is in a
nonrewarding situation.

Schizophrenia (129: *Circle one:* does or does
not) tend to run in families. Children with two
schizophrenic parents have about a (130) _____
percent chance of becoming schizophrenic. Current theory and research concerning an organic
basis for schizophrenia focus on the neurotransmitter (131) _____ine. According to the
dopamine theory of schizophrenia, schizophrenics
may (132) u_____ more dopamine than
normal people do. Overutilization stems from

either a greater–than–normal number of dopamine (133) _____ors in the brain, or from greater–than–normal sensitivity to dopamine. A group of drugs called the (134) _____azines are often effective in treating schizophrenia. Researchers believe that phenothiazines work by blocking the action of (135) do_____ receptors.

## SECTION 9: Personality Disorders

**OBJ. 10:** Personality disorders, like personality traits, are characterized by enduring patterns of (136) be_____. Personality disorders are inflexible, (137) mal_____ive behavior patterns that impair personal or social functioning and are a source of (138) dis_____ to the individual or to others.

The defining trait of the (139) _____oid personality is suspiciousness. Persons with (140) sch_____ personality disorders show oddities of thought, perception, and behavior. However, schizotypal personalities do not show bizarre (141) _____tic behavior. Social (142) _____al is the major characteristic of the schizoid personality. Persons with (143) _____oid personality prefer to be by themselves and do not develop warm, tender feelings for others.

Persons with (144) _____ial personality disorders persistently violate the rights of others and encounter conflict with the (145) l_____. They show little or no (146) g_____ or shame over their misdeeds and are largely undeterred by (147) _____ment.

Various factors seem to contribute to antisocial behavior. One is having an antisocial (148: *Circle one:* mother or father). Second is parental (149) re_____ion during childhood. Third is a pattern of inconsistent (150) _____line. Fourth is an organic factor. Research suggests that persons with antisocial personalities have (151: *Circle one:* higher or lower)–than–normal levels of arousal, which might explain why they are undeterred by most forms of punishment. (152) _____tive psychologists find that antisocial adolescents encode social information in ways that bolster their misdeeds. For example, antisocial adolescents tend to interpret other people's behavior as (153) _____ning, even when it is not.

## Answer Key to *Chapter Review*

1. six
2. statistically
3. unacceptable
4. perception (or interpretation)
5. self–defeating
6. demonological
7. possessed
8. retribution
9. witchcraft
10. exorcism
11. organic
12. psychodynamic
13. Hippocrates
14. brain
15. Kraepelin
16. psychodynamic
17. psychological
18. unconscious
19. humanistic
20. symptomatic
21. normal
22. learning
23. Cognitive
24. Information
25. retrieving (or manipulating)
26. irrational
27. errors
28. pessimism
29. Statistical
30. Psychiatric
31. observable
32. neuroses
33. reliability
34. Szasz
35. medical

36. physical (physiological, biological)
37. Subjective
38. sympathetic
39. phobias
40. control
41. generalized
42. obsessive–compulsive
43. post–traumatic
44. agoraphobia
45. social
46. sweating
47. heart
48. obsession
49. compulsion
50. stress
51. flashbacks
52. repression
53. unconscious
54. conditioned
55. Mineka
56. Evolutionary
57. external
58. anxiety
59. do
60. natural
61. adopted
62. gamma-aminobutyric
63. inhibitory
64. consciousness
65. Dissociative
66. personality
67. depersonalization
68. *Eve*
69. repression
70. think
71. attention
72. somatoform
73. cannot
74. conversion
75. hypochondriasis
76. physical
77. belle
78. hypochondriasis
79. psychodynamic
80. self–handicapping
81. emotions

82. depression
83. bipolar
84. energy
85. interest
86. pessimism
87. Major
88. weight
89. retardation
90. unworthiness
91. Bipolar
92. elation
93. flight
94. ideas
95. normal
96. attributional
97. neurotransmitters
98. anger
99. reinforced
100. Iinactivity
101. Seligman
102. helplessness
103. internal
104. stable
105. global
106. serotonin
107. noradrenaline
108. excesses
109. elevating
110. college students
111. women as men
112. depression
113. psychological
114. options
115. more
116. thought
117. perception
118. motor
119. three
120. disorganized
121. delusions
122. hallucinations
123. dtupor
124. eaxy
125. felusions
126. id
127. ego

128. fantasy
129. does
130. 35
131. dopamine
132. utilize
133. receptors
134. phenothiazines
135. dopamine
136. behavior
137. maladaptive
138. distress
139. paranoid
140. schizotypal
141. psychotic
142. withdrawal
143. schizoid
144. antisocial
145. law
146. guilt
147. punishment
148. father
149. rejection
150. discipline
151. lower
152. Cognitive
153. threatening

# EXERCISE 1: MATCHING DISORDER CATEGORIES

In the first column is a list of types of psychological disorder. In the second column are major categories of psychological disorders. Write the letter signifying the appropriate major category of psychological disorders in the blank space to the left of the type of psychological disorder. Answers are given below.

| | | | |
|---|---|---|---|
| _____ 1. | Conversion disorder | A. Anxiety Disorders |
| _____ 2. | Major depression | B. Dissociative Disorders |
| _____ 3. | Depersonalization disorder | C. Gender–Identity Disorders |
| _____ 4. | Post–traumatic stress disorder | D. Mood Disorders |
| _____ 5. | Dissociative fugue | E. Paraphilias |
| _____ 6. | Agoraphobia | F. Personality Disorders |
| _____ 7. | Obsessive–compulsive disorder | G. Schizophrenia |
| _____ 8. | Dissociative identity disorder | H. Somatoform Disorders |
| _____ 9. | Schizotypal personality | |
| _____ 10. | Hypochondriasis | |
| _____ 11. | Dissociative amnesia | |
| _____ 12. | Bipolar disorder | |
| _____ 13. | Catatonic schizophrenia | |
| _____ 14. | Panic disorder | |
| _____ 15. | Generalized anxiety disorder | |
| _____ 16. | Antisocial personality | |

## Answer Key to Exercise 1

| | | |
|---|---|---|
| 1. F | 6. A | 12 .C |
| 2. C | 7. A | 13. E |
| 3. B | 8. B | 14. A |
| 4. A | 9. D | 15. A |
| 5. B | 10. F | 16. D |
| | 11. B | |

# EXERCISE 2: SYMPTOMS AND DISORDER

In the first column is a list of symptoms of types of psychological disorders. In the second column are various types of psychological disorders. Write the letter of the type of psychological disorder in the appropriate blank space. Note that more than one type of psychological disorder may apply. Answers are given below.

___ 1. Waxy flexibility
___ 2. Flashbacks
___ 3. Nervousness
___ 4. Weight loss
___ 5. Free–floating anxiety
___ 6. Loss of a sense of one's personal identity
___ 7. Pressured speech
___ 8. Vivid, abundant hallucinations
___ 9. Delusions of persecution
___ 10. Delusions of unworthiness
___ 11. Sudden anxiety attacks in the absence of threatening stimuli
___ 12. Lack of guilt over misdeeds
___ 13. Elation
___ 14. Hallucinations
___ 15. Lack of energy
___ 16. Suspiciousness
___ 17. La belle indifférence
___ 18. Compulsive behavior
___ 19. Social withdrawal
___ 20. Fear of public scrutiny
___ 21. Physical complaints
___ 22. Loose associations
___ 23. Giddiness

A. Phobic disorder
B. Panic disorder
C. Generalized anxiety disorder
D. Obsessive–compulsive disorder
E. Post–traumatic stress disorder
F. Dissociatve amnesia
G. Dissociative identity disorder
H. Depersonalization disorder
I. Conversion disorder
J. Hypochondriasis
K. Major depression
L. Bipolar disorder
M. Disorganized schizophrenia
N. Catatonic schizophrenia
O. Paranoid schizophrenia
P. Paranoid personality
Q. Schizoid personality
R. Antisocial personality

## Answer Key to Exercise 2

| | | | |
|---|---|---|---|
| 1. N | 7. L | 13. L | 19. K, M, N, O, Q |
| 2. E | 8. M | 14. M, N, O | 20. A |
| 3. A, B, C, D, E, etc. | 9. O | 15. K | 21. J |
| 4. K | 10. K | 16. O, P | 22. M, N, O |
| 5. C | 11. B | 17. I | 23. M |
| 6. F, H | 12. R | 18. D | |

| Idioms | Explanation |
|---|---|
| 482 set foot | arrived at |
| 499 lie ahead | will happen very soon |
| 499 to be rid of | to remove |

| Cultural References | Explanation |
|---|---|
| 482 instant-cash cards | bank cards which can be used in bank machines to withdraw money from a person's account and receive the cash without the services of a bank teller |
| 482 the boy next door | this is an expression used in the U.S. to refer to a nice, friendly, intelligent young man |
| 482 Salem, Massachusetts... burned as a witch | a play has been written about the "witch trials" that occurred in Salem, Mass. |
| 484 Mafia | an organized crime group |
| 485 Stir slightly | this is a phrase frequently used in recipes (directions for creating particular dishes) |
| 491 Sani-Flush | the brand name for a chemical mixture which is used to clean toilets |
| 494 The Three Faces of Eve | This movie was being shown in the 1950s |
| 501 wrong sign | refers to the astrological signs which indicate personality traits of people according to when they were born |
| 501 coworkers | people who work together in the same company |
| 501 Marquis de Sade | lived and wrote during the French Revolution (late eighteenth century) |
| 501 punk rock group | refers to current musical groups |
| 501 The Naked and the Dead | this is actually the name of a book written in the late 1940 by the American writer Norman Mailer |
| 501 "hot lines" | special telephone numbers which can be called for special emergency purposes |

| Phrases and Expressions (Different Usage) | |
|---|---|
| 482 Strip-teasers | women whose jobs entail removing their clothes; they usually perform their acts in a nightclub |
| 483 by reason of | because of |

| Phrases and Expressions (Different Usage) | |
|---|---|
| 484 "out of the blue" | unexpectedly; without warning |
| 484 "out to get you" | looking for you in order to kill you |
| 484 almost unheard of | was not condoned; was not proper |
| 484 And the "Patient" | and the patient died |
| 484 was to lie dormant | was not to be considered |
| 484 in full sway | the accepted model |
| 489 stage fright | fear of being in front of people |
| 490 midair | between elevator stops |
| 490 creepy-crawlies | bugs |
| 491 loath to venture out | afraid to go out of |
| 491 feel spent | feel extremely tired; exhausted |
| 491 descend from nowhere | occur without warning |
| 491 free-floating | without attachment |
| 494 feel whole | feel like one complete person |
| 494 break out with hives | have an allergic reaction consisting of red areas on the skin |
| 495 stands outside | feels as though he or she is outside of his or her self |
| 495 come to | begin to |
| 496 meaningful whole | a complete unified identity with meaning |
| 496 go from doctor to doctor | continuously search for a doctor by visiting one and then another |
| 497 were at work | were operating |
| 497 to serve a purpose | to accomplish something; to have a reason for occurring |
| 498 certain ends | specific results |
| 498 taking a person's mind off | redirecting; causing the person to not think about |
| 498 something all too real | an actual or real illness |
| 498 run-of-the-mill | common |
| 498 fitting | natural and appropriate |
| 498 blue | a little depressed |
| 498 "down in the dumps" | a little depressed |
| 498 rotting away from disease | slowly dying from a disease |
| 498 carrying jokes too far | allowing a joke to psychologically hurt someone |
| 499 "get a word in edgewise" | speak quickly because the other person talks all the time |
| 499 other side of the coin | the other part of the same disorder |
| 499 "on the way down" | as they move into depression |
| 499 overly concerned | too concerned (negative) |
| 499 becomes turned inward | becomes directed toward the person himself or herself |

Chapter 13  Psychological Disorders

| Page | Term | Meaning |
|---|---|---|
| 499 | **bridges** | connects |
| 499 | **to fall short** | to not reach |
| 499 | **does not work out** | is not successful |
| 501 | **...loused it up** | caused, or was responsible for, the bad experience |
| 501 | **making small talk** | talking about things that are not serious, but are introductory at a gathering |
| 501 | **chops the problem down to a manageable size** | causes the problem to be very specific and one that can be deal with |
| 501 | **out of touch with reality** | disconnected from the immediate circumstances |
| 501 | **slit her wrists** | cut the place in the wrists where it is difficult to stop the bleeding and is an indication, therefore, of a wish to die |
| 502 | **earphone** | telephone on her ear |
| 502 | **tightly knit** | connected by associations |
| 502 | **jumbled** | confused |
| 502 | **"bugged" his walls with "radios"** | installed machines in his walls that could listen to and record what he was saying |
| 502 | **wrapped up in** | focused only on |
| 506 | **nonsensical speech** | speech that has no meaning |
| 506 | **grossly disorganized** | extremely disorganized |
| 506 | **hold onto jobs** | maintain their employment |
| | **"loners"** | people who prefer to be alone most of the time |
| 506 | **Striking features** | noticeable characteristics |
| 507 | **One promising avenue of research** | one direction of research that might be important |
| 507 | **payoff** | positive result |

Chapter 13 Psychological Disorders

1.  All of the following statements about psychological disorders are true **EXCEPT**:
    (a) They are caused by specific events.
    (b) They interfere with daily functioning.
    (c) They cause emotional distress.
    (d) They can be either behavioral or mental.

2.  A psychologist argues that patterns of normal and abnormal behavior are acquired by the same processes, although people who acquire abnormal behavior patterns have different experiences from those who acquire normal behavior patterns. This psychologist probably adheres to the _____ model.
    (a) learning
    (b) psychodynamic
    (c) organic
    (d) cognitive

3.  An advantage of the current edition of the DSM, as compared to earlier editions, is that it
    (a) specifies more precisely when a diagnosis should be made.
    (b) is fully acceptable to psychologists.
    (c) is based on the social–learning model.
    (d) deals only with disorders that have psychological causes.

4.  According to the text, the most widespread phobia among adults is
    (a) speech anxiety.
    (b) claustrophobia.
    (c) agoraphobia.
    (d) fear of injections.

5.  Dan has a problem in which he encounters heavy sweating and a pounding heart—both for no apparent reason. Dan would probably be diagnosed as having a(n)_____ disorder.
    (a) phobic
    (b) panic
    (c) generalized anxiety
    (d) obsessive compulsive

6.  A difference between a phobic disorder and a fear is that the phobic response
    (a) is out of proportion to the actual danger.
    (b) involves cognitive as well as behavioral reactions.
    (c) is characterized by rapid heart rate.
    (d) encourages avoidance of the feared object or situation.

7.  By definition, all dissociative disorders involve
    (a) massive repression of unacceptable impulses.
    (b) a sudden, temporary change in consciousness or identity.
    (c) the presence of at least two conflicting personalities.
    (d) malingering.

8.  In which of the following does the individual feel unreal and separated from her or his body?
    (a) depersonalization disorder
    (b) schizotypal personality disorder
    (c) dissociative identity disorder
    (d) schizoid personality disorder

9.  Mary believes that she is suffering from a serious stomach or intestinal disease, because she has difficulty keeping food down and has unusual sensations in these regions of the body. However, repeated visits to physicians have not uncovered evidence of any medical disorder. Mary is most likely to be diagnosed as suffering from
    (a) conversion disorder.
    (b) malingering.
    (c) anorexia nervosa.
    (d) hypochondriasis.

10. Mood disorders are primarily characterized by disturbance in
    (a) thought processes.
    (b) biological processes.
    (c) expressed emotions.
    (d) motor responses.

Chapter 13  Psychological Disorders  353

11. The feature that differentiates bipolar disorder from other disorders is
    (a) suicide attempts.
    (b) severe bouts of depression.
    (c) delusional thinking.
    (d) rapid flight of ideas.

12. Deficiencies of _____ are most likely to set the stage for both types of mood disorders discussed in the text.
    (a) adrenaline
    (b) noradrenaline
    (c) serotonin
    (d) dopamine

13. Which of the following statements about suicide is most accurate?
    (a) Suicide attempts frequently follow "exit events."
    (b) People who attempt suicide are psychotic.
    (c) Most people who threaten suicide are just seeking attention.
    (d) Most people with suicidal thoughts eventually attempt suicide.

14. Schizophrenic disorders are known primarily by disturbances in
    (a) motor responses.
    (b) thought.
    (c) expressed emotions.
    (d) physical functioning.

15. A person with _____ is most likely to show confused, jumbled thinking.
    (a) agoraphobia
    (b) paranoid schizophrenia
    (c) paranoid personality disorder
    (d) schizoid personality disorder

16. Evidence seems clearest that schizophrenics
    (a) produce more dopamine than normal people do.
    (b) have a greater number of dopamine receptors in the brain than normal people do.
    (c) are more sensitive to dopamine than normal people are.
    (d) utilize more dopamine than normal people do.

17. The defining trait of the paranoid personality disorder is
    (a) social withdrawal.
    (b) oddities of thought.
    (c) suspiciousness.
    (d) self–absorption.

18. Feeling paralyzed when there is no physical reason is a symptom of a(n) _____ disorder.
    (a) somatoform
    (b) personality
    (c) anxiety
    (d) mood

19. Whch of the following is **NOT** a biological risk factor for schizophrenia?
    (a) problem pregnancy
    (b) winter births
    (c) twin births
    (d) genetic history of the disorder

20. A _____ theorist is most likely to focus on the ways in which antisocial adolescents process social information.
    (a) humanistic–existential
    (b) social–learning
    (c) psychodynamic
    (d) cognitive

Answer Key to *Posttest*

| | |
|---|---|
| 1. A | 11. D |
| 2. A | 12. C |
| 3. A | 13. A |
| 4. C | 14. B |
| 5. B | 15. B |
| 6. A | 16. D |
| 7. B | 17. C |
| 8. A | 18. A |
| 9. D | 19. C |
| 10. C | 20. D |

| | |
|---|---|
| Dissociative identity disorder | Specific phobia |
| Multiple personality disorder | Social phobia |
| Insanity | Claustrophobia |
| Schizophrenia | Acrophobia |
| Psychological disorders | Agoraphobia |
| Hallucination | Panic disorder |
| Ideas of persecution | Generalized anxiety disorder |

| | |
|---|---|
| Persistent fear of a specific object or situation. | A disorder in which a person appears to have two or more distinct identities or personalities that may alternately emerge. |
| An irrational, excessive fear of public scrutiny. | The previous DSM term for *dissociative identity disorder*. |
| Fear of tight, small places. | A legal term descriptive of a person judged to be incapable of recognizing right from wrong or of conforming his or her behavior to the law. |
| Fear of high places. | A psychotic disorder characterized by loss of control of thought process and inappropriate emotional responses. |
| Fear of open, crowded places. | Patterns of behavior or mental processes that are connected with emotional distress or significant impairment in functioning. |
| The recurrent experiencing of attacks of extreme anxiety in the absence of external stimuli that usually elicit anxiety. | A perception in the absence of sensory stimulation that is confused with reality. |
| Feelings of dread and foreboding and sympathetic arousal of at least 6 months duration. | Erroneous beliefs that one is being victimized or persecuted. |

356   Chapter 13   Psychological Disorders

| | |
|---|---|
| Obsession | Dissociative disorders |
| Compulsion | Dissociative amnesia |
| Post-traumatic stress disorder | Malingering |
| Acute stress disorder | Dissociative fugue |
| Concordance | Depersonalization disorder |
| GABA | Somatoform disorders |
| Benzodiazepines | Conversion disorder |

| | |
|---|---|
| Disorders in which there are sudden, temporary changes in consciousness or self-identity. | A recurring thought or image that seems beyond control. |
| A dissociative disorder marked by loss of memory or self-identity; skills and general knowledge are usually retained. Previously termed *psychogenic amnesia*. | An apparently irresistible urge to repeat an act or engage in ritualistic behavior, such as hand washing. |
| Pretending to be ill to escape duty or work. | A disorder that follows a distressing event outside the range of normal human experience and that is characterized by features such as intense fear, avoidance of stimuli associated with the event, and reliving the event. PTSD. |
| A dissociative disorder in which one experiences amnesia and then flees to a new location. Previously termed *psychogenic fugue*. | A disorder, like PTSD, that is characterized by feelings of anxiety and helplessness and caused by a traumatic event. Unlike PTSD, acute stress disorder occurs within a month of the event and lasts from 2 days to 4 weeks. |
| A dissociative disorder in which one experiences persistent or recurrent feelings that one is not real or is detached from one's own experiences or body. | Agreement. |
| Disorders in which people complain of physical problems even though no physical abnormality can be found. | An inhibitory neurotransmitter that is implicated in anxiety reaction. |
| A disorder in which anxiety or unconscious conflicts are "converted" into physical symptoms that often have the effect of helping the person cope with anxiety or conflict. | A class of drugs that reduce anxiety; minor tranquilizers. |

| La belle indifférence | Attributional style |
|---|---|
| Hypochondriasis | Neuroticism |
| Major depression | Delusions |
| Psychomotor retardation | Stupor |
| Bipolar disorder | Paranoid schizophrenia |
| Manic | Disorganized schizophrenia |
| Learned helplessness | Catatonic schizophrenia |

| | |
|---|---|
| One's tendency to attribute one's behavior to internal or external factors, stable or unstable factors, and so on. | A French term descriptive of the lack of concern sometimes shown by people with conversion disorders. |
| A personality trait characterized largely by persistent anxiety. | Persistent belief that one has a medical disorder despite lack of medical findings. |
| False, persistent beliefs that are unsubstantiated by sensory or objective evidence. | A severe depressive disorder in which the person may show loss of appetite, psychomotor behaviors, and impaired reality testing. |
| A condition in which the senses and thoughts are dulled. | Slowness in motor activity and (apparently) in thought. |
| A type of schizophrenia characterized primarily by delusions–commonly of persecution–and by vivid hallucinations. | A disorder in which the mood alternatives between two extreme poles (elation and depression). Also referred to as manic-depression. |
| Disorganized delusions and vivid hallucinations. | Elated, showing excessive excitement. |
| Striking impairment of motor activity. | A model for the acquisition of depressive behavior, based on findings that organisms in aversive situations learn to show inactivity when their operants go unreinforced. |

| | |
|---|---|
| Waxy flexibility | Eating disorders |
| Personality disorders | Anorexia nervosa |
| Paranoid personality disorder | Bulimia nervosa |
| Schizotypal personality disorder | Sexual dysfunctions |
| Schizoid personality disorder | Hypoactive sexual desire disorder |
| Antisocial personality disorder | Female sexual arousal disorder |
| Avoidant personality disorder | Male erectile disorder |

| | |
|---|---|
| Psychological disorders that are characterized by distortion of the body image and gross disturbance in eating patterns. | A feature of catatonic schizophrenia in which persons maintain postures into which they are placed. |
| A life-threatening eating disorder characterized by refusal to maintain a healthful body weight, intense fear of being overweight, a distorted body image, and, in females, lack of menstruation. | Enduring patterns of maladaptive behavior that are sources of distress to the individual or others. |
| An eating disorder characterized by recurrent cycles of binge eating followed by dramatic measures to purge the food. | A disorder characterized by persistent suspiciousness, but not involving the disorganization of paranoid schizophrenia. |
| Persistent problems in becoming sexually aroused or reaching orgasm. | A disorder characterized by oddities of thought and behavior, but not involving bizarre psychotic behaviors. |
| A sexual dysfunction characterized by lack of interest in sexual activity. | A disorder characterized by social withdrawal. |
| A sexual dysfunction characterized by difficulty in becoming sexually aroused, as defined by vaginal lubrication, or in sustaining arousal long enough to engage in satisfying sexual relations. | The diagnosis given a person who is in frequent conflict with society, yet who is undeterred by punishment and experiences little or no guilt and anxiety. |
| A sexual dysfunction characterized by difficulty in becoming sexually aroused, as defined by achieving erection, or in sustaining arousal long enough to engage in satisfying sexual relations. | A personality disorder in which the person is generally unwilling to enter relationships without assurance of acceptance because of fears of rejection and criticism. |

# Chapter 14

# Methods of Therapy

Directions: This *PRETEST* will give you feedback about how well you understand Chapter 14. In order to enhance your mastery of Chapter 14, complete all the sections of this chapter of the Study Guide. Then you can take the *POSTTEST* and compare your results.

1. Asylums often had their origins in European
   (a) prisons.
   (b) churches.
   (c) bedlams.
   (d) monasteries.

2. According to the text, humanitarian reform movements for mental patients began in the _____ century.
   (a) seventeenth
   (b) eighteenth
   (c) nineteenth
   (d) twentieth

3. Psychodynamic therapies all
   (a) view internal conflict in terms of unconscious forces.
   (b) encourage clients to lie back on a couch or a recliner and to engage in free association.
   (c) assume that internal conflict impairs clients' efforts to lead productive lives.
   (d) assume that people are rational beings who can become aware of their drives.

4. Abreaction is also known as
   (a) catharsis.
   (b) the compulsion to utter.
   (c) response prevention.
   (d) Mellaril.

5. According to the text, the "cardinal rule" of a traditional psychoanalysis is that
   (a) the client must recline on a couch.
   (b) unconscious conflicts are made conscious.
   (c) no thought is to be censored.
   (d) the transference relationship must be resolved.

6. The person–centered therapist's ability to accurately reflect clients' experiences and feelings is termed
   (a) congruence.
   (b) empathic understanding.
   (c) countertransference.
   (d) frame of reference.

7. Smith and Glass found that about _____ percent of the clients receiving person–centered therapy were "better off than people who were left untreated."
   (a) 65
   (b) 75
   (c) 85
   (d) 95

8. Virginia Satir is a major innovator in
   (a) modern psychoanalytic approaches.
   (b) Gestalt therapy.
   (c) family therapy.
   (d) transactional analysis.

9. According to _____, people attempt to justify certain basic life positions.
   (a) Gestalt therapy
   (b) cognitive therapy
   (c) transactional analysis
   (d) functional analysis

10. Who is the author of *I'm OK—You're OK*?
    (a) Carl Rogers
    (b) Fritz Perls
    (c) Eric Berne
    (d) Thomas Harris

11. According to the text, the person who wrote that many people are depressed because they are pessimistic and tend to minimize their own accomplishments is a
(a) cognitive therapist.
(b) traditional psychoanalyst.
(c) behavior therapist.
(d) transactional analyst.

12. The technique of modeling is most likely to be used in
(a) Gestalt therapy.
(b) systematic desensitization.
(c) social–skills training.
(d) encounter groups.

13. The self–control technique of _____ is a strategy that is aimed at the reinforcements that maintain behavior.
(a) response prevention
(b) stimulus control
(c) successive approximations
(d) covert sensitization

14. The text presents participant modeling as an alternative to
(a) social–skills training.
(b) systematic desensitization.
(c) operant conditioning.
(d) "Grandma's method."

15. According to the evaluations reported in the text, the *most* effective of the following therapy methods is
(a) Gestalt therapy.
(b) transactional analysis.
(c) the encounter group.
(d) behavior therapy.

16. Phenothiazines are usually prescribed for patients with
(a) panic disorder.
(b) major depression.
(c) bipolar disorder.
(d) schizophrenia.

17. Ugo Cerletti is credited as the originator of a treatment whose use is now generally limited to patients who show
(a) "run–of–the–mill" anxiety and tension.
(b) bipolar disorder.
(c) major depression.
(d) antisocial personality disorder.

18. Monoamine oxidase inhibitors appear to work by blocking the activity of an enzyme that breaks down
(a) dopamine.
(b) noradrenaline.
(c) acetylcholine.
(d) ACTH.

19. According to the text,
(a) the prefrontal lobotomy has been shown to be more useful than chemotherapy with agitated patients.
(b) ECT is the preferred treatment for patients with major depression.
(c) minor tranquilizers should be used to treat ordinary anxiety and tension.
(d) all forms of biological therapy seem to have side effects or other kinds of problems associated with their use.

20. Your friend Phil wants to consult with someone who is highly likely to be critically acquainted with psychological theory. According to the text, the group of professionals most likely to fit this description are
(a) psychologists.
(b) psychiatrists.
(c) psychiatric social workers.
(d) psychoanalysts.

**Answer Key to *Pretest***

| | |
|---|---|
| 1. D | 11. A |
| 2. B | 12. C |
| 3. C | 13. D |
| 4. A | 14. B |
| 5. C | 15. D |
| 6. B | 16. D |
| 7. B | 17. C |
| 8. C | 18. B |
| 9. C | 19. D |
| 10. D | 20. A |

In Chapter 14 psychotherapy is defined. The text discusses the history of the treatment of persons showing abnormal behavior, referring to the ancient and medieval treatments that reflected the demonological model, and tracing modern history from asylums to mental hospitals and the community mental–health movement.

Psychodynamic therapies owe their origin to Sigmund Freud. They are based on the view that our problems largely reflect early childhood experiences and internal conflicts. Freud used methods such as free association and resolution of a transference relationship to help clients root out conflicts and develop more appropriate ways of relating to other people. Modern psychodynamic approaches tend to be briefer and less intense. Modern psychoanalysts also tend to be more direct than Freud.

Humanistic–existential therapies focus on the quality of clients' subjective, conscious experiences, and on what clients are experiencing today—in "the here and now." Humanistic–existential therapies include Carl Rogers' nondirective person–centered therapy, Eric Berne's transactional analysis (TA), and Fritz Perls' highly directive Gestalt therapy.

Cognitive therapies tend to focus on the beliefs, attitudes, and automatic types of thinking that create and compound clients' problems. In his rational–emotive therapy, Albert Ellis points out that our beliefs about events, as well as the events themselves, shape our responses to them. Aaron Beck focuses on clients' cognitive errors, pointing out, for example, how their minimizing of their accomplishments and their pessimistic assuming that the worst will happen heightens feelings of depression. In cognitive restructuring, clients are shown how their interpretations of events lead to maladaptive responses and are then helped to rethink their situations so that they can generate more adaptive overt behavior.

The goals of behavior therapy are discontinuation of maladaptive behavior and acquisition of adaptive behavior—with or without benefit of self–insight. The behavior–therapy methods highlighted in the text include fear–reduction methods, aversive conditioning, operant conditioning, social–skills training, and a number of self-control techniques.

Problems in determining the effectiveness of psychotherapy are outlined. Then various kinds of therapy are evaluated as compared to no treatment and as compared to other forms of therapy.

Group therapy methods are shown to vary with the needs of clients and theoretical orientations of therapists. Two types of group approaches are discussed in detail: encounter groups and family therapy.

Biological therapies include chemotherapy (drugs), electroconvulsive therapy (ECT), and psychosurgery. Chemotherapy is shown to be useful with schizophrenia and severe mood disorders, although its usefulness with common anxiety and tension is questioned. Despite side effects, the ECT is still used in many cases of major depression when antidepressant drugs fail. The prefrontal lobotomy—the most frequently used form of psychosurgery—has been largely discontinued.

## LEARNING OBJECTIVES

| | What Is Therapy? In Search of That "Sweet Oblivious Antidote" |
|---|---|
| 1. Define *psychotherapy*. | |

2. Trace the history of the treatment of abnormal behavior from ancient to contemporary times.

## Psychodynamic Therapies

3. Describe the goals and methods of Freud's traditional *psychoanalysis*.

4. Compare and contrast traditional psychoanalysis with modern psychodynamic approaches.

## Humanistic-Existential Therapies

5. Explain what the *humanistic–existential therapies* have in common.

6. Describe the goals and methods of Rogers' *person-centered therapy*.

7. Describe the goals and methods of Berne's *transactional analysis*.

8. Describe the goals and methods of Perls' *Gestalt therapy*.

## Cognitive Therapies

9. Explain what the cognitive therapies have in common.

10. Describe the goals and methods of Ellis's *rational–emotive therapy*.

11. Describe the goals and methods of Beck's *cognitive therapy*.

12. Describe the method of cognitive restructuring.

## Behavior Therapy: Adjustment Is What You Do

13. Describe the goals of *behavior therapy*.

14. Describe behavior–therapy methods of reducing fears.

15. Describe the behavior–therapy method of *aversive conditioning*.

16. Describe some behavior–therapy methods of *operant conditioning*.

17. Describe behavior–therapy self–control methods.

## Group Therapies

18. Explain the advantages of group therapy.

19. Describe *encounter groups* and *family therapy*.

## Does Psychotherapy Work?

20. Evaluate methods of psychotherapy and behavior therapy.

## Biological Therapies

21. Describe various methods of drug therapy, and when they are used.

22. Describe *electroconvulsive therapy,* and when it is used.

23. Discuss *psychosurgery.*

24. Evaluate the biological therapies.

25. Discuss multicultural issues and psychotherapy.

**Additional Notes**

## What Is Therapy? In Search of That "Sweet Oblivious Antidote"

- History of Therapies

## Psychodynamic Therapies

1. Traditional Psychoanalysis

2. Women and Psychotherapy

3. Modern Psychodynamic Approaches

## Humanistic–Existential Therapies

1. Person-Centered Therapy

2. Transactional Analysis

3. Gestalt Therapy

## Cognitive Therapies

1. Rational-Emotive Therapy

2. Cognitive Therapy

3. Cognitive Restructuring

## Behavior Therapy: Adjustment Is What You Do

   1. Fear-Reduction Methods

   2. Aversive Conditioning

   3. Operant Conditioning Procedures

   4. Self-Control Methods

## Group Therapies

   1. Encounter Groups

   2. Couple Therapy

   3. Family Therapy

## Does Psychotherapy Work?

1. Problems in Conducting Research on Psychotherapy

2. Analyses of Therapy Effectiveness

## Biological Therapies

1. Drug Therapy

2. Electroconvulsive Therapy

3. Psychosurgery

4. Does Biological Therapy Work?

## Psychology and Modern Life

1. Psychotherapy in the New Multicultural United States

2. Ethnic Matching of Clients and Therapists

# KEY TERMS AND CONCEPTS

## What Is Therapy?

1. Psychotherapy _____

2. Asylums _____

## Psychodynamic Therapies _____

3. Psychoanalysis _____

4. Abreaction _____

5. Catharsis _____

6. Free association _____

7. Resistance _____

8. Interpretation _____

9. Wish fulfillment _____

10. Phallic symbol _____

11. Manifest content _____

12. Latent content _____

13. Ego analyst _____

## Humanistic–Existential Therapies _____

14. Person–centered therapy _____

15. Unconditional positive regard _____

16. Empathic understanding _____

17. Frame of reference _____

18. Genuineness _____

19. Congruence _____

20. Transactional analysis _____

21. Parent (in TA) _____

22. Child (in TA) _____

23. Adult (in TA) _____

24. Transaction _____

25. Complementary (in TA) _____

26. Gestalt therapy _____

27. Dialogue (in Gestalt therapy) _____

## Cognitive Therapies

28. Cognitive therapy _____

29. Rational–emotive therapy _____

## Behavior Therapy

30. Behavior therapy _____

31. Systematic desensitization _____

32. Hierarchy _____

33. Modeling _____

34. Aversive conditioning _____

35. Rapid smoking _____

36. Token economy _____

37. Successive approximations _____

38. Self–monitoring _____

39. Behavior rehearsal _____

40. Feedback _____

41. Biofeedback training _____

42. Functional analysis _____

## Group Therapies

43. Encounter group _____

44. Family therapy _____

## Does Psychotherapy Work?

45. Meta–analysis _____

## Biological Therapies

46. Rebound anxiety _____

47. Antidepressant _____

48. Monoamine oxidase (MAO) inhibitors _____

49. Tricyclic antidepressants _____

50. Serotonin-uptake inhibitors _____

51. Sedative _____

52. Electroconvulsive therapy (ECT) _____

53. Psychosurgery _____

54. Prefrontal lobotomy _____

## SECTION 1: What Is Therapy?

**OBJ. 1:** The text defines psychotherapy as a systematic interaction between a therapist and a client that brings (1) _____ical principles to bear on influencing the client's thoughts, feelings, or behavior. Psychotherapy helps the client overcome (2) ab_____ behavior or adjust to problems in living.

**OBJ. 2:** Ancient and medieval treatments of psychological disorders often reflected the (3) _____gical model. They involved cruel practices such as the (4) ex_____ of the Middle Ages. The first institutions intended primarily for the mentally ill were called (5) _____ms. Asylums often had their origins in European (6) _____aries. St. Mary's of (7) Be_____ is the name of a well–known London asylum.

Humanitarian reform movements began in the (8) _____eenth century. Philippe (9) P_____ unchained the patients at the asylum called La Bicêtre. The reform movement in the United States was led by schoolteacher Dorothea (10) _____. Mental (11) _____tals replaced asylums in the United States. Today as many patients as possible are maintained in the community. The community movement was in part stimulated by the Community (12) M_____–_____ Centers Act of 1963.

## SECTION 2: Psychodynamic Therapies

**OBJ. 3:** Psychodynamic therapies are based on the thinking of Sigmund (13) _____. They are based on the view that our problems largely reflect early childhood experiences and internal (14) con_____s. Freud's method of psychoanalysis attempts to shed light on (15) _____cious conflicts that are presumed to lie at the roots of clients' problems. Freud also sought to replace impulsive and defensive behavior with (16) _____ng behavior. Freud also believed that psychoanalysis would allow clients to engage in (17) _____sis or abreaction—that is, to spill forth the (18) _____ic energy theorized to have been repressed by conflicts and guilt.

The chief psychoanalytic method is (19) _____ association. The cardinal rule of free association is that no thought is to be (20) _____ed. In this way, material that has been (21) _____sed should eventually come to the surface of awareness. But the ego's continuing tendency to repress threatening material leads to the countervailing force of (22) _____nce.

Freud considered (23) _____s to be the "royal road to the unconscious." In dreams, unconscious impulses were expressed as a form of wish (24) _____ment. Objects in dreams were thought to be (25) _____s of unconscious wishes. The perceived content of a dream is termed its (26) _____t content. The presumed symbolic content of a dream is termed its hidden or (27) _____t content.

Freud also found that people generalized feelings toward other men onto him, and Freud termed this generalization of feelings (28) _____ence. Freud termed the analyst's transference of feelings onto clients (29) _____ference.

**OBJ. 4:** Contemporary psychodynamic approaches tend to be (30: *Circle one:* longer or briefer) and (31: *Circle one:* more or less) intense than Freud's. However, many of them still focus on revealing (32) un_____ conflicts and on breaking down psychological resistance. Modern psychodynamic therapists focus more on the (33) e_____ as the "executive" of personality. For this reason, many modern psychodynamic therapists are considered ego (34) _____ sts.

## SECTION 3: Humanistic–Existential Therapies

**OBJ. 5:** Humanistic–existential therapies focus on the quality of clients' (35) _____ tive, conscious experience. (36) <u>Psy</u>_____ therapies tend to focus on the past, and particularly on early childhood experiences. (37) <u>Humanistic–</u>_____ therapies, however, focus on what clients are experiencing today—on "the here and now."

**OBJ. 6:** Person–centered therapy was originated by (38) _____ _____ s. Person–centered therapy is a (39: *Circle one:* directive or nondirective) method that provides clients with a warm, accepting atmosphere that enables them to explore and overcome roadblocks to self–actualization. The characteristics shown by the person–centered therapist include (40: *Circle one:* conditional or unconditional) positive regard, (41) <u>em</u>_____ understanding, (42) <u>gen</u>_____, and (43) _____ence.

The goals of person–centered therapy include (44) <u>self–es</u>_____, self–acceptance, and (45) <u>self–ac</u>_____ation.

**OBJ. 7:** Transactional analysis (TA) was originated by (46) <u>E</u>_____ _____. TA focuses on people's life (47) _____ons (such as "I'm OK—You're not OK"), and on how people play (48) _____s to confirm unhealthful life positions. TA hypothesizes that there are (49) _____ ego states. TA encourages clients to function according to their rational (50: *Circle one:* "child," "adult," or "parent") ego states, rather than their impulsive (51: *Circle one:* "child," "adult," or "parent") ego states or their moralistic (52: *Circle one:* "child," "adult," or "parent") ego states. In the most healthful transactions, or social exchanges, people relate to one another as (53: *Circle one:* children, adults, or parents).

**OBJ. 8:** Gestalt therapy was originated by (54) _____ _____ s. Gestalt therapy provides (55: *Circle one:* directive or nondirective) methods that are designed to help clients integrate conflicting parts of the (56) _____ity. In the Gestalt technique of the (57) <u>d</u>_____, people undertake a verbal confrontation between conflicting parts of the personality. Clients are instructed to pay attention to their body (58) <u>l</u>_____, such as their facial expressions, in order to gain insight into their true feelings. Perls saw the content of dreams as (59) _____ned parts of the personality.

## SECTION 4: Cognitive Therapies

**OBJ. 9:** Cognitive therapists focus on the (60) <u>be</u>_____s, attitudes, and (61) _____tic types of thinking that create and compound their clients' problems.

**OBJ. 10:** (62) <u>Rational–</u>_____ therapy is one type of cognitive therapy. It was originated by (63) _____ _____. Rational–emotive therapy confronts clients with the ways in which (64) _____nal beliefs contribute to problems such as anxiety, depression, and feelings of hopelessness. Ellis's methods are (65: *Circle one:* nondirective or directive).

**OBJ. 11:** Psychiatrist Aaron Beck has focused on ways in which cognitive errors or (66) <u>dis</u>_____s heighten feelings of (67) <u>de</u>_____. Beck notes the pervasive influence of four basic types of cognitive errors that contribute to clients' miseries: selective (68) _____tion of the world as a harmful place; (69) <u>over</u>_____zation on the basis of a few examples; (70) <u>mag</u>_____tion of the significance of negative events; and (71) _____tist thinking, or looking at the world in black and white rather than in shades of gray.

Beck also encourages clients to see how their (72: *Circle one:* exaggerating or minimizing) of accomplishments and their (73: *Circle one:* optimism or pessimism) are self-defeating.

**OBJ. 12:** In cognitive (74) re_____ing, clients are shown how their interpretations of events lead to maladaptive responses. Then they are helped to rethink their situations so that they can generate more adaptive (75) be_____.

Cognitive therapists have devised a number of methods to help people get in touch with fleeting thoughts, such as (76) "_____ing movies."

Many theorists consider cognitive therapy to be a collection of techniques that belong within the province of (77) be_____ therapy. Some members of this group prefer the name (78) "cog_____ _____ior therapy." However, there is a difference in focus between many cognitive therapists and behavior therapists. To behavior therapists, the purpose of dealing with client cognitions is to change overt (79) be_____. Cognitive therapists assert that (80) _____tive change is in and of itself an important goal.

**SECTION 5: Behavior Therapy**

**OBJ. 13:** Behavior therapy is also referred to as behavior (81) _____tion. Behavior therapy is defined as the systematic application of principles of (82) _____ing to bring about desired behavioral changes. Behavior therapists insist that their methods be established by (83) _____tation and that therapeutic outcomes be assessed in terms of (84) ob_____ble, measurable behavior. Behavior therapists attempt to help clients discontinue self-defeating, (85) mal_____ive behavior patterns and to acquire (86) _____ive behavior patterns.

**OBJ. 14:** The text describes three behavior-therapy methods for reducing fears: (87) _____ing, in which a client is bombarded with fear-arousing stimuli; systematic (88) de_____tion, in which a client is gradually exposed to more fear-arousing stimuli; and (89) p_____ modeling, in which a client observes and then imitates a model who handles fear-arousing stimuli. Systematic desensitization was developed by (90) _____ _____, who assumed that maladaptive anxiety responses are learned or conditioned. Wolpe reasoned that these anxiety responses could be unlearned by means of (91) _____ conditioning or extinction. In counterconditioning, a response that is (92: *Circle one:* compatible or incompatible) with anxiety is made to occur under conditions that usually elicit anxiety. Muscle (93) _____ation is incompatible with anxiety. In systematic desensitization, clients confront a (94) h_____y of anxiety-evoking stimuli while they remain relaxed.

**OBJ. 15:** In the behavior-therapy method of aversive conditioning, undesired responses are decreased in frequency by being associated with (95) _____ive stimuli. An example of aversive conditioning is (96) r_____ smoking, in which cigarette smoke is made aversive by means of puffing every six seconds.

**OBJ. 16:** In behavior-therapy operant-conditioning methods, desired responses are (97) _____ced and undesired responses are (98) _____shed. Two examples are the use of the (99) t_____ economy and of successive approximations.

In social-skills training, behavior therapists decrease social anxiety and build social skills through operant-conditioning procedures that employ (100) _____-monitoring, coaching, modeling, (101) _____ playing, (102) _____ rehearsal, and (103) _____back. In (104) _____ness training, clients learn to express themselves and seek their legitimate rights.

Through (105) _____back training (BFT), therapists help clients become more aware of, and gain control over, various bodily functions.

"Bleeps" or other electronic signals are used to (106) r_____ bodily changes in the desired direction. The (107) _____ograph (EMG) monitors muscle tension. The (108) _____ograph (EEG) monitors brain waves and can be used to teach people how to produce (109) _____a waves, which are associated with relaxation.

**OBJ. 17:** In behavior–therapy self–control methods, clients first engage in a (110) _____nal analysis of their problem behavior. A functional analysis helps them learn what stimuli trigger and (111) _____ain the behavior. Then clients are taught how to manipulate the antecedents and (112) _____nces of their behavior, and the behavior itself, to increase the frequency of desired responses and decrease the frequency of undesired responses.

Self–control methods that are aimed at stimuli that trigger unwanted behavior include: (113) re_____ of the stimulus field; avoiding powerful stimuli that trigger habits; and (114) _____lus control. Strategies aimed at the problem behavior itself include: response (115) pre_____, in which the unwanted behavior is made impossible; use of (116) _____ing or incompatible responses; chain breaking; and successive (117) _____ations. Strategies aimed at reinforcements include: reinforcement of desired behavior; (118) re_____ cost; "Grandma's method"; covert sensitization; and covert (119) _____ment.

## SECTION 6: Group Therapies

**OBJ. 18:** The methods and characteristics of group therapy reflect the clients' needs and the (120) _____ical orientation of the group leader. There are a number of advantages to group therapy. Group therapy can be more (121) _____ical than individual therapy, allowing several clients to be seen at once. Clients may draw upon the (122) exp_____ of other group members as well as the knowledge of the therapist. Too, clients can receive (123) em_____al support from other group members.

**OBJ. 19:** (124) En_____ groups seek to promote personal growth by heightening awareness of one's own feelings and needs and those of others. This goal is sought through intense (125) con_____ions in which strangers relate to one another by expressing genuine feelings and stripping off each other's social masks. Encounter groups have been found harmful rather than helpful in many cases.

Family therapy usually uses a (126) _____ems approach to boost family members' coping skills and self-esteem, and to promote the growth of each member. In family therapy, clients are encouraged to tolerate each other's (127) _____ness, and are given insight into how one family member often becomes the (128) "_____fied patient" or scapegoat for family problems.

## SECTION 7: Does Psychotherapy Work?

**OBJ. 20:** There are many problems in evaluating methods of therapy. The ideal method for evaluating treatments is the (129) _____ment. In ideal experiments, subjects are (130) b_____ as to the treatment they are receiving. It can also be difficult to identify the (131) _____mes of therapy, especially when they are defined as self–insight. Smith and Glass used an averaging technique referred to as (132) m_____=_____sis to weigh the results of dozens of outcome studies on types of therapy.

Smith and Glass found that people who receive psychoanalysis show greater well–being than (133) _____ percent of those who are left untreated. Psychoanalysis is most effective with clients who are (134: *Circle one:* well– or poorly) educated, highly verbal, and (135: *Circle one:* highly or poorly) motivated. About (136) _____ percent of clients receiving person– centered therapy were better off than people left untreated. People receiving TA were better off than about (137) _____ percent of people left untreated, and people receiving Gestalt therapy showed greater well–being than about 60 percent of those who were left untreated.

Critics of psychodynamic and humanistic–existential methods assert that it has not been shown that their benefits can be attributed to the (138) th_____ methods per se. Benefits may derive from the common factors in many types of therapy, such as showing warmth, (139: *Circle one:* encouraging or discouraging) exploration, and combating feelings of (140) h_____ness. And so the benefits of therapy could stem largely from the (141) _____ship with the therapist.

A number of studies of cognitive therapy show that modification of (142) _____nal beliefs decreases emotional distress. Researchers who have analyzed studies that compare cognitive, psychodynamic, and humanistic–existential approaches to the treatment of anxiety and depression have generally found that (143) _____ approaches foster greater improvements.

Smith and Glass found behavior–therapy techniques somewhat (144: *Circle one:* more or less) effective than psychodynamic or humanistic–existential methods. About (145) _____ percent of those receiving behavior–therapy treatments showed greater well–being than people who were left untreated. Psychodynamic and humanistic–existential approaches seem to foster (146: *Circle one:* less or greater) self–insight than behavior therapy. Behavior–therapy techniques show relatively (147: *Circle one:* inferior or superior) results in problems such as phobias, sexual dysfunctions, and management of institutionalized populations.

## SECTION 8: Biological Therapies

**OBJ. 21:** The use of drugs in the treatment of abnormal behavior is termed (148) _____ _____rapy. (149: *Circle one:* minor or major) tranquilizers are usually prescribed for outpatients who complain of anxiety or tension. (150) V_____ and other minor tranquilizers are theorized to depress the activity of the 151) _____ nervous system, which, in turn, decreases sympathetic activity. Many patients who have regularly used minor tranquilizers encounter (152) re_____ anxiety when they discontinue.

Major tranquilizers are sometimes referred to as (153) anti_____ drugs. In most cases, major tranquilizers reduce agitation, (154) del_____s, and hallucinations. Major tranquilizers that belong to the chemical class of (155) _____iazines are thought to work by blocking the action of the neurotransmitter (156) _____ine in the brain. In many cases, the blocking of dopamine action leads to symptoms like those of (157) _____son's disease. (158: *Circle one:* Minor or Major) tranquilizers have permitted thousands of schizophrenics to lead productive lives in the community.

(159) Anti_____ drugs have relieved many instances of major depression. Antidepressants are believed to work by increasing the amounts of the neurotransmitters (160) nor_____ine and (161) _____nin available in the brain. Antidepressants have also been found useful in many instances of the anxiety disorder called (162) p_____ disorder and in some cases of (163) e_____ing disorders.

Lithium helps flatten out the cycles of (164) m_____ behavior and depression found in (165) _____ar disorder. Lithium appears to moderate the level of (166) _____line available to the brain.

**OBJ. 22:** Electroconvulsive therapy (ECT) was

introduced by Ugo (167) C_____ in 1939. ECT uses electric shock to produce (168) _____ions. Since the advent of major tranquilizers, use of ECT has been generally limited to patients with (169) _____ sion. ECT is controversial because it impairs (170) m_____ and nobody knows why it works. Today, ECT tends to be used only when (171) anti_____ drugs fail. (172) Uni_____ ECT appears to have relatively fewer side effects.

**OBJ. 23:** Psychosurgery was pioneered by Antonio Egas (173) M_____. The best-known technique is called the (174) pre_____ omy. The prefrontal lobotomy has been used with severely disturbed patients and severs the nerve pathways that link the prefrontal (175) _____s of the brain to the (176) _____mus. Today, the prefrontal lobotomy has been largely discontinued because of the advent of major tranquilizers and because of (177) s_____ effects.

**OBJ. 24:** (178) Drug_____ has a distinct place in the treatment of abnormal behavior. Unfortunately, (179: *Circle one:* minor or major) tranquilizers, used for common anxiety and tension, are frequently abused. Patients rapidly develop (180) _____ance for these drugs, and the drugs do nothing to show them how to manage their problems in more productive ways. In spite of the controversies that surround ECT, supporters note that there is evidence that it brings many immobilized patients out of their depression when (181) anti_____ drugs fail. ECT patients have a (182: *Circle one:* higher or lower) mortality rate following treatment than depressed people who do not receive ECT.

**Answer Key to *Chapter Review***

1. psychological
2. abnormal
3. demonological
4. exorcism
5. asylums
6. monasteries
7. Bethlehem
8. eighteenth
9. Pinel
10. Dix
11. hospitals
12. Mental–Health
13. Freud
14. conflicts
15. unconscious
16. coping
17. catharsis
18. psychic
19. free
20. censored
21. repressed
22. resistance
23. dreams
24. fulfillment
25. symbols
26. manifest
27. latent
28. transference
29. countertransference
30. briefer
31. less
32. unconscious
33. ego
34. analysts
35. subjective
36. Psychodynamic
37. Humanistic–existential
38. Carl Rogers
39. nondirective
40. unconditional
41. empathic
42. genuineness
43. congruence
44. self–esteem
45. self–actualization
46. Eric Berne
47. positions
48. games
49. three
50. "adult"
51. "child"
52. "parent"
53. "adults"
54. Fritz Perls
55. directive
56. personality
57. dialogue
58. language
59. disowned
60. beliefs
61. Aautomatic
62. Rational–emotive
63. Albert Ellis
64. irrational
65. directive
66. distortions
67. depression
68. perception
69. overgeneralization
70. magnification
71. absolutist
72. Mminimizing
73. pessimism
74. restructuring
75. behavior
76. running
77. behavior
78. cognitive behavior
79. behavior
80. cognitive

81. modification
82. learning
83. experimentation
84. observable
85. maladaptive
86. adaptive
87. flooding
88. desensitization
89. participant
90. Joseph Wolpe
91. counter–conditioning
92. incompatible
93. relaxation
94. hierarchy
95. aversive
96. rapid
97. reinforced
98. extinguished
99. token
100. self
101. role
102. behavior
103. feedback
104. assertiveness
105. biofeedback
106. reinforce
107. electromyograph
108. electroencephalograph
109. alpha
110. functional
111. maintain
112. consequences
113. restriction
114. stimulus
115. prevention
116. competing
117. approximations
118. response
119. reinforcement
120. theoretical
121. economical
122. experiences
123. emotional
124. Encounter
125. Confrontations
126. systems

127. differentness
128. identified
129. experiment
130. blind
131. outcomes
132. meta–analysis
133. 70–75
134. well
135. highly
136. 75
137. 72
138. therapy
139. encouraging
140. helplessness
141. relationship
142. irrational
143. cognitive
144. more
145. 80
146. greater
147. superior
148. Drug therapy
149. Minor
150. Valium
151. central
152. rebound
153. antipsychotic
154. delusions
155. phenothiazines
156. dopamine
157. Parkinson's
158. Major
159. Antidepressant
160. noradrenaline
161. serotonin
162. panic
163. eating
164. manic
165. bipolar
166. noradrenaline
167. Cerletti
168. convulsions
169. major depression
170. memory
171. antidepressant
172. Unilateral

173. Moniz
174. prefrontal lobotomy
175. lobes
176. thalamus
177. side
178. Drug therapy
179. minor
180. tolerance
181. antidepressant
182. lower

| Idioms | |
|---|---|
| 525 | shore (ing) up | reinforce (ing) |
| 526 | go (gone) mad | become insane |
| 527 | shed light on | make more understandable |
| 528 | make up | comprise |
| 555 | wind up | end up; finish |

| Cultural References | |
|---|---|
| 524 | Quakers | a religious group who are known for their active concern for humanitarian issues. |
| 549 | Fats Domino | a popular singer and piano player |
| 553 | voter referendum | a vote of "yes" or "no" on a proposed law by the registered voters in the election district |
| 553 | found its way to the ballot box | became an issue that the public would vote on in local elections |
| 553 | witch doctors, palm reader | people in Africa who were thought to have magical powers, people who interpret lines in the palm of the hands in terms of future events |
| 553 | self-help books | a book which focuses on a specific problems and solutions |
| 554 | Elvis Presley | a singer who was popular in the 1950s and 1960s who died and has maintained a following-people |
| 554 | U.F.O. | unidentified flying object |

| Phrases and Expressions (Different Usage) | |
|---|---|
| 520 | out on the town | going places for entertainment |
| 520 | to take the lead | to direct the discussion and emphasis themselves |
| 520 | uplifting experience | exciting and happy experience |
| 520 | is no | is not a |
| 522 | pops into | enters |
| 522 | face to face | two people looking at one another |
| 522 | places major burden... on... shoulders | expects Brad to direct his own therapy |
| 522 | Role-playing | imagining a social situation and acting it |
| 522 | squarely in the eye | directly |
| 522 | a matter of chance | not carefully planned |
| 522 | brings... to bear on influencing | using... in order to influence This is an overwhelming |

| Phrases and Expressions (Different Usage) | |
|---|---|
| 522 | quite a mouthful | This is an overwhelming statement, isn't it? |
| 523 | not based on, say, | not based on, for example |
| 523 | aimed at | relevant to |
| 523 | As such | as this, |
| 523 | not meet demands ... life | not function in terms of supporting themselves and, therefore, not having money for food and shelter |
| 523 | human warehousing | to provide only a place to stay; no care |
| 523 | mushroomed in population | increased in number |
| 525 | go for a stroll on a lazy afternoon | walk slowly and leisurely on an afternoon in which they did not have to work |
| 525 | to take in the sights | to look at the "entertainment" |
| 525 | want to visit | it was their habit to visit |
| 525 | running amok | becoming confused, disorganized and more insane |
| 525 | seemed foreign and frightening | appeared too unfamiliar and scary |
| 525 | follow-up care | care which followed their release on a continuous basis |
| 525 | a "revolving door" | they left the hospital feeling all right, became disturbed again and returned to the hospital |
| 525 | outlook | prospect |
| 525 | looks brighter | appears optimistic |
| 526 | to bulwark the ego against | to protect the ego from |
| 526 | torrents of energy | large amounts of energy |
| 526 | loosed by the id | released by the id |
| 526 | no matter how | it did not matter how trivial... or |
| 526 | trivial... personal | personal |
| 526 | par for the course | what was expected |
| 526 | plucking | taking; pulling |
| 526 | weighs upon the heart | causes depression |
| 527 | been dammed up | to have been restrained |
| 527 | the inner workings of | the operation of |
| 527 | to spill forth | to release |
| 527 | blocked insight | stopped; insight that cannot occur |
| 527 | may eventually surface | may eventually be revealed |
| 527 | "My mind is blank" | there are no thoughts in my mind |
| 527 | compulsion to utter | compulsion to say something that reveals a hidden feeling |
| 527 | tips the balance in favor of | changes the balance so that the person speaks about it |

Chapter 14    Methods of Therapy

| 527 | deep-seated feelings | feelings that are very deep |
|-----|----------------------|-----------------------------|
| 527 | the "royal road..." | the best way |
| 527 | a father figure | a substitute for a father |
| 527 | a two-way street | the feelings are from the client to the therapist and they are also from the therapist to the client |
| 527 | sex object | an impersonalized person to enjoy sexually |
| 528 | not give... "a chance " | not allow time and experience to know the new person and refuse to continue to develop the relationship |
| 528 | plead not guilty of encouraging | say that he or she did not encourage |
| 528 | grist for the therapeutic mill | information for the therapist to use in treatment |
| 529 | frankly | candidly; I shall be direct and say this, even though it may be negative |
| 529 | ratio of cost to benefits | the relationship of the cost to the results received |
| 529 | fashion desired traits | create the traits that they want |
| 530 | has a way of influencing | often influence; (it is characteristic for this to happen) |
| 530 | Given this view | accepting this opinion |
| 530 | roadblocks placed in the path of | hindrances that are preventing |
| 530 | don masks and facades | act falsely |
| 530 | seen but not heard | be quiet and unobtrusive and not express our feelings; |
| 530 | might be unleashed | might be released |
| 530 | by setting aside | by not considering |
| 532 | paints a lurid scene | describes a terrible experience |
| 532 | "top dog" | a boss |
| 532 | "underdog" | a person who has nothing |
| 532 | Don't take chances... | don't experiment |
| 533 | Stick with what you have | remain the way you are |
| 533 | get out of this rut | remove yourself from the boring routine |
| 533 | clear the path | open the way; make it possible |
| 533 | spent in worrying | used in worrying |
| 533 | shape our responses to them | are responsible for what we do about them |
| 533 | be fleeting | quick in appearing and quick in disappearing |
| 533 | hard to catch | hard to notice |
| 533 | the worst will happen | the worst event will happen |
| 533 | pin down | notice and pay attention |
| 534 | laid off at work | lost their jobs |
| 534 | blown out of proportion | exaggerate |
| 534 | get going in the morning | start to function in the morning |
| 535 | run all right | be all right |
| 535 | in the long run | most of the time |

| 535 | scaled down | reduced |
|-----|-------------|---------|
| 535 | Along the way | as he did this |
| 535 | pave the way for | prepare for; create the conditions for; make it possible for |
| 535 | "exploding" at the slightest provocation | express anger in an unacceptable manner at something that is not important |
| 536 | of tying | of connecting |
| 536 | rely heavily | rely a lot |
| 536 | build... relationships | develop relationships |
| 537 | armchair adventurer | one who satisfies the need for adventure by sitting and reading or watching TV |
| 537 | twinges of discomfort | feelings of discomfort |
| 538 | would-be-quitters | the people who are trying to stop |
| 538 | an everyday hair dryer | an ordinary hair dryer |
| 538 | at six-month follow-ups | every six months |
| 539 | walk all over you? | take advantage of you? |
| 541 | bottle up | repress |
| 541 | make a scene | cause a disturbance |
| 540 | humdrum activities | boring activities |
| 540 | to no avail | but it was not successful |
| 542 | go window-shopping | look at window displays in stores and think about buying but don't |
| 543 | is curbed | is curtailed; stopped |
| 543 | shred your credit cards | destroy your credit cards |
| 543 | Break the chain | stop the habit |
| 543 | cut out | eliminate |
| 543 | Why give yourself something for nothing? | Why do you require something from yourself and not give something to yourself? |
| 543 | Your most hated cause | organization that you do not like or agree with |
| 543 | no veggies, no dessert | if you don't eat your vegetables, you can't have any dessert |
| 543 | like clockwork | at regular times |
| 544 | run into troubles | have trouble |
| 544 | ships in the night...out of the darkness... | a metaphor; know each other for a short time and never see each other again |
| 544 | en masse | everyone at the same time |
| 545 | to rip it off | to remove it |
| 545 | in unison | together; all speaking at one time |
| 545 | the bad apple... the barrel | a metaphor |
| 546 | as time goes on | as time passes |
| 546 | on their own | without help |
| 546 | have a stake in believing | want to believe because that is what they do |
| 547 | fare better | do better; feel better |

1. A leader of the humanitarian reform movement in the United States was
   (a) Philippe Pinel.
   (b) Dorothea Dix.
   (c) Sigmund Freud.
   (d) William Tuke.

2. A woman client complains to her therapist, "Who do you think you are—my father?" Sigmund Freud would probably characterize her behavior as an example of
   (a) transference.
   (b) reaction formation.
   (c) projection.
   (d) resistance.

3. Sigmund Freud remarked, "Where id was, there shall ego be." According to the text, Freud meant that
   (a) all unconscious ideas should be made conscious.
   (b) feelings of guilt should be removed.
   (c) coping behavior should replace impulsive behavior.
   (d) defense mechanisms should be destroyed.

4. A person has a dream in which she is flying. According to Sigmund Freud, the perceived subject matter of a dream—in this case, flying—is its _____ content.
   (a) manifest
   (b) objective
   (c) symbolic
   (d) latent

5. Which of the following is an example of the application of operant conditioning to therapy?
   (a) transference
   (b) analysis of social transactions
   (c) selective abstraction
   (d) biofeedback training

6. Congruence may be defined as
   (a) honesty in interpersonal relationships.
   (b) a fit between one's behavior and feelings.
   (c) ability to perceive the world from a client's frame of reference.
   (d) genuine acceptance of the client as a person.

7. A relative of yours is considering seeing a person–centered therapist, but wonders if person–centered therapy is right for him. You note that person–centered therapy seems to be most effective with _____ clients.
   (a) psychotic
   (b) poorly motivated
   (c) middle–class
   (d) well–educated

8. In transactional analysis, when two people relate to one another as adults, there is said to be a
   (a) crossed transaction.
   (b) confirmed exchange.
   (c) complementary transaction.
   (d) transference relationship.

9. According to Albert Ellis, the central factors in our problems are
   (a) genetic factors.
   (b) maladaptive habits.
   (c) unconscious conflicts.
   (d) irrational beliefs.

10. A client fantasizes an experience in order to get in touch with automatic, fleeting thoughts. This technique is termed
    (a) the dialogue.
    (b) running a movie.
    (c) introspection.
    (d) abreaction.

11. Behavior rehearsal is most similar in meaning to
    (a) practice.
    (b) role playing.
    (c) modeling.
    (d) countertransference.

12. The technique of modeling is connected with
    (a) person–centered therapy.
    (b) traditional psychoanalysis.
    (c) social–skills training.
    (d) encounter groups.

13. The technique called _____ is an example of aversive conditioning.
    (a) "Grandma's method"
    (b) restriction of the stimulus field
    (c) operant conditioning
    (d) rapid smoking

14. Tom cut down on his cigarette intake by simply pausing between puffs. This technique is an example of
    (a) successive approximations.
    (b) chain breaking.
    (c) response prevention.
    (d) avoiding stimuli that trigger unwanted behavior.

15. Which of the following is **NOT** a problem in evaluating the effectiveness of traditional psychoanalysis?
    (a) The effectiveness of therapy varies with the effectiveness of the therapist.
    (b) Persons receiving psychoanalysis are not blind to the treatment they are receiving.
    (c) A traditional psychoanalysis may require many years to complete.
    (d) Statistical techniques apply to short–term therapies, but not to long–term therapies.

16. According to the studies analyzed by Smith and Glass, the **LEAST** effective form of therapy is
    (a) Gestalt therapy.
    (b) psychoanalysis.
    (c) cognitive therapy.
    (d) behavior therapy.

17. Valium and other minor tranquilizers are thought to depress the activity of the _____, which, in turn, decreases, sympathetic activity.
    (a) central nervous system
    (b) parasympathetic nervous system
    (c) adrenal medulla
    (d) adrenal cortex

18. Phenothiazines are thought to work by blocking the action of
    (a) acetylcholine.
    (b) noradrenaline.
    (c) dopamine.
    (d) serotonin.

19. The use of _____ might lead to symptoms like those of Parkinson's disease.
    (a) ECT
    (b) the prefrontal lobotomy
    (c) lithium carbonate
    (d) major tranquilizers

20. A friend of yours is concerned about academic pressures and asks you if you know of anyone who can prescribe tranquilizers. You try to convince him not to resort to drugs to handle college, but you also inform him that _____ are licensed physicians, and thus capable of prescribing drugs.
    (a) psychologists
    (b) psychiatrists
    (c) psychiatric social workers
    (d) psychoanalysts

**Answer Key to *Posttest***

1. B
2. A
3. C
4. A
5. D
6. B
7. D
8. C
9. D
10. B
11. A
12. C
13. D
14. B
15. D
16. A
17. A
18. C
19. D
20. B

| | |
|---|---|
| Psychotherapy | Wish fulfillment |
| Asylum | Phallic symbol |
| Psychoanalysis | Manifest content |
| Catharsis | Latent content |
| Free association | Ego analyst |
| Resistance | Person-centered therapy |
| Interpretation | Unconditional positive regard |

| | |
|---|---|
| A primitive method used by the id to attempt to gratify basic instincts. | A systematic interaction between a therapist and a client that brings psychological principles to bear on influencing the client's thoughts, feelings, or behavior to help that client overcome abnormal behavior or adjust to problems in living. |
| A sign that represents the penis. | An institution for the care of the mentally ill. |
| In psychodynamic theory, the reported content of dreams. | Freud's method of psychotherapy. |
| In psychodynamic theory, the symbolized or underlying content of dreams. | Another term for abreaction, which is the expression of previously repressed feelings. |
| A psychodynamically-oriented therapist who focuses on the conscious, coping behavior of the ego instead of the hypothesized, unconscious functioning of the id. | In psychoanalysis, the uncensored uttering of all thoughts that come to mind. |
| Carl Rogers's method of psychotherapy, which emphasizes the creation of a warm, therapeutic atmosphere that frees clients to engage in self-exploration and self-expression. | The tendency to block the free expression of impulses and primitive ideas—a reflection of the defense mechanism of repression. |
| Acceptance of the value of another person, although not necessarily acceptance of everything the person does. | An explanation of a client's utterance according to psychoanalytic theory. |

| | |
|---|---|
| Empathic understanding | Adult (in TA) |
| Frame of reference | Transaction |
| Genuineness | Complementary |
| Congruence | Gestalt therapy |
| Transactional analysis | Dialogue |
| Parent (in TA) | Cognitive therapy |
| Child (in TA) | Rational-emotive therapy |

| | |
|---|---|
| In TA, a rational, adaptive ego state. | Ability to perceive a client's feelings from the client's frame of reference. A quality of the good person-centered therapist. |
| In TA, an exchange between two people. | One's unique patterning of perceptions and attitudes, according to which one evaluates events. |
| In TA, descriptive of a transaction in which the ego states of two people interact harmoniously. | Recognition and open expression of the therapist's own feelings. |
| Fritz Perls's form of psychotherapy, which attempts to integrate conflicting parts of the personality through directive methods designed to help clients perceive their whole selves. | A fit between one's self-concept and behaviors, thoughts, and emotions. |
| A Gestalt therapy technique in which clients verbalize confrontations between conflicting parts of their personality. | A form of psychotherapy that deals with how people interact and how their interactions reinforce attitudes, expectations, and "life positions." TA. |
| A form of therapy that focuses on how clients' cognitions (expectations, attitudes, beliefs, etc. ) lead to distress and may be modified to relieve distress and promote adaptive behavior. | In TA, a moralist ego state. |
| Albert Ellis's form of cognitive psychotherapy which focuses on how irrational expectations create anxiety and disappointment and which encourages clients to challenge and correct these expectations. | In TA, an irresponsible, emotional ego state. |

| | |
|---|---|
| Behavior therapy | Self-monitoring |
| Systematic desensitization | Behavior rehearsal |
| Hierarchy | Biofeedback training |
| Modeling | Functional analysis |
| Aversive conditioning | Encounter group |
| Token economy | Family therapy |
| Successive approximations | Meta-analysis |

| | |
|---|---|
| Keeping a record of one's own behavior to identify problems and record successes. | Systematic application of the principles of learning to the direct modification of a client's problem behaviors. |
| Practice. | Wolpe's method for reducing fears by associating a hierarachy of images of fear-evoking stimuli with deep muscle relation. |
| The systematic feeding back to an organism of information about a bodily function so that the organism can gain control of that function. BFT. | An arrangement of stimuli according to the amount of fear they evoke. |
| A systematic study of behavior in which one identifies the stimuli that trigger problem behavior and the reinforcers that maintain it. | A behavior-therapy technique in which a client observes and imitates a person who approaches and copes with feared objects or situations. |
| A type of group that aims to foster self-awareness by focusing on how group members relate to each other in a setting that encourages open expression of feelings. | A behavior-therapy technique in which undesired responses are inhibited by pairing repugnant or offensive stimuli with them. |
| A form of therapy in which the family unit is treated as the client. | A controlled environment in which people are reinforced for desired behaviors with tokens that may be exchanged for privileges. |
| A method for combining and averaging the results of individual research studies. | In operant conditioning, a series of behaviors that gradually become more similar to a target behavior. |

| | |
|---|---|
| Rebound anxiety | Psychosurgery |
| Antidepressant | Prefrontal lobotomy |
| Monoamine oxidase inhibitors | Abreaction |
| Tricyclic antidepressants | Rapid Smoking |
| Serotonin-uptake inhibitors | Self-actualization |
| Sedative | Lithium |
| Electroconvulsive therapy | Feedback |

| | |
|---|---|
| Surgery intended to promote psychological changes or to relieve disordered behavior. | Strong anxiety that can be experienced after someone stops taking tranquilizers. |
| The severing or destruction of a section of the frontal lobe of the brain. | Acting to relieve depression. |
| In psychoanalysis, expression of previously repressed feelings and impulses to allow the psychic energy associated with them to spill forth. | Antidepressant drugs that work by blocking the action of an enzyme that breaks down noradrenaline and serotonin. MAO. |
| An aversive conditioning for quitting smoking in which the would-be quitter inhales every 6 seconds, thus rendering once-desirable cigarette smoke aversive. | Antidepressant drugs that work by preventing the re-uptake of noradrenaline and serotonin by transmitting neurons. |
| Developing to one's fullest potential. | Antidepressant drugs that work by blocking the re-uptake of serotonin by presynaptic neurons. |
| A drug used to control the symptoms in a manic episode and, in maintenance therapy, to even out the mood swings and reduce recurrence of future manic or depressive states in bipolar disorder. | Relieving nervousness or agitation. |
| In assertiveness training, information about the effectiveness of a response. | Treatment of disorders like major depression by passing an electric current (that causes a convulsion) through the cead. ECT. |

Directions: This *PRETEST* will give you feedback about how well you understand Chapter 15. In order to enhance your mastery of Chapter 15, complete all the sections of this chapter of the Study Guide. Then you can take the *POSTTEST* and compare your results.

1. Which is the most accurate statement about stress?
   (a) Stress is the painful price we must pay for living.
   (b) The most stressed people are usually unaware of stress.
   (c) Some stress is necessary to keep us alert and occupied.
   (d) All stress is harmful to the body.

2. Since they are life changes, increased income and going on a vacation
   (a) should not both be experienced during the same year.
   (b) are about as stressful as personal injury and illness.
   (c) both lower the stress experienced by the individual.
   (d) both require adaptation.

3. When Richter placed rats into uncomfortably warm or cold water, they could swim for about
   (a) a few minutes.
   (b) two to four hours.
   (c) twenty to forty hours.
   (d) eighty hours.

4. In Albert Ellis's A-B-C approach, the *B* stands for
   (a) behavior.
   (b) beliefs.
   (c) bargaining.
   (d) balance.

5. Research on the effects of Type A behavior must be interpreted with caution because it
   (a) shows that Type B people are more concerned with the quality of life.
   (b) shows that Type A people earn more money.
   (c) is correlational, not experimental.
   (d) relies on statistical techniques.

6. As compared to Type B individuals, Type A people tend to
   (a) perceive time as passing more rapidly.
   (b) eat more slowly.
   (c) seek out more positive information about themselves.
   (d) be more willing to share power.

7. Nancy has just had a frightening experience in which she thought her car was going off the road. Which of the following is likely to be happening inside her?
   (a) Her respiration rate is decreasing.
   (b) Her blood pressure is decreasing.
   (c) Her digestive processes are speeding up.
   (d) Her blood flow is shifting away from her skeletal musculature.

8. Unrelieved stress during the _____ may lead to diseases of adaptation and death.
   (a) fight–or–flight reaction
   (b) exhaustion stage
   (c) resistance stage
   (d) alarm reaction

9. High pepsinogen levels are implicated in
   (a) cancer.
   (b) hypertension.
   (c) ulcers.
   (d) asthma.

10. Hypertension predisposes victims to all of the following, **EXCEPT**
    (a) arteriosclerosis.
    (b) strokes.
    (c) heart attacks.
    (d) ulcers.

11. A vascular headache is caused by
    (a) muscle tension.
    (b) change in blood supply to the head.
    (c) injury.
    (d) chronic stress.

12. Corticotrophin–releasing hormone is secreted by the
    (a) pituitary gland.
    (b) adrenal medulla.
    (c) hypothalamus.
    (d) adrenal cortex.

13. The proteins that attack invading foreign agents are called
    (a) antibodies.
    (b) antigens.
    (c) pathogens.
    (d) steroids.

14. Which of the following best summarizes research concerning the relationship between Type A behavior and cardiovascular disorders?
    (a) Type A behavior heightens the risk for all cardiovascular disorders with the exception of coronary heart disease.
    (b) Type A behavior decreases the risk for all cardiovascular disorders with the exception of coronary heart disease.
    (c) Studies agree that Type A behavior increases the risk for cardiovascular disorders.
    (d) Some studies suggest that Type A behavior increases the risk of cardiovascular disorder, whereas other studies suggest that Type A behavior has no effect or may decrease the risk.

15. The risk factors for AIDS are defined in terms of
    (a) behavior.
    (b) mental illness.
    (c) family history.
    (d) patterns of consumption.

16. People are **LEAST** likely to comply with medical instructions when
    (a) the physician is friendly.
    (b) the physician is authoritarian.
    (c) symptoms are highly visible.
    (d) they believe that the treatment will work.

17. Which of the following is most likely to enhance the likelihood of seeking medical advice?
    (a) The patient is a woman.
    (b) The symptoms do not interfere with one's life.
    (c) The patient fears that the symptoms may be life–threatening.
    (d) The physician appears competent, but emotionally cold and disinterested.

18. One alternately tenses and relaxes muscles in the relaxation method of
    (a) biofeedback training.
    (b) progressive relaxation.
    (c) autogenic training.
    (d) meditation.

19. Orne–Johnson exposed meditators and nonmeditators to intermittent loud noises. The meditators
    (a) showed no stress reaction.
    (b) showed a less intense stress reaction than nonmeditators.
    (c) stopped showing a stress reaction sooner.
    (d) showed a more intense stress reaction than nonmeditators.

20. Jane shows a typical Type A behavior pattern and would like to alter it. The text recommends all of the following as ways to cope with Type A behavior, **EXCEPT**
    (a) leaving home for work as late as possible.
    (b) using an alarm clock with a softer alarm.
    (c) using work breaks to exercise or meditate.
    (d) spacing chores out.

Chapter 15 explores the field of health psychology—the relationships between psychological factors (e.g., stress, overt behavior, and attitudes) and the prevention and treatment of physical illness. The first section concerns sources of stress such as daily hassles (sources of aggravation) and life changes; pain and discomfort; frustration and conflict; irrational beliefs which can give rise to or heighten feelings of anxiety and depression; and the Type A behavior pattern, which is characterized by a sense of time urgency, hostility, and self-destructive behavior patterns.

There are numerous psychological moderators of the effects of stress. Persons with high self-efficacy expectations cope better. Psychologically hardy business executives show commitment, challenge, and control (an internal locus of control). Humor appears to buffer the impact of stress. Predictability of stressors apparently permits us to brace ourselves and find ways of coping. Social supports of various kinds are also of help.

Stress influences our physical well-being by increasing sympathetic arousal—as described in Hans Selye's general adaptation syndrome or Walter Cannon's fight–or–flight reaction. The endocrine system becomes involved through secretion of steroids, adrenaline, and norepinephrine. The immune system destroys pathogens, recognizes pathogens, and causes inflammation. Steroids suppress the functioning of the immune system.

Stress, in association with predisposing factors, can give rise to or exacerbate illnesses such as ulcers and hypertension. It also appears that stress can exert some influence over the course of cancer, although scientists do not suggest that stress causes cancer.

Health psychologists also study patient behavior, including factors that determine seeking of medical advice, the conceptualization of illness, and compliance with medical advice. The aspects of the "sick role" are enumerated. Ways of enhancing physician–patient relationships are explored.

Ways of coping with stress are outlined in the Psychology and Modern Life section.

# LEARNING OBJECTIVES

| | |
|---|---|
| | **Health Psychology** |
| 1. Define *health psychology*. | |
| | **Stress: Presses, Pushes, and Pulls** |
| 2. Define *stress*. | |
| 3. Enumerate the sources of stress. | |
| 4. Describe the various psychological moderators of the impact of stress. | |
| 5. Describe the general adaptation syndrome. | |

6. Describe the functions of the immune system.

7. Describe the effects of stress on the immune system.

8. Describe the relationships between psychological factors and illnesses such as headaches, cardiovascular disorders, and cancer.

## A Multifactorial Approach to Health and Illness

## Compliance with Medical Advice

9. Describe the factors that determine whether we shall seek help when we feel ill.

10. Describe the ways in which we conceptualize illness.

11. Describe factors that contribute to compliance with medical instructions and procedures.

## Psychology and Modern Life

12. Describe how psychologists help people control irrational thoughts as a way of coping with stress.

13. Describe how psychologists help people lower arousal as a way of coping with stress.

14. Describe various ways of modifying the Type A behavior pattern.

15. Explain how exercise can help people cope with stress.

## Health Psychology

## Stress: Presses, Pushes, and Pulls
1. Sources of Stress: Don't Hassle Me?

2. Psychological Moderators of Stress

3. The General Adaptation Syndrome

4. Effects of Stress on the Immune System

## A Multifactorial Approach to Health and Illness
1. Human Diversity and Health: Nations within the Nation

2. Headaches

3. Coronary Heart Disease

4. Asthma

5. Cancer

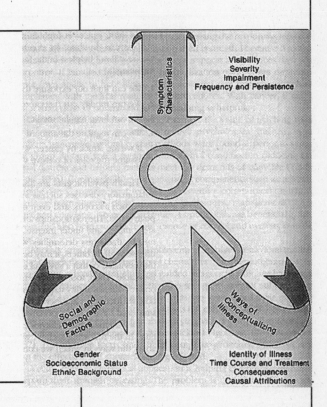

## Compliance with Medical Advice

1. Encouraging Compliance by Enhancing Physician-Patient Interactions

## Psychology and Modern Life
- Ways of Coping with Stress

# KEY TERMS AND CONCEPTS

## Health Psychology

1. Health psychology _____

2. Pathogens _____

## Stress: Presses, Pushes, and Pulls

3. Stress _____

4. Eustress _____

5. Daily hassles _____

6. Uplifts _____

7. Conflict _____

8. Approach–approach conflict _____

9. Vacillate _____

10. Avoidance–avoidance conflict _____
_____

11. Approach–avoidance conflict _____
_____

12. Multiple approach–avoidance conflict _____
_____

13. Catastrophize _____

14. Type A behavior _____

15. Self–efficacy expectations _____

16. Psychological hardiness _____

17. Locus of control _____

18. "Internals" _____

19. Internal locus of control _____

20. "Externals" _____

21. General adaptation syndrome _____
_____

22. Alarm reaction _____

23. Fight–or–flight reaction _____

24. Resistance stage _____

25. Exhaustion stage _____

26. Immune system _____

27. Leukocytes _____

28. Antigen _____

29. Antibodies _____

30. Inflammation _____

31. Psychoneuroimmunology _____

## A Multifactorial Approach to Health and Illness

32. Socioeconomic status _____

33. Migraine headache _____

34. Serum choesterol _____

34. Hypertension _____

## Additional Terms

_____
_____
_____
_____
_____
_____
_____
_____
_____
_____
_____
_____
_____
_____
_____
_____
_____
_____
_____
_____

Directions: Consider each of the following statements. Circle the T if it is true and the F if it is false. Answers and explanations follow the exercise.

NOTE: I'm going to be impossibly "tricky," so keep in mind that this is a learning exercise for you, and not a real test! The items along with the explanations of the correct answers are intended to enhance your "test-wiseness."

T F 1. According to the text, if we become ill and require hospitalization, like Norman Cousins did, it is most healthful for us to refuse routine medical tests and leave the hospital as soon as we feel that we can.

T F 2. Stress is harmful.

T F 3. A "daily hassle" is synonymous with a "life change."

T F 4. Life changes are to be avoided, if we wish to remain healthy.

T F 5. The research links between life changes and illness are correlational, not experimental.

T F 6. Richter found that in water at room temperature, most rats can swim for about 80 hours.

T F 7. For most people, the stresses of commuting are severe.

T F 8. People who have never encountered frustration are most tolerant of frustration.

T F 9. An approach–approach conflict is the most stressful form of conflict.

T F 10. According to Ellis, most of our miseries are caused by activating events.

T F 11. It is easier to evade life's responsibilities and problems than to face them and undertake more rewarding forms of self-discipline.

T F 12. Type A people become restless when they see others working slowly.

T F 13. Psychological factors can moderate the impact of sources of stress.

T F 14. It has been shown experimentally that high self–efficacy expectations are accompanied by low levels of adrenaline and norepinephrine in the bloodstream.

T F 15. People in whom high self–efficacy expectations are experimentally induced complete tasks more successfully than people of comparable ability but lower self–efficacy expectations.

T F 16. Psychologically hardy individuals show a tendency to involve themselves in, rather than experience alienation from, whatever they are doing or encountering.

T F 17. Of the three aspects of psychological hardiness that help people resist stress, Hull and his colleagues argue that commitment and challenge are the ones that make the most difference.

T F 18. Psychologically hardy people tend to have an external locus of control.

T F 19. According to Allport, "The essence of humor is that one spares oneself the [emotional responses] to which the situation would naturally give rise and overrides with a jest the possibility of such an emotional display."

T F 20. In an important psychological study of the moderating effects of humor on stress by Canadian psychologists Rod Martin and Herbert Lefcourt, students with a greater sense of humor, and who produced humor in difficult situations, were less affected by negative life events than other students.

T F 21. In the Weiss study, rats that received shock without warning showed greatest ulceration.

T F 22. If you get married, you will live longer.

T F 23. The GAS consists of three stages: an adaptation stage, a resistance stage, and an exhaustion stage.

T F 24. The alarm reaction involves a number of body changes that are initiated by the brain and further regulated by the endocrine system and the sympathetic division of the autonomic nervous system.

T F 25. The hypothalamus secretes corticotrophin–releasing hormone, which, in turn, stimulates the pituitary gland to secrete adrenocorticotrophic hormone.

T F 26. The parasympathetic division of the ANS activates the adrenal medulla, causing a mixture of adrenaline and norepinephrine to be released.

T F 27. In their research, psychologists frequently use the amount of cortisol in the saliva or urine as a biological measure of stress.

T F 28. In their research, psychologists use the amount of cortisol in the adrenal glands as a biological measure of stress.

T F 29. One way in which we combat physical disorders is by producing white blood cells that routinely engulf and kill pathogens.

T F 30. The foreign agents that are recognized and destroyed by leukocytes are called antibodies.

T F 31. Steroids heighten the functioning of the immune system.

T F 32. The single most frequent kind of headache is the migraine headache.

T F 33. Arousal of the sympathetic division of the ANS heightens the blood pressure.

T F 34. People whose families show a history of cardiovascular disease are more likely to develop cardiovascular disease themselves.

T F 35. According to the text, the research links between Type A behavior and cardiovascular disorders are currently in disarray.

T F 36. Asthma attacks can be triggered by stress.

T F 37. Cancer rates have been skyrocketing.

T F 38. A study of children with cancer found that a significant percentage had encountered severe life changes within a year of the diagnosis, often involving the death of a loved one or the loss of a close relationship.

T F 39. Stress can cause cancer.

T F 40. Women are more likely to seek medical help than men.

**Answer Key to True-False *Exercise***

ANSWER      COMMENT

1. F  Although Cousins' experiences are used to show how he took charge of his own treatment, the text cautions that Cousins knew a great deal about medicine and that readers are not advised to follow his example in the event of illness.

2. F  Some stress ("eustress") is good for you, according to the text. Therefore, this statement is too all-inclusive.

3. F  The text points out that daily hassles differ from life changes in two ways. What are they?

4. F  The text points out that *high numbers* of life changes place us in higher risk groups. Even so, there is no experimental evidence that high numbers of life changes directly cause illness in people.

5. T  Again, this is why we cannot assume that life changes cause illness.

6. T  A simple statement of fact from the text.

7. F  The text states that they are "mild," and so this statement is exaggerated.

8. F  The text states that people who *have* encountered frustration and found that they can cope with it are more tolerant.

9. F  This is actually the least stressful kind of conflict. Why?

10. F  Ellis notes that activating events may *initiate* problems, but that our irrational beliefs are more to blame.

11. F  This is one of Ellis's *irrational* beliefs!

12. T  This is one "side effect" of their sense of time urgency.

13. T  Sure they can.

14. T  Here the "trick" is to carefully check out the adjectives "high" and "low."

15. T  Again, the task is to check out the relationships between the words "high," "more," and "lower."

16. T  This is what is meant by their sense of commitment.

17. F  Only half true! Hull argues that their senses of commitment and *control*—not challenge— make the difference.

18. F  *Internal*, not *external*.

19. F  Freud, not Allport, made the statement, which is quoted accurately. (In true-false items, all parts of the statement must be true if the statement is to be considered true.)

20. T  You need to check out the names of the researchers (accurate) as well as the relationships between "greater" and "less" (all accurate).

21. T  The study was run by Weiss and the results as reported in the statement are consistent with what is stated in the text.

22. F  Again we have correlational evidence. Therefore, while it is true that married men live longer than single men, it may be that the factors that lead to the decision to get married, and not marriage itself, make the difference. Also, the findings are less clear-cut for women, so the statement is also too general.

23. F  Tricky! Yes, there are three stages, but the adaptation stage *is* the resistance stage; the alarm reaction has been omitted from the list.

24. T  All parts true (a difficult question!).

25. T  Another difficult item, with all parts true. It may help to recall, from Chapter 3, that the hypothalamus secretes many releasing factors that cause the pituitary to secrete related hormones.

26. F  The sympathetic division, not the parasympathetic division, does this.

27. T  A simple statement of fact.

28. F  Cortisol is produced by the adrenal glands.

29. T  This is one of the functions of the immune system.

30. F  They are called antigens, not antibodies.

31. F  Steroids *suppress* the functioning of the immune system.

32. F  The muscle-tension headache is more common.

33. T  A simple statement of fact.

34. T  There is a genetic risk factor.

35. T  Various studies show different findings.

36. T  This is a simple statement of fact.

37. F  Actually, many better-educated people have been modifying their behavior and placing themselves in lower risk categories for many kinds of cancer.

38. T  Stress does appear to exacerbate the course of cancer.

39. F  Although stress appears to exacerbate the course of cancer (see the previous item), there is no evidence that stress *causes* cancer.

40. T  This is a factual gender difference that is reported in the text.

# CHAPTER REVIEW

**SECTION 1: Health Psychology**

**OBJ. 1:** The field of health psychology studies the relationships between (1) _____ical factors (e.g., stress, behavior, and attitudes) and the prevention and treatment of physical illness.

**SECTION 2: Stresses: Presses, Pushes, and Pulls**

**OBJ. 2:** In psychology, (2) s_____ is the demand made on an organism to adapt, to cope, or to adjust. Some stress is healthful and keeps us alert and occupied. Selye refers to healthful stress as (3) _____ss.

**OBJ. 3:** Many sources of stress largely reflect external factors—daily (4) _____les, life changes, pain and discomfort, frustration, and conflict. Others, such as (5) ir_____ beliefs and Type (6) _____ behavior, are self–imposed.

(7) D_____ hassles are notable daily conditions and experiences that are threatening or harmful to a person's well–being. The opposite of hassles are (8) _____ts. Life changes differ from daily hassles in that many life changes are (9) _____ive and desirable, whereas hassles are all negative. (10) L_____ changes are also more isolated than daily hassles. Holmes and Rahe constructed a scale to measure (11) life–_____ units. Very stressful events include (12) _____ of a spouse (100 units), divorce (73 units), and (13) m_____ (50 units). Holmes and Rahe found that people who "earned" (14) _____ or more life–change units within a year according to their scale were at greater risk for illness. Critics note that the links between hassles, life changes, and illness are (15) _____tional, not experimental. Rather than hassles and life changes causing illness, it could be that people who are (16) pre_____ed toward medical or psychological problems encounter more hassles and

amass more life–change units.

(17) C_____ is being torn in two or more directions by opposing motives. An (18) approach–_____ conflict is the least stressful form of conflict. An (19) _____–avoidance conflict is more stressful because one is motivated to avoid each of two negative goals. However, avoiding one requires (20) _____ing the other. The same goal can produce both approach and avoidance motives, as in the (21) _____–_____ conflict. The most complex form of conflict is the (22) m_____ approach–avoidance conflict, in which each of several alternative courses of action has its promising and distressing aspects.

Ellis notes that our (23) _____fs about events, as well as the events themselves, can be a source of stress. Events can (24) _____vate irrational belief systems that cause or compound stresses. Ellis's first irrational belief is that you need sincere love and (25) ap_____ almost all the time from the people who are important to you. The second is that you must be thoroughly competent, adequate, and achieving.

Type A behavior is characterized by a sense of time (26) _____cy, competitiveness, and (27) ag_____ness. Type B people, by contrast, relax (28: *Circle one:* less or more) readily and focus (29: *Circle one:* less or more) on the quality of life.

**OBJ. 4:** There (30: *Circle one:* is or is not) a one–to–one relationship between the amount of stress we experience and physical illness or psychological distress. Our (31) self–_____ expectations are our perceptions of our capacities to bring about change. People with higher self-efficacy expectations tend to cope better with stress.

Kobasa and her colleagues have found that psychologically hardy executives differ from the nonhardy in three ways: Hardy individuals are high in (32) _____ment (they involve themselves in, rather than experience alienation from, what they are doing); hardy individuals are high in challenge; hardy individuals are (33: *Circle one:* high or low) in perceived control over their lives.

Being able to predict the onset of a stressor (34: *Circle one:* increases or decreases) its impact upon us.

Social support (35: *Circle one:* does or does not) buffer the effects of stress. Numerous studies have found a lower mortality rate for (36: *Circle one:* single or married) men.

**OBJ. 5:** The concept of the general adaptation syndrome (GAS) was originated by (37) S_____. The GAS consists of 38) _____ stages. These stages are the (39) a_____ reaction, a resistance stage, and the (40) _____tion stage. The alarm reaction (41) m_____izes or arouses the body for defense. Cannon had earlier termed this alarm system the (42) _____–or–_____ reaction.

The alarm reaction involves a number of body changes that are initiated by the brain and further regulated by the (43) _____rine system and the (44) _____etic division of the autonomic nervous system. Under stress, the hypothalamus secretes (45) _____trophin–releasing hormone (CRH), which, in turn, stimulates the pituitary gland to secrete (46) adr_____co-trophic hormone (ACTH). ACTH then acts upon the adrenal cortex, causing it to release (47) _____sol and other steroids that help the body respond to stress by fighting (48) in_____tion and allergic reactions. Two other hormones that play a major role in the alarm reaction are secreted by the adrenal medulla: (49) ad_____ine and (50) nor_____rine.

In the (51) _____tion stage, or resistance stage, of the GAS, the body attempts to restore lost energy and repair whatever damage has been done. All of us eventually reach the (52) _____tion

stage when stress persists. With exhaustion, the (53) para_____tic division of the ANS may become predominant.

**OBJ. 6:** The immune system has a number of functions that help us combat (54) _____ease. The immune system produces (55) _____ blood cells that routinely engulf and kill pathogens. White blood cells are technically termed (56) _____ytes. The immune system "remembers" foreign agents so that future combat will be more efficient. Pathogens that are recognized and destroyed by leukocytes are called (57) _____ens. Some leukocytes produce (58) _____dies, or specialized proteins that bind to their antigens and mark them for destruction. The immune system also causes (59) _____tion when injury occurs by increasing the flow of blood to the damaged area. The increased blood supply brings in large numbers of (60) _____ blood cells to combat invading microscopic life forms.

**OBJ. 7:** A new field of study addresses the relationships between psychological factors and the immune system: (61) psycho_____nology. One of the major concerns of psychoneuroimmunology is the effects of stress on the (62) _____e system.

One of the reasons that stress eventually exhausts us is that it stimulates us to produce (63) _____oids. Steroids (64: *Circle one:* enhance or suppress) the functioning of the immune system. Dental students in one study showed (65: *Circle one:* higher or lower) immune–system functioning during stressful school periods than immediately following vacations.

## SECTION 3: A Multifactorial Approach to Health and Illness

**OBJ. 8:** The most common kind of headache is the (66) _____–_____sion headache. Most other headaches, including the migraine, are vascular in nature—stemming from changes in

the (67) b_____ supply to the head.
(68) Mi_____ headaches have preheadache phases during which there is decreased blood supply to the head, and headache phases, during which the (69) _____ries are dilated, increasing the flow of blood. Behavioral methods such as progressive (70) _____tion help headaches by decreasing muscle tension. (71) _____back training that alters the flow of blood to the head has been used effectively to treat migraine headache.

Arousal of the (72) _____tic division of the ANS heightens the blood pressure. Hypertension predisposes victims to other (73) car_____lar disorders such as (74) art_____rosis, heart attacks, and strokes. Blood pressure appears to be higher among (75: Circle one: African Americans or white people).

There are several risk factors for cardiovascular disease: family history; (76) phy_____gical conditions such as obesity, hypertension, and high levels of serum (77) _____erol; patterns of consumption, such as heavy drinking and smoking; Type (78) _____ behavior; and work (79) o_____ (e.g., overtime work and assembly–line labor). We can profit from behavior modification that is intended to reduce the risk factors, such as stopping smoking; weight control; reducing (80) hy_____sion; lowering (81) s_____ cholesterol; modifying Type A behavior; and exercise.

People who develop ulcers under stress often have higher (82) pep_____ levels than those who do not. Asthma is a respiratory disorder which is often the result of an (83) _____ic reaction in which the main tubes of the windpipe––the bronchi—contract, making it difficult to breathe. Asthma attacks (84: Circle one: can or cannot) be triggered by stress.

People (85: Circle one: can or cannot) inherit dispositions toward developing cancer, but many behavior patterns, such as smoking, drinking, and eating animal fats, heighten the risk for cancer. Numerous studies connect stressful life events to the onset of cancer in people, but this research has been criticized in that it is (86) ret_____tive. Experimental research with animals shows that once cancer has affected the individual, stress can (87: Circle one: accelerate or retard) its course.

## SECTION 4: Compliance with Medical Advice

OBJ. 9: Reluctance to seek health care is related to fear of what the doctor might find; to social and demographic factors, such as (88) _____der, socioeconomic status, and ethnic background; to characteristics of the (89) _____toms; and to the ways in which we tend to (90) con_____ize illness. Women are (91: Circle one: less or more) likely to seek medical help than men. People of (92: Circle one: lower or higher) socioeconomic status are more willing to seek medical help. Four symptom characteristics also help determine whether we shall seek medical help: (93) _____ity of the symptom (e.g., whether it is on the face or torso); perceived (94) sev_____ of the symptom; (95) _____rence of symptoms with the person's life; and frequency and (96) _____tence of the symptoms.

OBJ. 10: The first factor in conceptualizing illness is the (97) _____ty of the illness. Our ideas about what is wrong with us provide a framework for the (98) inter_____ of symptoms. Accurate conceptualization of the (99) c_____ of a disease is important to maintaining an adequate treatment regimen. We often fail to seek medical advice when we conceptualize the consequences of the illness to be minor, as in the case of cold symptoms, or life-threatening. Causal attributions for illnesses are important because they influence (100) _____tive behavior as well as seeking of proper treatment.

OBJ. 11: Patients are (101: Circle one: less or more) likely to adhere to advice from physicians who are perceived as competent, friendly, warm, and concerned. Patients are (102: *Circle one:* less or more) likely to comply with instructions from physicians whom they perceive as authoritarian and condescending. Patients are (103: *Circle one:* less or more) likely to comply with medical instructions when illness is severe. Patients are (104: *Circle one:* less or more) likely to comply with instructions when they believe that the instructions will work. Patients are likely to discontinue medications when they encounter (105) s_____ effects, especially when the side effects are (106: *Circle one:* expected or unexpected).

## SECTION 5: Psychology and Modern Life

**OBJ. 12:** Describe how psychologists help people control irrational thoughts as a way of coping with stress. (107) Mei_____ suggests a three–step procedure for controlling the irrational and catastrophizing thoughts that heighten stress: first, develop awareness of these thoughts through careful self–examination; second, prepare thoughts that are (108) in_____ with the irrational thoughts, and practice saying them firmly to yourself; and third, (109) r_____ yourself with a mental pat on the back for effective changes in beliefs and thought patterns.

**OBJ. 13:** The three ways for lowering arousal discussed in the text are (110) med_____, (111) bio_____, and (112) pro_____ relaxation. Meditation seems to focus on the (113) _____tive components of a stress reaction, whereas biofeedback can be directed at various (114) _____logical functions, such as heart rate and muscle tension. Progressive relaxation focuses on reducing (115) m_____ tension.

In progressive (116) re_____, people purposefully tense a muscle group before relaxing it. This sequence allows them to 1) develop (117) _____ness of their muscle tensions; and

2) differentiate between feelings of (118) t_____ and relaxation.

**OBJ. 14:** Type A behavior is identified by a sense of (119) _____ urgency, (120) hos_____, and hard–driving, self–destructive behavior patterns. The first step in coping with a sense of time urgency is (121) con_____ing and replacing the beliefs that support it. Other methods include engaging in (122: *Circle one:* less or more) social activities with family and friends, visiting museums and art galleries, and reminding yourself daily that life is by nature unfinished and that you do not need to have all your projects finished on a given date. Suggestions for dealing with hostility include telling your family and children that you love them, making some new friends, and looking for the beauty and joy in things.

**OBJ. 15:** Exercise, particularly (123) _____bic exercise, can enhance our psychological well being and help us cope with stress as well as foster physical health. Aerobic exercise is any kind of exercise that requires a sustained increase in the consumption of (124) o_____. The major physiological effect of exercise is the promotion of (125) _____ness. (126) _____ascular fitness, or "condition," means that the body can use greater amounts of oxygen during vigorous activity and pump more blood with each heart beat.

(127) De_____ is characterized by inactivity and feelings of helplessness. (128) E_____ is the "opposite" of inactivity. Success at exercise may also help alleviate feelings of (129) _____ness. The benefits of exercise may also help people cope through enhancing feelings of physical well–being, improving physical health, and enhancing one's sense of (130) c_____ over one's body.

1. psychological
2. stress
3. eustress
4. hassles
5. irrational
6. A
7. Daily
8. uplifts
9. positive
10. Life
11. life–change
12. death
13. marriage
14. 300
15. correlational
16. predisposed
17. Conflict
18. approach–approach
19. avoidance–avoidance
20. approaching
21. approach–avoidance
22. multiple
23. beliefs
24. activate
25. approval
26. urgency
27. aggressiveness
28. more
29. more
30. is not
31. self-efficacy
32. commitment
33. high
34. decreases
35. does
36. married
37. Selye
38. three
39. alarm
40. exhaustion
41. mobilizes
42. fight–or–flight

43. endocrine
44. sympathetic
45. corticotrophin–releasing hormone
46. adrenocortico-trophic hormone
47. cortisol
48. inflammation
49. adrenaline
50. norepinephrine
51. adaptation
52. exhaustion
53. parasympathetic
54. disease
55. white
56. leukocytes
57. antigens
58. antibodies
59. inflammation
60. white
61. psychoneuro–immunology
62. immune
63. steroids
64. suppress
65. lower
66. muscle–tension
67. blood
68. Migraine
69. arteries
70. relaxation
71. Biofeedback
72. sympathetic
73. cardiovascular
74. arteriosclerosis
75. African Americans
76. physiological
77. cholesterol
78. A
79. overload
80. hypertension
81. serum
82. pepsinogen
83. allergic
84. can
85. can
86. retrospective

87. accelerate
88. gender
89. symptoms
90. conceptualize
91. more
92. higher
93. visibility
94. severity
95. interference
96. persistence
97. identity
98. interpretation
99. causes
100. preventive
101. more
102. less
103. more
104. more
105. side
106. unexpected
107. Meichenbaum
108. incompatible
109. reward
110. meditation
111. biofeedback
112. progressive
113. cognitive
114. physiological
115. muscle
116. relaxation
117. awareness
118. tension
119. time
120. hostility
121. confronting
122. more
123. aerobic
124. oxygen
125. fitness
126. Cardiovascular
127. Depression
128. Exercise
129. helplessness
130. control

| | Idioms | |
|---|---|---|
| 579 | turn out | become; result in |
| 574 | bring about | cause |
| 574 | draw on | use |
| 579 | shut off | stop operating |
| 590 | to defend off | to defeat; to protect against |
| 597 | stick to | persevere with |

| | Cultural References | |
|---|---|---|
| 567 | loan installments | monthly payments to repay a loan |
| 567 | taxes | money people pay to support |
| 567 | | the government |
| 567 | property investments | purchasing property to receive income |
| 567 | stock-market swings | prices of stocks tend to go up and down together |
| 567 | retirement | a person stops working and lives on saved money and social security payments |
| 567 | in-laws | the parents of a spouse |
| 572 | volley like a | hit the ball back and forth |
| 579 | tennis pro | over the net like professional |
| 579 | low-interest loans | loans made with low costs |
| 579 | Three Mile Island | the name of a place where a nuclear reactor is situated |
| 588 | Overtime work | additional hours of work at higher pay |
| 588 | assembly-line labor | work in a factory where a person attaches a part to an item before the moving table carries the item to the next worker |
| 597 | mow the grass | people who do not live in the city have grass around their houses which they cut. |
| 601 | climbing the corporate ladder | continually obtaining higher positions in a business |
| 602 | jumping rope | swinging the jumping over a rope. |
| 604 | cross-country skiing | it is a sport where a person moves in a "walking" fashion on level ground covered with snow. |
| 604 | postal workers | people who work for the U.S. Post Office |
| 604 | longshoremen | people who are employed to unload cargo from ships |

| | Phrases and Expressions (Different Usage) | |
|---|---|---|
| 564 | a springboard for discussion | something said to start a discussion |
| 565 | overtax | put too large a burden upon |

| | Phrases and Expressions (Different Usage) | |
|---|---|---|
| 566 | last straw that will break camel's back | final part of a load that causes a person not to function |
| 566 | so goes the saying | this is the expression |
| 567 | too much of a good thing | attaining success in many areas in the same time period |
| 567 | marrying Mr. or Mrs. Right | marrying the perfect mate |
| 567 | propel you into a state of bliss | make you extremely happy |
| 567 | one on top of the other | one added to the other |
| 567 | from all walks of life | from different economic and social groups |
| 567 | baseline | the same situation for all |
| 567 | dampen our moods | depress us a little |
| 567 | rival explanations | different explanations |
| 570 | easy-going | relaxed and flexible |
| 570 | psychologically hardy | psychologically strong |
| 570 | "damned if you did and damned if you didn't?" | it would be bad if you did it and bad if you didn't do it |
| 570 | being torn in two or more directions | there are two or more directions in which you want to go |
| 570 | you cheap or uncommitted | that you don't want to spend money (when friends think you should) |
| 571 | this so-and-so | terrible person |
| 572 | flunking | failing |
| 572 | opt for | decide on taking |
| 572 | cash will soon be jingling in your pockets | you will soon be earning money |
| 572 | no-good | terrible |
| 572 | our personal doorways to distress | our own methods for causing ourselves distress |
| 572 | go the way you want them to go | occur the way that you want |
| 573 | one eye glued firmly on the clock | look at the clock continually in order to always know the time |
| 573 | bat the ball back and forth | hit the ball over the net to someone who hits it back |
| 573 | motto | private rule |
| 573 | pace themselves | insure that there will be periods of time between stress |
| 574 | no one-to-one relationship | no relationship of amount of stress to to illness |
| 574 | to withstand stress | not be hurt by stress |
| 574 | hardy and nonhardy | emotionally strong and emotionally weak |
| 574 | threat to security | method of causing insecurity |

Chapter 15  Health Psychology

| Phrases and Expressions (Different Usage) | | Additional Terms | |
|---|---|---|---|
| 574 | buffers between themselves | shields between themselves; a protection | | |
| 574 | "a merry heart doeth good like a medicine" | a happy person is healthy | | |
| 603 | avoid rush-hour jams | do not travel when everyone else is traveling to work | | |
| 603 | car-pool | share your car or ride in someone else's car | | |
| 603 | back to back | a class immediately after the first | | |
| 603 | Space chores | allow time periods between tasks or jobs | | |
| 603 | Set aside | choose; decide on | | |
| 603 | up to us | it is our responsibility | | |
| 603 | stand ready | are always ready | | |
| 603 | hold divergent and set opinions | have different opinions which are very strong | | |
| 604 | cursing | swearing; (using blasphemy) | | |
| 604 | Play to lose | play a game in a way that you will lose | | |
| 604 | gorge on high-fat foods | eat too much fat food | | |
| 604 | short bursts | short intensive periods | | |
| 606 | tracking | researching | | |
| 606 | If... have a family history of | if members of your family before you had | | |
| 606 | stick to it | to continue to do it | | |
| | old-timers | people who have been doing it for a long time | | |

| Additional Terms | | | |
|---|---|---|---|
| | | | |

1. Hassles differ from life changes in that
   (a) hassles require adaptation.
   (b) hassles are a source of stress.
   (c) life changes occur more frequently.
   (d) life changes can be positive as well as negative.

2. In order to develop their life–change units scale, Holmes and Rahe created a baseline by assigning 50 units to
   (a) death of a spouse.
   (b) marriage.
   (c) taking on a high mortgage.
   (d) divorce.

3. A list of ten irrational beliefs that can make us miserable was compiled by
   (a) Albert Bandura.
   (b) Donald Meichenbaum.
   (c) Julian Rotter.
   (d) Albert Ellis.

4. Type A people are characterized by
   (a) need for affiliation.
   (b) secretion of excessive ACTH.
   (c) competitiveness and impatience.
   (d) predisposition toward alcoholism.

5. As compared to Type B people, Type A people
   (a) perceive time as passing more rapidly.
   (b) earn less money.
   (c) smoke less frequently.
   (d) are better adjusted in their marriages.

6. Psychologically hardy individuals show all of the following, **EXCEPT**
   (a) competitiveness.
   (b) commitment.
   (c) control.
   (d) challenge.

7. Which of the following is **NOT** a risk factor for cardiovascular disorders?
   (a) low serum cholesterol
   (b) family history of cardiovascular disease
   (c) hypertension
   (d) physical inactivity

8. The so–called common migraine headache is identified by
   (a) muscle tension in the shoulders and back of the neck.
   (b) hypertension.
   (c) sudden onset and throbbing on one side of the head.
   (d) sensory and motor disturbances that precede the pain.

9. Which of the following is a component of the alarm reaction?
   (a) muscles relax
   (b) adrenaline is secreted
   (c) blood coagulability decreases
   (d) heart rate decreases

10. Which of the following is characterized by dominance of the parasympathetic branch of the autonomic nervous system?
    (a) fight–or–flight reaction
    (b) resistance stage
    (c) alarm reaction
    (d) exhaustion stage

11. According to the text, stress is seen as possibly influencing the course of, but not causing, all of the following, **EXCEPT**
    (a) cancer.
    (b) ulcers.
    (c) heart attacks.
    (d) asthma.

12. According to the text, asthma attacks can be triggered by all of the following, **EXCEPT**
    (a) pepsinogen.
    (b) laughing.
    (c) an allergic reaction.
    (d) stress.

13. According to the text, so–called diseases of adaptation are caused by
    (a) daily hassles and life changes.
    (b) fear that one will contract the disease.
    (c) genetic factors.
    (d) a combination of stress and some predisposing factor.

14. Bacteria and viruses are examples of
    (a) antigens.
    (b) antibodies.
    (c) leukocytes.
    (d) pathogens.

15. The immune system has all of the following functions, **EXCEPT**
    (a) producing white blood cells.
    (b) producing red blood cells.
    (c) causing inflammation.
    (d) recognizing pathogens.

16. Which of the following suppresses the functioning of the immune system?
    (a) leukocytes
    (b) vaccination
    (c) steroids
    (d) relaxation

17. If a physician wants his or her patients to comply with medical advice, she or he ought to
    (a) behave in an authoritarian manner.
    (b) explain the rationales for the advice.
    (c) discourage questions.
    (d) belong to a prestigious medical group.

18. According to the text, one reason that many psychologists object to the medical model of psychological disorders is that
    (a) research has shown that abnormal behavior is caused by pathogens.
    (b) physicians are frequently clumsy in physician–patient relationships.
    (c) it is most helpful to remove the sources of stress confronting the patient.
    (d) the medical model sometimes backfires by relieving patients of their normal responsibilities.

19. When Goleman and Schwartz exposed meditators and nonmeditators to a stress–producing film, they found that meditators
    (a) showed no response to the film at all.
    (b) showed consistently lower levels of arousal than nonmeditators.
    (c) showed consistently higher levels of arousal than nonmeditators.
    (d) recovered normal levels of arousal more rapidly than nonmeditators.

20. The concept of locus of control was initially defined by
    (a) Albert Bandura.
    (b) Julian Rotter.
    (c) Donald Meichenbaum.
    (d) Edmund Jacobson.

**Answer Key to *Posttest***

1. D
2. B
3. D
4. C
5. A
6. A
7. A
8. C
9. B
10. D
11. A
12. A
13. D
14. D
15. B
16. C
17. B
18. D
19. D
20. B

| | |
|---|---|
| Health psychology | Approach-approach conflict |
| Pathogen | Vacillate |
| Stress | Avoidance-avoidance conflict |
| Eustress | Approach-avoidance conflict |
| Daily hassles | Multiple approach-avoidance conflict |
| Uplifts | Catastrophize |
| Conflict | Type A behavior |

| | |
|---|---|
| A type of conflict in which the goals that produce opposing motives are positive and within reach. | The field of psychology that studies the relationships between psychological factors (e.g., attitudes, beliefs, situational influences, and behavior patterns) and the prevention and treatment of physical illness. |
| Move back and forth. | A microscopic organism (e.g., bacterium or virus) that can cause disease. |
| A type of conflict in which the goals are negative, but avoidance of one requires approaching the other. | The demand that is made on an organism to adapt. |
| A type of conflict in which the same goal produces approach and avoidance motives. | Stress that is healthful. |
| A type of conflict in which each of a number of goals produces approach and avoidance motives. | Notable daily conditions and experiences that are threatening or harmful to a person's well-being. |
| To interpret negative events as being disastrous; to "blow out of proportion." | Notable pleasant daily conditions and experiences. |
| Behavior characterized by a sense of time urgency, competitiveness, and hostility. | Being torn in different directions by opposing motives. Feelings produced by being in conflict. |

| Self-efficacy expectations | Fight-or-flight reaction |
|---|---|
| Psychological hardiness | Resistance stage |
| Locus of control | Exhaustion stage |
| Internals | Immune system |
| Externals | Leukocytes |
| General adaptation syndrome | Antigen |
| Alarm reaction | Antibodies |

| | |
|---|---|
| An innate adaptive response to the perception of danger. | Our beliefs that we can bring about desired changes through our own efforts. |
| The second stage of the GAS, characterized by prolonged sympathetic activity in an effort to restore lost energy and repair damage. Also called the adaptation stage. | A cluster of traits that buffer stress and are characterized by commitment, challenge, and control. |
| The third stage of the GAS, characterized by weakened resistance and possible deterioration. | The place to which an individual attributes control over the receiving of reinforcers—either inside or outside the self. |
| The system of the body that recognizes and destroys foreign agents (antigens) that invade the body. | People who perceive the ability to attain reinforcements as being largely within themselves. |
| White blood cells. | People who perceive the ability to attain reinforcements as being largely outside themselves. |
| A substance that stimulates the body to mount an immune-system response to it. | Selye's term for a hypothesized three-stage response to stress. GAS. |
| Substances formed by white blood cells that recognize and destroy antigens. | The first stage of the GAS, which is triggered by the impact of a stressor and characterized by sympathetic activity. |

# Chapter 16  Social Psychology

Directions: This *PRETEST* will give you feedback about how well you understand Chapter 16. In order to enhance your mastery of Chapter 16, complete all the sections of this chapter of the Study Guide. Then you can take the *POSTTEST* and compare your results.

1. The text defines attitudes in terms of the following components, with the exception of _____ components.
   (a) behavioral
   (b) biological
   (c) cognitive
   (d) emotional

2. People are most likely to act in accordance with their attitudes when
   (a) their attitudes are general.
   (b) their attitudes are weak.
   (c) they have a vested interest in the outcome.
   (d) their attitudes are inaccessible.

3. One religious teacher believes that children are more likely to adhere to their own religion's beliefs when they are also taught opposing beliefs. Another religious teacher believes that it is dangerous to teach children's opposing beliefs. Research concerning persuasion shows that two–sided arguments have the advantage of
   (a) offering peripheral cues for persuasion.
   (b) conditioning the audience.
   (c) appealing to the intellect only, not the emotions.
   (d) showing the audience how to refute the opposition's arguments.

4. A characteristic of people who are readily persuaded by others is
   (a) low social anxiety.
   (b) low self–esteem.
   (c) individuation.
   (d) diffusion of responsibility.

5. If a behavior is low in consensus then
   (a) the behavior is disagreed with when seen.
   (b) most people behave that way.
   (c) few people behave that way.
   (d) only certain environments allow the behavior to appear.

6. According to the psychoanalytic interpretation of the Holocaust, the Germans
   (a) displaced unconscious hostility toward their fathers onto Jews.
   (b) were a twentieth–century embodiment of historic European antisemitism.
   (c) were imitating the behavior of antisemitic models.
   (d) found it easier to attend to, and remember, instances of minority–group behavior that were consistent with their prejudices.

7. According to the feature on interracial relationships, the _____ woman is presented by "Madison Avenue" (the U.S. advertising establishment) as the epitome of sexual beauty.
   (a) "well–scrubbed" brunette
   (b) slim, blond, white
   (c) exotic, foreign–looking
   (d) Asian

8. In studies of stereotypes, whites viewed lower–class African Americans as
   (a) ambitious.
   (b) responsible.
   (c) sly.
   (d) self–pitying.

9. Luchins had subjects read different stories about "Jim" in order to study
   (a) cognitive dissonance.
   (b) diffusion of responsibility.
   (c) the primacy effect.
   (d) factors that contribute to attraction.

10. We tend to make an external attribution for behavior when that behavior is low in
    (a) distinctiveness.
    (b) dissonance.
    (c) consensus.
    (d) consistency.

11. Which of the following is defined in the text as an attitude?
    (a) discrimination
    (b) attraction
    (c) imbalance
    (d) evaluation apprehension

12. Research shows that women undergraduates generally see themselves as
    (a) heavier than the figure that is most attractive to males.
    (b) slimmer than the figure that is most attractive to males.
    (c) having the figure that is most attractive to males.
    (d) having the figure that is considered ideal by other women.

13. Physically attractive people are perceived as _____ than other people.
    (a) poorer parents
    (b) having less stable marriages
    (c) more mentally healthy
    (d) more likely to commit crimes

14. In an early phase of his research on obedience to authority, Milgram recruited 40 men. Of these men, _____ percent complied with the demands of an authority figure to deliver the highest levels of electric shock to an innocent "learner."
    (a) 25
    (b) 45
    (c) 65
    (d) 85

15. When Milgram moved the site of his research on obedience from Yale University to a storefront in a nearby city,
    (a) no one complied with the demands of the authority figure.
    (b) fewer subjects complied with the demands of the authority figure.
    (c) more subjects complied with the demands of the authority figure.
    (d) the results were about the same.

16. The tendency to conform to incorrect group judgments increases as the group expands to _____ members.
    (a) 8          (b) 18
    (c) 80         (d) 800

17. According to Robert Zajonc's view of social facilitation, the presence of others influences us by
    (a) causing evaluation apprehension.
    (b) increasing our levels of arousal.
    (c) making us anonymous.
    (d) creating diffusion of responsibility.

18. According to the text, when a jury is deadlocked the members may eventually make a decision according to the
    (a) majority–wins scheme.
    (b) truth–wins scheme.
    (c) two–thirds majority scheme.
    (d) first–shift rule.

19. The "risky shift" refers to the finding that
    (a) attitudes become polarized during a group process.
    (b) people undergo deindividuation when they are members of a mob.
    (c) people behave recklessly when ordered about by an authority figure.
    (d) group decisions are often riskier than individual decisions.

20. Mob behavior appears to be characterized by all of the following, EXCEPT
    (a) reduced self–awareness.
    (b) focusing of individual attention on the group process.
    (c) arousal due to noise and crowding.
    (d) heightened concern for social evaluation.

Social psychology concerns the nature and causes of our behavior and mental processes in social situations.

The first section concerns attitudes. The "A–B problem" refers to the fact that behavior cannot be directly predicted from knowledge of attitudes. It is shown that attitudes are acquired through learning and cognitive appraisal. Attitudes may be changed by persuasive messages that rely on central cues, such as information; and on peripheral cues, such as the qualities of the communicator. Balance theory and cognitive–dissonance theory both suggest that we are motivated to keep our attitudes and behaviors in harmony. Prejudice is an attitude that leads people to evaluate groups negatively and to discriminate against them.

Social perception concerns the factors that influence our perceptions of other people. It is shown how primacy and recency effects contribute to our social perceptions. Next it is shown how we make dispositional and situational attributions for behavior, and that we tend to underestimate the role of situational factors in accounting for the behavior of others.

We use body language to communicate and to persuade.

We see that physical attractiveness and attitudinal similarity are the two most important factors in interpersonal attraction. We tend to expect positive things from attractive people— that "Good things come in pretty packages." We tend to ask out and get married to people who are similar to us in attractiveness.

Obedience to authority and conformity are two behavior patterns of interest to psychologists who study social influence. Classic studies by Milgram and Asch suggest that we are more likely to comply with the demands and the norms set by others than we might expect.

Some of the effects of group behavior include social facilitation (especially when we are apprehensive about how others may evaluate us) and social loafing (which sometimes occurs when we are anonymous). Group decision–making tends to be characterized by polarization and the risky shift. Mobs appear to function by creating deindividuation in individual members, and we are less likely to help others when we are members of a group rather than alone. A central factor in group behavior appears to be diffusion of responsibility.

## LEARNING OBJECTIVES

1. Define *social psychology*.

| **Attitudes** |
|---|
| 2. Define *attitude* and explain what is meant by the A–B problem. |
| 3. Discuss the origins of attitudes. |

4. Discuss ways in which attitudes may be changed by means of persuasion.

5. Define *prejudice* and discuss the origins of prejudice.

## Social Perception

6. Explain the *primacy* and *recency effects* on social perception.

7. Differentiate between *dispositional* and *situational attributions*, and explain the biases that are found in the attribution process.

8. Explain the role of body language in social perception.

## Interpersonal Attraction: Liking and Loving

9. Discuss factors that contribute to interpersonal attraction.

## Social Influence

10. Describe the Milgram studies on obedience to authority, and discuss factors that contribute to obedience.

11. Describe the Asch studies on *conformity*, and discuss factors that contribute to conformity.

## Group Behavior

12. Discuss factors that contribute to *social facilitation* and *social loafing*.

13. Discuss social–decision schemes in group decision making.

14. Discuss these factors as they contribute to the group decision–making process: *polarization* and the *risky shift*.

15. Discuss the factors that contribute to *groupthink*.

16. Discuss the factors that contribute to mob behavior.

17. Discuss the factors that contribute to helping behavior.

18. Discuss the factors that contribute to the bystander effect.

**Additional Notes**

## Attitudes

1. The A–B Problem: Do We Do as We Think?

2. Origins of Attitudes

3. Changing Attitudes through Persuasion

4. Prejudice

## Social Perception

1. Primacy and Recency Effects:
   The Importance of First Impressions

2. Attribution Theory: You're Free
   but I'm Caught in the Middle?

3. Body Language

## Interpersonal Attraction: Liking and Loving

1. Physical Attractiveness:
   How Important Is Looking Good?

2. Similarity: Do "Opposites Attract": or Do "Birds of
   a Feather Flock Together"?

3. Reciprocity: If You Like Me, You Must Have
   Excellent Judgment

4. Love: Doing What Comes...Culturally?

## Social Influence

1. Obedience to Authority: Does Might Make Right?

2. Conformity: Do Many Make Right?

## Group Behavior

1. Social Facilitation: Monkey See, Monkey Do Faster?

2. Group Decision Making

3. Polarization and the Risky Shift

4. Groupthink

5. Mob Behavior and Deindividuation

6. Altruism and the Bystander Effect: Some Watch While Others Die

## Psychology and Modern Life

1. Gender Polarization: Gender Stereotypes and Their Costs

2. Machismo/Marianismo Stereotypes and Hispanic Culture

# KEY TERMS AND CONCEPTS

1. Social psychology _____

## Attitudes

2. Attitude _____

3. A–B problem _____

4. Stereotype _____

5. Elaboration likelihood model _____

6. Fear appeal _____

7. Selective avoidance _____

8. Selective exposure _____

9. Foot-in-the-door technique _____

10. Prejudice _____

11. Discrimination _____

## Social Perception

12. Social perception _____

13. Primacy effect _____

14. Recency effect _____

15. Attribution _____

16. Attribution process _____

17. Dispositional attribution _____

18. Situational attribution _____

19. Fundamental attribution error _____

20. Actor–observer effect _____

21. Self–serving bias _____

22. Consensus _____

## Interpersonal Attraction: Liking and Loving

23. Attraction _____

24. Matching hypothesis _____

25. Reciprocity _____

26. Romantic love _____

27. Triangular model of love _____

28. Consummate love _____

## Social Influence

29. Social influence _____

30. Conformity _____

31. Social norms _____

## Group Behavior

32. Social facilitation _____

33. Evaluation apprehension _____

34. Diffusion of responsibility _____

35. Social–decision scheme _____

36. Polarization _____

37. Risky shift _____

38. Groupthink _____

39. Deindividuation _____

40. Altruism _____

## Additional Notes

_____

_____

_____

_____

_____

_____

_____

_____

_____

_____

_____

_____

_____

_____

_____

_____

_____

# CHAPTER REVIEW

**SECTION 1: Introduction**

**OBJ.1 :** Social psychology is the study of the nature and causes of our behavior and (1) m_____ processes in (2) _____al situations.

**SECTION 2: Attitudes**

**OBJ. 2:** Attitudes can be defined as enduring mental (3) _____ations of people, places, or things that evoke feelings and influence (4) _____vior. When we are free to do as we wish, our behavior (5: *Circle one:* is or is not) most often consistent with our attitudes. According to the (6) A_____ problem, the link between attitudes and behavior tends to be weak. Factors that influence the likelihood that we can predict behavior from attitudes include the attitudes' specificity and strength, whether when people have a (7) v_____ed interest in the outcome of behavior based on their attitudes, and the (8) _____ility of the attitudes.

**OBJ. 3:** Attitudes may be acquired through conditioning, observational learning, and (9) cog_____ appraisal. Attitudes toward national groups can be influenced by (10) _____ing them with positive or negative words. Parents often (11) re_____ children for doing or saying things that are consistent with their own attitudes. We also acquire attitudes by observing friends and the mass media. Early attitudes tend to serve as cognitive (12) _____ors; we judge later points of view in terms of how much they (13) d_____ from the first set.

**OBJ. 4:** Petty and Cacioppo have devised the (14) _____tion _____hood model for understanding the processes by which people examine the information in persuasive messages. According to this view, there are central and (15) _____ral routes to persuading others to change attitudes. That is, there are two ways of responding to, or (16) _____ting, persuasive messages. The (17) _____ral route views elaboration and possible attitudinal change as resulting from conscientious consideration of arguments and evidence. The (18) _____ral route involves elaboration of the objects of attitudes by associating them with positive or negative cues.

Repeated messages generally "sell" (19: *Circle one:* better or worse) than messages delivered once. (20) Two–_____d arguments, in which the communicator recounts the arguments of the opposition in order to (21) re_____ them, can be especially effective when the audience is at first uncertain about its position. People tend to show greater response to (22) e_____al appeals than to purely factual presentations, especially when emotional appeals offer concrete advice for avoiding negative consequences. Audiences also tend to believe arguments that appear to (23: *Circle one:* be in agreement with, or run counter to) the personal interests of the communicator.

Persuasive communicators tend to show (24) ex_____, trustworthiness, attractiveness, or (25) _____ity to the audience. People show selective avoidance of and selective (26) ex_____ to communicators. They avoid communicators whose messages (27: *Circle one:* agree or disagree) with their own attitudes. They seek communicators whose outlooks (28: *Circle one:* agree or disagree) with their own. People are more readily persuaded when they are in a (29: *Circle one:* good or bad) mood. People who are easily persuaded frequently show (30: *Circle one:* high or low) self–esteem and (31: *Circle one:* high or low) social anxiety. They also tend (32: *Circle one:* to be, or not to be) highly concerned with what the persuader might think of them if they fail to comply.

According to the (33) _____–in–the–door effect, people are more likely to accede to large requests after they have acceded to smaller requests. Perhaps initial compliance causes them to view themselves as people who help under these sorts of circumstances.

**OBJ. 5:** Prejudice is an (34) at_____ toward a group. Prejudice can involve negative (35) ev_____tion; negative affect; avoidance behavior; and denial of access to privileges, which is termed (36) _____nation. A (37) _____type is a fixed, conventional idea about a group that can lead us to make certain assumptions about group members we have not met.

Sources of prejudice include attitudinal (38: *Circle one:* similarity or dissimilarity). We tend to assume that members of outgroups hold attitudes that are (39: *Circle one:* similar or dissimilar) to our own. Other sources may include social and (40) ec_____ conflict; an authoritarian society in which minority group members serve as (41) _____goats; social learning from parents; and the tendency to divide the social world into two categories: "us" and "them." We also tend to assume that members of out–groups are (42: *Circle one:* more or less) similar to one another in their attitudes than are the members of our own in–groups.

## SECTION 3: Social Perception

**OBJ. 6:** The psychology of social (43) _____tion concerns our perception of others. We often perceive others in terms of first impressions; this is an example of the (44) _____cy effect. In a classic experiment on the primacy effect, (45) L_____ had subjects read different stories about "Jim." However, fading memories sometimes allow more recent information to take precedence; this is the so–called (46) _____cy effect.

**OBJ. 7:** Our inference of the motives and traits of others through the observation of their behavior is called the (47) _____tion process. When we make dispositional attributions, we attribute people's behavior to (48: *Circle one:* internal or external) factors, such as their personality traits and decisions. When we make (49) _____nal attributions, we attribute people's behavior to their circumstances or external forces.

Certain biases operate in the attribution (50) _____ss. The so–called (51) _____tal attribution error is the tendency to attribute too much of other people's behavior to dispositional factors. Another is the (52) actor–_____er effect. According to the actor–observer effect, we tend to attribute the behavior of others to internal, (53) _____nal factors, whereas we tend to attribute our own behavior to external, (54) _____nal factors. According to the (55) self–_____ing bias, we are more likely to ascribe our successes to internal, dispositional factors but our failures to external, (56) _____nal influences.

Our attribution of behavior to internal or external causes is also influenced by the behavior's (57) _____sus, consistency, and (58) dis_____ness. We are likely to attribute behavior to internal factors when it is (59: *Circle one:* high or low) in consensus, that is, when few people act that way; when it is (60: *Circle one:* high or low) in consistency, that is, when the person behaves that way consistently; and when it is (61: *Circle one:* high or low) in distinctiveness, that is, when a person acts similarly in different situations.

**OBJ. 8:** At an early age we learn to "read" body language. People who feel (62: *Circle one:* positively or negatively) toward one another tend to position themselves close together and to touch. Women are (63: *Circle one:* more or less) likely than men to touch other people when they are interacting with them. Waitresses in one study received

(64: *Circle one:* higher or lower) tips when they touched patrons on the hand or the shoulder while making change. Gazing into another's eyes can be a sign of love, but a so–called (65) h_____ stare is an aversive challenge.

## SECTION 4: Interpersonal Attraction

**OBJ. 9:** In social psychology, (66) _____tion has been defined as an attitude of liking (positive attraction) or disliking (67) (_____tive attraction). In our culture, (68: *Circle one:* obesity or slenderness) is found attractive in both men and women, and tallness is valued in (69: *Circle one:* men or women). Women generally see themselves as (70: *Circle one:* slimmer or heavier) than the figure that is attractive to most males. Men actually prefer women to be somewhat (71: *Circle one:* slimmer or heavier) than women expect. Women prefer men to be somewhat (72: *Circle one:* slimmer or heavier) than men expect. We tend to find the same people (73: *Circle one:* more or less) attractive when they are smiling. Socially dominant college men are rated as being (74: *Circle one:* attractive or unattractive) by college women. Assertive college women (75: *Circle one:* are or are not) rated as being attractive by most college men. Nevid found that college undergraduates are relatively (76: *Circle one:* more or less) concerned about their partner's physical attractiveness when they are involved in short–term sexual relationships. However, when they are involved in long–term, meaningful relationships, traits such as honesty and warmth play (77: *Circle one:* more or less) prominent roles. (78: *Circle one:* Men or Women) tend to place greater emphasis on characteristics such as professional status, consideration, dependability, kindness, and fondness for children.

We are more attracted to good–looking people. We tend to assume that attractive people are (79: *Circle one:* more or less) likely to be talented and (80: *Circle one:* more or less) likely to engage in criminal behavior. (81: *Circle one:* Attractive or Unattractive) college students are more likely to rate themselves as prone toward developing problems and psychological disorders. According to the (82) _____ing hypothesis, we tend to seek dates and mates at our own level of attractiveness. The matching tendency seems to be motivated largely by fear of (83) _____tion.

We are (84: *Circle one:* more or less) attracted to people who share our attitudes. Social (85) in_____ is the area of social psychology that studies the ways in which people alter the thoughts, feelings, and behavior of others. Areas within the study of social influence include (86) ob_____ and conformity.

**OBJ. 10:** Most people comply with the demands of authority figures, even when these demands seem immoral, as shown in the studies on obedience run by Stanley (87) M_____ at (88) _____e University. Of 40 men participating in an early phase of his research, (89) _____ percent complied with the authority figure's demands all the way up to the highest level of electric shock. It turns out that the only people who received electric shock during Milgram's studies were the (90) "_____ers."

The following factors appear to have contributed to obedience in the Milgram studies: subjects' history of socialization, lack of (91) _____al comparison, perception of experimenters as being legitimate (92) _____ity figures, the (93) foot–in–the–_____ technique, inaccessibility of values, and the presence of (94) _____ers that separated "teachers" from their victims.

**OBJ. 11:** In Asch's studies of conformity to group pressure, (95) _____ percent of the subjects agreed with an incorrect majority judgment at least once. People experience increasing pressure to conform to group norms and opinions as groups grow to (96) _____ people. (97: *Circle one:* Men or Women) are more likely to conform. The presence of at least (98) _____ person(s) who share(s) one's minority view, and familiarity with the tasks at hand, decrease conforming behavior.

## SECTION 6: Group Behavior

**OBJ. 12:** Social (99) _____ tion refers to the effects on performance that result from the presence of others. According to Zajonc, the presence of others influences us by increasing our levels of (100) _____ sal. We may also be concerned that the other people present are evaluating our performance—a phenomenon termed (101) ev_____ _____ sion. However, Latané and other researchers have found that task performance may decline when we are (102) _____ mous members of a group. This phenomenon is referred to as social (103) _____ ing.

**OBJ. 13:** Social psychologists have discovered a number of rules, or (104) so_____ – _____ sion schemes, that seem to govern group decision making. In the (105) _____ - wins scheme, the group arrives at the decision that was initially supported by the majority. In the (106) _____ -wins scheme, the group comes to recognize that one approach is objectively correct as more information is provided and opinions are discussed. The (107) _____ - _____ ds majority scheme is frequently adopted by juries, who tend to convict defendants when two-thirds of the jury initially favors conviction. In the (108) _____ -shift rule, the group tends to adopt the decision that reflects the first shift in opinion expressed by any group member. According to the first–shift rule, a deadlocked jury may eventually follow the lead of the (109) _____ st juror to change his position.

**OBJ. 14:** A number of phenomena tend to occur during group decision-making processes. One is termed (110) _____ ation, or the taking of extreme positions by group members. Another is the tendency for groups to take (111: *Circle one:* more or less) risky actions than the average group member would take if he or she were acting as an individual. This phenomenon is known as the (112) _____ _____ ft. Groups may take riskier actions than individual group members would because of diffusion of (113) _____ ility.

**OBJ. 15:** Groupthink is usually (114: *Circle one:* realistic or unrealistic) and can lead to flawed decisions. Groupthink is usually instigated by a dynamic group leader. It tends to be fueled by the perception of (115) _____ nal threats to the group or to those the group wishes to protect. The perception of external threat heightens group (116) co_____ ness and serves as a source of stress. When under stress, group members (117: *Circle one:* tend or tend not) to weigh carefully all their options.

The following factors contribute to groupthink: feelings of (118: *Circle one:* vulnerability or invulnerability), group belief in its rightness, discrediting of (119) _____ tion opposed to the group's decision, pressures on group members to conform, and stereotyping of members of the (120) out_____ .

**OBJ. 16:** Gustave Le Bon characterized a mob as a (121) "b_____ with many heads." As members of a mob, we may experience (122) _____ duation, which is a state of reduced self–awareness and lowered concern for social (123) ev_____ tion. Factors that lead to deindividuation include anonymity, (124) _____ sion of responsibility, a high level of (125) ar_____ due to noise and crowding, and focusing of individual attention on the group process.

**OBJ. 17:** Helping behavior is otherwise termed (126) _____ ism. We are more likely to help others when we are in a (127: *Circle one:* good or bad) mood.

**OBJ. 18:** According to the (128) _____ der effect, people are less likely to aid others in distress when they are members of crowds. A powerful case in point is the tragedy of Kitty (129) Ge_____, who was stabbed to death while some 40 neighbors did nothing to help. One reason for failure to help is that in a crowd there is diffusion of (130) re_____ity. We are more likely to help people in need when we think we are the only one available, when we have a(n) (131: *Circle one:* clear or unclear) view of the situation, and when we (132: *Circle one:* are or are not) afraid that we shall be committing a social blunder.

## Answer Key to *Chapter Review*

| | |
|---|---|
| 1. mental | 41. scapegoats |
| 2. social | 42. more |
| 3. representations | 43. perception |
| 4. behavior | 44. primacy |
| 5. is | 45. Luchins |
| 6. A–B | 46. recency |
| 7. vested | 47. attribution |
| 8. accessibility | 48. internal |
| 9. cognitive | 49. situational |
| 10. associating | 50. process |
| 11. reinforce (or reward) | 51. fundamental |
| 12. anchors | 52. actor-observer |
| 13. deviate | 53. dispositional |
| 14. elaboration likelihood | 54. situational |
| 15. peripheral | 55. self-serving |
| 16. elaborating | 56. situational |
| 17. central | 57. consensus |
| 18. peripheral | 58. distinctiveness |
| 19. better | 59. low |
| 20. two-sided | 60. high |
| 21. refute | 61. low |
| 22. emotional | 62. positively |
| 23. run counter to | 63. more |
| 24. expertise | 64. higher |
| 25. similarity | 65. hard |
| 26. exposure | 66. attraction |
| 27. disagree | 67. negative |
| 28. agree | 68. slenderness |
| 29. good | 69. men |
| 30. low | 70. heavier |
| 31. high | 71. heavier |
| 32. to be | 72. slimmer |
| 33. foot | 73. more |
| 34. attitude | 74. attractive |
| 35. evaluation | 75. are not |
| 36. discrimination | 76. more |
| 37. stereotype | 77. more |
| 38. dissimilarity | 78. women |
| 39. dissimilar | 79. more |
| 40. economic | 80. less |

81. Unattractive
82. matching
83. rejection
84. more
85. influence
86. obedience
87. Milgram
88. Yale
89. 65
90. teachers
91. social
92. authority
93. foot-in-the-door
94. buffers
95. 75
96 right
97. women
98. one
99. facilitation
100. arousal
101. evaluation apprehension
102. anonymous
103. loafing
104. social-decision
105. majority-wins
106. truth-wins
107. two–thirds
108. first–shift
109. first
110. polarization
111. more
112. risky shift
113. responsibility
114. unrealistic
115. external
116. cohesiveness
117. tend not
118. invulnerability
119. information
120. outgroup
121. beast
122. deindividuation
123. evaluation
124. diffusion
125. arousal
126. altruism
127. good
128. bystander
129. Genovese
130. responsibility
131. clear
132. are not

# MATCHING EXERCISE CONCEPTS AND EXAMPLES

In the first column are a number of concepts in social psychology. In the second column are instances of behavior that serve as examples of these concepts. Match the example with the appropriate concept by writing the letter of the example in the blank space to the left of the concept. Answers are given below.

CONCEPT

___ 1. Prejudice
___ 2. Bystander effect
___ 3. Cognitive dissonance
___ 4. Discrimination
___ 5. Conformity
___ 6. Dispositional attribution
___ 7. Emotional appeal
___ 8. Foot–in–the–door technique
___ 9. Matching hypothesis
___10. Nonbalance
___11. Primacy effect
___12. Propinquity
___13. Reciprocity
___14. Evaluation apprehension
___15. Effort justification
___16. Risky shift
___17. Situational attribution
___18. Deindividuation
___19. Diffusion of responsibility
___20. Fundamental attribution error
___21. The first–shift rule
___22. Buffer
___23. Inaccessibility of attitudes
___24. A–B problem
___25. Groupthink

EXAMPLE

A. A person assumes that someone who bumped into him did so on purpose.
B. A man does not ask a beautiful woman out for fear of rejection.
C. A committee takes a greater gamble than any member would take acting alone.
D. A person asks a small favor to prepare someone to grant a larger favor later.
E. A new worker is late and the boss conceptualizes him as "a late person."
F. John blames his mood on the weather.
G. A person does not come to the aid of a crime because many people surround the victim.
H. Joan likes Jim much more after he tells her that he likes her very, very much.
I. Patty Hearst's attitudes become radicalized after she is coerced into attitude–discrepant behavior.
J. A mob member adopts the norms of the crowd.
K. A person is paid too little for his work and begins to think that his work has high intrinsic value because of the low pay.
L. A student wears blue jeans because "everyone" is wearing them.
M. An athlete runs faster because he is concerned that fellow racers are aware of his performance.
N. A man assumes that a woman will not be assertive in the business world.
O. The man in item N, above, chooses not to hire a woman.
P. A dentist shows photos of diseased gums to convince patients to improve their oral hygiene.
Q. A person falls in love with someone who works in the same office.
R. Jim disagrees with Joan, but Joan doesn't care because she is indifferent toward Jim.
S. A group with a dynamic leader ignores the evidence and makes foolish decisions.
T. A person becomes so aroused as a member of a mob that he completely forgets his personal moral values.
U. A psychologist cannot predict a voter's behavior because the voter's political beliefs are very generalized.
V. A "teacher" in the Milgram study shocks the "learner" because the learner is out of sight, behind a wall.
W. A deadlocked jury votes to convict a defendant after one person who had previously thought the defendant not guilty changes his mind.

**Answer Key to *Matching Exercise***

| | | |
|---|---|---|
| 1. N | 11. E | 21. W |
| 2. G | 12. Q | 22. V |
| 3. I, K | 13. H | 23. T |
| 4. O | 14. M | 24. U |
| 5. L | 15. K | 25. S |
| 6. A | 16. C | |
| 7. P | 17. F | |
| 8. D | 18. J | |
| 9. B | 19. G | |
| 10. R | 20. A | |

| Idioms | Explanation |
|---|---|
| 611 put off | postpone |
| 612 leans toward | indicates a preference for |
| 615 run counter to | be opposite of |
| 616 drop by | go to; come to |
| 636 put an end to | stop |
| 638 to "push around" | to control and demand |

| Cultural References | Explanation |
|---|---|
| 613 blue jeans | most common informal clothing in the U.S. culture |
| 613 preppy sweaters | sweaters wore by people who went to expensive private high schools and colleges |
| 613 frizzies | very tight curls in the hair |
| 614 college appreciation course | college music appreciation course |
| 615 pop tune | popular music (as opposed to classical music) |
| 615 Chrysler or General Motors...Toyotas and Hondas | manufacturers of automobiles |
| 616 Peter Jennings ... Tom Brokaw... Dan Rather | new commentators on the three primary stations |
| 616 Szechuan tidbits, the nouveau Fresno film, the disco party | special Chinese food, new and important movie, the party at a discotheque |
| 616 sign petitions | people who sign this state-ment want the government to act on an issue |
| 617 voting booth | private area where a person votes |
| 619 The King and I | a musical comedy popular in the 1950s |
| 619 defense attorneys | the lawyers defending the accused person in court |
| 619 jury | group citizens selected to make judgments about the innocence of a defendant |
| 619 curfew | the time when a person is to be home |
| 629 1920's "flapper" era | after World War I when women dressed boyish and had more freedom |
| 632 Mel Gibson or Julia Roberts | current movie stars |
| 637 dorm food | food service in dormitory not a restaurant or at home |
| 642 car model | different styles of cars |
| 642 SAT scores | Scholastic Aptitude Test scores |

| Cultural references | |
|---|---|
| 643 lynchings | mobs of people killing other people |
| 644 Big Apply | a nickname for New York City |
| 645 our home town | a town where a person lived when a child or an adult |

| Phrases and Expressions (Different Usage) | |
|---|---|
| 610 hurts sales | the product won't sell well |
| 610 take others to task | criticize others |
| 610 falls short of our ideals | is not what we think it should be |
| 610 Beauty is in the eye of the beholder | a person seems beautiful to another person because the other person believes it |
| 610 social norm | what is normal for the culture |
| 610 doubles as | also has the function of being |
| 610 make conversation | talking to get to know each other |
| 610 been around | had a very active social life; known a lot of men |
| 611 And so begins a relationship | and the relationship begins |
| 611 turning the other off | saying or doing something that will cause the other person not to be interested anymore |
| 611 narrow-minded | believe that their religion is the only true religion |
| 611 If the truth be known | if you want to know the truth |
| 611 tangled web of deception | confusing situation in which each person is deceiving the other |
| 611 ever after? | forever? |
| 612 makes much difference | will cause change in what the government does |
| 612 "get out the vote" | encourage people to vote |
| 612 media blitzes | many advertisements close together on radio, TV, and newspapers |
| 612 It does...little good | supporters who do not vote can not help |
| 612 "worked up" | excited |
| 613 by keeping them under the table | by not discussing them |
| 613 go their separate ways | part; not see each other |
| 613 somehow un-American | they are not respecting the American ideal |
| 613 cognitive anchors | cognitive bases |
| 613 mold the ways | create the ways |
| 614 So too do | also, the...ads do that |
| 614 familiarity breeds content/contempt | we become bored with what we know very well. |

| | | |
|---|---|---|
| 615 | grisly films | terrible, bloody films |
| 615 | vested interests | self-centered beliefs |
| 615 | prick up our ears | listen intently |
| 615 | homely models? | ugly or unattractive model |
| 616 | spongelike | like a sponge, absorbs |
| 616 | tube feeds them | is on the television |
| 616 | by buttering you up | persuade someone by complementing them |
| 616 | a sip of wine | a small drink of wine |
| 616 | tail end of a date | the last few minutes of a date |
| 616 | wine that was sold at its time | wine that was sold at the time when the taste is best |
| 616 | enrich the lives of every door-to-door salesperson | always buy something from sales people who come to the home |
| 616 | get you off the hook | you will not be asked to do anything else |
| 616 | mount a campaign | begin a campaign |
| 616 | Giving an inch...to go for a yard | give a little and other people may expect you to give a lot |
| 616 | wrecking crew | people whose job it is to destroy a building |
| 616 | primed for | prepared for |
| 616 | and stick to your guns | and not change your mind |
| 616 | it works the other way | it is also the reverse |
| 616 | leaves us | causes us to be |
| 616 | to sweep it under the rug | to hide it |
| 617 | falling for | believing |
| 617 | charitable donation | money that is given to a charity |
| 618 | "airheads" | not intelligent |
| 619 | boorish | awkward and clumsy |
| 619 | was a cad forever | would always be socially unskilled |
| 619 | make or break us | establish us as wonderful or as awful |
| 619 | an exception to a rule | not part of our real character |
| 619 | to "make up for it" | to compensate for it; to create a better image |
| 619 | to take precedence | to be more important |
| 620 | snap judgments | opinions made quickly |
| 620 | networks of forces acting on ourselves | pressures that affect us |
| 621 | as being forced into combat | having to argue and disagree |
| 622 | "of their own making" | to be their responsibility |
| 622 | to a fluke | to an accidental incident that appears unrelated to the actual outcome |
| 622 | ironic twist | an outcome that you did not expect |
| 622 | "uptight" | tense and worried |
| 622 | "hang loose" | to be flexible and not worry |

| | | |
|---|---|---|
| 623 | privy to a conversation | overhear a conversation |
| 623 | toying with his hair | playing with his hair |
| 623 | is not having any of what she is selling | does not want what she is selling |
| 623 | hard stares | unrelenting stares |
| 626 | that is, a meeting of the minds | two people have similar opinions and ideas |
| 628 | are beheld | are seen ; are thought of |
| 628 | a hunch | the back bent forward a little |
| 629 | fancy men | like men |
| 629 | a hallmark | a distinguishing characteristic |
| 630 | outside of the mainstream | not among the accepted groups in society |
| 630 | go hand in hand | go together |
| 630 | throw up our hands in despair | not care about improving |
| 630 | So don't abandon the ship | don't stop trying |
| 632 | you're not alone | you're not the only person who feels that way |
| 632 | left to blend in with the wallpaper | be on a less equal basis with |
| 632 | look-alike | imitation |
| 632 | kinks in a relationship | disagreements and unresolved issues |
| 632 | can iron them out | can be worked out |
| 632 | swerve from our expectations | do not do what we expect |
| 635 | ground to a halt | stopped |
| 635 | break-in | use of force to enter a locked building |
| 635 | cover-up | concealment |
| 635 | come to grips with | tried to understand |
| 635 | for the sake of science | because you wanted to help science |
| 636 | running the gamut | being all degrees |
| 636 | having some misgivings | think that it wasn't a good idea |
| 636 | What to do? | "What should I do?" |
| 636 | Not at all | no, that was not true |
| 636 | barged into | went into, quickly and with anger |
| 636 | were in on | knew |
| 636 | hard truths | unfortunate facts |
| 636 | experimenter's ground | the experiment's territory |
| 636 | on their own | alone |
| 636 | dingy storefront | small, unpainted |
| 636 | at the behest of | at the request of |
| 637 | gurgling a bit | making hunger noises |
| 637 | was riveted on the chore | focused on the task |
| 637 | trust your eyes | trust what you were seeing |
| 637 | caved in | stopped participating in the experiment |
| 637 | went along with | do what people expect |

1. Which of the following most nearly expresses the relationship between attitudes and behaviors?
   (a) People always behave in ways that are consistent with their attitudes.
   (b) People always change their attitudes so that they are consistent with their behavior.
   (c) There is no relationship between attitudes and behaviors.
   (d) People are likely to act in accord with strong, specific attitudes.

2. Which of the following is a central cue for persuading people to drink Coke or Pepsi?
   (a) providing information about the taste of the drink
   (b) having a rock star deliver a television commercial
   (c) Sshowing attractive, slender people drinking the soda
   (d) using a person with a fine voice to sell the product

3. People tend to be easy to persuade when they
   (a) have high self-esteem.
   (b) focus on the needs and feelings of the persuader.
   (c) have low social anxiety.
   (d) focus on their own needs and feelings.

4. Which of the following is NOT a characteristic of a successful persuasive speaker?
   (a) aggressiveness
   (b) trustworthiness
   (c) attractiveness
   (d) similarity to audience

5. An attibution for behavior is
   (a) a disagreement.
   (b) a way to reduce prejudice.
   (c) an explanation about why people do things.
   (d) cognitive dissonance.

6. Which of the following sources of prejudice is reflected in the statement, "It is easier to attend to, and remember, instances of behavior that are consistent with our prejudices than it is to reconstruct our mental categories"?
   (a) assumptions of dissimilarity
   (b) social conflict
   (c) authoritarianism
   (d) information processing

7. One form of behavior that results from prejudice is called
   (a) authoritarianism.
   (b) deindividuation.
   (c) attitude–discrepant behavior.
   (d) discrimination.

8. Which of the following statements reflects a clear dispositional attribution?
   (a) "Something got the best of him."
   (b) "He did what he thought was right."
   (c) "He did it that way because of the weather."
   (d) "He could not refuse the money."

9. Attributing too much of other people's behavior to dispositional factors is called
   (a) the fundamental attribution error.
   (b) the actor–observer effect.
   (c) internalization.
   (d) evaluation apprehension.

10. The central factor in attraction is
    (a) personal honesty.
    (b) reciprocity.
    (c) physical appearance.
    (d) propinquity.

11. Which of the following is true about standards for attractiveness in our culture?
    (a) Tallness is an asset for women.
    (b) Women prefer their dates to be about the same height as they are.
    (c) Women prefer their men somewhat heavier than men expect.
    (d) Men prefer their women somewhat heavier than women expect.

12. In their dating practices, people tend to ask out persons who are similar in attractiveness largely because of
(a) fairness.
(b) fear of rejection.
(c) balance theory.
(d) evaluation apprehension.

13. Important experiments on obedience to authority were carried out by
(a) Stanley Milgram.
(b) Solomon Asch.
(c) Abraham Luchins.
(d) John Dollard.

14. In the experiments on obedience to authority run at Yale University, who received electric shock?
(a) learners
(b) teachers
(c) experimenters
(d) confederates of the experimenters

15. Conformity is defined as
(a) obedience to authority.
(b) deindividuation.
(c) behavior in accordance with social norms.
(d) diffusion of responsibility.

16. When we are members of a group, we are most likely to engage in social loafing when
(a) we experience evaluation apprehension.
(b) our level of arousal increases.
(c) we are anonymous.
(d) the leader is an authority figure.

17. When juries are deadlocked, they are most likely to arrive at a verdict by means of the
(a) two–thirds rule.
(b) majority–wins scheme.
(c) first–shift rule.
(d) truth–wins scheme.

18. Groups are thought to make risky decisions because
(a) needed information is rarely shared in the group process.
(b) group members experience evaluation apprehension in regard to other group members.
(c) strong group leaders tend to have their way.
(d) responsibility for the decisions is diffused.

19. All of the following appear to lead to deindividuation, **EXCEPT**
(a) a low level of arousal.
(b) anonymity.
(c) diffusion of responsibility.
(d) focusing of individual attention on the group process.

20. The case of Kitty Genovese illustrates
(a) cognitive–dissonance theory.
(b) group decision–making.
(c) the bystander effect.
(d) the principle of social loafing.

**Answer Key to *Posttest***

1. D
2. A
3. B
4. A
5. C
6. D
7. D
8. B
9. A
10. C
11. D
12. B
13. A
14. B
15. C
16. C
17. C
18. D
19. A
20. C

| | |
|---|---|
| Social psychology | Selective exposure |
| Attitude | Foot-in-the-door technique |
| A–B problem | Prejudice |
| Stereotype | Discrimination |
| Elaboration likelihood model | Social perception |
| Fear appeal | Primacy effect |
| Selective avoidance | Recency effect |

Chapter 16  Social Psychology    433

| | |
|---|---|
| Deliberately seeking and attending to information that is consistent with one's attitude. | The field of psychology that studies the nature and causes of individual thoughts, feelings, and overt behavior in social situations. |
| A method for inducing compliance in which a small request is followed by a larger request. | An enduring mental representation of a person, place, or thing that evokes an emotional response and affected behavior. |
| The belief that a person or group, on the basis of assumed racial, ethnic, sexual, or other features, will possess negative characteristics or perform inadequately. | The issue of how well we can predict behavior on the basis of attitudes. |
| The denial of privileges to a person or group because of prejudice. | A fixed, conventional idea about a group. |
| A subfield of social psychology that studies the ways in which we form and modify impressions of others. | The view that persuasive messages are evaluated (elaborated) on the basis of central and peripheral cues. |
| The tendency to evaluate others in terms of first impressions. | A type of persuasive communication that influences behavior on the basis of arousing fear instead of rational analysis of the issues. |
| The tendency to evaluate others in terms of the most recent impression. | Diverting one's attention from information that is inconsistent with one's attitudes. |

| | |
|---|---|
| Attribution | Consensus |
| Attribution process | Attraction |
| Dispositional attribution | Matching hypothesis |
| Situational attribution | Reciprocity |
| Fundamental attribution error | Romantic love |
| Actor-observer effect | Triangular model of love |
| Self-serving bias | Consummate love |

| | |
|---|---|
| General agreement. | A belief concerning why people behave in a certain way. |
| In social psychology, an attitude of liking or disliking. | The process by which people draw inferences about the motives and traits of others. |
| The view that people tend to choose persons similar to themselves in attractiveness and attitudes in the formation of interpersonal relationships. | An assumption that a person's behavior is determined by internal causes such as personal attitudes or goals. |
| In interpersonal attraction, the tendency to return feelings and attitudes that are expressed about us. | An assumption that a person's behavior is determined by external circumstances such as the social pressure found in a situation. |
| An intense, positive emotion that involves sexual attraction, feelings of caring, and the belief that one is in love. | The tendency to assume that others act predominantly on the basis of their dispositions, even when there is evidence suggesting the importance of their situations. |
| Sternberg's view that love involves combinations of three components; intimacy, passion, and decision/commitment. | The tendency to attribute our own behavior to situational factors but to attribute the behavior of others to dispositional factors. |
| The ideal form of love within Sternberg's model, which combines passion, intimacy, and commitment. | The tendency to view one's successes as stemming from internal factors and one's failure as stemming from external factors. |

# Chapter 17  Applied Psychology

Directions: This *PRETEST* will give you feedback about how well you understand Chapter 17. In order to enhance your mastery of Chapter 17, complete all the sections of this chapter of the Study Guide. Then you can take the *POSTTEST* and compare your results.

1. The single largest group of applied psychologists consists of _____ psychologists.
   (a) industrial/organizational
   (b) environmental
   (c) clinical
   (d) community

2. Community psychologists differ from clinical psychologists in that community psychologists
   (a) are concerned about the causes of abnormal behavior.
   (b) focus on the prevention of abnormal behavior.
   (c) receive training in the treatment of abnormal behavior.
   (d) consider what resources are available to treat abnormal behavior.

3. Which of the following is likely to make it more difficult for an athlete to achieve a peak performance?
   (a) training to achieve excellent physical condition
   (b) training to improve athletic skills
   (c) relaxing muscle groups that are not directly involved in the performance
   (d) trying hard to achieve a peak performance on a particular occasion

4. The main difference between high density and crowding is the
   (a) number of people present.
   (b) gender of the people who are present.
   (c) level of arousal of the individual.
   (d) individual's interpretation of the situation.

5. According to psychologists in human factors, good codes have each of the following characteristics, **EXCEPT**
   (a) variability.
   (b) meaningfulness.
   (c) multidimensionality.
   (d) detectability.

6. Theory Y is based on the assumption that
   (a) organizations should adapt features of the Japanese workplace to the realities of the U.S. workplace.
   (b) worker apathy and misbehavior stem from shortcomings of the organization.
   (c) workers develop from individuals capable of concrete thought to individuals capable of abstract thought.
   (d) pay and praise are less important than financial rewards.

7. According to the text, the greatest cause of conflict at work is
   (a) lack of input into organizational policies.
   (b) humdrum, assembly–line activities.
   (c) poor use of criticism.
   (d) bias in the appraisal process.

8. According to the text, the first step in marketing research is
   (a) targeting a consumer population.
   (b) packaging a product.
   (c) task analysis of consumer behavior.
   (d) determining the factors that contribute to an effective advertising campaign.

9. The lowest decibel level that can rupture one's eardrums is
(a) 150.
(b) 250.
(c) 350.
(d) 450.

10. Auto fumes may impair children's intellectual functioning because of the presence of
(a) lead.
(b) sulfur dioxide.
(c) carbon dioxide.
(d) mercury.

11. Extremes of heat can lead to all of the following conditions, **EXCEPT**
(a) heat exhaustion.
(b) a heart attack.
(c) constriction of blood vessels in the skin.
(d) dehydration.

12. Studies in the effects of temperature suggest that mild changes
(a) have no effect, but large changes facilitate behavior.
(b) facilitate behavior, but large changes have no effect.
(c) and large changes both impair behavior.
(d) facilitate behavior, but large changes impair behavior.

13. In the experiment on population density that was run by Worchel and Brown, which group of subjects reported that they felt **LEAST** crowded?
(a) subjects who saw a violent film
(b) subjects who saw an unarousing film
(c) subjects who saw a humorous film
(d) subjects who saw a film with sexual content

14. Which of the following groups requires the least amount of personal space?
(a) women
(b) people who feel that they are not in control of their lives
(c) violent prisoners
(d) anxious people

15. How far apart do people tend to remain during impersonal business contacts?
(a) less than 11/2 feet
(b) 11/2 feet to 4 feet
(c) 4 to 12 feet
(d) 12 feet or more

16. Community mental–health centers were created during the
(a) 1890s.
(b) 1920s.
(c) 1940s.
(d) 1960s.

17. When psychologists attempt to deal with psychological problems by addressing issues such as unemployment, lack of education, drug abuse, teenage pregnancy, marital conflict, and substandard housing, they are using _____ prevention.
(a) preemptive
(b) primary
(c) secondary
(d) tertiary

18. Whose name is used to label the rules concerning the grounds for being found not guilty by reason of insanity?
(a) M'Naghten
(b) Peel
(c) Hinckley
(d) Forensic

19. Placing students in resource–rich environments and allowing them to work on their own to discover basic principles is referred to as
(a) expository teaching.
(b) discovery learning.
(c) the recitation method.
(d) the taxonomic approach.

20. The following measures help to motivate students, **EXCEPT**
(a) assuring that students can fulfill their needs for affiliation and belonging.
(b) encouraging students to see the links between their own efforts and achievements.
(c) recognizing that students' backgrounds can give rise to various patterns of needs.
(d) grading students on their achievements, and not on their presumed abilities.

Answer Key to *Pretest*

| | | | | | | |
|---|---|---|---|---|---|---|
| 1. C | 4. D | 7. C | 10. A | 13. B | 16. D | 19. B |
| 2. B | 5. A | 8. A | 11. C | 14. A | 17. B | 20. D |
| 3. D | 6. B | 9. A | 12. D | 15. C | 18. A | |

Applied psychologists use psychological knowledge and methods to solve problems in the world outside the laboratory. It is noted that clinical, counseling, and health psychologists are all applied psychologists. However, the areas of applied psychology discussed in this chapter include industrial/organizational (I/O) psychology, human factors, consumer psychology, environmental psychology, community psychology, forensic psychology, sports psychology, and educational psychology.

I/O psychologists consider the relationships between people and work, and the efficiency of organizations. They assist in the recruitment, training, and appraisal of personnel, noting the importance of objective evaluation of skills and performance. Organizational theories include classic theories, contingency theories, and human–relations theories.

Human factors psychologists are concerned with the creation of person–machine systems and work environments that are efficient and safe. Consumer psychologists analyze consumer (buyer) behavior and develop ways to stimulate people to make purchases of particular brands.

Environmental psychologists are concerned about our interrelationships with the physical environment. They note how aspects of the environment facilitate or impair human functioning. High noise levels, extremes of temperature, air pollution, and crowding all create certain physical hazards. However, they are also aversive stimuli that function as stressors and, as such, they tend to reduce feelings of attraction and to generally impair social interactions.

Community psychologists tend to focus on education and the marshalling of community resources to prevent abnormal behavior patterns. Forensic psychologists apply psychological expertise within the criminal–justice system. They are concerned with issues such as factors influencing eyewitness testimony and its interpretation, the recruitment and training of police personnel, and evaluation of the competence of individuals to participate in their own defense. Sports psychologists analyze and facilitate athletic performances and team organizations. They help athletes handle choking and increase the likelihood of peak performances through techniques such as athletic training, relaxation training, and positive visualization.

Educational psychologists apply psychological expertise to facilitate the processes of learning and memory in the academic setting. They conduct research into the effectiveness of various kinds of teaching practices and ways of managing classrooms. They evaluate the needs of exceptional students and help find ways to meet them. They study the reliability and validity of ways of testing and grading.

## LEARNING OBJECTIVES

1. Define *applied psychology*.

2. Explain the functions of industrial/ organizational (I/O) psychologists.

**Industrial/Organizational Psychology**

3. Describe some of the influences on I/O psychology.

4. Describe contributions of I/O psychologists in the areas of recruitment and placement.

5. Describe the contributions of I/O psychologists in the areas of training and instruction.

6. Describe the contributions of I/O psychologists in appraisal of workers' performance.

7. Describe various organizational theories.

8. Describe the sources of stress in the workplace and their effects.

**Human Factors**

9. Describe criteria for evaluating person–machine systems and work environments.

10. Describe criteria for evaluating the coding in displays.

**Consumer Psychology**

11. Describe the functions of consumer psychologists.

**Environmental Psychology**

12. Describe the functions of environmental psychologists.

13. Describe research findings concerning the effects of noise.

14. Describe research findings concerning the effects of temperature.

15. Describe research findings concerning the effects of odors.

16. Describe research findings concerning the effects of crowding.

## Community Psychology

17. Describe the functions of community psychologists.

## Forensic Psychology

18. Describe the functions of forensic psychologists.

## Sports Psychology

19. Describe the functions of sports psychologists.

20. Explain how sports psychologists help athletes achieve peak performances.

## Educational Psychology

21. Describe the functions of educational psychologists.

22. Describe ways of motivating and managing students in classrooms.

23. Describe ways of enhancing planning and teaching.

24. Discuss some issues in teaching exceptional students.

25. Discuss issues involving the use of tests and grades.

26. Describe ways to prevent rape and AIDS.

**Additional Notes**

## Industrial/Organizational Psychology

1. Currents in Industrial/Organizational Psychology

2. Recruitment and Placement

3. Training and Instruction

4. Appraisal of Workers' Performance

5. Organizational Theory

## Human Factors

1. Criteria for Evaluating Person–Machine Systems and Work Environments

2. Criteria for Evaluating the Coding in Displays

## Consumer Psychology

1. Task Analysis of Consumer Behavior

2. Marketing Research

## Environmental Psychology

1. Environmental Activism

2. Noise

3. Temperature

4. Of Aromas and Air Pollution

5. Crowding and Personal Space

## Community Psychology

- Levels of Prevention

## Forensic Psychology

- The Insanity Plea

## Sports Psychology

1. Task Analysis of Athletic Performances

2. How Sports Psychologists Help Athletes Handle "Choking"

3. Positive Visualization

4. Peak Performance

## Educational Psychology

1. Teaching Practices

2. Classroom Management

3. Planning and Teaching

4. Teaching Exceptional Students

5. Tests and Grades

## Psychology and Modern Life

1. Primary Prevention of Rape

2. Primary Prevention of AIDS

# KEY TERMS AND CONCEPTS

1. Applied psychology _____

### Industrial/Organizational Psychology

2. Industrial psychology _____

3. Organizational psychology _____

4. Organizational analysis _____

5. Task analysis _____

6. Halo effect _____

7. Classic organization theory _____

8. Bureaucracy _____

9. Contingency theories _____

10. Human–relations theories _____

11. Theory Y _____

12. Theory Z _____

### Human Factors

13. Human factors _____

### Consumer Psychology

14. Consumer psychology _____

### Environmental Psychology

15. Environmental psychology _____

16. Personal space _____

### Community Psychology

17. Community psychology _____

18. Primary prevention _____

19. Secondary prevention _____

20. Tertiary prevention _____

### Forensic Psychology

21. Forensic psychologist _____

### Sports Psychology

22. Sports psychologists _____

### Educational Psychology

23. Educational psychology _____

24. Discovery learning _____

25. Expository teaching _____

26. Self–fulfilling prophecy _____

27. Instructional objective _____

28. Taxonomy _____

29. Recitation _____

30. Exceptional students _____

31 Mainstreaming _____

32. Least-restrictive placement _____

33 Norm-referenced testing _____

34. Criterion-referenced testing _____

### Additional Notes

_____

_____

_____

_____

_____

_____

_____

_____

_____

_____

_____

_____

_____

_____

_____

_____

_____

_____

_____

_____

## SECTION 1: Introduction

**OBJ. 1:** (1) _____ied psychologists use psychological knowledge and methods to solve problems in the world outside the laboratory. (2) C_____ psychologists are the largest subgroup of applied psychologists. (3) _____ling psychologists apply psychological knowledge to help people with academic, vocational, and adjustment problems. (4) H_____ psychologists apply psychological knowledge to the prevention and treatment of illness.

## SECTION 2: Industrial/Organizational Psychology

**OBJ. 2:** (5) Industrial/_____tional (I/O) psychologists are employed by corporations and other groups to help in matters such as recruitment, worker appraisal, motivation, job satisfaction, and organizational efficiency.

**OBJ. 3:** I/O psychology is born of movements such as the twentieth–century testing movement, which has focused on the measurement of (6) _____dual differences in personality and aptitudes. People whose personal attributes (7) f_____ the requirements of their jobs are better adjusted in their work and more productive. Second is the (8) human–_____s movement, which conveys the thinking of the humanistic psychologists Carl Rogers and Abraham (9) M_____. Their philosophy suggests that the workplace should provide an opportunity for individuals to reach their potential, express unique (10) t_____ts, and find (11) self–_____ment. Third is the (12) industrial–_____ring movement, which has sparked interest in efficient, user–friendly person–machine systems and prompted psychologists to become involved in (13) h_____ factors.

(14) _____ral principles have been used in industry to train workers in step–by–step fashion, to modify problem work behaviors, and to make sure that workers are rewarded for targeted behaviors. The influences of cognitive psychology are being felt in issues ranging from biases in the (15) _____sal of worker performance to the ways in which workers' (16) _____tion–processing capacities impact on the design of work environments.

**OBJ. 4 :** I/O psychologists facilitate recruitment procedures by analyzing jobs, specifying the (17) sk_____s and personal (18) at_____s that are needed in a position, and constructing tests and interview procedures that are likely to determine their presence in candidates. Personnel tests most likely to be used by organizations include tests of (19) in_____tual abilities, spatial and mechanical abilities, perceptual accuracy, motor abilities, and personality and interests. Tests of (20) me_____ comprehension are appropriate for many factory and construction workers. Tests of motor abilities are useful for jobs that require strength, (21) coor_____ of the limbs, rapid (22) re_____on time, or dexterity. Interest inventories such as the (23) _____/Campbell Interest Inventory predict adjustment in various occupations.

**OBJ. 5:** Worker training and (24) _____tion is the most commonly reported way of enhancing productivity. Training provides workers with appropriate (25) _____lls. Training programs usually follow when managers identify a (26) n_____ for improved performance in a job. A formal needs assessment has three components: (27) _____tional analysis, (28) t_____ analysis, and person or worker analysis. Once learning objectives are established, psychologists help devise ways to gain and maintain the (29) at_____ of workers, to present materials in step–by–step fashion, to promote retention, and to (30) ev_____ the effectiveness of the training program.

**OBJ. 6:** Workers fare (31: *Circle one:* better or worse) and productivity is (32: *Circle one:* enhanced or impaired) when workers receive individualized guidance and reinforcers are based on accurate appraisal of their performance. Criticism of workers' performance should be delivered (33) con_____ively. Poor use of (34) cr_____ is the greatest cause of conflict at work. Workers respond best to criticisms that are (35: *Circle one:* general or specific), prompt, and considerate.

A number of biases are at work in appraisal. One is a tendency for supervisors to focus on the *worker* rather than the worker's (36) per_____. The tendency to rate workers according to general impressions (e.g., of liking or disliking) is an example of the (37) _____o effect. Behavioral I/O psychologists suggest that the criteria for appraisal be totally (38)_____tive. A second bias in the appraisal procedure is the tendency to evaluate workers according to how much (39) _____rt they put into their work.

**OBJ. 7:** The formal and informal characteristics of organizations may be thought of as (40) _____ts—consistent ways in which they respond to economic, political, and other challenges. Three broad approaches to organizing businesses are in sway today: (41) cl_____ organization theory, (42) _____gency theories, and human–relations theories.

(43) _____ic organization theories propose that there is one best way to structure an organization—from the skeleton outward. Classic organization theories frequently rely on a (44) bu_____, which frees workers from favoritism and nepotism and enables them to make long-range plans. Other elements of classic

organization theories include the (45) _____ion of labor and the (46) dele_____ of authority.

(47) Con_____ theories hold that there are many valid ways to structure organizations. They see organizational approaches as (48) _____gent on organizational goals, workers' characteristics, and the overall political or economic environment.

(49) Human–_____s theories begin their structuring with the individual. The text considers three human–relations approaches: McGregor's Theory (50) _____, Argyris' (51) _____ental theory, and Ouichi's Theory Z. Theory Y is based on the assumption that workers (52: *Circle one:* are or are not) motivated to take responsibility for their work behavior and that worker apathy and misbehavior stem from shortcomings of the organization. Theory Y argues that management should structure the organization so that organizational goals will be (53) _____ruent with workers' goals. Argyris suggests that organizations are structured efficiently when they allow their workers to (54) d_____. Argyris notes that workers develop from passive to (55) _____ve organisms; from (56) _____dent to independent organisms; from organisms capable of dealing with concrete issues to organisms capable of dealing with (57) _____ct issues; and from organisms with few abilities to organisms with many abilities. Theory Z combines some of the positive features of the (58) _____ese workplace with some of the realities of the American workplace. Ouichi's theory suggests that American firms should offer (59: *Circle one:* short–term or long–term) employment.

**OBJ. 8:** (60) _____al stressors in the workplace include poor lighting, air pollution, crowding, noise, and extremes of temperature. (61) _____ual stressors include work overload, boredom, conflict about one's work, excessive responsibility, and lack of forward movement. (62) G_____ stressors include irritating relationships with supervisors, subordinates, and peers. (63) _____tional stressors include lack of opportunity to participate in decision making, ambiguous or conflicting company policies, too much or too little organizational structure, low pay, racism, and sexism.

On a (64) _____tive level, stressed workers can experience anxiety, depression, frustration, fatigue, and boredom. On a cognitive level, stress decreases (65) _____tion span, impairs (66) con_____ion, and interferes with decision making. Physiological effects include (67: low or high?) blood pressure and the "diseases of (68) _____tion" discussed in Chapter 15. The (69) _____tional effects include absenteeism, alienation from co–workers, decreased productivity, and turnover.

## SECTION 2: Human Factors

**OBJ. 9:** In evaluating the efficiency and safety of equipment, human–factors psychologists use (70) _____mance criteria, (71) physio_____ criteria, subjective criteria, and accident and injury criteria. Performance standards involve the (72) qu_____ of the performance made possible by the design. Physiological standards involve the (73) ph_____ changes caused by operating the equipment. (74) _____tive criteria include psychological factors, such as boredom and job satisfaction.

**OBJ. 10:** Good codes are readily (75) _____ted or sensed. Good codes can be (76) _____inated from other symbols of the kind. Good codes are (77) com_____ with our expectations. Good codes have (78) _____fulness; they symbolize the information in question. Good codes are (79) _____ized, or used universally. Good codes are (80) _____sional; they employ two or more dimensions.

## SECTION 3: Consumer Psychology

**OBJ. 11:** (81) C_____ psychology applies psychological methods to the investigation and modification of consumer behavior and mental processes. Consumer psychologists investigate questions such as why consumers are (82) l_____ to one brand or another and how consumer (83) _____tudes toward products can be modified.

Consumer psychologists undertake (84) t_____ analyses of consumer behavior. Consumer behavior involves these steps: deciding to make a purchase, selecting the (85) b_____, shopping, buying, and evaluating the product. Advertising and packaging is used to help consumers tell (86) _____nds apart and to encourage them to make a purchase.

(87) _____ting research targets a consumer population, draws representative samples, and measures their responses to product names, ads, packages, and the products themselves are measured. Consumer psychologists also study the factors in advertisements that enhance their (88) _____siveness.

## SECTION 4: Environmental Psychology

**OBJ. 12:** Environmental psychologists study the ways in which people and the (89) _____al environment influence each other.

**OBJ. 13:** Environmental psychologists apply knowledge of sensation and (90) p_____tion in the design of environments that induce positive emotional responses and contribute to performance. The (91) d_____ (dB) is used to express the loudness of noise. Prolonged exposure to (92) _____ dB can damage hearing. High noise levels can (93: *Circle one:* increase or decrease) the blood pressure and cause stress–related illnesses. Children exposed to loud noise from low–flying airplanes in their schools may show hearing loss and impairments in (94) l_____ing and memory.

**OBJ. 14:** Extremes of heat make excessive demands on our bodies' (95) _____ atory systems, leading to conditions such as (96) de_____ tion, heat exhaustion, heat stroke, and heart problems. When it is too cold, the (97) _____ lism increases; we shiver; and blood vessels in the skin (98: *Circle one:* dilate or constrict). Hot and cold temperatures are both aversive events that (99: *Circle one:* increase or decrease) arousal. Moderate shifts in temperature are mildly arousing and have generally (100: *Circle one:* positive or negative) effects on performance. But extreme temperatures (101: *Circle one:* facilitate or impair) performance and activity levels.

**OBJ. 15:** The lead in auto fumes may impair children's (102) in_____ tual functioning. Carbon monoxide decreases the capacity of the blood to carry (103) o_____ and impairs learning ability. Odorous air pollutants, like other forms of aversive stimulation, (104: *Circle one:* increase or decrease) feelings of attraction and (105: *Circle one:* increase or decrease) aggression.

**OBJ. 16:** In his "rat (106) _____ rse," Calhoun allowed rats to reproduce with no constraints except for the limited space of their laboratory environment. Beyond a critical population, the (107) mor_____ rate rose and the social structure broke down.

Environmental psychologists use the term (108) d_____ to refer to the number of people in an area. They use the term (109) _____ ding to suggest a high–density social situation that is aversive. Whether we feel crowded depends on who is thrown in with us and our (110) _____ tation of the situation. In a study reported in the text, densely– seated people who could attribute their (111) a_____ to films they were watching reported feeling less crowded than those who could not. A sense of (112) c_____ over a high–density situation helps us cope with the stress. Women find high density (113: *Circle one:* more or less) aversive than men do.

As compared with suburbanites and rural folk, people who live in a big city encounter greater (114) _____ lus overload and fear of crime.

(115) Pe_____ space is an invisible boundary, something like a bubble, that surrounds you. You are likely to become anxious and angry when others invade your (116) _____ ce. Personal space serves protective and (117) com_____ tive functions. People sit and stand (118: *Circle one:* closer to or farther from) people of the same race, similar age, or similar socioeconomic status. Personal space invasions lead to stress, as reflected by (119: *Circle one:* higher or lower) levels of arousal.

**SECTION 5: Community Psychology**

**OBJ. 17:** Community psychologists focus on the (120) _____ ion of psychological problems. Community (121) _____ – _____ Centers (CMHCs) were created in the 1960s to deal with psychological problems in the community rather than the mental hospital. Prevention takes place at (122) _____ levels: primary, secondary, and (123) _____ ary. (124) _____ ary prevention aims to deter problems before they start. (125) _____ ary prevention aims to catch psychological problems in their formative stages and to stay their advancement. (126) T_____ prevention deals with psychological problems that have ripened.

**SECTION 6: Forensic Psychology**

**OBJ. 18:** Forensic psychologists apply psychological knowledge to the functioning of the (127) _____ – _____ ice system. Forensic psychologists apply knowledge concerning (128) _____ tion processing in the investigation of the use of eyewitness testimony. They apply social psychological knowledge in the investigation of the ways in which the behavior of judges, attorneys, and defendants influence (129) j_____ decisions.

Forensic psychologists apply knowledge of personality, personality assessment, and the psychology of learning to facilitate the (130) re_____ment and training of police officers. Some psychologists apply therapy methods to help police find ways of coping with (131) _____ss.

A number of forensic psychologists apply knowledge of abnormal behavior in testifying as to the (132) com_____ of defendants to stand trial or participate in their own defense, and as to whether defendants should be found not guilty by reason of (133) in_____ty. In pleading insanity, lawyers use the so–called (134) M'_____ rules.

# SECTION 7: Sports Psychology

**OBJ. 19:** (135) _____ts psychologists apply psychological methods and knowledge to the study and modification of the behavior and mental processes of people involved in sports. Sports psychologists do (136) _____sk analyses of athletic performances just as I/O psychologists do task analyses of work performances. Sports psychologists help athletes to focus their (137) _____tion on their performance and not the crowd; use cognitive strategies such as mental practice and (138) _____tive visualization to enhance performance; handle their emotions; enhance team (139) cohe_____; and handle "choking."

**OBJ. 20:** Peak performances are characterized by intense (140) conc_____; ability to screen out the crowd and, as appropriate, the competitors; a sense of (141) c_____ over the situation; lack of pain and fatigue; and the sense that time has slowed down. Peak performances can elude athletes who "try too hard." It helps to enhance endurance, fine–tune physical skills, regulate the breathing, (142) r_____ muscle groups that

are unessential to performance, and spend some practice time picturing oneself performing flawlessly under adverse conditions.

# SECTION 8: Educational Psychology

**OBJ. 21:** Educational psychologists apply knowledge from many areas of psychology to the processes of (143) t_____ing and (144) l_____ing.

Educational psychologists help instructors find ways of teaching effectively by first analyzing the (145) _____mes of learning. Some psychologists argue in favor of (146) _____ery learning, or placing children in resource–rich environments and allowing them to work on their own to discover basic principles. Others prefer to rely on (147) ex_____ teaching, or the orderly setting forth of facts and ideas.

**OBJ. 22:** Some educational psychologists suggest that teachers can find ways of motivating students if they consider how they can foster (148) _____tive attitudes toward learning activities and how the activities can help meet students' (149) _____ds.

Teachers can help motivate students by making classrooms and lessons interesting and inviting; by assuring that students can fulfill their needs for affiliation and belonging; by encouraging students to perceive the links between their own efforts and their (150) _____ments; and by helping students set attainable short–term (151) g_____s. Classrooms become more manageable when concrete (152) _____ures and rules are spelled out to students. Young students need concrete examples. Educational psychologists also devise ways for dealing with defiant and violent students, as through the use of behavior (153) _____cation.

**OBJ. 23:** Educational psychologists advise teachers to specify instructional (154) _____tives. A classification system, or (155) ta_____, of instructional objectives divides them into three domains: cognitive, (156) _____tive (emotional), and psychomotor (concerning the development of physical abilities and skills).

There are various teaching formats. In the (157) re_____ approach, teachers pose questions that students answer. Other formats include the lecture approach, group discussion, seatwork and homework, and individualized instruction. (158) _____alized instruction is usually prized because of the presumably ideal teacher–to–student ratio.

It (159: *Circle one:* has or has not) been shown that teachers who know more about a subject do a better job of teaching it. Students of teachers who know more about classroom management and who present material in a clear, organized way learn (160: more or less?) than students of poor managers and disorganized teachers.

**OBJ. 24:** The term (161) _____nal student applies to students whose needs are special because of physical and health problems, communication problems, behavior disorders, specific learning disabilities, mental retardation, or—at the other intellectual extreme—(162) g_____ness.

The practice of placing exceptional students in educational environments that are as normal as possible is referred to as (163) _____ming. Since the passage of Education for All Handicapped Children Act, exceptional children have been placed in the (164) _____ _____tive placement.

**OBJ. 25:** (165) _____dized tests are used to assess broad learning ability and to see how well children are reading or computing math problems as compared to agemates. These tests can be norm–referenced or (166) _____ion–referenced. Students' performances on (167) _____–referenced tests are compared with the average performance of others. In (168) criterion–_____ed testing, test–takers' scores are compared to a fixed performance standard.

Educational psychologists study the reliabil-

ity and (169) _____ity of various kinds of tests, such as multiple–choice tests versus essay tests. Long tests are (170: *Circle one:* more or less) reliable than short tests. The grading of multiple–choice tests is more (171: *Circle one:* subjective or objective) than the grading of essay tests. The grading of essays, like the appraisal of workers, can also be influenced by the (172) h_____ effect—that is, the teacher's general impression of the student.

Grades give students (173) _____back as to how much they have achieved and affect their self–esteem and motivation.

## Answer Key to *Chapter Review*

| | |
|---|---|
| 1. Applied | 33. constructively |
| 2. Clinical | 34. criticism |
| 3. Counseling | 35. specific |
| 4. Health | 36. performance |
| 5. Organizational | 37. halo |
| 6. individual | 38. objective |
| 7. fit | 39. effort |
| 8. human-relations | 40. traits |
| 9. Maslow | 41. classic |
| 10. talents | 42. contingency |
| 11. self-fulfillment | 43. Classic |
| 12. industrial engineering | 44. bureaucracy |
| 13. human | 45. division |
| 14. Behavioral | 46. delegation |
| 15. appraisal | 47. Contingency |
| 16. information-processing | 48. contingent |
| 17. skills | 49. Human-relations |
| 18. attributes | 50. Y |
| 19. intellectual | 51. Developmental |
| 20. mechanical | 52. are |
| 21. coordination | 53. congruent |
| 22. reaction | 54. develop |
| 23. Strong | 55. active |
| 24. instruction | 56. dependent |
| 25. skills | 57. abstract |
| 26. need | 58. Japanese |
| 27. organizational | 59. long–term |
| 28. task | 60. Environmental |
| 29. attention | 61. Individual |
| 30. evaluate | 62. Group |
| 31. better | 63. Organizational |
| 32. enhanced | 64. subjective |

65. attention
66. concentration
67. high
68. adaptation
69. organizational
70. performance
71. physiological
72. quality
73. physical
74. Subjective
75. detected
76. discriminated
77. compatible
78. meaningfulness
79. standardized
80. multidimensional
81. Consumer
82. loyal
83. attitudes
84. task
85. brand
86. brands
87. Marketing
88. persuasiveness
89. physical
90. perception
91. decibel
92. 110–120
93. increase
94. earning
95. circulatory
96. dehydration
97. metabolism
98. constrict
99. Iincrease
100. positive
101. impair
102. intellectual
103. oxygen
104. decrease
105. increase
106. universe
107. mortality
108. density
109. crowding
110. interpretation
111. arousal
112. control
113. less
114. stimulus

115. Personal
116. space
117. Ccommunicative
118. closer to
119. higher
120. prevention
121. Mental–Health
122. three
123. tertiary
124. Primary
125. Secondary
126. Tertiary
127. criminal–justice
128. information
129. jury
130. recruitment
131. stress
132. competence
133. insanity
134. M'Naghten
135. Sports
136. task
137. attention
138. positive
139. cohesiveness
140. concentration
141. control
142. relax
143. teaching
144. learning
145. outcomes
146. discovery
147. expository
148. positive
149. needs
150. achievements
151. goals
152. procedures
153. modification
154. objectives
155. taxonomy
156. affective
157. recitation
158. Individualized
159. has not
160. more
161. exceptional
162. giftedness
163. mainstreaming
164. least restrictive

165. Standardized
166. criterion-referenced
167. norm-referenced
168. criterion-referenced
169. validity
170. more
171. objective
172. halo
173. feedback

## EXERCISE 1: ORGANIZATION THEORIES

*Directions:* The text discusses three theories of organization, which are listed below. Following are statements about organization. Match the statement with the appropriate theory by writing the number of the theory in the blank space to the left of the statement.

| 1. Classic organization theories | 2. Contingency theories | 3. Human–relations theories |
|---|---|---|

_____ A.  There are many valid ways to structure organizations.

_____ B.  Efficient organizational structure will reflect the cognitive processes of individuals as these processes are applied to problem solving, decision making, and the quests for self–expression and self–fulfillment.

_____ C.  There is one best way to structure an organization—from the skeleton outward.

_____ D.  American firms should offer long–term (if not lifetime) employment when possible.

_____ E.  The behavior of the organization cannot be predicted or controlled without taking into account the characteristics, and needs, of the individual worker.

_____ F.  Efficient organization requires the division of labor and the delegation of authority.

_____ G.  Organizations must consider factors such as organizational goals, workers' characteristics, and the overall political or economic environment in arriving at an efficient structure.

_____ H.  Workers are motivated to take responsibility for their work behavior; worker apathy and misbehavior stem from shortcomings of the organization.

## EXERCISE 2: CHARACTERISTICS OF GOOD CODES

*Directions:* The text assigns six characteristics to good codes. The characteristics are listed below. Following are explanations of these characteristics. Match the characteristic with the appropriate explanation by writing the number of the characteristic in the blank space to the left of the explanation.

1. Compatibility
2. Detectability
3. Discriminability
4. Meaningfulness
5. Multidimensionality
6. Standardization

_____ A.  Codes are made easier to recognize when they employ two or more characteristic features, such as shape and color.

_____ B.  Good codes symbolize the information in question.

_____ C.  Good codes can be readily distinguished from other symbols of the kind.

_____ D.  Good codes are readily noticed or sensed.

_____ E.  Good codes are consistent with our expectations.

_____ F.  Good codes are used universally.

| **Answer Key to *Exercise 1*** | | **Answer Key to *Exercise 2*** | |
|---|---|---|---|
| A. 2 | E. 3 | A. 5 | D. 2 |
| B. 3 | F. 1 | B. 4 | E. 1 |
| C. 1 | G. 1 | C. 3 | F. 6 |
| D. 3 | H. 3 | | |

## EXERCISE 3: True or False?

Below are a number of statements concerning the chapter on applied psychology. Circle the T for those that are true, and the F for those that are false. Answers and comments follow.

T F  1. Industrial/organizational psychologists make up the single largest subgroup of applied psychologists.

T F  2. The main difference between clinical psychologists and community psychologists is that clinical psychologists work in hospitals.

T F  3. People whose skills are adequate for a job will be well adjusted in the job, regardless of their interests and other personal attributes.

T F  4. Supervisors tend to rate employees on the basis of their work performance only.

T F  5. Employees who are satisfied with their jobs have lower absenteeism and turnover rates.

T F  6. Tests of perceptual accuracy are useful for evaluating applicants for clerical positions, such as bank tellers and secretaries.

T F  7. Interest in an occupation suggests the presence of the aptitudes required to excel in that occupation.

T F  8. A formal needs assessment has three components: (1) organizational analysis, (2) economic analysis, and (3) person or worker analysis.

T F  9. Setting concrete goals at high but attainable levels can render work challenging but keep stress within acceptable limits.

T F 10. The concept of the quality circle originated in Japan.

T F 11. In job sharing, multiple workers fill one job.

T F 12. There is one best way to structure an organization.

T F 13. Contingency theories hold that there are many valid ways to structure organizations.

T F 14. Japanese career paths tend to be relatively nonspecialized, allowing for sideways movement and variety.

T F 15. Organizational stressors in the workplace include work overload, boredom, conflict about one's work, excessive responsibility, and lack of forward movement.

T F 16. The text suggests that decaffeinated coffee should be color-coded green or blue.

T F 17. Advertising is used only to encourage consumers to make a purchase.

T F 18. Consumer psychologists have found that it doesn't matter whether a commercial is likable or irritating.

T F 19. After eight hours of exposure to 110 to 120 dB your hearing may be damaged.

T F 20. When it is extremely cold, blood vessels in the skin dilate, increasing flow of blood to the periphery.

## Answer Key to *Exercise 3*

1. F   Clinical psychologists do, as pointed out in the introductory section of the chapter.

2. F   The main difference is that community psychologists focus on prevention.

3. F   Not necessarily. The job may bore us or disinterest us.

4. F   1) rating the worker due to feelings about worker; 2) rate the worker on effort not performance.

5. T   Did the statement look to easy to be correct?

6. T   The "trick" is knowing what is meant by "perceptual accuracy."

7. F   Not at all. (But it would be nice, wouldn't it?)

8. F   Tricky! Two parts are true, but the second part should read "task analysis," not economic analysis.

9. T   A complex, annoying type of item, but all parts are true.

10. F   It was ironically first brought to Japan by an American, H. Edwards Deming.

11. T   A simple matter of knowing a definition.

12. F   This is true only according to classic organization theory. The item, as stated, is too broad.

13. T   Here we have the qualification lacking in item 12.

14. T   A statement taken verbatim from the text; all parts are true.

15. F   Tricky! These stressors are presented in the text as individual stressors, not organizational stressors.

16. T   The point is that green and blue are "cool colors," suggesting lack of stimulating caffeine.

17. F   Advertising *is* used to encourage customers to make purchases, but not *only* for this purpose.

18. T   Is only necessary that the consumer remember what the product is and when to use it.

19. T   Statements with qualifiers such as "may be" are more likely to be true than absolute statements.

20. F   The opposite is true. The vessels constrict, decreasing blood flow to the periphery of the body.

# ESL—BRIDGING THE GAP

| Idioms | | Explanation |
|---|---|---|
| 657 | time off | free time away from work |
| 666 | lay off | remove from employment |
| 674 | broke out | occurred unexpectedly |

| Cultural | | Explanation |
|---|---|---|
| 656 | Russell Baker | current humorist for New York Times |
| 660 | IBM | International Business Machines |
| 667 | New Mexico | a state in southwestern part of U.S. |
| 670 | Pepsico | manufacturer of Pepsi Cola |
| 670 | baby-boomers | adults who were born after World War II, in the 1950's; there were an unusual number of babies born at that time |
| 670 | soft drinks | |
| 675 | harems | collection of females cared for by one male |
| 676 | shake hands | gesture of greeting in U.S. |
| 676 | eye contact | look directly at the other person's eyes when speaking or listening |
| 677 | Big Brother | organizations to help children who do not have family advantages |
| 677 | Parents Anonymous | organization to help parents cope with problems with children |
| 679 | streetwalkers | prostitutes |
| 679 | repeal the insanity plea | abolish the legal defense to a criminal charge that the defendant was insane and therefore not responsible for actions |
| 681 | John McEnroe | former U.S. tennis champion |
| 681 | Penn State | Pennsylvania State University |
| 681 | facing its second loss | had lost one football game and was probably going to lose this one |
| 681 | Iowa | University of Iowa provides useful experience |
| 683 | place kicker | a football play who scores by kicking the ball between the goal posts |
| 683 | Pittsburgh Steelers | a professional football team |
| 683 | North Carolina State | North Carolina State University |
| 683 | Standardized tests | tests that are the same in every part of U.S. |

| Phrases and Expressions (Different Usage) | | |
|---|---|---|
| 656 | clockwise | in the direction of the hands of the clock |
| 656 | counterclock-wise | in the opposite direction of the clock hands |
| 656 | "smart sticks" | controls |
| 656 | to gas up | to put gas in the car |
| 656 | to pop open | to open |

| Phrases and Expressions (Different Usage) | | |
|---|---|---|
| 656 | left to chance | not planned |
| 657 | is born of | is the result of |
| 657 | on the one hand | as one...as the other |
| 657 | develop our bents | develop our interests and potential |
| 657 | has sparked interest | has caused interest |
| 657 | step-by-step | one activity at a time |
| 657 | raises | increases in salary |
| 657 | bonuses | extra money for good performance |
| 657 | are spelled out | are clearly indicated |
| 657 | morale rises | moral increases |
| 657 | impact on | effect |
| 657 | nepotism reigns | hiring relatives occurs a lot |
| 658 | an invasion of privacy | asking very personal questions |
| 658 | zero in on | decide on |
| 660 | for their own sake | for that reason only |
| 660 | acted upon | used |
| 660 | in a given job title | in a specific job |
| 660 | barehanded gardeners | gardeners with no gloves on |
| 661 | And it does turn out | and it is true |
| 662 | have...characters of their own | every organization has a unique personality |
| 662 | familylike | like a family |
| 662 | by stripping away layers of | by reducing in stages |
| 662 | "leaner and meaner" | thin and unpleasant |
| 662 | "lean and hungry" looks | increase profits by eliminating jobs |
| 666 | economic downturn | less money for everyone |
| 666 | "cubbyholed" | same job to do all the time |
| 666 | sideways movement | changing the job a person does without paying more |
| 666 | left to their own devices | given no directions |
| 666 | "winner-take-all" | managers make all the decisions and have benefits that workers don't have |
| 666 | I was griping | I was complaining |
| 666 | switches difficult to throw? | handles difficult to turn? |
| 667 | that housed all the codes | place where codes are |
| 668 | | |
| 668 | runs contrary | is against |
| 668 | the saving grace | what justifies |
| 668 | Which telegraphs itself as the best | which is the most appropriate symbol |

| Page | Phrase | Meaning |
|------|--------|---------|
| 668 | return to the drawing board | try again to create an appropriate design |
| 670 | national advertising blitz | intensity nationwide advertising |
| 670 | does sex sell? | Are sexy ads effective in selling products |
| 670 | jeans ads? | ads for blue jeans |
| 670 | meet one's needs | satisfies the consumer |
| 672 | pushed back forests | cut down trees |
| 673 | our impact has mushroomed | people's influences have increased |
| 674 | make change for a quarter | give two dimes and a nickel or five nickels |
| 674 | blowout | tire on car pops (loses air) |
| 674 | Angered people | people who are angry |
| 674 | pop its cap | cap comes off suddenly |
| 674 | climes | climates |
| 675 | simply grapple with | consider only |
| 675 | the occasional advance | occasional attempt of the male to begin a sexual relationship |
| 676 | is thrown in with us | in the space where we are |
| 676 | of being packed in | of being in a crowd |
| 676 | to catch a snooze | sleep for a short time |
| 676 | Farming, anyone? | Would anyone like to operate a farm? |
| 677 | sever ties | disconnect the connections |
| 677 | to spawn problems | to create problems |
| 677 | to stay their advancement | to prevent their advancement |
| 677 | gets out of hand | becomes uncontrollable |
| 677 | have ripened | have completely developed |
| 679 | high burnout rate | a large number who become exhausted |
| 679 | public voices skepticism | people express skepticism |
| 681 | outplay | play better than |
| 681 | cost him matches? | cause him to lose games? |
| 681 | landed him | gave him a job |
| 681 | booted the ball | kicked the ball |
| 682 | is being carried out in slow motion | is occurring slower than reality of the movement |
| 683 | resource-rich environment | environment which contains stimulating material |
| 683 | marshal students' needs | assess students' needs |
| 683 | short-term goals | immediate objectives |
| 686 | "judgment calls" | decision is based on the judgment of the personal who is making the decision |

## Additional Terms from the Text

| | |
|---|---|
| | |
| | |
| | |

## Additional Terms from the Text

| | | |
|---|---|---|
| | | |

1. Industrial/organizational psychologists with a(n) _____ approach are likely to argue that the workplace, like other arenas of life, should provide an opportunity for individuals to reach their potential, express unique talents, and find self–fulfillment.
   (a) behavioral
   (b) cognitive
   (c) human–relations
   (d) industrial–engineering

2. According to the text, industrial/organizational psychologists have found that tests of _____ are useful in evaluating candidates for jobs that require strength, coordination of the limbs, rapid reaction time, or dexterity.
   (a) perceptual accuracy
   (b) motor abilities
   (c) intellectual abilities
   (d) personality attributes

3. Training programs usually follow when managers identify a need for improved performance in a given job. Which of the following is **NOT** a component of a formal needs assessment?
   (a) economic analysis
   (b) task anaylsis
   (c) worker analysis
   (d) organizational analysis

4. When they are evaluated by their superiors, workers respond best to criticisms that are
   (a) delayed.
   (b) generalized.
   (c) subjective.
   (d) considerate.

5. One of the cognitive biases in the process of worker appraisal is the tendency to
   (a) assume that women workers are superior in mechanical skills.
   (b) judge workers on the basis of the effort they make.
   (c) hire on the basis of nepotism.
   (d) allow workers to form quality circles.

6. The concept of the quality circle was initiated by
   (a) Deming.
   (b) Ouichi.
   (c) McGregor.
   (d) Argyris.

7. As compared to the U.S. workplace, Japanese organizations tend to
   (a) offer more specialized career paths.
   (b) foster a "winner–take–all" approach.
   (c) offer permanent employment.
   (d) encourage flextime.

8. It has become commonplace for decaffeinated coffee to be designated by the color orange in restaurants. The color orange falls short as a code because of its lack of
   (a) standardization.
   (b) detectability.
   (c) compatibility.
   (d) discriminability.

9. Consumer psychologists found that the most important aspect of TV commercials in fostering sales is whether the viewer
   (a) finds the commercial entertaining.
   (b) remembers the product and when to use it.
   (c) sees something with which he or she can identify.
   (d) develops an attitude of liking toward the brand name.

10. Under high noise levels,
    (a) feelings of attraction increase.
    (b) blood pressure decreases.
    (c) learning and memory are facilitated.
    (d) helping behavior decreases.

11. Which of the following was **NOT** a result of unrestricted population growth in Calhoun's "rat universe"?
    (a) Female rats sought increased sexual activity.
    (b) The mortality rate rose.
    (c) There were unhealthful changes in organs.
    (d) Family structure broke down.

12. Close friends and everyday acquaintances tend to remain _____ feet apart during their interactions.
    (a) less than 1 1/2
    (b) 1 1/2 feet to 4
    (c) 4 feet to 12
    (d) more than 12

13. In the Middlemist experiment on invasion of personal space, one of the operational measures of heightened arousal was
    (a) dryness in the mouth.
    (b) self–report of "butterflies in the stomach".
    (c) delay of onset of urination.
    (d) elevated electrodermal response.

14. When community psychologists work with teachers and others to sensitize them to early signs of psychological problems or abuse, they are using _____ prevention.
    (a) preemptive
    (b) primary
    (c) secondary
    (d) tertiary

15. The functions of the clinical psychologist and the community psychologist are most similar in the practice of _____ prevention.
    (a) preemptive
    (b) primary
    (c) secondary
    (d) tertiary

16. Daniel M'Naghten tried to assassinate
    (a) Grover Cleveland.
    (b) Robert Peel.
    (c) Gerald Ford.
    (d) Margaret Thatcher.

17. In the technique of positive visualization, an athlete
    (a) imagines going through a flawless performance under adverse conditions.
    (b) distracts himself or herself from the performance.
    (c) develops an imaginary "safe scene" that reduces the stress of the performance.
    (d) trains to increase peripheral vision.

18. The orderly setting forth of facts and ideas is referred to as
    (a) the recitation method.
    (b) expository teaching.
    (c) discovery learning.
    (d) meeting instructional objectives.

19. Classrooms become more manageable when teachers
    (a) know more about their subjects.
    (b) are aware of principles of classical and operant conditioning.
    (c) spell out concrete procedures and rules to students.
    (d) use individualized instruction.

20. Acquisition of knowledge is an example of a(n) _____ instructional objective.
    (a) cognitive
    (b) affective
    (c) psychomotor
    (d) preliminary

Answer Key to *Posttest*

1. C
2. B
3. A
4. D
5. B
6. A
7. C
8. C
9. B
10. D
11. A
12. B
13. C
14. C
15. D
16. B
17. A
18. B
19. C
20. A

| | |
|---|---|
| Applied psychology | Bureaucracy |
| Industrial psychology | Contingency theories |
| Organizational psychology | Human-relations theories |
| Organizational analysis | Theory Y |
| Task analysis | Theory Z |
| Halo effect | Human factors |
| Classic organization theories | Consumer psychology |

| | |
|---|---|
| An administrative system characterized by departments and subdivisions whose members frequently are given long tenure and inflexible work tasks | The application of fundamental psychological methods and knowledge of the investigation and solution of human problems. |
| Theories that hold that organizational structure should depend on factors such as goals, workers' characteristics, and the overall economic or political environment. | The field of psychology that studies the relationships between people and work. |
| Theories that hold that efficient organizations are structured according to the characteristics and needs of the individual worker. | The field of psychology that studies the structure and functions of organizations. |
| McGregor's view that organization goals should be congruent with workers' goals. | Evaluation of the goals and resources of an organization. |
| Ouchi's view that adapts positive features of the Japanese workplace to the U.S. workplace. | The breaking down of a job or behavior pattern into its component parts. |
| The field that studies the efficiency and safety of person-machine systems, and work environments. | The tendency for one's general impression of a person to influence one's perception of aspects, or performances by, that person. |
| The field of psychology that studies the nature, causes, and modification of consumer behavior and mental processes. | Theories that hold that organizations should be structured from the skeleton (governing body) outward. |

| | |
|---|---|
| Environmental psychology | Sports psychology |
| Personal space | Educational psychology |
| Community psychology | Discovery learning |
| Primary prevention | Expository teaching |
| Secondary prevention | Self-fulfilling prophecy |
| Tertiary prevention | Instructional objective |
| Forensic psychology | Mainstreaming |

| | |
|---|---|
| The field of psychology that studies the nature, causes, and modification of the behavior and mental processes of people involved in sports. | The field of psychology that studies the ways in which people and the environment influence each other. |
| The field of psychology that studies the nature, causes, and enhancement of teaching and learning. | An invisible boundary that surrounds a person and serves protective functions. |
| Bruner's view that children should work on their own to discover basic principles. | A field of psychology, related to clinical psychology, that focuses on the prevention of psychological problems and the maintenance of distressed persons in the community. |
| Ausubel's method of presenting material in an organized form, moving from broad to specific concepts. | In community psychology, the deterrence of psychological problems. |
| An expectation that is confirmed because of the behavior of those who hold the expectation. | In community psychology, the early detection and treatment of psychological problems. |
| A clear statement of what is to be learned. | In community psychology, the treatment of ripened psychological problems. |
| The practice of placing exceptional students in educational environments that are as normal as possible. | The field that applies psychological knowledge within the criminal justice system. |

# Appendix A

# Statistics

Directions: This *PRETEST* will give you feedback about how well you understand Appendix A. In order to enhance your mastery of Appendix A, complete all the sections of this chapter of the Study Guide. Then you can take the *POSTTEST* and compare your results.

1. All of the following are concerns of descriptive statistics, **EXCEPT**
   (a) frequency distributions.
   (b) measures of variability.
   (c) measures of central tendency.
   (d) statistically significant differences.

2. In a frequency polygon, the number of scores in a class interval is represented by a
   (a) line.
   (b) rectangular solid.
   (c) point.
   (d) many–sided geometric figure.

3. What is the mean of the following set of scores: 4, 12, 8, 16, 32, 3, 2?
   (a) 12.8
   (b) 11.0
   (c) 10.6
   (d) 8.0

4. The high score of a distribution minus the low score is the
   (a) deviation.
   (b) variability.
   (c) range.
   (d) standard deviation.

5. Which of the following is the formula for the standard deviation? The square root of the sum of
   (a) *d* divided by *N*.
   (b) *d* squared divided by *N*.
   (c) *d* divided by *N* squared.
   (d) *d* squared divided by *N* squared.

6. On the Stanford Binet Intelligence Scale, about _____ percent of the scores lie within 16 points from the mean.
   (a) 34
   (b) 50
   (c) 68
   (d) 95

7. Jim finds that the longer he runs the less he weighs. The relationship between time running and weight may be described as a _____ correlation.
   (a) positive
   (b) negative
   (c) normal
   (d) frequency

8. The Stanford Binet and Wechsler scales show reliability coefficients closest to
   (a) +0.90.
   (b) +0.70.
   (c) 0.00.
   (d) -0.90.

9. In order to determine the validity of a psychological test, scores are correlated with scores attained
   (a) by another tester.
   (b) on an alternate form.
   (c) on another testing occasion.
   (d) on an external criterion.

10. As the difference between the means of two group grows larger, the likelihood that their difference is statistically significant
    (a) increases.
    (b) decreases.
    (c) remains the same.
    (d) cannot be determined from the given information.

**Answer Key to *Pretest***

| | | | |
|---|---|---|---|
| 1. D | 4. C | 7. B | 10. A |
| 2. C | 5. B | 8. A | |
| 3. B | 6. C | 9. D | |

Appendix A begins with a vignette that demonstrates the futility of using sophisticated statistical techniques when our samples do not represent the intended populations. Statistics is the science that obtains and organizes numerical measurements. It lies at the heart of data analysis in psychology. Appendix A discusses descriptive statistics and inferential statistics.

Descriptive statistics includes methods for determining the central tendency (average) of a group of measures, and their variability. Inferential statistics permits us to draw conclusions (or inferences) about populations from data taken from representative samples. For instance, we can use inferential statistics to find out whether the differences between the mean (average) scores of two samples are "statistically significant"—that is, unlikely to be due to chance fluctuation.

The section on descriptive statistics first explains how to organize a frequency distribution. Then formulas for deriving three measures of central tendency are presented: the mean, the median, and the mode. Two measures of variability are then presented: the range and the standard deviation.

The bell–shaped or "normal" curve is presented. Its applications for understanding the distribution of intelligence test scores are outlined. The normal curve is presented with skewed (slanted) distributions.

The correlation coefficient describes a mathematical relationship between two variables. Correlations may be positive and negative, strong and weak. The scatter diagram permits a visual display of correlational data.

## LEARNING OBJECTIVES

1. Define *statistics, descriptive statistics*, and *inferential statistics.*

2. Arrange data in a frequency distribution, using class intervals.

3. Graphically represent a frequency distribution by drawing a histogram or a polygon.

4. Compute three measures of central tendency (types of averages): the mean, median, and mode.

5. Explain when the median and mode are more appropriate measures of central tendency than is the mean.

6. Compute two measures of variability: the range and the standard deviation.

7. Describe the central tendencies and variability of a normal curve.

8. Know the percentage of cases that lie between various points on the normal curve.

9. Explain the function of a correlation coefficient.

10. Show how correlation coefficients varying between +1.00 and -1.00 describe the strength and direction of a relationship between two variables.

11. Explain the difference between correlation and cause and effect.

12. Define and differentiate between *population* and *sample*.

13. Explain the impact of the size of the difference between group means on the statistical significance of that difference.

14. Explain the impact of the size of the standard deviations of groups on the statistical significance of the difference between the group means.

15. Refer to Chapter 2 to explain how psychologists use random and stratified sampling of populations to draw representative samples.

1. Statistics _____

2. Sample _____

3. Population _____

4. Range _____

5. Average _____

### Descriptive Statistics

6. Descriptive statistics _____

7. Frequency distribution _____

8. Frequency distribution _____

9. Histogram polygon _____

10. Mean _____

11. Median _____

12. Mode _____

13. Bimodal _____

14. Range _____

15. Standard deviation _____

### The Normal Curve

16. Normal distribution _____

17. Normal curve _____

### The Correlation Coefficient

18. IQ score _____

19. Correlation coefficient _____

### Inferential Statistics

20. Infer _____

21. Inferential statistics _____

22. Statistically significant difference _____

23. Random sampling _____

24. Stratified sampling _____

# CHAPTER REVIEW

**OBJ. 1:** The science that obtains and organizes numerical measurements or information is termed (1) _____ tics. (2) _____ tive statistics is the branch of statistics that provides information about a distribution of scores. Inferential statistics is the branch of statistics concerned with the confidence with which conclusions about samples may be extended to the (3) _____ tions from which the samples were drawn.

## SECTION 1: Descriptive Statistics

**OBJ. 2:** A frequency distribution orders scores from lowest to highest, and then scores according to (4) c_____ intervals.

**OBJ. 3:** Both in frequency histograms and in frequency polygons, the class intervals are typically drawn along the (5: *Circle one:* horizontal or vertical) axis and the number of scores in each class is drawn along the (6: *Circle one:* horizontal or vertical) axis. The horizontal axis is also referred to as the (7: *Circle one:* X or Y) axis. The vertical axis is also called the (8: *Circle one:* X or Y) axis. In a (9) _____ am, the number of scores in each class interval is represented by a rectangular solid. In a frequency polygon the number of scores in each class interval is plotted as a (10) _____ on.

**OBJ. 4:** There are three measures of central tendency: the (11) m_____, (12) _____ n, and (13) _____ e. The mean is attained by adding all the scores in a distribution, then dividing the sum by the (14) _____er of scores. The median is the (15) _____dle case in a frequency distribution, or the score beneath which (16) _____ percent of the cases fall. The (17) m_____ is the most frequently occurring score in a distribution. A distribution with two modes is labeled (18) _____al.

**OBJ. 5:** The median or (19) m_____ may be a more accurate measure of (20) _____ral tendency than the mean when distributions have a few extreme cases. The (21) m_____ of a distribution is the measure of central tendency that is most greatly distorted by a few extreme scores.

**OBJ. 6:** There are two main measures of variability in a distribution: the (22) r_____ and the (23) _____rd deviation. The range is attained by (24) _____ting the lowest score in the distribution from the highest score. The standard deviation (S.D.) is calculated by the following formula: S.D.= [The square root of] the Sum of (25) ____ squared [divided by] (26)_____. In this formula, *d* equals the deviation of each score from the (27) m_____ of the distribution. *N* equals the (28) n_____ of scores in the distribution.

## SECTION 2: The Normal Curve

**OBJ. 7:** In a (29) n_____ distribution, the mean, median, and (30) m_____ all lie at the same score. Scores cluster most heavily near the (31) _____n. They fall off rapidly at first, then taper off more gradually. A normal distribution is also called a normal (32) _____ve, and it has the shape of a (33) b_____. Normal curves theoretically depict (34) ch_____ variation. IQ tests have nearly normal distributions of scores with a mean of (35) _____ points. The S.D. of the Wechsler scales is (36) _____ points, and the S.D. of the Stanford–Binet is (37) _____ points.

**OBJ. 8:** Slightly more than two of every three cases fall within (38) _____ standard deviation(s) of the mean. About (39) _____ percent of the cases lie within two standard deviations of the mean. About (40) _____ percent of the scores or cases lie outside two standard deviations from the mean.

## SECTION 3: The Correlation Coefficient

**OBJ. 9:** The (41) c_____ coefficient is a number that can vary from (42) _____ to -1.00. A correlation coefficient indicates the degree (strong to [43] _____) and direction (positive or [44] _____) of the relationship between two variables. In a positive correlation, one variable increases as the other variable (45: *Circle one:* increases or decreases). In a negative correlation, one variable increases as the other variable (46: *Circle one:* increases or decreases).

**OBJ. 10:** A correlation coefficient of +1.00 indicates a perfect (47: *Circle one:* positive or negative) correlation between variables. A correlation coefficient of -1.00 indicates a (48) p_____ _____ correlation.

Correlation coefficients of at least (49) _____ are considered high. Correlation (50) _____ents of (51) _____ to 0.60 are considered moderate. Correlation coefficients below (52) _____ are considered weak.

**OBJ. 11:** Correlation coefficients show only the direction and the strength of the (53) _____ship between two variables. Correlation coefficients do not show (54) c_____ and effect. The two variables that are correlated could each have been caused by other influences. Psychologists usually use (55) _____al research in order to determine cause and effect.

## SECTION 4: Inferential Statistics

**OBJ. 12:** A (56) _____tion is defined as a complete group of organisms or events. A (57) s_____ is defined as part of a population. (58) In_____ statistics uses mathematical techniques to permit statements about populations from which samples have been drawn.

**OBJ. 13:** A (59) _____cally significant difference between group means is defined as a difference that is unlikely to be due to chance fluctuation. The bigger the difference, the (60: *Circle one:* more or less) likely it is to be due to chance. Expressed in more technical terms, the probability that the difference between group means is statistically significant (61: *Circle one:* increases or decreases) as the difference between the group means increases.

**OBJ. 14:** The variabilities of two groups also has an impact on whether differences between their (62) _____ns are statistically significant. The likelihood that the difference between group means is statistically significant increases as the standard deviations of the groups (63: *Circle one:* increases or decreases). In other words, the greater the variability within each group, the (64: *Circle one:* more or less) likely it is that differences between group means are statistically significant.

**OBJ. 15:** Samples must adequately (65) _____sent the populations from which they were drawn, if we are to be able to generalize from the samples to those (66) _____ions. Psychologists attempt to draw representative samples by means of random sampling or (67) _____ied sampling. A (68) _____ sample is defined as one which is drawn in such a way that every member of the population being sampled has an equal chance of being selected. A stratified sample is one in which known subgroups within a population are represented in (69) pro_____ to their numbers in the population.

Answer Key to *Chapter Review*

---

1. statistics
2. Descriptive
3. populations
4. class
5. horizontal
6. vertical
7. X
8. Y
9. histogram
10. polygon
11. mean
12. median
13. mode
14. number
15. middle
16. 50
17. mode
18. bimodal
19. mode
20. central
21. mean
22. range
23. standard
24. subtracting
25. d
26. *N*
27. mean
28. number
29. normal
30. mode
31. mean
32. curve
33. bell
34. chance
35. 100
36. fifteen
37. sixteen
38. one
39. 95
40. 5
41. correlation
42. +1
43. weak
44. negative
45. increases
46. decreases
47. positive
48. perfect negative
49. 0.60
50. Coefficients
51. 0.40
52. 0.40
53. relationship
54. cause
55. experimental
56. population
57. sample
58. Inferential
59. statistically
60. less
61. increases
62. means
63. decreases
64. less
65. represent
66. populations
67. stratified
68. random
69. proportion

Below are the major league baseball standings as of June 15 in a recent year. Use them to work the problems below. Then check your answers against the answer key at the bottom of the previous page.

### Major League Baseball Standings

**American League**

**National League**

**Eastern Division**

| | W. | L. | Pct. | G.B. |
|---|---|---|---|---|
| Yankees | 35 | 21 | .625 | – |
| Milwaukee | 31 | 24 | .564 | 3 1/2 |
| Boston | 29 | 27 | .518 | 6 |
| Cleveland | 27 | 27 | .500 | 7 |
| Baltimore | 28 | 29 | .491 | 7 1/2 |
| Toronto | 27 | 28 | .491 | 7 1/2 |
| Detroit | 26 | 28 | .481 | 8 |

**Eastern Division**

| | W. | L. | Pct. | G.B. |
|---|---|---|---|---|
| Montreal | 33 | 20 | .623 | – |
| Pittsburgh | 32 | 23 | .582 | 2 |
| Philadelphia | 28 | 24 | .538 | 4 1/2 |
| Mets | 26 | 28 | .481 | 7 1/2 |
| Chicago | 23 | 30 | .434 | 10 |
| St. Louis | 20 | 36 | .357 | 14 1/2 |

**Western Division**

| | W. | L. | Pct. | G.B. |
|---|---|---|---|---|
| Kansas City | 36 | 22 | .621 | – |
| Chicago | 29 | 28 | .509 | 6 1/2 |
| Oakland | 29 | 29 | .500 | 7 |
| Seattle | 27 | 31 | .466 | 9 |
| Texas | 26 | 32 | .448 | 10 |
| Minnesota | 23 | 34 | .404 | 12 1/2 |
| California | 21 | 34 | .382 | 13 1/2 |

**Western Division**

| | W. | L. | Pct. | G.B. |
|---|---|---|---|---|
| Houston | 33 | 22 | .600 | – |
| Cincinnati | 32 | 25 | .561 | 2 |
| Los Angeles | 32 | 25 | .561 | 2 |
| San Diego | 25 | 33 | .431 | 9 1/2 |
| San Francisco | 24 | 33 | .421 | 10 |
| Atlanta | 23 | 32 | .418 | 10 |

1. Compute the mean number of games won in each division of each league.

2. Compute the mean percentage of games won for each league.

3. Compute the median number of games lost in each league.

4. Compute the modal number of lost games in each division of each league.

5. Compute the standard deviation of number of games won by the teams of the American League East and then of the National League East.

1.  American East: 29    National East: 27
    American West: 27.29    National West: 28.17

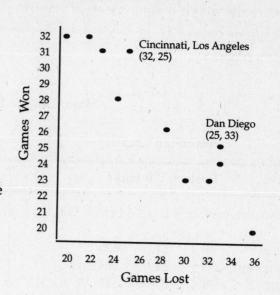

2.  These are both .500. Why?

3.  American: 28      National: 26.5

4.  American East: 27, 28    National West: No mode

5.  American East: 2.88    National East: 4.62

6.  The scatter diagram shows the relationship between games won and games lost for the twelve National League teams. It is a very high negative relationship. Why isn't it a perfect negative relationship?

1. _____ is defined as the science that is concerned with obtaining and organizing numerical measurements.
   (a) Sampling
   (b) Statistics
   (c) Descriptive statistics
   (d) Inferential statistics

2. In a histogram, the number of scores in each class interval is represented as a(n)
   (a) point.
   (b) line.
   (c) rectangular solid.
   (d) irregular polygon.

3. The _____ of a frequency distribution is defined as the score beneath which 50 percent of the cases fall.
   (a) median
   (b) mode
   (c) average
   (d) mean

4. Which measure of central tendency is most affected by the addition of a few extreme scores?
   (a) norm
   (b) mode
   (c) median
   (d) mean

5. In calculating the standard deviation of a distribution, $d$ is defined as the
   (a) number of scores in the distribution.
   (b) range of each score.
   (c) distance between the high score and the low score.
   (d) deviation of each score from the mean.

6. A normal distribution of IQ scores has a mean of 100 and a standard deviation of 15. About _____ percent of the scores lie below 100.
   (a) 50
   (b) 68
   (c) 84
   (d) 95

7. The _____ allows us to represent the relationship between parental income and children's SAT scores as a single number.
   (a) frequency distribution
   (b) scatter diagram
   (c) correlation coefficient
   (d) frequency polygon

8. A researcher finds a correlation of +2.00 between intelligence and achievement for a sample of children. This correlation coefficient indicates a(n)
   (a) weak positive relationship.
   (b) moderate to strong positive relationship.
   (c) perfect positive relationship.
   (d) error in computation.

9. Which is the most accurate statement of the relationship between correlation and cause and effect?
   (a) The stronger the correlation between two variables, the more likely it is that one causes the other.
   (b) If two variables are not correlated, it is unlikely that one causes the other.
   (c) If two variables are correlated, they are each caused by a third variable.
   (d) Correlational research is the best way of determining cause and effect.

10. The smaller the standard deviations of two groups, the _____ likely it is that the difference in the _____ is statistically significant.
    (a) more; means
    (b) less; means
    (c) more; standard deviations
    (d) less; standard deviations

**Answer Key to *Posttest***

| | |
|---|---|
| 1. B | 6. A |
| 2. C | 7. C |
| 3. A | 8. D |
| 4. D | 9. B |
| 5. D | 10. A |

| | |
|---|---|
| Sample | Median |
| Population | Mode |
| Range | Bimodal |
| Average | Standard deviation |
| Descriptive statistics | Normal distribution |
| Frequency distribution | Normal curve |
| Mean | Correlation coefficient |

Appendix A  Statistics

| | |
|---|---|
| The score beneath which 50% of the class fall. | Part of a population. |
| The most frequently occurring number or score in a distribution. | A complete group from which a sample is selected. |
| Having two modes. | A measure of variability; the distance between extreme measures or scores. |
| A measure of the variability of a distribution. | Central tendency of a group of measures, expressed as mean, median, and mode. |
| A symmetrical distribution in which approximately 68% of cases lie within a standard deviation of the mean. | The branch of statistics that is concerned with providing information about a distribution of scores. |
| Graphic presentation of a normal distribution, showing a bell shape. | An ordered set of data that indicates how frequently scores appear. |
| A number between -1.00 and +1.00 that indicates the degree of relationship between two variables. | A type of average calculated by dividing the sum of scores by the number of scores. |